JOURNAL FOR THE STUDY OF THE OLD TESTAMENT
SUPPLEMENT SERIES
320

Editors
David J.A. Clines
Philip R. Davies

Executive Editor
John Jarick

Editorial Board
Richard J. Coggins, Alan Cooper, J. Cheryl Exum, John Goldingay,
Robert P. Gordon, Norman K. Gottwald, Andrew D.H. Mayes,
Carol Meyers, Patrick D. Miller

GENDER, CULTURE, THEORY
9

Editor
J. Cheryl Exum

Sheffield Academic Press

Wise, Strange and Holy

The Strange Woman and the Making of the Bible

Claudia V. Camp

Journal for the Study of the Old Testament
Supplement Series 320

Gender, Culture, Theory 9

For Rebecca

daughter

trickster

wise, strange

holy

Copyright © 2000 Sheffield Academic Press

Published by Sheffield Academic Press Ltd
Mansion House
19 Kingfield Road
Sheffield S11 9AS
England

Typeset by Sheffield Academic Press
and
Printed on acid-free paper in Great Britain
by Bookcraft Ltd
Midsomer Norton, Somerset

British Library Cataloguing in Publication Data

A catalogue record for this book is available
from the British Library

ISBN 1-84127-166-7 cl
1-84127-167-5 pb

CONTENTS

PREFACE

This book has been about a dozen years in process, beginning before it knew it would grow up to be a book. Its roots lie in the work of my earlier book on Woman Wisdom, *Wisdom and the Feminine in the Book of Proverbs*, also published by the grace of folks at Sheffield (1985). On those pages the Strange Woman already appeared, though subsumed in an (at the time perhaps necessary) apologetic on behalf of female Wisdom (I use the capital to indicate the figure of wisdom personified). A subsequent invitation from Cheryl Exum to 'write something on the trickster' opened the door for a new way of viewing the relationship between the two female figures in Proverbs. This more dialectical mode offered, I felt, the possibility of pushing past the patriarchal blockade in the biblical construction of gender. This essay, only slightly changed over the years, was to be the core of this new book; it is now Chapter 2.

With this essay, my approach to the relationship of the book of Proverbs to the rest of the canon also reversed itself. Whereas in *Wisdom and the Feminine* I had sought to understand Proverbs' female imagery by means of other biblical women, now Woman Wise and Strange guided my reading of narrative texts; the union of two women generated Chapters 3 and 4 on Samson and Solomon and their loves. In the last part of the book, on the other hand, something different has happened, the result of what I took at first to be a rather fanciful impulse to invert the Strange Woman paradigm and consider *Israelite* women *estranged*. I did not know when I began that study that I would find a whole new dialectic at work: no longer strange and wise, but strange and *holy*. Nor did I realize the implications this would have for imagining the institutional dynamics at work in the shaping of what would become canonical literature. I could now think of priests as well as sages. It made things much more complicated and also much more interesting.

I think it could be said that *Wisdom and the Feminine* anticipated, though unconsciously and often in an unsophisticated way, the current scholarly interest in postexilic studies and in feminist analysis of female imagery in that period. Also rudimentary in that earlier book, but likewise crucial in my own intellectual development and to my self-understanding within the discipline, were efforts, undertaken once more here, to find the methodological means to understand both the period and its literature by means of each other: that is, to overcome the breach between literary and historical methodologies; that is, to provide myself the pleasure I find in doing both historical and literary analyses. I hope, in the last 15 years, that I've gotten better at both endeavors, and at putting them together, but you will find here, as before, no methodological grand plan, no unified theory. Then as now I have followed my nose, tracking questions as they arose, and using what was at hand that seemed to work to answer them.

'Ideological criticism' is a convenient term for much of what I do, if by it one means the attempt to trace a perceived logic of ideas lying under the surface of the texts, somewhere between the surface structure of New Criticism and the deep structure of structuralism, though including a bit of both. Ideological criticism also implies a politics, which as a feminist I do not disavow. Systems of logic empower and disempower, but usually more complexly than it appears to ideologues. I am interested in this complexity. It is why I feel compelled to consider history, in spite of the odds against saying anything intelligible—or at any rate 'provable'—about the period in question. The effort to do this has delayed this book by a good two or three years, as scholars in postexilic studies have issued forth their historical reconstructions *du jour* at an ever-increasing rate, a state of affairs at once fascinating and depressing for one ever on the verge of completing a manuscript.

Ideological criticism does not, though, always capture the fullness of my experience in producing this work, nor, I hope, yours in reading it. There have been times when I have laughed out loud at some reading the biblical text has provoked me to. God only knows whether the joke was sitting there 'in' the text waiting for my eye, or whether it is the product only of my own skewed view of things. My daughter and even my students often laugh at things I say, the absence of any humorous intention on my part notwithstanding. I consider this response preferable to its alternative, the rolled eyes that indicate my hopeless outmodedness. Perhaps the biblical authors would as well. By the same token, I have sometimes wept. Again and again in my readings Solomon takes his sword to the child. In spite of textual efforts to justify this bloody division, however, the narrative never entirely suppresses the horror of the one who wields what Mieke Bal calls the s/word. And yes, I have wept for Moses and Aaron as well as for Dinah and Miriam, for Samson as well as for his burned bride. It is, finally, the laughter and the tears that keep me at the task of biblical interpretation, when politics and ideology would have driven me long since away.

It will come as no surprise that a project of this duration has depended on varied sorts of support from many people. Biblical studies would be a far less hospitable enterprise without the long labor of our colleagues at Sheffield Academic Press. Thanks to Cheryl Exum for her enthusiastic response to my manuscript. My department at Texas Christian University has for two decades been a model and a marvel of collegiality in a profession that is not always kind, and in a part of the country that is not always feminist-friendly. My student assistants over the past few years, Mary Certain and Sara Steen, deserve mention and thanks for their congenial reliability and organizational skills I'll never have. I have never received anything other than encouragement from my colleagues here or further afield. I offer special thanks for their long friendship to Toni Craven, Danna Nolan Fewell, Carole Fontaine and Andy Fort. Thanks also to Gary Phillips for comments on an earlier version of the manuscript. I have a friend and colleague beyond compare in David Gunn, who not only took the risk of publishing my dissertation 15 years ago, but who has read more versions of the present work than he or I would care to count, has performed admirably as adopted soccer-uncle to my daughter Rebecca, and has willingly sacrificed body and soul to an absolutely essential 'one more glass of wine' on occasions too numerous to mention. Rebecca has grown up with this book; she and my husband Jeffrey have always provided the motivation to call it a day and get on home, as well as, finally, the necessity to get this thing finished so I can once more fully share their lives.

Portions of this book have appeared previously. Chapter 1 is a revised and expanded version of Claudia V. Camp, 'What's So Strange About the Strange Woman?', in David Jobling, Peggy Day and Gerald T. Sheppard (eds.), *The Bible and the Politics of Exegesis* (Cleveland, OH: Pilgrim Press, 1991): 17-32. Used by permission of Pilgrim Press. An earlier version of Chapter 2 was published as Claudia V. Camp, 'Wise and Strange: An Interpretation of the Female Imagery in Proverbs in Light of Trickster Mythology', *Semeia* 42 (1988): 14-36,

A note on translation and transliteration: Translations of the Hebrew text are mine, sometimes more than others colored by long familiarity with the RSV/NRSV tradition. Transliterations are not scientific, to make them more accessible to the non-specialist reader.

ABBREVIATIONS

AB	Anchor Bible
BETL	Bibliotheca ephemeridum theologicarum lovaniensium
Bib	*Biblica*
BibInt	*Biblical Interpretation: A Journal of Contemporary Approaches*
BR	*Bible Review*
BZAW	Beihefte zur *ZAW*
CBQ	*Catholic Biblical Quarterly*
CBQMS	*Catholic Biblical Quarterly*, Monograph Series
ETR	*Etudes théologiques et religieuses*
FOTL	The Forms of the Old Testament Literature
GCT	Gender, Culture and Theory Series
GKC	*Gesenius' Hebrew Grammar* (ed. E. Kautzsch, revised and trans. A.E. Cowley; Oxford: Clarendon Press, 1910)
HAR	*Hebrew Annual Review*
HTR	*Harvard Theological Review*
ICC	International Critical Commentary
JBL	*Journal of Biblical Literature*
JPS	Jewish Publication Series
JSOT	*Journal for the Study of the Old Testament*
JSOTSup	*Journal for the Study of the Old Testament*, Supplement Series
NCB	New Century Bible
OBO	Orbis biblicus et orientalis
OTL	Old Testament Library
OTS	*Oudtestamentliche Studiën*
SBL	Society of Biblical Literature
SBLDS	SBL Dissertation Series
SBLSS	SBL Semeia Studies
SBT	Studies in Biblical Theology
TynBul	*Tyndale Bulletin*
UBSMS	United Bible Societies, Monograph Series
USQR	*Union Seminary Quarterly Review*
VT	*Vetus Testamentum*
VTSup	*Vetus Testamentum*, Supplements
ZAW	*Zeitschrift für die alttestamentliche Wissenschaft*

INTRODUCTION

Every culture constructs a view of the world, a set of categories and boundaries that gives identity and meaning to its members. Every culture also has to deal with anomalies that blur the boundaries, as well as sociopolitical realities that challenge the order. An intense preoccupation with identity boundaries within certain segments of the community in Second Temple Judah[1] remains manifest in canonical representations of strange women. This book examines the paradigmatic example of the Strange Woman and her counterpart in Proverbs, the female personification of Wisdom, and then turns these two figures as a hermeneutical lens onto narrative texts where issues of strangeness—whether of gender, ethnicity, sexuality or cultic activity—predominate. This reading strategy serves two purposes. It produces a series of deconstructive literary readings, which in turn provide a view into the ideological tensions of the postexilic period.[2]

Wisdom and Strangeness, personified as women, dominate the nine introductory chapters of the book of Proverbs. And they provide the overarching (metaphorical) conceptual framework for this book (see Chapters 1–2). While drawing on my previous work on Woman Wisdom (Camp 1985), my major focus here is her multifaceted negative

1. These are the segments, largely responsible for the origins of the canon, that will call themselves 'the Jews' and, ultimately, 'Israel'. The latter terms are, however, to a large degree anachronistic: 'Israel' as a national political entity no longer existed, while 'Israel' as religious Judaism was only in the highly contested process of coming into being. It is this contest, as it manifested itself in the Persian province of Yehud, that is the main setting for the analysis of this book.

2. The typical scholarly conventions for designating the time period have also recently come under fire (see Grabbe 1998c, with its references to other articles in that volume). What is the meaning of 'the Exile', and hence 'the postexilic period', if the Exile is in large part an ideological construct? What is the meaning of the 'Second Temple period' if we are not sure when the Second Temple was actually built? My own work will attend to the difficulties behind these terms, but must in the process risk their conventional use.

counterpart who is designated by the doubled epithet 'Strange Woman/
Alien Woman' (*'ishshah zarah/'ishshah nokriyyah*). The figures of
Woman Wisdom and the Strange Woman are not, however, simply
equal opposites; my readings of Proverbs and the narratives do not produce interpretations that show the Stranger's 'bad' to Wisdom's 'good',
but rather that deconstruct a variety of presumed moral, social and theological polarities. The argument of this book proceeds on several fronts
to lay out the biblical field of strangeness, and also show how it undermines itself. In the remainder of this Introduction, I offer the reader
three different but overlapping conceptual frameworks which inform
my work. I shall then conclude with a historical overview of the period
in question.

Wise and Strange, Strange and Holy:
Signs of Binary Breakdown

Let me begin by pointing to four ways in which the apparent binary of
wise–strange breaks down.

1. The binary of 'wise vs. strange' is an imperfect one. One expects
the antithesis of 'wisdom' to be 'folly' (cf. Scott 1972: 160-61). While
'folly' has a range of negative connotations, the sense of deadly evil
and fundamental 'otherness' associated with the concept 'strange' does
not inhere in it.[3] It is more difficult to predict what the opposite of
'strange' might be in biblical thought. The force of this term in any
given context has been the subject of some dispute and, indeed, it is
part of the project of this book to explore its possibilities, both when it
stands in conjunction with wisdom and when it does not. The most
notable alternative to wisdom as the antithesis of strangeness is the
notion of holiness found in the priestly literature. The conceptual pair of
strange and holy thus also requires explication.

2. The apparent dichotomy of the concepts wise and strange is further
broken down by their mutual embodiment in female figures. In virtually
all known cultures, and most certainly in the Mediterranean culture of
Israel, one of the most pervasive binaries is that of 'male vs. female'.

---

3.   It comes as a surprise in Prov. 9, for example, when the figure theretofore
referred to as the Strange Woman is suddenly cast as Folly. The connotative force
of the latter term shifts rather dramatically in that equation: by dint of context, folly
is rhetorically pressed into the mold of strangeness.

Moreover, in a thought-world as interested in logical antitheses as that of Proverbs, one might expect the personification of its governing opposition to be actualized in terms of opposing genders. The fact that Wisdom and the Stranger are joined as Woman becomes, then, of more than passing interest (see Chapter 4). In fact, a close reading of the concepts of wisdom and strangeness as feminized in Proverbs reveals more ambiguity to their relationship than at first appears. The male reader is certainly advised to embrace Wisdom and avoid the Stranger, but telling them apart may be trickier than it seems. In Chapter 2, I shall use folklore's trickster figure as a lens for interpreting this relationship.

3. The third mode of deconstructing the wise–strange polarization is that of narrative. The Bible contains a significant number of texts dealing with women who are 'strange' in one or more senses of the term and who often either appear alongside women associated with wisdom, or whose encompassing narratives deal with the problem of wisdom. The ambiguity that lurks under the surface of Proverbs is, in particular, boldly highlighted in the stories of Samson (see Chapter 3) and Solomon (see Chapter 4), the former a full embodiment of a trickster. In both cases, the opposition between wise and strange apparent at least on the surface of Proverbs breaks down. Discernment of the difference becomes difficult; whether or not there *is* a real difference is opened to question.

4. Finally, the wise (or holy) vs. strange dichotomy breaks down when set into the social and political dynamics of postexilic Judah. This was a time of struggle over Jewish identity formation, including the use of a powerful rhetoric of Othering in the interest of defining and controlling 'Us'. The struggle took place on more than one level, with attempts to limit at the outer edges those who qualified for community membership, as well to limit to a small inner circle those with claim to priestly status. In both cases, however, the lines tended to blur and slip: those called 'foreign' were often residents of the land; those called 'strange' were often former members of a priestly lineage. Wisdom and holiness as designators of insider status could be fragile categories indeed; the canon proves them needy of considerable literary-ideological shoring up. Importantly for our purposes, this poetic and mythic task was not only carried out in gendered terms, but, insofar as both Wisdom and Strangeness were figured as female, in terms that reproduced the blurring and slippage it attempted to eliminate.

Issues of Method and Interpretation

As a second approach to the conceptual underpinnings of my project, I shall try to unpack in this section three major interpretive and related methodological issues that emerge when the elements discussed above are woven together into a more complex web.

1. As noted, through its female images, Proverbs establishes a basic thematic relationship, and apparent opposition, between wisdom and strangeness. This tensive relationship provides a hermeneutical key that opens up the ideologic of other texts as well. Wisdom in Proverbs is explicitly associated with restricting sex to marriage, speaking truth, maintaining one's inheritance, living in righteousness and, indeed, gaining life itself. One would expect the opposite of 'wisdom' to be 'folly', as, indeed, it is in the individual proverbs of Proverbs 10–30, as well as in 9.13-18, the concluding poem of the introductory chapters. The more frequent poetic embodiment of Wisdom's counterpart as the *Strange* Woman, however (2.16; 5.3, 20; 6.2; 7.5), complicates the picture. Strangeness is a rich and varied concept in Hebrew (see Chapter 1). It not only represents the opposite of the typical wisdom attributes and values just mentioned, but also raises issues of ethnicity and national identity (who is a true 'Israelite'?), of faithful worship of Yhwh as opposed to idolatry, and of practicing proper cult (including concern for authorized cultic leadership), issues that do not explicitly appear in Proverbs.

Although these latter concerns only appear explicitly outside Proverbs, many commentators have applied them to the interpretation of Woman Wisdom and the Strange Woman, usually as part of an effort to locate the historically elusive poetry of Proverbs in the context of specific sociohistorical debates. The usual suspect in this case is the apparent fifth-century opposition to foreign marriages attested in the books of Ezra and Nehemiah. This move is not inappropriate—indeed, it will play a part in my own argument—but involves both historical and literary complications usually not accounted for. I shall treat the historical issues below and focus on the literary here. Two points need more attention than is typically given. The first of these, the ambiguous interrelationship of the now notably odd polarity of wisdom and strangeness has been mentioned above. The second concerns the hermeneutics of reading Proverbs through the lens of narrative, legal and prophetic texts.

The issue in this case has to do with intertextual methodology. There is no clear rationale, especially in the increasingly synchronic context of the emerging canon,[4] for reading Proverbs in light of other texts and then failing to turn the tables. Woman Wisdom and, especially, the Strange Woman are multifaceted figures in Proverbs, whose complexity tends to be reduced by unidirectional intertextuality (cf. Aichele and Phillips 1995: 11-15). A typical scholarly move reads the Strange Woman through the nationalistic filter of Ezra–Nehemiah, with its bias against foreign wives, thereby virtually ignoring the sexual aspects of the figure in favor of her meaning as an ethnic foreigner and perhaps idolater. One of the most obvious features of Hebrew Bible rhetoric, however, is its collapsing of language for illicit sex, illicit worship and intermarriage with foreigners, especially foreign women. Thus, in Chapter 1, I consider the various figurations of strangeness, sex and religion found in the Bible, attempting to explicate the complex linkages of Proverbs to other texts. Priestly literature makes a different, but equally interesting rhetorical move, designating as 'strange' those who are not of the proper priestly family (see Chapters 5–7). Sometimes this rhetoric is explicitly gendered, other times only implicitly. Focus on the Strange Woman will, I argue, allow for an integrated reading of the larger priestly construction of the holy by means of the strange. There is value, then, in maintaining the plurivocality of Proverbs's Strange Woman both on its own terms and for its potential to reverse the intertextual telescope. What are the results of giving a wisdom reading—a Strange Woman reading—to other texts dealing with strangeness?

2. A second significant issue that runs through the chapters of this book—virtually unavoidable given the embodiment of Wisdom and Strangeness as women—is the construction of gender. Although the wise woman–strange woman images smack of classic patriarchal virgin–whore stereotyping, the matter is more complex and, to my mind, more interesting. I have already suggested that the dichotomy of wise

---

4. Better might be the plural, emerging canon*s*, a case made with admirable clarity, given the paucity of data, by Philip Davies, in his recent *Scribes and Schools* (1998). This book appeared, unfortunately, after my own manuscript was all but complete. Thus, I have not been able to make full use of Davies's enormously valuable reconstruction of the development of the early Jewish canons and the scribes who produced them. I shall try at least to point to his contributions in footnotes.

and strange tends to break down in the ambiguity of telling one woman from another.

On one level, this is patriarchy at its worst: not two categories constructed for women, all-good or all-bad, but only one, all women as evil. The book's last section (Chapters 5–7) takes up this point of view by considering cases of Israelite women, Dinah and Miriam, who are symbolically 'made strange', one raped by a strange man, the other struck with the uncleanness of leprosy. There are two related points of interest here. First is the fact that each woman is a sister to a forebear of a priestly lineage (Levi and Aaron, respectively); second is the absence of wisdom from these narrative representations of strangeness and its replacement with the concern for holiness construed in a particular way, namely, purity of lineage. These facts raise the question of the social-institutional location of the likely audience(s) of these texts and their gender ideology (see further below).

On the other hand there is sometimes a play in the narratives on the 'evil woman' construction that may confuse (or perhaps even amuse?) contemporary feminist judgment. For one thing, there are men—Solomon and Samson—who go strange. In both cases, of course, great men are *led* astray by strange women; the logic is patriarchal, yet not simple-minded. Solomon's case is particularly interesting because he is the quintessential wise man, who before his fall has dealings with women who are both wise *and* strange (Bathsheba and the Queen of Sheba). Samson's is complicated because his estrangement, and thus his strange women, serve God's purposes against Israel's Philistine enemies. The question of whose side God is on at any given moment, and what that means for human behavior, is here called radically into question, in and through the image of the Strange Woman.

3. Finally, this book attempts to address the thematics of wisdom and strangeness, as related to the construction of gender, in terms of the developing institutional forms and shifting power relationships of postexilic Judah, mainly during the period of Persian rule (538–333 BCE), though with an eye toward the early Hellenistic as well. The last decade has seen considerable scholarly interest in this period. Although advances in understanding have been made, the paucity of our information leads as often to speculation as to assured results. My own approach will be circumspect, in a rather literal sense of that term. Rather than attempt a full-scale sociohistorical reconstruction into which I would set the literature, I shall try to maintain a consistent awareness of the circu-

larity of plumbing ideological literature for the data used to reconstruct the circumstances of its creation or redaction.

In taking this stance, I shall not avoid the circle; however, part of my interest is precisely in the intellectual and ideological process by which I as a contemporary reader undertake such a literature-based historical reconstruction. Thus, while I shall employ some of the sociohistorical categories of current biblical scholarship, I shall do so tentatively, trying to maintain a sense of their existence as *literary* entities. Further, whether literary or social-institutional, these are categories that almost certainly changed, whether on the ground or in the eyes of readers, over the time period under consideration.

'The eyes of readers' will be an important element in my circumspection. Part of my sociohistorical reconstruction will be a second-order reconstruction not of the authors or redactors of the texts, but of possible readers. In particular, I shall conjecture a 'wisdom reader' (one, that is, invested in Proverbs's way of thinking) for the Solomon and Samson narratives, and a 'priestly reader' for Miriam and Dinah. My readers are not necessarily ideal readers; that is, I do not suppose they are a direct construction of the narratives themselves, although (in some cases more than others) I suspect this argument could be made. My argument, rather, is one that combines (tentatively) intertextual and sociohistorical assumptions; my readers are constructions drawn from *other* texts whose social locations have been hypothesized by scholars.

My priestly reader, then, is a construction from texts generally agreed to have cultic interests, combined with the scholarly reconstruction of postexilic political leadership by those centered in the cult. This picture is complicated by what seem to have been conflicts among different groups who wished to claim this control, and between these groups and others, sometimes allied and sometimes not, whose claims to political control were grounded in secular authority, either in their positions as the 'heads of the fathers' households' or in their commission from the Persian imperial government. Part of the result of this authority struggle that is highly determinative for my version of a priestly reader is a concern for genealogy, a view of authority as derived from being born of the right seed.

My wisdom reader is drawn from my interpretation of Proverbs, one who is given to antitheses like wisdom and strangeness, yet also on some level realizes these cannot be sustained. The social location of this reader—a postexilic 'sage'—is not attested until much later (cf. Ben

Sira, c. 180 BCE); thus certain educated guesses about it can be made, while other questions remain. One of the best attempts to reconstruct the position, role, ideology and political relationships of the postexilic developers of the wisdom tradition (at least insofar as it is represented by Proverbs) is that of Jon Berquist (1995: 161-76). Largely by means of an ideological analysis that makes the most of the little available data, he argues that these sages belonged to a class of scribes with an international outlook and, in particular, an interest in maintenance of a social order aligned with Persian rule, but manifest in God's creation. Berquist sees these scribes as intellectuals, aware 'of the socially constructed nature of reality', and thus resistant to accepting either the temple or the canon as absolute authority for truth (164-66). On the other hand, as Davies argues, 'it will be among the scribes of the Jerusalem temple that the impetus for a literature of national identity will have developed' (1998: 68-69). Yet not all scribes who work for the temple are priests, with narrowly defined 'priestly interests'. Scribes are also needed for the running of the government and the business of the laity and, as a larger, wealthy lay class develops, for their education as well (Davies 1998: 15-36, 74-88). Moreover, as a social group of employees whose identity lay not wholly with their employers their literature may evidence the subtle commentary of ambiguity and satire (19).

The book of Proverbs was produced by scribes, possibly for a non-scribal audience, life lessons for a pious elite. It had, then, the possibility of a rather wide readership, the potential to condition the world-view of persons with otherwise varying interests. But, as I shall argue, there is more to the book, taken as a whole, than a collection of moral lessons. Proverbs does not focus on the temple, but it is not, in its redacted form, unconcerned with the matter of spatial purity; it does not focus on the Mosaic Torah, but it is not, as a book, unconcerned with matters of canon in general or Torah interpretation in particular.[5] If we focus on its female construction of Wisdom and Strangeness, generally considered part of the latest stage of its editing process, we are drawn to the question of the relationship of someone who reads—and reads the world—like this to other institutional matrices and political groups. How

---

5. By Davies's definition, the book of Proverbs, as a collection of writings categorized as 'Solomonic', put onto a single scroll and archived, *is* a 'canon' (1998: 135-36). I shall go further than this, however, and argue for a certain self-consciousness on the part of its copyists/archivists with respect to the (potentially disputed) authority of this particular canon.

does this person relate to the priests who offer the other major canonical perspective on strangeness, or to the persons who produced Ezra–Nehemiah, which describes both a version of the giving of the law and an actualized political opposition to marriages by 'Israelite' men to 'foreign' women?

My readings of Proverbs alongside other, narrative texts suggest that these relationships were not consistent. I shall not, then, claim to offer new conclusions regarding the postexilic period except perhaps the caution that things were far more complex than we, 2500 years later, can imagine. I shall, however, through a close reading of certain texts, try to unpack some of the ideological underpinnings and cross-currents that marked the era and its institutions, considering, in particular, the relationship of the sages to canons and cult.

Gendering Strangeness

Because my entrée into history is literarily determined, I offer here an overview of the variations in the conceptual field of strangeness and its entailments running through our present canonical literature that certainly impacted and were, indeed, probably generated in the postexilic period.[6]

6. Broadly speaking, the theoretical perspective that governs the following analysis is drawn from the work of George Lakoff and Mark Johnson on the operation of cognitive models that provide the means by which humans organize knowledge (Lakoff 1987; Lakoff and Johnson 1980). Though my work on 'strangeness' does not approach the level of technical sophistication made possible by their theory, it depends on certain aspects of it. For example, 'strangeness' can be seen as a 'cluster model' (Lakoff 1987: 74-76), that is, a combination of a number of cognitive models to form a more complex one (thus, 'strangeness' is 'defined' collectively by nationality/ethnicity, idolatry, sexual behavior and cultic proximity). The category of 'strangeness', moreover, is determined by several idealized cognitive models that are to some degree in conflict with one another or with social reality (e.g. 'proper marriage is marriage to another Israelite' vs. 'Israelite identity is predicated on blood ties that preclude marriage' or, alternatively, vs. the reality that what constitutes Israelite identity is in debate; cf. Lakoff 1987: 69-74); one must discover the logic by which these tensions could be managed if not resolved. Particularly when combined with female imagery, the idea of strangeness can be understood as a metonymic model (Lakoff 1987: 77-90), one, that is, that involves a 'stands-for' relationship. Thus, 'woman' stands for 'strangeness' in a variety of ways involving important cultural stereotypes (especially the danger and deceit of a sexually autonomous woman) and ideals (the contrast to the [sexually controlled and truthful]

Ethnicity[7] and marriage. With a few notable exceptions, biblical discourse typically takes it as a given that faithful 'Israelites' will separate themselves from national/ethnic foreigners, a separation whose most obvious social manifestation is the prohibition of intermarriage. This us-vs.-them ideology masks, however (and none too well), certain undermining realities.

The question of when one might begin to speak of an identifiable 'people of Israel' is currently under heated scholarly debate. It is certainly the case that, the assumption of the texts notwithstanding, the earliest purported period of Israel's emergence onto the historical scene (1200–900 BCE) was one in which material identity markers between one group and another were virtually non-existent.[8]

This utter lack of notable ethnic difference between an identifiable 'Israel' and their 'Canaanite' neighbors is mythologized in Genesis's stories about the consanguine origins of the different groups in the region. By the same token, the mythology of Israel as a family descended from one man (couple?) runs up against the fact that, when translated into historical terms, it would require centuries of unbroken incest. More likely is the scenario painted by Ezekiel's castigating rhetoric: 'Your mother was a Hittite and your father an Amorite' (16.45). We may not, that is, be able to imagine a pristine 'Israel' at any point in time; Israel emerged from and as a mixture. We are left with what appears in hindsight, but only in hindsight, as a paradox: on the one hand, so-called 'intermarriage' would have been the norm of the day

wise wife, by definition a 'non-stranger'). At a general level, what I take from Lakoff and Johnson is an approach to 'strangeness' as a culturally definitive category, a root metaphor for 'not-Us'. I assume that ideas others have taken to be items on a list of 'different meanings' of the term are in fact united by a logic or logics that can reveal larger insights into the construction of meaning in biblical literature.

7.   The term 'ethnicity' is an ambiguous one; it may suggest groupings of people based on race (but what is that?) or custom. I use it in uneasy conjunction with the equally unsatisfactory term 'nationality' (at what point might one begin to speak of a 'nation' of Israel, and what relationship to some sort of 'ethnic' distinction did that imply?). The problem in the terminology encapsulates the problem in the conception: in what sense are 'Israelites' Israelites?

8.   Cf. Coote and Whitelam (1987: 123-27) on the continuity in material culture between that of the new Early Iron Age highland settlements (often equated with 'early Israel') and that of the preceding Late Bronze, as well as between highland and lowland sites.

while, on the other, it is unlikely that the issue of 'intermarriage' could have been conceived as a matter of social policy.

In other words, the problem of 'boundaries' between peoples that could be 'breached' by intermarriage was a question of a later day and age. When, then, and for whom? The question remains open as to the degree of popular consensus about the ethnic or religious (as opposed to simply political) self-understanding of a 'people of Israel' before the time of late seventh-century Judah. Even if some such self-consciousness existed during the monarchic era, the populace would, nonetheless, have been sufficiently segmented that it would have been difficult, on a practical level, to think in terms of marriage between Israelites as inherently incestuous, despite the implications of the myth of The Family (but was there yet such a myth?). During the monarchic era, moreover, it is unlikely that the possibility of intermarriage with politically defined foreigners would have been a live one for most people. The problem during the monarchy was more likely that of deciding on advantageous marital relationships between different families of the propertied class. If intermarriage were an issue at this time, it left remarkably few literary remains, except for two flagship cases involving kings: Solomon, who was led astray by his foreign wives, and Ahab, the beleaguered husband of that paragon of wickedness, Jezebel.

Both these latter texts connect the practice of intermarriage—in both cases involving foreign *wives*, not husbands—with the worship of foreign gods. These narratives and the laws against intermarriage in Exod. 34.15-16 and Deut. 7.2-5 to which they seem to be related are dated by scholars, at the earliest, late in the monarchic era. The considerations above, however, indicate little sense in such legal restrictions in that period. Alexander Rofé (1988), moreover, has made a strong case for dating the Jezebel narrative in the postexilic period,[9] and my own reading of the Solomon material will be from a postexilic perspective.

---

9.   Rofé contrasts the account of Naboth's vineyard in 1 Kgs 21.1-16, which features Jezebel's murderous deceit, with the version recounted by Jehu in 2 Kgs 9.25-26, which blames only Ahaz. 1 Kgs 21 itself, moreover, is a composite narrative. The prophetic announcement of punishment and its immediate effects (vv. 17-29), like 2 Kgs 9, focus blame on Ahaz; references to Jezebel are awkwardly inserted, and make no reference to the Naboth incident. Linguistic evidence, as well as its strong and direct reliance on Torah literature, mark the Jezebel version as the later text, in which blame has been shifted, in typical postexilic rhetoric, to the foreign woman.

To be sure, the worship of gods other than or in addition to Yhwh provided a challenge to advocates of henotheism throughout the monarchic era and after. Even as official dogma (not to mention popular practice), henotheism (not to mention monotheism) was slow to take hold. It seems to win the day only in the Persian period, when the situation was, as we shall see, further complicated by struggles over membership in and leadership of the cultic and political structure in Judah. Here, then, is the ultimate reality undermining the Bible's 'Israelite vs. the foreigner' ideology: the problem of establishing 'true Israelite' identity was, at that time it came to matter, at least as great a problem internally—who had and made claims to Israeliteness?—as it was externally. These struggles were played out, in part, in rhetoric about marriage to outsiders, especially women. Thus, the question of intermarriage only achieved real practical force after the establishment of the Persian administration in Judah, at which time it came to stand at the center of the symbolic discourse of identity formation. Whether or not it ever, even at this point, substantially affected social policy remains uncertain. To these symbolic issues we now turn.

Right sex and right religion. Marriage, for a group of people struggling with identity, is a problem on a couple of levels. To the extent that the problem is defined simply as separation of one group from another, gender would not seem to be a central concern. Whether insider men marry outsider women or vice versa should be immaterial; the point is, no intermarriage should take place at all. Although this way of expressing things is evident at some points in the Bible (Deut. 7.3; Ezra 9.12; Neh. 13.25; and, notably for our purposes, Gen. 34), the most forceful textual voices speak solely in terms of the danger of the foreign woman. Even the Ezra and Nehemiah passages, which seem to quote Deuteronomy, are set in a narrative where marriage to foreign *women* is the only real issue.

There are probably several factors to explain this. In the Persian and early Hellenistic periods, these may have included practical matters of undesirable (in terms of certain interests) political alliances sealed by marriage or inheritance rights involving women. To such considerations we shall return below and in Chapter 1. For the moment, I shall focus on the broader cultural-symbolic level of the issue. Structural anthropology points to the notion of women as mediators of exchange in the arrangement of marriages (Lévi-Strauss 1963: 60-62, 83). Part of the sense of underlying danger comes from women's position at that margin of family (read: 'national') identity that must come into contact with and open up a channel to the alien group (cf. Williams 1982: 110-32). This sense of female danger would attach both to one's own daughters as well as to women marrying in. At a practical sociological level, however, since a family's daughters marry out (i.e. join the husband's household), the practice of 'our' women marrying 'foreign' men held relatively little danger of contaminating the group's cultural or religious life compared to that of the wife marrying in. On the other hand, the same practical considerations would indicate that intergroup marriage will always be a matter of exchange: 'we' could hardly expect 'them' to marry our daughters without reciprocation. Thus, the focus on refusing foreign *wives* must be seen as a matter of rhetoric more than policy.

The biblical canon is pervaded, moreover, with an ideological use of marriage as religious symbolism wherein God, as husband, chooses (what was supposed to be) a faithful Israel as wife. Crucially, as is evidenced in many texts, the failure of Israel to devote exclusive worship to Yhwh was metonymically connected to men's sexual relations with inappropriate women, variously defined—foreign women, prostitutes, adulteresses—and also metaphorically transformed into the image of Israel playing the harlot with foreign gods. Two symbolic moves have been made here, perhaps best described as metaphoric collapses. The first collapse is that of male into female. Once the marriage metaphor fully takes hold as a way of talking about the relationship of Israel and Yhwh, Israel is necessarily transformed into a woman and, one might note, seldom a good one. The challenge inherent in the marriage metaphor to Israel's normal sense of gender identity—the people defined by its *male* members—also raises the possibility of imaging the relationship of God and Israel as a homosexual one, a possibility repressed but not absent in certain texts (Eilberg-Schwartz 1994). Secondly, the issue of marrying the correct woman is conjoined with that of appropriate use of sexuality within the socially designated confines of that correct marriage. 'Right sex' carries this doubled significance—right marriage and right sexual practice—into the symbolic field of 'right religion', while struggling to stay upright before its now gender-bent altar.

Right sex and right ritual. Sexuality in the Bible has an inverse connection to ritual: 'right sex' with respect to ritual is sex disconnected from it by a combination of time (after nightfall) and purification

(Frymer-Kensky 1989: 91). Indeed, in what may be one of the most widely accepted fabrications of all time (Oden 1987: 131-53), the Bible makes its case against Israel's neighbors based in part on their lascivious ritual habits. Like the wage of a prostitute, however, sex slips in through the temple doors (cf. Deut. 23.18). Sex is, first of all, invisible. Because it would have been impossible to ascertain everyone's purity status on a regular basis, the restricting laws can have had but limited effectiveness, perhaps applied strictly only by the priests to themselves. In certain literary contexts, moreover, the images of strange fire (Lev. 10; see Chapter 5) and the Strange Woman (Prov. 7; see Chapter 1) open Israel's cultic life to the presence of sex precisely in its act of protestation. Language, restless under its ideological constraints, seeks to say what cannot be said.

Right sex and right language as a matter of life and death. As I have suggested, the metaphor of Israel as God's wife exerts extraordinary pressure on the conceptualization of proper—or, to be more precise, improper—religious practice. The words for 'play the harlot' and 'commit adultery' become virtually synonymous with 'worshiping foreign gods'. At the same time, particularly in texts showing connection to wisdom thought, language's reflection on itself takes a sexual turn.[10] Fundamental to the opposition of Woman Wisdom and Woman Stranger in Proverbs is the question of who speaks truth and who deceives. Deceitful language is imaged as sexual in both process and content. 'The lips of a strange woman drip honey and her speech is smoother than oil' (Prov. 5.3). Her offer, of course: illicit sex. The contrast begins to blur, however, when the protection offered by Wisdom's truth is itself purveyed in erotic terms familiar from the Song of Songs and Egyptian love poetry: 'Say to Wisdom, "You are my sister"; and call Insight your intimate friend' (Prov. 7.4; for 'sister' as an element of love language, see Song 4.9, 12; 5.1).

The business of good speech is at the heart of the wisdom tradition, as is evident in many proverbs as well as in the introduction to the book itself, where wisdom's most advanced practitioners are equipped to 'understand a proverb and a figure, the words of the wise and their riddles' (1.5-6). Wisdom's dependence on language is undermined, however, first by its seeming unwillingness to distinguish clearly between *effec-*

10. Cf. Williams's discussion of 'the feminine, sexuality and language' (1982: 114-23).

tive speech and *truthful* speech and, secondly, by the reality that language is always capable of a deceitful turn (Aletti 1977: 139-40). The encapsulation of the wisdom enterprise as the ability to understand 'proverb, figure and riddle' (Prov. 1.6) bespeaks this ambiguity. And, as Chapter 2 will elaborate, the difficulty in discerning the Wise Woman from the Strange, because of gender and sex, symbolically reproduces it. This is, we should note, a dilemma of significant proportion, for the capacity to distinguish truth from deceit is intertwined, by means of Proverbs's female imagery and sexual language, with the choice between life and death.

Biblical narrative is filled with women who deceive or connive: Rebekah, Tamar, Ms Potiphar, the midwives of Exodus, Rahab, Ruth, Bathsheba, Judith. Notable, however, is the fact that deceit's predicted entailments, particularly strangeness and death, are only inconsistently present. Some of these women are foreign, some are Israelite, and the ancestry of two is ambiguous. Some element of sexual deviance is involved in all but two cases. In every case, the actions of the women lead to the fulfillment of God's plan, though they themselves receive varying degrees of credit and castigation for it. Among the most interesting female characters to consider in this vein are Samson's women and Solomon's. In both cases, sexuality and language are rather pointedly inter-metaphorized, and precisely in wisdom's terms. In the Samson saga, these elements are tied directly to reflection on deceit (see Chapter 3), while for Solomon, the question of right religion is at issue (see Chapter 4).

Right sex, righteousness, inheritance and lineage. The discussion up to this point shows the direction here. If deceit can lead to life and the fulfillment of God's plan, and if the act of deceit metaphorically entails sex outside its acceptable social confines, then the moral equation of righteousness and marital faithfulness breaks down, as does the predictability of whose side God is really on. Complexity increases again when the further entailments of inheritance and lineage are considered. These two concepts serve to specify the broader mythological fields of life and death. Life and death show up in biblical ideology less in terms of an individual's physical existence (though 'length of days' is not irrelevant) than they do in the man's right to claim his share of honor and prosperity in the God-given land, and in the divine promise of heirs to continue this claim in his name.

Righteousness should guarantee these expectations. Typically framed in terms of obedience to God's commandments, this righteousness and its promises still hinge at certain points on right marriage and right sex. Failure to avoid the Strange Woman puts a man 'at the point of utter ruin in the public assembly' (Prov. 5.14) and dooms his tenure in the land:

> the wicked will be cut off from the land,
> and the treacherous rooted out of it (Prov. 2.22; cf. 2.16-21).

The penalty seems to have a doubled force: not only is the perpetrator excluded from the rights and honor of his citizenship, but, if Eilberg-Schwartz correctly nuances the term 'cut off' with the notion of infertility, his lineage is also jeopardized (1990: 148).[11] The two aspects are closely related, yet not perfectly equivalent. Whereas loss of status and material inheritance are open to community sanction, loss of fertility functions at a symbolic level; it is something only God can control. The difficulty in maintaining assurance about the direct relationship of sexual crime and its punishment is, however, manifest in biblical narrative: Hagar and Lot's daughters are 'wrong women' who mother non-chosen lineages; Tamar and Ruth are sexually aggressive outsiders who bear the chosen seed; the end result of Bathsheba's adultery (whether as victim or temptress) is the heir to David's throne; Solomon's forbidden relationships cost his heirs part, but only part, of his kingdom.

Woman as Strange

The studies in this book turn on the strange, specifically on strange women. Sometimes their strangeness manifests in the most obvious sense of that term, as ethnic outsiders vis-à-vis the people of Israel. I suggest, however, that female ethnic foreignness is intimately linked, via several different modes, to other significant conceptual fields: it is linked, by ideological framing, to worship of foreign gods; by metaphor,

---

11. Being 'cut off' may well include ostracism from the people, or even execution at God's hand. Eilberg-Schwartz's discussion, however, places the phrase in the context of the covenant with Abraham, which avers that any uncircumcised man will be 'cut off' (Gen. 17.14). Here, the covenant promise in focus is that of fertility: God's promise to Abraham (vv. 5-6) and even to the (circumcised but still excluded) Ishmael (v. 20) of abundant progeny. Eilberg-Schwartz notes the interpretation of 'cut off' as 'made infertile' by the medieval commentators Ibn Ezra and Rashi.

to sexual strangeness (adultery, prostitution and, in general, women's control of their own sexuality); by extension of the sexual metaphor, to deceitful language; by metonymy to correct ritual practice; by moral logic to evil; by onto-logic to death; and by patri-logic, to loss of inheritance and lineage.

The textual base of operation begins in Proverbs where, I shall argue, the idea of strangeness plays out in largely symbolic ways: real ethnic foreign women and their gods are less a concern than all the metaphoric implications associated with them. As a product of the postexilic period, Proverbs's concern with strangeness is, in significant measure, a reflection not only of the need to establish 'true Israeliteness' by defining differences between different (= right vs. wrong) kinds of Israelites, but also of the need to divide the world into manageable existential categories. On this agenda, wisdom images find common ground with priestly interests and, I would suggest, the literary trajectory from Proverbs to Ben Sira bespeaks a practical merger of these two, never entirely independent, modes of thought. There are, nonetheless, different emphases: the priests' concern for ritual purity is not coterminous with the sages' development of a moral ontology. Both interests thread through the narrative texts, however, adding yet further complexity to the breakdown of the imperfect 'wise vs. strange' binary. I propose, then, not simply a study of literary images but also, through them, an exploration of their social and institutional bases in the postexilic period. To a preliminary look at this sociohistorical context we now turn.

Constructing Strangeness in the Postexilic Period

The books of Ezra and Nehemiah, along with the prophetic books of Haggai, Zechariah, Malachi and Third Isaiah, are our most important sources for the situation in Judah during the first hundred or so years of Persian rule (538 to about 430).[12] Unfortunately, the prophetic books deal with only the early years of the period (up to about 480), and that often allusively. The words of Haggai (520 BCE) and Zechariah (520–518) presuppose the return of some of the descendants of those Ju-

---

12. There are also other political and economic documents and inscriptions, from Persia, Mesopotamia and Egypt, as well as seals and coins from Palestine, that give a larger picture of the period, with occasional insights into the circumstances in Judah. In addition, later sources such as Josephus and Greco-Roman writers are sometimes helpful. See Grabbe (1992: I, 27-73) for an overview.

dahites exiled to Babylon in the early sixth century. They call for the rebuilding of the temple, though they never mention its completion;[13] envision the establishment of a pure priesthood in the person of Joshua; and, in the case of Zechariah, apparently attempt to fan messianic hopes around the leadership of Zerubbabel, hopes that the silence of the texts indicates, however, were quickly extinguished. The little we can glean after this comes from Malachi, whose reports of famine and cultic corruption are usually regarded to come from the first half of the fifth century. This prophet also admonishes against men divorcing their wives and against marrying women who worship other gods. Accusation of foreign worship is also made in Isaiah 57, likely from this period. We shall take up that issue in Chapter 1, and turn here instead to the books of Ezra and Nehemiah, whose concern with foreign marriage, interestingly, does not seem to be grounded in foreign deities.

The books of Ezra and Nehemiah are highly tendentious accounts that have been heavily edited, if not often authored, by a hand much later than the mid-to-late fifth-century context they presuppose. Paradoxically, then, while the next hundred years appear to be a literary blank as far as the Bible goes, the literary and theological shaping of Ezra and Nehemiah may tell us more about the late *fourth* century (and perhaps even later) than they let on. Grabbe, for example, argues that these books conflate three originally independent cult and city 'founder legends'—involving, respectively, Joshua/Zerubbabel, Nehemiah and Ezra—each of whom was considered by some group or other to have 'returned and restored the cult and/or the city after an extended period of exile' (1998a: 187-89). Despite this critical assessment, Grabbe continues to make cautious use of these books as sources for the purported governorship of Nehemiah in Jerusalem (445–c. 430), though he is far less sanguine about the historical value of their report of Ezra's mission. Davies, in contrast, relates the Nehemiah material to events in the late fourth century, when, according to Josephus, marriage between the families of a Jerusalem priest and a Samarian Sanballat was at issue (cf. Neh. 13.28). He sees Ezra, who goes unmentioned in sources as late as the second century, as a reflection of scribal interests of that era (1998: 100-102; cf. Garbini 1988: 151-69).

13. Scholars have usually accepted 515 (or 516) as the date of completion of the temple, based on the chronology in Ezra 6, though this has now been challenged by Grabbe (1998a: 134).

It is not essential for my present purposes to make a firm decision on dating these books, although, independent of Davies, I have been increasingly interested in the relationship of the character of Ezra to the second-century Ben Sira. I am less certain of which century to put (a probably more historical) Nehemiah in. I shall, at different points, consider the implications of one or more of the suggested possibilities. More relevant to me is the development of certain key themes in these books in relationship to those themes in Proverbs and other narrative texts. My particular interest, of course, is in their treatment of so-called 'foreign' women, but also of the equally important—and, in my view, related—issues of canon and cult.

On the political front, the books of Ezra and Nehemiah register a significant conflict between those who had experienced Babylonian exile and those who had remained in the land or entered it during the intervening decades. As is now widely recognized, this conflict was not always between 'Jews' and 'foreigners', as the generalized references to 'foreign wives' might suggest (Blenkinsopp 1991a; Eskenazi and Judd 1994; Washington 1994). While there were no doubt some 'real' foreigners (Ashdodites, Ammonites, Moabites; cf. Neh. 13.23) with daughters—and land claims—to offer, there was also the relationship with Samaria to negotiate. This city was a center of provincial power that could challenge Jerusalem, but also the home of worshipers of Yhwh. Also important was the internecine conflict between one group of Yehudites, the descendants of the former land-owning aristocracy taken into exile, now returned, and another group of Yehudites, the peasants who, remaining, would have claimed by right of 50 years of sweat that same land. The lines of conflict were further complicated in Nehemiah's day, some 75–100 years after the first wave of return, by which time a fair amount of intermarriage among these various groups, likely for reasons of mutual advantage, had taken place. With sharp, though perhaps unintentional, irony, Ezra–Nehemiah entitles those with rights to membership in the community and access to its material resources 'the Exile' (*golah*); those to be disenfranchised are called 'the peoples of the land(s)' (*'ammey ha'arats[ot]*).

> By referring to the local non-*golah* Judaeans as 'peoples of the land(s)', the returning exiles effectively classified their Judaean rivals, together with the neighboring non-Judaean peoples (Ammonites, Moabites, Edomites, residents of Samaria, etc.), as alien to Israel (Washington 1994: 232-33).

The rhetoric reaches its peak in Ezra 9.1-2, where these peoples of the lands are anachronistically identified with the abominating inhabitants of the past, the native Canaanites, Hittites, Perizzites, Jebusites and Amorites.

The book of Ezra, in particular, asserts with vigor not only the authority of the returned exiles, but also the necessity of their maintaining purity of lineage, a 'holy seed' (9.2). Cultic membership and the attendant land rights were established, however fictitiously, in genealogical terms (Ezra 2 = Nehemiah 7). Ezra in effect transforms a struggle over power and material interests into a struggle over the definition of Jewish identity at a cultural-symbolic level, a struggle that was definitively mounted in terms of divorce of 'foreign' wives—definitively, though perhaps only symbolically. For it is possible one should credit (or blame) the editor of Ezra–Nehemiah with having created a transformative piece of literature, rather than assuming a historical person who actualized this radical social policy. Though we shall return to this point later on, the distinction is not crucial to my present argument. Whatever the historical veracity of Ezra's reported leadership of a mass divorce of foreign wives, the important fact for my purposes here is the power such political rhetoric had to shape a significant part of biblical thought.

Whether Ezra's attempt at social engineering was carried out at all, much less with the success recorded in Ezra 9–10, its image is boldly stamped onto the face of the emerging canon, whether in texts of compliance or resistance; it will provide a point of departure for all the biblical literature considered in this book. For good reason, then, a number of recent scholars have argued for a relationship between Ezra and Nehemiah's reported attempts to get rid of wives taken from outside the *golah* group and the depiction of the Strange Woman in Proverbs (Camp 1985; Blenkinsopp 1991a; Eskenazi and Judd 1994; Washington 1994). It will be my contention, for reasons developed in Chapter 1, that the Strange Woman figure is too multidimensional to be univocally linked to one historical moment. To the extent, however, that Ezra–Nehemiah's 'foreign wives' already represent a complicated linkage between gender and nationality in the construction of 'Jewish' identity, this material points in the direction that my analysis of the Strange Woman, both inside and outside Proverbs, will take.

There is a further complication to understanding the dynamics of power and identity in postexilic Judah, namely the struggle of a priestly caste divided both internally, for control of the temple, and over against the lay leadership represented by the heads of the 'fathers' houses' (the extended relational networks, at best fictively tied as 'kin'). As I shall argue in Chapters 5–7, there is a priestly logic in portions of the Pentateuch wherein the Strange Woman is used as part of the identity rhetoric that makes outsiders of those who might have considered themselves insiders. Interesting questions thus arise as to the relationship between the priests and those responsible for Proverbs, as well as between either of these groups and Ezra.

Several recent scholars have argued that the book of Proverbs, and especially its first nine chapters, represents the voice of the lay aristocracy (Albertz 1994; Berquist 1995; Maier 1995). It has been my contention as well that the dominance of the sexual imagery used to construct Proverbs's Strange Woman reflects a significant concern for male control of the household (Camp 1991), essentially a secular, patriarchal issue. Yet the author of Proverbs 7 is not, as I shall show, disinterested in matters of cultic purity. This does not make him a priest; it does point to an ideological alignment between the interest of the sage in right sex and the priest in right cult, an alignment that, as Chapters 5 and 6 will show, pervades the book of Numbers.

There has been a similar long-standing debate among scholars about whether Ezra should be considered a priest. Although he is referred to as both priest and scribe skilled in the law (typically both together, if only by dint of editorial insertion: Ezra 7.1-6, 11, 12, 21; 10.10, 16; Neh. 8.1-2, 9; 12.26), he never acts in a priestly role. Rather, his major activity of promulgating the law seems definitively scribal. This, and his status as Persian appointee, lead some to consider him a representative of lay interests in Judah (Berquist 1995; Douglas 1993). Yet the narrator not only calls him 'priest', but even assigns him to the lineage of Aaron. His rhetoric against foreign wives (9.11-14) is decidedly priestly.[14] It is possible that this priestly stylization is a later addition to

---

14. This passage contains allusions to a number of texts in Deuteronomy (Deut. 7.1; 18.9; 7.3; 23.6; 11.8; 6.11; 1.38-39), as well as to the priestly material in Lev. 18.24-30. I characterize Ezra's words as 'priestly', because the logic of his statement—the rationale for avoiding marriages with the peoples of the lands—hangs on the idea, from Leviticus, that the land is 'unclean' (*niddah*) with the uncleanness of its peoples and their 'abominations' (*to'ebot*); they have filled it with their 'impurity' (*tum'ah*). While 'abomination' is a term shared by Leviticus and Deuteronomy, 'impurity' is the language of the priests. Striking in Ezra's speech is the use of *niddah*, whose most typical referent is menstrual impurity. Here again Ezra makes a

the book of Ezra, but this only moves the question to a later day: who would want to make of Ezra a priest if he weren't one already? Alternatively, who invented the character of Ezra 'priest and scribe'?

Notable, I believe, is the joint association of Ezra both with the priesthood and with the promulgation of the Torah, both overlain with his political role as a Persian official appointee. Albertz has argued that the time of Ezra—which he accepts, with the text, as the mid-fifth century—was one that saw the formulation of the Torah as a compromise document, representing the interests of both priests and lay leaders (1994: 464-93). It was a document produced out of their common concern to maintain Persian blessing on their leadership by seeking some reconciliation of the factions that divided Judah. If Albertz is correct about the motivations for Torah-making, then modeling Ezra as part-priest, part-lay, part Persian was quite a useful thing to do. This characterization may, however, as Grabbe and Davies suggest, represent the myth-making of a later hand, rather than fifth-century historical reality.

This leaves us, finally, with the question of the relationship of the book of Ezra to Proverbs. The most obvious connection is their shared concern for the Strange Woman. But it is not clear the figure of the Strange Woman serves the same rhetorical purpose in both cases. The larger ideological pictures need to be considered and compared, in particular the question of the relationship of the wisdom tradition, often regarded as tangential to the canon, to a priestly scribe who is closely associated with the canon's promulgation. The later wisdom book of Ben Sira, which combines close literary and ideological ties to Proverbs with interests in both canon and cult, provides motivation to reconstruct the prior development of these relationships.[15] By tracking the figure of the Strange Woman through an assortment of otherwise apparently unrelated texts, I shall attempt to trace one thread through this tangled

---

priest-like appeal to a 'natural symbol' of impurity, female blood. *Niddah* does not occur, however, in Lev. 18.24-30, the main source for Ezra's ideology of the polluted land. It does occur a few verses earlier (Lev. 18.19), in its usual sense of menstrual uncleanness. Ezra's exegesis of Leviticus, then, by making meaning of the merely contiguous, specifies the land's uncleanness as *female* uncleanness in a way his source does not.

15. There are important precedents for my interests in the work of Leo Perdue on wisdom and cult (1977) and of Gerald Sheppard on wisdom as a hermeneutical construct to the canon (1980). Davies (1998) has now added a whole new dimension of sociological grounding to the discussion of the development of early Jewish canons with his discussion of scribes, libraries and archives.

history. The key to its unraveling, I shall suggest, lies not in a simple equation of a historical Ezra's elimination of foreign wives with Proverbs's rejection of the Strange Woman. It lies rather in exploring the fissures in the process of identity formation in postexilic Judah—the multilayered process of separating 'us' from 'them'—fissures encoded in the emerging canon and embodied in the multifaceted figure of the Strange Woman.

Part I

WOMAN WISDOM AND THE STRANGE WOMAN
IN THE BOOK OF PROVERBS

Introduction to Part I

The figures of female personified Wisdom and her counterpart, the 'Strange Woman', in the book of Proverbs provide a rare locus for analyzing elevated female imagery in the biblical tradition. Whereas elsewhere in the Bible goddesses are simply condemned, if not ignored, here both positive and negative traits of powerful female symbols are rhetorically limned. Yet it is my contention that there is more to be learned when these two female figures are read not as an absolute polarity, but in dialectical tension with each other; together they are a paradigm of paradox. As such, I shall argue, they provide a construct by which both to analyze significant portions of biblical literature and to take soundings into the social and political tensions and interests surrounding the canon's formation.[1] As the starting point for the rest of this book, then, the task of the two ensuing chapters on the book of Proverbs itself is to suggest the sociohistorical milieu and the hermeneutical possibilities of the figures of Woman Wisdom and the Strange Woman.

It has become a commonplace in recent years to connect the figure of the Strange Woman with the so-called marriage reforms of Ezra–Nehemiah, with increasing attention paid to the likelihood that the rhetoric against 'foreign wives' in the latter material may be part of a polemic of identity and power claims directed against some Jews by other Jews, rather than (at least exclusively) against actual national/ethnic foreigners.[2] At this point, however, I think we can begin to see this setting of Proverbs's Strange Woman in these postexilic power politics as the beginning of an analysis rather than the conclusion. Reconstruction of the work of Ezra and Nehemiah is, for one thing, highly contested at this

---

1.   When I speak of the 'canon' and its development in this book, I am thinking more or less of the Hebrew Bible as we now know it, including some sense of the authoritative force accorded to it. I have assumed this to be a long and conflict-ridden process, beginning in the Persian period and still at work on some level well into the Roman, though also, in major respects, complete by then (in the sense of having widely recognized collections of Torah, Prophets and Writings). Davies's (1998) work sharpens this considerably, however, with his attention to the several smaller canons, each with some (though not necessarily absolute) authority to somebody, that would have been consolidated along the way to the final whole.

2.   See Introduction; and Blenkinsopp 1991a; Eskenazi and Judd 1994; Washington 1994; cf. Camp 1985.

moment in scholarship. Did Nehemiah arrive in Jerusalem in 445, as his book implies, or not until the late fourth century, when other sources attest the conflict with the Samarians which so pervades this book? Did Ezra arrive in 458, which the most literal reading of the text suggests, or in 397, which would make more sense of other available data? Or not at all: is he, in other words, along with his reported divorce action against foreign wives, an invention of a much later day? Equally important is the fact that the rhetoric of strangeness—especially when it gets mixed up, as it so often does, with the rhetoric of gender and sexuality—creates a complex web of associations and meanings that I doubt were 'read' the same by all parties in all times and places, even in a period we tend (mistakenly, I think) to homogenize as 'the postexilic' (cf. Berquist [1995] for an importantly nuanced reconstruction of the time Judah spent 'in Persia's shadow').

Chapter 1 argues that, while the 'Ezra connection' must be appreciated as part of the background of Proverbs's Strange Woman, its purported report of mass divorce is indeed, for Proverbs, *back*ground. Focusing on Proverbs's rhetoric of strangeness shows that the theological vision of this book faces, rather, forward to a new (though not necessarily better) era of identity and gender politics. The concern of Chapter 2 is more purely literary, focusing on the subtle, perhaps now frozen, dialectic of Proverbs's female embodiments of wisdom and strangeness. Here we prepare to discover their more exuberant interplay in the Solomon and Samson narratives (Part II), as well as to perceive the differences involved when priestly literature pairs holiness, rather than wisdom, with strangeness (Part III).

Chapter 1

THE STRANGE WOMAN OF PROVERBS[*]

Interpretation of the figure of the Strange Woman (*'ishshah zarah/ 'ishshah nokriyyah*) in Proverbs has taken two main routes. The first has focused on debate about the contextual meaning of the terms in the repeated doubled epithet that designates her. *Zar* and *nokri*, here in their feminine forms with 'woman' (*'ishshah*), have a variety of connotations, often overlapping, in the Hebrew Bible. They can refer to persons of foreign nationality,[1] to persons who are outside one's own family household,[2] to persons who are not members of the priestly caste,[3] and

---

[*] The main lines of this chapter's argument were laid out in an earlier article (Camp 1991). The years since then have seen a spate of publications on the post-exilic period that have helped to refine my analysis. I have found particularly helpful historical works by Albertz (1994), Grabbe (1992) and Berquist (1995), as well as analyses by Eskenazi and Judd (1994) and Washington (1994) of the use of the rhetoric of 'foreignness' in the internal Jewish power struggle of this period. Davies (1998) should now be added to this list.

1. *Zar*: 2 Kgs 19.24; Isa. 1.7; 25.2, 5; 61.5; Jer. 5.19; 30.8; 51.51; Ezek. 7.21; 11.9; 28.7, 10; 30.12; 31.12; Hos. 7.9; Obad. 11; Joel 3.17; Job 15.19; Lam. 5.2. *Nkr*: Gen. 17.12, 27; Exod. 2.22; 12.43; 18.3; Lev. 22.12; Deut. 14.21; 15.3; 17.15; 23.21; 29.21; Judg. 19.12; 2 Sam. 15.19; 22.45, 46; 1 Kgs 8.41, 43; 11.1, 8; Isa. 2.6; 28.21; 56.3, 6; 60.10; 61.5; 62.8; Ezek. 44.7, 9; Obad. 11; Zeph. 1.8; Ps. 18.45, 46; 137.4; 144.7, 11; Ruth 2.10; Lam. 5.2; 2 Chron. 6.32, 33; Ezra 10.2, 10, 11, 14, 17, 18, 44; Neh. 9.2; 13.26, 27, 30.

2. *Zar*: Lev. 22.10, 12, 13; Deut. 25.5; 1 Kgs 3.18; Jer. 3.13; Ezek. 16.32; Hos. 5.7; Ps. 69.9; 109.11; Job. 19.13, 15, 17. *Nkr*: Gen. 31.15; Exod. 21.8; Ps. 69.9; Prov. 23.27; 27.2; Job. 19.15; Qoh. 6.2. Because adultery and harlotry—that is, sexual activity outside the prescribed familial boundaries—are sometimes used as symbols for religious faithlessness, this meaning of *zar/nkr* overlaps at points with the connotation 'outside the covenant' noted below.

3. *Zar* only: Exod. 29.33; 30.9, 33; Lev. 10.1; 22.10, 12, 13; Num. 1.51; 3.4, 10, 38; 17.5; 18.4, 7; 26.61. Because the priests are often conceptualized as of one

to deities or practices that fall outside the covenant relationship with Yhwh.[4] Which of these connotations, or which combination of connotations, applies to Proverbs? Focusing on foreign nationality, Boström (1935), for example, concluded that the Strange Woman was a worshiper of a foreign goddess, an argument taken up more recently by Blenkinsopp (1991a), though with much greater methodological sophistication. On the other hand, the recognition that neither *zar* nor *nokri* necessarily refers to a national foreigner, led Humbert (1937, 1939) to a minimalist reading of the terms in Proverbs. In many cases they simply refer to anyone other than oneself; hence, he argued, the *'ishshah zarah* is 'the wife of another'. Snijders (1954) offers yet a third possibility. He finds in *zar* and *nokri* a broad sense of deviation, faithlessness and the unknown: the Strange Woman represents all one must utterly avoid.

The motivation for the Strange Woman figure in Proverbs remains in debate, not only because of the range of connotations for *zar* and *nokri*, but also because the imagery used to construct her is so rich with varied implications. The most obvious images are those of sexual indiscretion, including a peculiar combination of accusations of adultery and prostitution. The Strange Woman 'forsakes the partner of her youth' (2.17) and allures her lover with the assurance that her husband 'has gone on a long journey' (7.19). Yet she also walks the streets 'decked out like a prostitute' (7.10), which would not, presumably, be the most usual way for a married woman to seek alternative sexual partnership. Complicating the matter is the fact that, in the Bible, rhetoric about sex often signifies larger issues of religious faith or faithlessness: Israel is construed as the faithless wife of husband Yhwh (see further below).

The discussion has been considerably advanced, though hardly settled, by a second, more recent line of inquiry that seeks to reconstruct the sociohistorical context in and to which the Strange Woman speaks. Scholars have reached a certain level of agreement in the past few years that the figure is the product of a postexilic Judean setting, her 'strangeness' alluding in some way to the tensions of that period. These tensions resulted from the return of some of the descendants of the exiled

---

family ('the sons of Aaron'), the connotation of *zar* as 'non-priest' is at points a subset of the connotation 'not of one's family'.

4.   *Zar*: Deut. 32.16; Isa. 1.4; 17.10; 28.21; 43.12; Ezek. 14.15; Hos. 8.12; Ps. 44.21; 58.4; 78.30; 81.10; Job. 19.27. *Nkr*: Gen. 35.2, 4; Deut. 31.16; 32.12; Josh. 24.20, 23; Judg. 10.16; 1 Sam. 7.3; Jer. 2.21; 5.19; 8.18; Mal. 2.11; Ps. 81.10; Dan. 11.39; 2 Chron. 14.2; 33.15.

Judean leadership group (the *golah*, 'exile') from Babylon. The return led, first, to the contested rebuilding of the Jerusalem temple and then to ongoing struggles for both power and survival between those who had returned, those who had remained in the land and those who had entered the land in the interim. At stake behind the more material concerns was the fundamental matter of Jewish identity—who would be regarded as inside and outside the congregation, and who would decide. The terms of these struggles did not remain unchanged, however, during the two hundred years of Persian rule of Judah (539–333), and conflicts continued after the arrival of the Greeks. I shall, at the end of this chapter, assess the current state of scholarly speculation on the date and social location of the Strange Woman poems in Proverbs. My larger interest, however, is in the rhetoric of strangeness, sexuality and religion as it is used to construct the national/ethnic identity of postexilic Judaism. Through analysis of this rhetoric, we shall not only explore the Strange Woman's social location—or location*s*—but also consider her literary-ideological role in the formation of a canonically based national identity.

Certain features of the female imagery in Proverbs seem to link the Strange Woman with postexilic prophetic polemic against foreign worship, perhaps especially goddess worship, with its presumed sexual rituals for fertility (Camp 1985: 265-69; Blenkinsopp 1991a: 464-65). She is located 'at the high places' (9.14); she sits by a doorway, with all its sexual implications (9.14); her bed is the focus of her attraction (7.17); and it is associated with her participation in a sacrificial cult (7.14). Similar imagery, particularly the depiction of ritual sex, is used by the postexilic author of Isaiah 57 to construct the picture of idolatrous Israel:

> Upon a high and lofty mountain,
> you have set your bed,
> and there you went up to offer sacrifice (Isa. 57.7).

In both cases, moreover, the female image is associated with Sheol, the realm of the dead (Prov. 2.18; 7.27; 9.18; Isa. 57.9). In other prophetic material from the early Persian period, Zech. 5.5-11 contains a vision of a woman with a name sounding much like Asherah (*harish'ah*, 'Wickedness'), flown to Babylon in an ephah. And, in terms reminiscent of Prov. 2.17, Mal. 2.13-16 enjoins against divorce of 'the wife of your youth', contextually (at least) linking this to preference for marriage to 'the daughter of a foreign god' (2.10-12).

In addition to comparisons with prophetic material, one might also cite Proverbs's own attribution of its instructions to Solomon, whose single sin, according to the text, was 'his addiction to foreign women' (*nashim nokriyyot*, 1 Kgs 11.1-8; Blenkinsopp 1991a: 457). These women led him to violate the deuteronomic law against intermarriage and fall prey to the inevitable consequence of syncretism (Deut. 7.3-4). Was Proverbs 1–9, then, pseudonymously formulated as 'a cautionary instruction of Solomon based on his own experience' (Blenkinsopp 1991a: 457)? In this case, intermarriage with worshipers of Asherah might be seen as Proverbs's motivating concern, its imagery of 'strange' sexuality functioning as symbolism for the idolatry that would presumably accompany such marital practice (so Blenkinsopp).

While the prophets' and Deuteronomist's rhetorical connection of illicit sex with illicit worship lurks in the background of Proverbs, to be sure, it is not altogether clear that a contemporary practice of foreign worship is the editor's real concern. Isaiah 57 and Zechariah 5 date to quite early in the postexilic period (about 520). Ezra and Nehemiah, at least 60–80 years later, do not mention foreign gods, even though they are apparently quite concerned with foreign marriage; nor, as I shall show, does Proverbs. There is, moreover, considerable evidence that the rhetoric of 'strangeness' was applied in the postexilic period at least as much to other Jews as to actual national foreigners. It was, that is, part of an internal struggle for control of 'Jewish' identity.

A study of the rhetoric connecting strangeness, sexuality and religion reveals a complex ideological web, a result that points away from the view that the Strange Woman refers directly either to the practice of ritual sex or to an actual foreign woman who, in a mixed marriage, might lead her Israelite husband into foreign worship. Instead, the figure operates at a less directly historically referential level of symbolism, consolidating a variety of images of female-identified evil into an archetype of disorder at all levels of existence. Indeed, the Strange Woman begins to carry the burden of theodicy, providing a means to shift responsibility for evil from Yhwh. This alternative interpretation is also suggestive, as I shall conclude, of class and power interests that can be at least broadly located in the political and theological dynamics of the postexilic period.

The Strange Woman and her 'Cult'

Several recent studies on 'sacred prostitution' help to clarify the identity of the woman in Proverbs 7, the most extended representation of

the *zarah/nokriyyah*. Phyllis Bird's (1989b) examination of harlotry as
a metaphor in the Hebrew Bible establishes conclusively that the *zonah*
('harlot'; cf. Prov. 7.10; 6.26; 23.27) is never associated with cultic
activity, and that even *qedeshah*, usually translated 'sacred prostitute',
means simply 'consecrated woman' ('hierodule', in Bird's terminology), among whose varied functions may or may not have been ritual
sex. Thus, she concludes, the association of sex and foreign cult in the
Hebrew Bible is polemical, not necessarily descriptive; it is a piece of
rhetoric originating with the eighth-century prophet Hosea. A more
general overview of the use of the sacred prostitution metaphor in
ancient sources by Robert Oden (1987: 131-53) reaches the same conclusion. As in Greek and patristic sources, 'sacred prostitution *as accusation* played an important role in defining Israel and Israelite religion
as something distinctive' (Oden 1987: 153).

Although Bird does not discuss Proverbs 7, extension of her argument allows us to draw two corollary inferences. This poem has been
the source of much interpretive debate because of its apparent linkage
of sexual activity with cultic ritual: a woman 'dressed as a prostitute'
seeks a sexual partner as some sort of culmination to her offering of
sacrifices in payment of vows. The passage has almost always been assumed to refer to ritual sexual activity associated with the cult of a
goddess of fertility and/or love. Bird's analysis relieves us, however
of any necessity to interpret this language literally. On the other hand,
Hosea's polemical rhetoric became increasingly naturalized over time
in Israelite thought. Religious faithlessness came to be understood, by
virtue of a dying metaphor, to be an almost literal referent of the language of sexual deviance (cf. Camp 1985: 265-71; Archer 1986). Thus,
we cannot deny the possibility that the illicit sexuality rendered in Proverbs is in some sense a cipher for the breaking of covenant faith with
Yhwh. The question of whether ritual sex associated with a goddess
cult was involved remains open to investigation. Bird's careful analysis
of the mixture of literal and allegorical sex-language in Hosea provides
a model for interpreting the multivalence of the Strange Woman: not
only must references to human sex acts be distinguished from theological rhetoric, but polemic that hurls accusations of illicit sex must be
distinguished from descriptions of actual cultic activity.

Karel van der Toorn (1989) has also argued against the existence of
'sacred prostitution' in ancient Israel. He proposes a novel interpretation of the Strange Woman in Proverbs 7 as a basically honest Israelite

matron who turns in desperation to an isolated act of harlotry in order to raise money to pay a vow to the temple. Although I find this particular thesis implausible and his argumentation for it unpersuasive, van der Toorn's work does provide a clue that might explain the woman's reference to her sacrifices and vows in 7.14. As part of her invitation to the young man, she says:

> Sacrifices of well-being are upon me;
> today I fulfill (*shillamti*) my vows.

What, then, is the relationship of the woman's sacrifices and her vows? The question of how to translate the tense of *shillamti* has been a crux for interpreters. Those who construe the woman as a goddess worshiper tend to read it as a modal ('I must fulfill'), the implication being that her sacrifices involved a vow of ritual sex in honor of the goddess, which she plans to fulfill with the young man.[5]

The significant move made by van der Toorn is to associate the vow instead with a typical act of Israelite piety that is, however, being funded by extraordinary means (1989: 194-97).[6] Although, as I have noted, the scenario of a proper Israelite matron picking up some pocket change with a little harlotry on the side seems improbable, his instinct to associate Prov. 7.14 with biblical rather than foreign ritual is attractive. Indeed, further investigation reveals that, in spite of widespread acceptance of some sort of fertility-worship theory,[7] this aspect of the Strange Woman's speech can be easily and well explained by reference to the biblical laws.

C.H. Toy (1899) noted long ago that her 'sacrifices of well-being' are instances of the sacrificial feasts described in Lev. 7.11-21. 'In the present instance its occasion is a vow which has just been fulfilled' (Toy 1899: 151), that must be eaten on the day of the offering or the next (Lev. 7.16). Unmentioned by Toy is the fact that the levitical law also

---

5.   Although the verb form is a perfect, usually translated as a past tense, van der Toorn notes that the modal usage is 'sparingly but sufficiently attested in Hebrew' (1989: 198).

6.   Van der Toorn suggests that vow-making is particularly a form of female devotion. That women make vows is clear; whether they do so more frequently than men remains unproved, but neither his argument nor mine depends on this point.

7.   See van der Toorn (1989: 197-201) for a review of recent literature.

requires that the flesh of the sacrifice be eaten by persons in the state of ritual cleanness (7.19-20). Thus, when the Strange Woman invites the young man to engage in sexual activity either the night before the sacrifice or the next night, between the two days of feasting, she invites him to commit with her a crime whose penalty is that 'that person shall be cut off (*krt*) from his people' (*me'am*; Lev. 7.20).[8] Proverbs describes a similar fate for the man who associates with Woman Stranger (Prov. 2.22; 5.14). As one of the wicked, he will be 'cut off' (*krt*), in this case 'from the land' (2.22), and in 'utter ruin in the assembly (*qahal*) and congregation (*'edah*)' (5.14), that is, alienated from the people.

The concept of ritual uncleanness associated with sexual activity—though here with a quite different motivation—is also found in the deuteronomic legislation, where the payment of a vow to the temple with 'the hire of a harlot (*zonah*) or the wages of a "dog"' is regarded as an abomination (*to'abat*) to Yhwh (Deut. 23.19 [Eng.: 18]).[9] In Leviticus, it is the act of sex itself that ritually defiles, while in Deuteronomy the problem lies in the person's deviance from prescribed sociosexual roles.[10] The overlap and distinction between what might be seen as two

---

8.   This interpretation of the passage removes much, if not all, of the burden long carried by the tense of the poor verb *shillamti*. Since the ultimate fulfillment of the 'peace offering' vow involves two days of feasting, it seems clear that this process is not yet in every sense complete at the time the woman accosts the young man. It is possible that she has already offered her sacrifice (though the lack of a verb in v. 14a leaves the phrase temporally ambiguous) and that the moment of the sacrifice constituted a technical completion, thus making appropriate a translation of the perfect verb in 14b with the English past tense. On the other hand, the 'today' (*hayyom*) of v. 14b may refer to the 24-hour period beginning that night (cf. 7.9) and ending the following evening, in which case the act of sacrifice has yet to take place and a translation of *shillamti* with modal force (so Boström 1935 and van der Toorn 1989) is appropriate. In any case, all we need to know for our purposes is that sometime 'today' the act has been or will be complete; hence my choice of the present tense, 'fulfill', rendered with the force of a perfect verb.

9.   It is in interpreting passages like Deut. 23.19 that van der Toorn's argument, in my view, runs astray. He sees this verse as evidence that 'among Israelites, the custom of paying vows by means of prostitution was a known phenomenon' (1989: 200). I have offered here what seems to me a far more natural interpretation, namely, that prostitutes sometimes made vows and then attempted to pay them with the proverbial wages of sin.

10.   Recent studies on sex and cultic impurity include Wenham (1983); Milgrom (1989); and Frymer-Kensky (1989).

primary symbols—that of 'stain' in the former text and 'deviation' in the latter—deserves scrutiny.[11] That particular investigation of 'sexual cultics' lies mostly outside our present scope, though I shall suggest at least one implication of it below. Of significance for this moment is the fact that both of these pieces of legislation apply to the vow of Woman Stranger in Prov. 7.14. We have already seen that she proposes to defile —ultimately defile—both herself and the young man with sex during the period of feasting. But now we also see that she has paid or will pay her vow to the temple (the sequence matters nowhere near as much as past commentators have fretted) with the 'hire of a harlot'.

With these two links between the Strange Woman's words and biblical cultic regulations rather firmly established, another somewhat more tenuous one may be suggested. The sensual attraction in the woman's speech is enhanced, in 7.17, with the allure of a bed perfumed with 'myrrh, aloes and cinnamon'. Although, on the one hand, this is typical love-talk such as that found in Ps. 45.9 (Eng.: 8; the royal lover's robes are 'fragrant with myrrh and aloes and cassia') and Song 4.14 (the beloved is compared to a garden of spice and fruit, including 'myrrh and aloes'), the background of cultic violation already invoked suggests another allusion as well. In Exod. 30.22-33, a recipe is provided for the 'holy anointing oil' to anoint the cultic objects and to consecrate the priests, 'Aaron and his sons'. The oil is to be made of myrrh, cinnamon, aromatic cane, cassia and olive oil, that is, with two of the Strange Woman's three ingredients. The connection might seem stretched but for the following line that concludes the legislation on oil:

> Whoever compounds any like it or whoever puts any of it on an outsider (*zar*) shall be cut off (*krt*) from his people (*me'am*) (v. 33).

Here, as elsewhere in the priestly writings, our variegated term *zar*, when applied to persons, means 'outsider to the priesthood, layperson'. The penalty for disobedience, being 'cut off from one's people', clearly connects this law, however, with the levitical legislation on peace offerings and, hence, with the *zarah* of Proverbs 7.

If Prov. 7.14 is related not to foreign worship, but rather to defilement of the Israelite cult, an unexpected twist is added to our mysterious Strange Woman and the question of her sociohistorical setting is

---

11. For an analysis of symbolic modalities related to the human experience of evil, see Ricoeur (1967: 18).

further complicated. Whatever the merit of the argument that interprets this figure as a foreigner and goddess worshiper, we now find that she is also a violator of not just one, but a whole series of Israelite cultic laws as well. In this reading, then, she appears not as a foreign woman, but as an Israelite, though a peculiarly and intentionally deviant one. The 'foreign worship' interpretation is also undercut, insofar as 7.14 is the only verse in Proverbs 1–9 that could be construed as a reference to such presumed practices.

The poet of ch. 7, then, clearly assumes that readers will be familiar with both deuteronomic and priestly legislation and, indeed, see them as pieces of a single fabric that can be wrapped around this female figure. Thus, we see an author who is a student and interpreter of Torah and, more specifically, one with a special investment in pieces of legislation dealing with cultic purity. This insight into the poet's larger literary world will have implications for understanding the sociohistorical context of the figure of the Strange Woman.

Strangeness, Sex and Religion in the Context of the Canon

A fuller understanding of the function of the Strange Woman figure may be available by comparing the rhetoric that constructs her with that of other biblical texts. If one takes the language of Proverbs at face value, the question of what makes the Strange Woman strange centers around the sexual behavior of her and her partner, sometimes but not always in connection to cultic practice. It is also true, however, that elsewhere in the Bible illicit sex stands allegorically or metaphorically for non-Yahwistic worship, which is sometimes said to be caused by association (sex and/or marriage) with 'foreign' women. In fact, an overview of the biblical writings on this matter reveals more than one rhetorical strategy for connecting strangeness, sex and religion. We can, I suggest, identify two basic modes or logics at work, with variations and sometimes in combination. The first I shall label 'metaphoric–metonymic', the second, 'social-functional'. Based on this analysis, it will be my argument that, although the significance of sexuality in Proverbs is not entirely literal, it functions more complexly and powerfully than as a mere allegory for faithless worship.

The Rhetorical Logic of Metaphor and Metonym
The pre-exilic prophetic rhetoric of Hosea and Jeremiah adopts the strategy of representing idolatry (and foreign political alliances) as

wantonly illicit sex, either adultery or prostitution. In these cases, the female figure does not represent either a foreign woman or a foreign goddess. To the contrary, Hosea's Gomer can only be understood as an Israelite and, thus, as a metaphor for the people of Israel, who have joined themselves with a foreign deity (indeed, at least for Hosea and Jeremiah, the male deity, Baal).[12] The people are thus represented in female form (perhaps a derogatory comment in itself), and a wanton one at that, but intermarriage is not an issue (even though it may have been a causal force). These prophets do also speak of 'real' sexual activity, although not directly in the form of ritual sex in the cultic context.[13] Their castigations are, rather, directed against men who commit adultery or consort with prostitutes (e.g. Jer. 5.7-8; Hos. 4.2). Thus, the two inherently independent practices of idolatry and illicit sex are brought into a metonymic relationship that compounds the force of the metaphoric equation of idolatry and adultery against Yhwh, as well as making indirectly the polemical accusation of ritual sexual activity. This powerful combination of metaphor, metonym and hyperbolic accusation can be seen in Hos. 4.12-14:

> My people consult a piece of wood,
> and their divining rod gives them oracles.
> For a spirit of whoredom has led them astray,
> and they have played the whore, forsaking their God.
> They sacrifice on tops of mountains,
> and make offerings upon the hills,
> under oak, poplar and terebinth,
> because their shade is good.
> Therefore your daughters shall play the whore,
> and your daughters-in-law commit adultery.

12. The gender of the foreign deity is complicated by the narrative in Jer. 44.15-19 that shows a conversation between the prophet and women who worship 'the queen of heaven'' (cf. 7.18). These passages may indeed point to the practice of goddess worship, either at the time of Jeremiah or his editor. If so, it did not condition the prophet's rhetoric, which otherwise consistently refers to Baal (14 times).

13. Van der Toorn (1989: 202-204) raises the interesting possibility that a (quite secular) prostitution service was run by temple personnel for the purpose of enhancing temple revenues. Similarly, for Bird (1989b: 88), Hos. 4.11-14 suggests 'that prostitutes found the rural sanctuaries an attractive place to do business, quite possibly by agreement with the priests'. Both scholars caution against taking evidence for such activities as sign of authorized sexual ritual.

> I will not punish your daughters when they play the whore,
> nor your daughters-in-law when they commit adultery;
> for the men themselves go aside with whores,
> and sacrifice with hierodules;[14]
> thus a people without understanding comes to ruin.

Aspects of this trifold rhetorical barrage appear in the exilic prophet Ezekiel and the postexilic prophet Third Isaiah, but with variations. Third Isaiah plays up the dimension of ritual sexual activity in the service of idols (57.1-13). He does not, however, activate the metonym of non-cultic promiscuity, nor is the idolatry = adultery metaphor foregrounded, though both may be alluded to.[15] Because of this, the gender of the reprobates is not figured definitively as female; thus the earlier tension of men 'playing the harlot' is gone.[16] It is possible, as Blenkinsopp argues, that Third Isaiah speaks against the practice of goddess worship, but one cannot draw a firm conclusion based entirely on what may be no more than polemical assertions of ritual sexual activity.

In Ezekiel, all references to adultery and harlotry are within the illicit sex = idolatry metaphor, although the prophet expands this vehicle to such unprecedented, pornographic lengths as to virtually reify it. Unlike the earlier prophets, he does not allude to actual human sexual acts; thus the polemic against ritual sex drops out along with accusations of literal extramarital sex.[17] Ezekiel introduces, however, a new element into the sex–religion rhetoric. His picture is not simply one of a promiscuous female Israel, but of an impure Israel. This impurity is suggested by the depiction of the woman 'in her blood', as well as by the reference to her mixed heritage, as daughter of a Canaanite and a Hittite. It

---

14. This translation is from the NRSV, except for this word; where I have substituted Bird's 'hierodules' for the overloaded 'temple prostitutes'.

15. The Hebrew of Isa. 57.3 is corrupt, reading literally, 'sons of a sorceress, seed of an adulterer, and she played the whore'.

16. Whatever the original sense of 57.3, the focus after that shifts to the faithlessness of the 'sons', rather than, as in Hosea, remaining on that of the mother. The verbal form also shifts in Third Isaiah, who uses a more literal second masculine plural to address his audience, rather than the metaphorical third or second feminine singular of the earlier prophets.

17. Though cf. Gravatt (1994: 198-214), who argues that the punishment described for the female-personified Jerusalem, divinely inspired gang-rape, alludes to the experience of real women in war.

is from such impurities, of both substance and lineage, that the new temple envisioned by Ezekiel must remain free.[18] And, in this rhetoric, we locate one of the sites where woman qua woman comes to represent the strange. The symbolic logic is both convoluted and remarkable: the impurity of a woman's blood is juxtaposed to the impurity of foreignness, a natural bodily function equated with ethnic otherness. But the ethnic Other is Israel herself! This collusion of evil, ethnicity and gender in Ezekiel has the effect of forcing 'the people of Israel to see themselves as "other" while simultaneously allowing or even creating for a male audience a certain distance from this picture' (Gravatt 1994: 280).

The Rhetorical Logic of Social Functionality
In Deut. 7.1-5, we find a second mode of relating the ideas of strangeness, sex and religion. Here the functional connection is made between religious syncretism and intermarriage (whether of Israelite men to foreign women *or* vice versa), but this connection is not figuratively extended. In other words, this text expresses the conviction that marriage to foreigners will lead to foreign worship without metaphorizing foreign worship as adultery or prostitution, or envisioning ritual sex, or construing the foreign woman as a goddess. As we have observed in the Introduction, it is hard to imagine this law emerging before the Persian period. Whom, after all, would the list of unmarriageable inhabitants of the land (7.1) refer to in the monarchic era?[19] It seems rather to express the ideology of a group newly arrived in the land—not, of course, the 'original 12 tribes', but the returned *golah*—in relation to those who then possessed it.

Rhetorical Combinations and Variations
The logic of 1 Kings 11 seems at first glance closely related to Deuteronomy 7. Here again a functional connection is drawn between for-

---

18. See further Galambush's (1992) thoroughly detailed analysis of the gender imagery in Ezekiel, especially her attention to this prophet's unique focus on the defilement of the temple.

19. Scholars agree that the book of Deuteronomy began to take shape no earlier than the period of the late monarchy, and reached its final form even later. The list of banned nations in 7.1 is a variant of many such lists of Israel's predecessors in the land. Archaizing rather than archaic, its rhetorical purpose needs to be considered.

eign marriage and foreign worship: it is Solomon's foreign wives who lead him astray religiously. Unlike Deuteronomy, however, which legislates against any sort of spousal exchange, the concern in the Solomon narrative is with wives alone, as also in Exodus 34 (see below). Unlike Exodus 34, however, illicit sex is not the problem in the Solomon story and, indeed, the boundary between licit and illicit sex is problematized: the sort of sexual activity that would normally be legitimate, sex within marriage, is delegitimated when it occurs with the 'wrong' women, namely strange (= foreign) ones. The one-sided focus on Israelite men's marriage to foreign wives in 1 Kings as compared to Deuteronomy's reciprocal formula requires explanation. It seems reasonable to consider the relationship of this narrative to the actions against 'foreign' wives reported in Ezra–Nehemiah (see below).

Exodus 34.11-16 again appears to make the same functional point as Deuteronomy 7 about intermarriage and syncretism (including a similar, though not quite identical, list of unmarriable indigenes), but with two important variations. First, as noted, the problem is expressed only in terms of Israelite men taking foreign wives. Secondly, the metaphor of 'playing the harlot' is introduced. The in-marrying foreign wives will play the harlot with their gods, and the sons of the Israelites will then play the harlot with them also. This doubled use of the key phrase both insinuates the practice of ritual sex by the foreign wives while construing idolatry as (female) adulterous behavior by (male) Israelites. Exodus 34 thus combines in a convoluted way the functional logic of Deuteronomy with metaphoric–metonymic rhetoric of the pre-exilic prophets. It thereby moves, as we shall see, in the direction of the even more baroque Numbers 25.

The relatively simple, social-functional ideology of exclusion in Deuteronomy 7 has, then, been coopted into a yet larger cultural agenda, still to be elaborated, through the rhetorical moves in 1 Kings 11 and Exodus 34. Malachi adds yet another variation on the theme with two contiguous passages, the first admonishing against marrying 'the daughter of a foreign god' (2.10-12) and the second against divorcing 'the wife of your youth', also referred to as 'your wife by covenant' (2.13-16). Again, then, we find the concern for marrying the proper *woman*, rather than for exclusivist marriage in general. It is often assumed that the first passage is causally relate to the second—men are divorcing their (Jewish) wives to marry foreign women who worship other gods —and that this reflects circumstances around or just before the presumed fifth-century time of Nehemiah and Ezra. But this is not explicitly stated and Ezra–Nehemiah, for all its vehemence against foreign wives, never mentions foreign gods or divorce of Jewish women. On analogy with, though different from, the combined logics of Exodus 34, this connection may be seen as quite ideologically purposeful on the part of an editor, without referring to specific social practices at some given time or at any time at all. There is not space here to work through all the issues involved with interpreting and dating this passage of Malachi. I shall make only certain points relevant to the present discussion. First, in contrast to the pre-exilic prophets, Malachi's logic is functional rather than metaphoric: the problem seems to be with the marriages of human men to human women (though the phrase 'daughter of a foreign god' is odd).[20] Thus, the people addressed are constructed literalistically, as male, rather than imaged, paradoxically, as female. Also different from most of the texts considered so far, the sinful outcome of mixed marriage and divorce of in-group wives is not the worship of foreign gods as such, but rather the profaning of Yhwh's sanctuary (2.11) and the failure to produce 'godly seed' (2.16). The underlying concern for a pure temple thus resembles Ezekiel and also, as we shall see, Ezra–Nehemiah; 'holy seed' is also at stake in Ezra. In Malachi, then, we no longer have an act of sociosexual deviance, adultery, functioning as a symbol for religious deviance. Rather, we have an act of communal deviance, intermarriage, rhetorically commandeered as a source of pollution. The logic, in other words, is priestly.

I have suggested that the shift in the discourse from the reciprocal prohibition against marital exchange of both daughters and sons to one against foreign women in particular represents a larger agenda than simply that of theopolitical exclusivism of the *golah* community over against the people of the land, though it is certainly related to it. What we see here is what might be called worldview discourse, that is, a discourse that naturalizes the ethos of exclusivism and *golah* rights by anchoring it in natural symbols and other already accepted 'realities'.[21] Gender difference and (not unrelated) ideas about sexual purity, espe-

---

20. The rhetoric is literalistic, but still, perhaps, not literal: David Gunn (personal communication) raises the possibility that the 'covenant wife' to whom Malachi's listeners have been unfaithful may in fact be the Torah.

21. I adapt here the concepts 'worldview' and 'ethos' from Geertz (1973), who analyzes them as the mutually reinforcing components of a religious symbol system.

cially when writ cosmic, not only serve the purpose well, but also have the power to outlast the specific circumstances in which they are first used. The books of Ezra and Nehemiah provide an important locus for observing this process.

It would seem at first glance that the concern for exogamy in Ezra and Nehemiah does no more than reiterate that of Deuteronomy. Both, indeed, quote Deuteronomy's reciprocal formula (Ezra 9.12; Neh. 10.31 [Eng.: 30]; 13.25). However, even their seemingly 'literal' reference to intermarriage, in the form of social regulation, already shows evidence of a gender bias that casts it in the direction of the worldview discourse it will become: in spite of the nod to Deuteronomy, it is only foreign *wives* against whom action is taken, and Nehemiah even alludes to the sin of Solomon, caused by 'such women', to justify this action (Neh. 13.26). The latter is one instance of the naturalizing rhetoric just mentioned: the assumption must be that 'everyone knows' what happened to Solomon.

The question, however, is how to explain this narrowing of the intermarriage prohibition and how, if at all, it relates to any particular historical reality. The focus on foreign *wives* alone is not altogether explained by the presumed need for a separate and pure community. Scholars have offered several interrelated explanations on the presumption that the books of Ezra and Nehemiah represent a real historical action against foreign wives in the mid-fifth century. It may, for example, represent a sociological situation in which Judean men were marrying women from outside the *golah*, but not reciprocating with their daughters, perhaps because the 'foreign' brides brought as dowries actual land holdings titularly claimed by members of the community of returned exiles (Camp 1985: 241; cf. Smith-Christopher 1994 on the social dynamics of 'marrying up'). Also related to the land issue are the postexilic laws that allow women to inherit property; thus, marriage to an outsider woman could alienate the patrilineal inheritance (Washington 1994: 235-36). At a very basic level, there may have been a problem of sex ratio: how many women returned with the men from Babylon (Eskenazi and Judd 1994)? Whatever combination of such factors may have been at play, what is notable about Ezra and Nehemiah is their resistance on the ideological grounds of *golah*-exclusivity to practices that would often have been materially advantageous to *golah* members themselves. There are obviously larger issues of identity (and control thereof) also at stake (Eskenazi and Judd 1994).

Many recent commentators resist, however, an easy identification between the apparently similar concerns of Ezra and Nehemiah. Those who accept some sort of fifth-century 'marriage crisis' usually credit it to Nehemiah, whose interests are usually understood to be political. He appears to be motivated by the desire for the prestige and power of Jerusalem over against Samaria, for the exclusivity of the *golah* over against the people of the land and, indeed for his own power over against that of other individuals (Grabbe [1998a: 154-82] is especially cynical). Thus, he expresses concern for the fact that the children of mixed marriages were learning foreign languages instead of the language of Judah (Neh. 13.23-24), as well as objecting to the defilement of the priesthood by improper marriage. Worth noting, however, is the fact that the particular priestly marriage condemned by Nehemiah was to the daughter of Sanballat, governor of Samaria, but apparently a worshiper of Yhwh. Here, as always, one must consider carefully who is calling whom 'foreign'. For Nehemiah, the issue is defined to a significant degree in territorial terms (Albertz 1994: 530), though not without religious concerns, especially those, like mixed marriage and proper cult, related to Torah-observance. In this, Nehemiah parallels closely the interests of the Solomon text he cites.

It is certainly possible to argue that Nehemiah's concerns for the temple and his animosity toward Samarians reflect the circumstances of some later day. His conflict with Sanballat, in particular, is as easy to locate in the late fourth century, when a Sanballat III (as opposed to the fifth-century Sanballat I) was governor of Samaria and a temple was built at Mount Gerizim, near Shechem. According to Josephus, a son of the later Sanballat married a daughter of the Jerusalem high priest. Conflict with Samarians flared again during the second-century period of Jewish home rule of John Hyrcanus (134–104 BCE), who is said to have destroyed the Gerizim sanctuary. These alternative possibilities for dating at least parts of the book of Nehemiah do not affect my argument at this point, though they point to the fact that the struggle for control of both identity and power continued for more than another century, and flared at least sporadically even much later (cf. Davies 1998: 100).

The book of Ezra makes gendered symbolic moves that further transform the political discourse of separation into a worldview constructed out of female otherness. First, Ezra extends the social-functional rhetoric of Deuteronomy and 1 Kings against intermarriage past the point of functionality. One of Ezra's colleagues, Shecaniah, claims, 'We have broken faith with our God and have married foreign women from the peoples of the land...' (10.2). Intermarriage with foreign women, in other words, is itself seen as the act of breaking faith, rather than as simply the first step toward apostasy; the women themselves are the problem. Here is a move analogous to Ezekiel's description of female Israel 'in her blood', one that begins to represent woman qua woman as symbol of the strange. With Ezra, we also begin to see the blending of the anti-exogamy rhetoric of Deuteronomy with the priestly concerns of Ezekiel. Ezra couples his stance against foreign women with rhetoric from the Holiness Code of Lev. 18.24-30. He calumniates the peoples of the lands in the priestly terms of 'uncleanness', 'pollution' and 'abominations', with all their loaded associations not only of illicit sex and foreign worship, but also of sheer 'mixed'-ness. For perhaps the first time, moreover (depending on what one makes of the meaning and date of Mal. 2.15), he articulates a concern, also grounded in the priestly ideology of avoiding mixed categories, for the production of 'holy seed' (9.2), that is, children of unmixed lineage.

Here the issue of limiting Jewish identity to the *golah* is clearly expressed; the anachronistic list of early inhabitants of the land of Canaan who are unfit for marital partners can refer to nothing other than citizens of the former nation of Judah who did not experience the Exile (cf. Deut. 7.1). At the same time, the threat of loss of property and community status to those who do not cooperate with the divorce action (10.8) bespeaks the more material concern for inheritance as well. Yet the question of the historicity of this account looms large, especially given the lack of reference to Ezra in important Jewish writings where Nehemiah's work is known (e.g. the second-century Ben Sira or 2 Maccabees). Whatever the case may be, this tale of mass divorce of women construed as foreign consolidates the rhetoric against exogamy with the rhetoric of uncleanness in a new and powerful way.[22] To single out

22. Smith-Christopher (1994) stresses, as I have, the priestly rhetoric in the book of Ezra. He argues further that Ezra's radical separatism indicates, from a sociological point of view, the perspective of a poor and marginal group. This may indeed be the case, though I doubt one can generalize, as he does, that 'the exile group was the relatively *disadvantaged* one of the two (or more) groups involved in the marriages' (Smith-Christopher 1994: 261). It may suggest that *Ezra's* group,

women in the rhetoric against exogamy and combine it with the rhetoric of impurity has the effect of defining Woman as all that is Not-Israel.

The chronological relationship of Numbers 25 to the postexilic literature just discussed cannot be absolutely established, though I shall argue in Part III that it is among the latest. However that may be, the narrative represents, rhetorically at least, a grand finale to the extraordinary range of figurations of strangeness, sex and religion we have considered thus far. On one level, it stands in the lineage of prophetic rhetoric, returning to the complexity of Hosea and Jeremiah, whose depictions of Israel's faithlessness waver between the image of the wanton female and descriptions of lustful men. Bird (1989b: 75) notes the special incongruity of Num. 25.1: 'While Israel dwelt at Shittim, the people began to play the harlot with the daughters of Moab.' As in the earlier prophetic texts, a cross-gendered 'female' Israel 'plays the harlot'; it is the rhetoric of idolatry. But, in a quick volte-face to Ezra, the harlot is played, not with a foreign male god, but with foreign human women! With its subject suddenly men once more, the verb takes on (though not without some tension) its literal sexual connotation. The next verse jerks the reader back once more to the religious dimension: we are told that Israel participated in worship of the Moabite gods. Sex and worship are thus juxtaposed so as to produce the implication of ritual sex. 'Thus Israel yoked itself to the Baal of Peor' (v. 3): the passage's opening fanfare of 'playing the harlot' is here finally confirmed as religious apostasy. The full range of symbolic logics in the pre-exilic prophets has thus been invoked, with a bit of Third Isaiah and Ezra thrown in for good measure. In contrast to the earlier prophets, however, whose varying figurations stand in tensive relationship to each other, Numbers 25 has collapsed and reified the language. The contiguity of its first three sentences creates an absolute equation: sex with foreign women = promiscuity = ritual sex = idolatry.

Have we forgotten the Strange Woman's pollution of the sanctuary? No, indeed. Apparently unable to fit every rhetorical permutation into only three verses, the author of Numbers 25 concludes the chapter with

however large that was and in whatever century they lived, represented a relatively disadvantaged group of the *golah*. Indeed, their extreme claims to wealth and prestige (cf. Grabbe 1998a: 138-42), as well as their unlikely power to instigate mass divorce does rather call fairy tales to mind. But their voice, nonetheless, somehow came to claim a disproportionate hearing in the canon.

the more expansive narrative about an Israelite man, Zimri, who brings his Midianite wife, Cozbi, into the tabernacle precincts, only to be run through most suggestively by the spear of Phineas, the high priest's son (on this text, see further, Chapter 5). The polluting threat to the holy place—construed here as the combined strangeness of sex, gender and nationality—is eliminated by the Israelite holy man.

Woman Stranger as Metaphor in the Book of Proverbs

Where, then, does Proverbs's Strange Woman stand in relation to this complex rhetoric of strangeness, religion and sexuality? The two distinctive rhetorics that we have considered, with their combinations and variations, should make us cautious, in the first instance, about an assumption that Proverbs addresses in a transparent way a postexilic practice of exogamy that threatened the self-proclaimed 'Jewish' community with the worship of foreign gods or goddesses imported by foreign wives. The rhetorical analysis offered above has made the historical credibility of all the biblical texts that envision such a scenario ideologically suspect and, in the texts where we expect a clear report of such a problem, like Ezra and Nehemiah, it does not occur. The 're-membered' danger of goddess worship from bygone days may indeed lend its aura to the construction of Proverbs's Strange Woman. It is, however, not mentioned in Proverbs (once the cultic reference in Prov. 7 is recontextualized), nor in the literature assumed to be most closely related to it. There is nothing in Proverbs, moreover, of the gender paradox present in the prophetic indictment of faithless Israel. In Proverbs, the audience is all male, all the time.

If the angst that produced Proverbs's Strange Woman is not worship of other gods, is it, then, some version of the exogamy conflicts evident in Nehemiah and Ezra, either the problem of the *golah*'s political power in the face of competing power bases (Nehemiah), or of a priestly identity ideology of pure *golah* seed and unpolluted land and temple (Malachi; Ezra; Neh. 13; cf. Ezekiel)? On the one hand, Proverbs seems to have little of Ezra–Nehemiah's interest in constructing identity boundaries in (pseudo-) historicized nationalistic terms. This would seem to suggest that it was written at some remove from them—perhaps temporal, perhaps ideological, perhaps both.

There is, on the other hand, a line of symbolic development that cannot be ignored. We have observed, first of all—at least as implicit in

Ezekiel's imagery of female pollution of the temple and in Ezra's equation of foreign marriage with covenant faithlessness resulting in pollution of the land—a conceptual move that identifies Woman with the Strange. From here it is but a short step to Proverbs, where the 'strange women' of Ezra and Nehemiah are poetically condensed into *the* Strange Woman. The point can be stated in more theoretical terms (cf. Lakoff and Johnson 1980: 25-40). The shifting metonymic associations of woman with strangeness—women's blood standing for all pollution, foreign wives standing for all things foreign, adulterous women standing for idolatrous Israel—have reified into an 'ontological metaphor': Strangeness is a Woman.

Along these lines I would re-evaluate Blenkinsopp's important reference to the sin of Solomon as a basis for Proverbs's instructions, an allusion also made in Neh. 13.26 (1991a: 457). While 1 Kings 11 makes the causal connection between foreign wives and foreign worship, thus reinforcing a crucial division between what is proper to Israel and what is not, Neh. 13.23-27 focuses on the connection of foreign wives and foreign language, a much more practical concern. Proverbs, on the other hand, makes the metaphorical connection between woman and the strange, thus identifying woman as that which is not proper to 'Israel'.[23] National/ethnic distinction has been assimilated to and named by gender distinction. This is, I would conjecture, a relatively late development. But whose development is this, and what purposes does it serve?

A comparison with Malachi is instructive, especially in terms of the shift in subject in the otherwise similar imagery in Mal. 2.14 and Prov. 2.17. In Malachi, the active partner is the man, who is blamed for Yhwh's unwillingness to accept cultic offerings:

> Why is this? Because Yhwh was witness between you and the wife of your youth (*'eshet ne'ureka*), to whom you have been faithless, though she is your companion and your covenant wife (*haberteka we'eshet beriteka*).

23. This radical naming of 'us' as male occurs, I would argue, in spite of the presence of Woman Stranger's counterpart in Proverbs, Woman Wisdom. The latter figure can be understood in either of two ways. By one account, she is merely property, like a wife, to be 'acquired' by a man: in this sense not counted in communal self-definition. Seen otherwise, however, Woman Wisdom is not merely counterpart but rather counter*point* to Woman Stranger, a construction of 'us' as 'good woman'. The interplay of these equal opposites will be the concern of Chapter 2.

The context connects this judgment with a preceding one against those who marry 'the daughter of a foreign god', and thereby are 'faithless to one another, profaning the covenant of our fathers' (2.10). With this act, 'abomination has been committed in Israel and in Jerusalem; for Judah has profaned the sanctuary of Yhwh, which he loves' (2.11). Marital faithlessness, then, becomes part of the rhetoric of religious infidelity and temple pollution, but in a much more literalistic way than in the preexilic prophets. Similar language occurs in Prov. 2.16-17, but the gender dynamic shifts. Here it is the Strange Woman (*'ishshah zarah/ nokriyyah*), not her partner, who forsakes the 'companion of her youth' (*'alluph ne'ureha*) and forgets 'the covenant of her God' (*berit 'elo-heha*).[24]

How should we understand the changed gender and symbolic dynam-ics in Proverbs 2? It seems, first of all, an exercise in irrelevance to imagine the Judean poet castigating a foreign woman who forgets her marital vows and/or her devotion to her (foreign) deity. Alternatively, taken out of context, it is possible to construe this verse in terms of the prophetic allegory, with the woman forgetful of her marital covenant representing the people of Israel acting in covenant faithlessness. Such an understanding is hard to square with the context, however, which assumes a male listener who is being persuaded against a future liaison with a woman who has forgotten (in parallel) her youthful companion and the covenant of her god. While Malachi depicts the husband's faith-lessness, Proverbs depicts the wife's. Unlike the daughter of a strange god in Malachi, moreover, who awaits the pleasure of her prospective husband, Woman Stranger accosts, deceives and seduces. Although the identification of marital and religious faithlessness is similar to that in Malachi, Proverbs's focus on female agency, rather than male, suggests that decisions about exogamy—over which women had little control—are not the main concern. The issue at stake here is not marriage to the proper (i.e. religio-political in-group) wife, or worship of the proper god. Rather, the issue is social control of women's and young men's sexual behavior, a concern evident throughout Proverbs's introductory poems (in addition to the Strange Woman passages, see also the poem on marital fidelity [5.5-19]; the contrast between the prostitute and the adulteress [6.26]; and the description of the consequences for 'going in'

---

24. The choice of alternative words for 'companion' (*haberteka* in Mal. 2.14 and *'alluph* in Prov. 2.17) can be explained by the needs of alliteration and asso-nance.

to the 'wife of another' [6.27-35]). The argument is patriarchal in the fullest sense, involving both men's control of women and also the older generation's males controlling the younger's (Newsom 1989: 145).

The rhetorical emphasis in the construction of Proverbs's Woman Stranger, then, is on the connotation of *zar/nokri* as outsider to the family household. All the language of sexuality in Proverbs 1–9 has socio-sexual deviance—prostitution and adultery—as its primary referent. The woman is depicted as *zarah* because, as an adulteress and prostitute, she acts in ways that are alien to the family structure, a structure that itself is a fundamental defining feature of what is 'our own', not-strange (cf. Snijders 1954: 68, 78, 88-104; Wright 1979). In Proverbs, strangeness, not of nationality but of gender, is given its fullest expression. It seems unlikely, however, that these texts describe the actions of a particular given woman. The language of deviant sexual behavior *is* being used symbolically, but not merely as a cipher for deviant (= foreign) worship. It is, rather, symbolic of the forces deemed destructive of patriarchal control of family, property and society. Because control of women's sexuality is the sine qua non of the patriarchal family, it is no accident that the forces of 'chaos' are embodied in a woman who takes control of her own sexuality.

Indeed, it would seem that the purpose of the poem in Proverbs 7 is to project into a single figure the greatest evil imaginable, even at the expense of realistic description, by portraying an improbable combination of sexually deviant activities. That the Strange Woman in Proverbs 7 (cf. 2.17) is about to commit an act of adultery against her own husband seems clear, an act which in itself is bad enough. But this is adultery of the worst kind: no passionate love affair (however improbable that may have been in any case) but calculated, anonymous sex with a stranger, and an innocent lad at that. We learn of her marital status only at the end of her speech; it is with her wantonness that we are first impressed. Notice, however, that she is not a professional prostitute, but is only 'dressed' as one.[25] Had she been a 'pro' the sage's depiction of utter evil would have been undercut, for the professional prostitute does have a place in a patriarchal world, even if it is a liminal one. Not protected by any man, she is also not obligated to any man; she is the

25. Bird's (1989b) analysis of the allegorical marriage of Hosea and Gomer reveals that the various modes of sexual deviance are interrelated in a similar manner in this prophetic text: Gomer is not a professional prostitute, but rather a wanton woman; only gradually does the context move us to understand her as an adulteress.

'institutionally legitimated "other woman"' (Bird 1989b: 79; Niditch 1979: 147). Far more dangerous is the woman who exists within the boundaries of male-controlled sexuality, but who decides for herself to opt out of them. Such is the wife 'dressed as a prostitute' in Proverbs 7.[26]

There is yet one more piece to the puzzle of sexuality and strangeness that will complete our picture of woman embodied in the full paradigm of sexual evil available in exilic and postexilic literature. The one who is *zar* can be not only foreign, not only outside the family, but also outside the priesthood. In a general sense, of course, all women are *zarot* on this level, as well as in terms of their natural bodily functions. Like Ezekiel, Malachi, Ezra and Numbers, Proverbs 7 expresses anxiety about the pollution of the temple by women's strangeness. In contrast, however, to the involuntary pollutions of blood or foreign birth purveyed by the female in these other texts, Proverbs's Strange Woman is portrayed as an active creator of her own alien status and an intentional polluter of holy space, engaging in sex during the feast of her peace offering, bringing her harlot's hire to the temple to pay her vows, and compounding the priestly anointing oil to perfume her illicit sexual encounter.

Given how fully the meanings associated with sexuality and strangeness are articulated and interwoven in Proverbs 1–9, it becomes important to ask to what extent and in what manner any of these represent a sociohistorical 'reality'. I have already suggested that, whatever concerns our poet–editor may have had for exogamy and foreign worship, Proverbs does not reflect the same sort of perceived crisis as that expressed by other postexilic writers. This suggestion is confirmed by the shift in imagery from the 'real' foreign women of Malachi and Ezra–Nehemiah (however literarily constructed they may actually be) to the almost mythical figure in Proverbs: the wisdom book seems to express less of a current situation and much more of an increasingly mythicized memory of a time when, as it were, the bad women were really bad. Woman Stranger of Proverbs is a full-blown force of evil, an evil that manifests death in sexual form. Because of the chronological telescoping effected by myth, however, one era of the past becomes conflated with another and with the present as well. Thus, 'memories' of the for-

26. The point is reaffirmed in Prov. 6.26 by the negative comparison between the 'woman of prostitution', who may be had for a loaf of bread, and 'the wife of another', who 'stalks a man's very life'.

eign women who led our ancestors astray at Moab, of the foreign women who turned Solomon's heart from God and of the 'daughter of a foreign god' who caused Malachi to castigate our fathers' (grandfathers'?) generation meld into an image of all that is dangerous to us in the present and future.[27] In such an interpretation of Proverbs, it is not so much a matter of illicit sex serving as an allegory for dalliance with strange gods (or goddesses), or of ritual sex, or of intermarriage as an act of covenant infidelity, but rather of a female image that evokes this metonymic memory and thus functions as a symbol for every danger that threatens the well-being of the community (as defined, of course, by those in charge).

The sociohistorical veracity of the association of strangeness with adultery and harlotry must be assessed in an analogous way. Against van der Toorn, I think it is unlikely that we should imagine a social situation in which married women regularly engaged in acts of harlotry. Although it is certainly true that laws are often enacted to counter some existing practice, what information we have about the postexilic period suggests to me that in Proverbs 7 we are confronting not a social reality of wanton wives but rather a sociopsychological reality of men threatened by a multiply stressed social situation, including internal religio-political power struggles, economically oppressive foreign rule and, as time went on, the pressures of cultural assimilation associated with emerging Hellenism. We might describe the psychological dynamics in this way: The need to maintain familial and social stability in the face of enormous disruptive forces created in the male leaders and thinkers of the community a fear of chaos that was projected into an external, but nonetheless imaginary, object of fear—the woman who goes strange in the sense of deciding to stand outside the family structure as defined by its sexual roles and restrictions.

Finally, the sage's close association with, if not membership in, the priestly caste completes the linkage of Woman, Strangeness and Sex. Precisely because all women are *zarot* to the sons of Aaron, Woman

27. That such 'memories' of the dastardly foreign female were held in high regard by members of the later wisdom tradition is evident in the fact that Ben Sira's hymn to the ancestors contains allusions both to Phineas's assassination of Cozbi (Num. 25.6-18; Sir. 44.23-25) and to the demise of Solomon, who gave women dominion over his body (1 Kgs 11; Sir. 47.19). The latter text demonstrates the conflation of sexual and national 'strangeness': in Sirach, sex replaces nationality as the defining evil of Solomon's women.

becomes a 'natural' target on which to project evil. But, just as Woman Stranger's vile adultery is not a depiction of women's actual activities, so also her deliberate violations of cultic regulations do not represent the acts of a flesh-and-blood woman. Rather they represent the worst forms of defilement our cultically inclined sage can imagine. Along with the accusations of wanton adultery, this depiction of the cultic violator must be taken as polemical, not descriptive, an expression of male anxiety as one generation attempts to pass its ideology of control to the next.[28] Although, in the biblical laws, defilement can come in many forms, from both men and women, here Woman—particularly in her sexual nature—becomes the embodiment of defilement. The metaphor has now been fully realized, but also reified: Woman is Strange.

Death, Yhwh and the Strange Woman

One final step is necessary to reveal the depth and significance of the ideological identification of Woman and Strangeness, and that is to suggest its theological dimensions. We must consider the relationship of Woman Stranger to Death and Sheol in light of their connection to Yhwh. A rather unexpected connection—of Isaiah 28 to Proverbs 1–9—provides the basis for our reflection. This chapter of Isaiah is notable for its concentration of wisdom vocabulary, most obviously its reference to 'teaching knowledge' (v. 9) and its description of Yhwh as 'wonderful in counsel and excellent in wisdom' (v. 29). More specifically, however, Isaiah 28 contains a series of images and vocabulary that are also used in connection with Woman Wisdom and the Strange Woman (and strange man) in Proverbs.

Isaiah 28.14 attacks 'men of scoffing' (*latson*). 'To scoff' (*lyts*) is a verb favored by Proverbs (18 of its 28 biblical usages occur here). The nominal form (*latson*) occurs only twice in addition to Isa. 28.14, both times in Proverbs. The key text is Prov. 1.27, where, like the prophet, Woman Wisdom challenges 'scoffers who delight in scoffing'.[29] Be-

---

28. See Newsom's (1989) analysis of the intergenerational aspects of Proverbs's discourse.

29. In spite of the similarity in epithet, Isaiah envisions a different audience than Proverbs: the former addresses 'those who rule this people in Jerusalem' (28.14), while the latter castigates recalcitrant youth, 'the simple' (1.22). If the Isaiah passage is postexilic, as it shows signs of being, then its contrast with Proverbs is

cause of the failure of Jerusalem's leaders, Isaiah asks rhetorically on Yhwh's behalf, 'Whom will he teach knowledge?' and cynically promises that the divine message will come 'on jabbering lips and in another tongue (*la'agey saphah / lashon 'aheret;* Isa. 28.10-11). In Proverbs, Yhwh does not need to speak in an alien language, for Woman Stranger's smooth lips and tongue (Prov. 5.3; 6.24; 7.21; cf. 2.16) offer a quite comprehensible message. The imagery of the snare is also prominent in both pieces of material. Because of the people's failure to listen to Yhwh's warnings, Isa. 28.13 claims that the divine word will cause them to 'go and fall backward and be broken and baited (*yqsh*) and snared (*lkd*)'. In Proverbs, the word pair *yqsh/lkd* (as in Isaiah in the niphal) is applied to the people's own words, which 'bait' and 'snare' them when they go surety for a neighbor—or a stranger (*zar*; 6.1-2; cf. 6.5; 1.17). The imagery of the snare (*pah*) also helps to create one of the sage's most powerful warnings against the seductive speech of the Strange Woman:

> With much seductive speech she persuades him;
> with her smooth talk she compels him.
> All at once he follows her...
> as a bird rushes into the snare
> he does not know it means his life (7.21-23).

The most important point for our purposes is that Isaiah 28 contains one of the contexts outside Proverbs where the word pair *zar/nokri* occurs.[30] The chapter describes a situation in which the leaders of Ephraim, likened to drunkards (vv. 1, 3, 7-9),[31] make 'a covenant with Death, an agreement with Sheol' (vv. 15, 18). Because of this, Yhwh will rise up

> to do his deed—strange (*zar*) is his deed!
> to work his work—alien (*nokriyyah*) is his work! (28.21)

It is not only this word pair that anticipates the Proverbs poems; so also does Isaiah's mythicized Death–Sheol language that is so similar to

---

another example of changing circumstances over the course of that era: the political struggle evident in the attack on 'scoffing' leaders has shifted to a patriarchal attack on 'scoffing' youth.

30. Other references include Isa. 61.5; Jer. 5.19; Obad. 11; Ps. 69.9; 81.10; Job. 19.15; Lam. 5.2.

31. Cf. Prov. 23.33, where drunkenness is said to cause one's eyes to see *zarot*. Though the term is usually translated as an abstraction ('strange things'), it is in a grammatical form that could as easily be construed 'strange women'.

its use in Prov. 2.18; 5.5; 7.27 and 9.18, where the house of Woman Stranger—who forgets 'the covenant of her God'—is imaged as the maw of Mot (McKane 1970: 287-88).

The continuity of images between Isaiah and Proverbs helps call attention, however, to a significant difference between them. In Isaiah it is Yhwh who speaks a fatal word in a foreign tongue, while in Proverbs this word issues from the enticing mouth of Woman Stranger. Similarly, Isaiah portrays the deity doing the strange deed and working the alien work in response to the people's covenant with Death and Sheol, while Proverbs moves the burden of strangeness to the Deadly One herself. I would suggest, then, that we see manifest in Proverbs a pattern of late postexilic theological thought in which evil, whether in the form of strange deeds or deadly words, is removed from the character of the deity and responsibility for it is ascribed to a quasi-human, quasi-mythical incarnation of evil. The language of death, shades and Sheol, which may have had its origin in the cult of a goddess (so Blenkinsopp) or some other chthonic deity (so McKane), is transformed in Proverbs to articulate a force—defined here as female—that begins to split the religious cosmos into a dualistic moral system. Both cause and effect of this split is the willingness to use female images to represent absolute good or absolute evil. Thus are defined the categories with which real women will have to live for centuries to come.

Proverbs and the Strange Woman in the Postexilic Period

What does this comparative literary analysis of gender and strangeness tell us about the date, social milieu and ideological force of the Strange Woman in the book of Proverbs? I have argued that the image's symbolic density, coupled with its lack of direct reference to foreign women or foreign worship, suggests a date and setting later than the politicization of marriage to non-*golah* women by Nehemiah (and Ezra?) in the fifth (or fourth?) century. This analysis builds on previous work of mine in which I suggested the possibility of dating the compilation of Proverbs as late as the Hellenistic period (Camp 1991).[32] Maier (1995) has also recently argued for a relatively late date, though she finds that an early-fourth-century setting accounts as well or better for the same considerations. I do not dispute her reasoning, but only caution against

---

32. For the sake of clarity, I should perhaps note that this argument departs from that of my earlier work on the subject (cf. Camp 1985: 233-54).

squeezing too much historical specificity from literary texts written in a period about which we know so little. Much depends, I would say now, on how early we can imagine an upper class in Judah with the leisure for the kind of literate education presupposed by Proverbs (cf. Davies's discussion of non-scribal schools [1998: 79-82]). For my purposes here, the difference between an early-fourth-century as opposed to a late-fourth-century date is negligible. My interest is in trying to understand the larger ideological matrix of which Proverbs and its Strange Woman are a part. On this score, I offer five observations, all of which point into the concerns of the rest of this book.

First, the juxtaposition of the personifications of female Wisdom and Strangeness in Proverbs 1–9 is a means of constructing identity, of dividing 'us' from 'them', but at a fundamental level. The Strange Woman image in particular draws on the prophetic heritage of equating strange religion with strange sex, specifically in the form of Woman Israel who goes, in the same gesture, sexually and religiously strange. It is also tied to the postexilic rejection of the 'foreign' wife as both agent and sign of the subversion of community boundaries and temple purity. Proverbs goes farther than other postexilic texts, however, in extending this social-functional symbolism into the realm of a moral ontology; that is, while Proverbs clearly remains concerned with on-the-ground social behaviors and relationships, the significance given to in-group and out-group status is intensified by identification with personified forces of good and evil. In this sense, Proverbs does not so much look back to the attempted exclusion of non-*golah* wives described in Ezra–Nehemiah, when the struggle for control of Jewish identity was still in heated process, as it looks forward to a new era of well-established class divisions, with its need to preserve and maintain the orders of lineage, inheritance and generational control. This is the sort of context in which men have the luxury of objectifying Woman with equal measures of adulation and damnation for the purpose of encouraging young men to cling to their class interests as they cling to the wives of their youth. Thus, the construction of Woman as Sexual Stranger comes to the fore. Still, I would argue that there is more at stake than pedagogical rhetoric. In the context of the emerging canon, Woman as Sexual Stranger is inexorably linked to Woman as Ethnic Stranger and to Israel as Estranged Wife. These multiple negativities, set in opposition to the divine origin of Woman Wisdom, lend ontological force to both figures.

Woman Divided is well on her way to becoming a construct of the cosmos as a whole.

Secondly, I have argued, based on comparing Proverbs 1–9 with Isaiah 28, that one motivation for this emerging dualism is the problem of theodicy. But whose problem is this? Rainer Albertz contends that the 'theologized wisdom' of Proverbs 1–9 and the book of Job represents the 'personal theology of the upper class' (1994: 507-17), a piety marked by a sincere concern for the moral life and especially the care for the poor, but one still presupposing upper-class wealth and influence. Job, he argues, reflects the economic crisis that characterized the second half of the fifth century (cf. Neh. 5), when some if not many of the righteous rich experienced their own financial difficulties in the face of less scrupulous neighbors. Although Albertz casts Proverbs 1–9 in the same class setting as Job, he does not apply his theodicy analysis to this material. Proverbs 1–9 is typically read as a more optimistic precursor to Job and, indeed, most likely served an exhortative pedagogical purpose quite well. At the same time, however, it also fits into Albertz's theodicy model, as an alternative response to the upper-class question 'why me?' Unlike either the Job of the narrative, who adopts the wisdom stance of stoic silence, or the Job of the poem, who works through his grief with laments (Albertz 1994: 515), the 'Job' of Proverbs is offered the embodied solace of Wisdom's breast—better than jewels!— and the knowledge that the righteous wise man, whatever his material fate, can trust in her support against the equally embodied force of evil and death. It is the latter, not Yhwh, who brings one to ruin. As far as dating goes, while the retribution theory characteristic of much of Proverbs certainly precedes Job, I am less certain that its particular feminized construction of good and evil does. Job could have used a Strange Woman to blame.

A third consideration raised by my analysis is that of the relationship of the editor of Proverbs to the temple and its priesthood. Berquist (1995: 170-73) and Maier (1995: 259-69) have argued that the voice of Proverbs is the voice of the upper-class laity, not that of the priests. While I agree that the pedagogical and theodic purposes of the poems represent upper-class interests, I think the question of their relationship to the cult needs more nuancing. In the first place, once a hereditary hierocracy is established, 'priestly' interests can hardly be disengaged from class ones. As Grabbe notes, the priestly aristocracy would have been one segment of society with the leisure for the intellectual pursuits scholars often associate with the wisdom tradition and with interpretation of the law (1996: 31-34). The scribal class would also have been an important crossover group: some scribes would have been priests, while other, non-priestly scribes would have worked with or for the temple in various capacities. Though not focused on cultic affairs Proverbs witnesses to the importance both of cultic obligation ('Honor Yhwh with your substance' [3.9]) and of cultic purity (7.14; see above). The sense that female-identified strangeness represents not only a threat to the security of the community's boundaries, but also of contamination at its holy center, resonates with the logic of Ezekiel, priestly words of Ezra, Malachi and Numbers 25. It does not take a priest to have concern for such things, but it does take a person with allegiance to the cult and a personal investment in matters of purity. If Proverbs does represent an alliance of laity and priesthood, then circumstances have changed from the time of Nehemiah, whose antagonism against foreign wives found special focus in those wed by priests.

Fourthly, Proverbs 1–9 manifests in a couple of different ways an interest in the formation and interpretation of religious canons. I have argued that ch. 7's overdetermined depiction of the Strange Woman's strangeness incorporates issues from no less than three Torah texts. That all of these are priestly texts is of no small interest. Maier argues further that Prov. 6.20-35 is a midrash-style interpretation of the decalogue on theft, adultery and coveting the wife of one's neighbor, with an introductory exhortation that recalls the Shema in Deut. 6.6-9 (1995: 255). Here, she observes, Proverbs 'deals with the figure of the Strange Woman in the context of Jewish ethics'. These laws are hardly universal ones, however; they speak with the voice of the propertied class. Proverbs offers, then, examples of Torah interpretation that reflect both particular priestly interests as well as those of the larger lay upper class. If Torah interpretation is indeed implicit—i.e. taken for granted—in Proverbs 1–9, then another hermeneutical possibility opens up as well, namely that Woman Wisdom may be read as a personification of Torah and the covenant-breaking Strange Woman as its rejection. [33] This identification is explicitly made and elaborated by Ben Sira in the second century, but may also be at work, albeit less definitively, in Proverbs.

33. David Gunn, personal communication.

In addition to Proverbs's obvious interest in Torah exegesis, there is also evidence that its editors had a larger sense of purpose and literary self-consciousness in their formation of the book itself. Here again, interest in both the upper-class environment as a whole and the temple itself come into play. On the one hand, the book is framed by images of wise women who build the patriarchal house and bring success to the men who embrace them: Woman Wisdom in the introductory poems of Proverbs 1–9 is structurally matched by the wise queen mother and the wise wife in the concluding poems of Proverbs 31 (Camp 1985: 186-91). Indeed, if the voice of exalted Woman Wisdom is heard as the authorizing voice of the book, one might be expected to draw the inference that the book itself is holy, as the women who build houses are holy.

A different sort of structural analysis of Proverbs offers another perspective, in which Proverbs's 'house' can be seen as Yhwh's house. In a series of three articles Patrick Skehan[34] argued that the literary structure of Proverbs 1–9 can be visualized as seven columns, thus embodying the 'seven pillars' with which Woman Wisdom is said to build her house (Prov. 9.1). This seven-pillar edifice, moreover, 'fronts' a book that, in its entirety, is also structured to accord with the measurements of an architectural entity, namely, the temple of Solomon, as described in 1 Kings 6. Solomon's temple, in other words, has been 'read' as the book of Proverbs, which is also understood as Wisdom's house.

If both these structuring devices—woman's house and Yhwh's house —were intentionally embedded in Proverbs, it would suggest an editor whose concern to reconcile lay and priestly interests matched, according to Albertz's analysis, that of the editor of the Torah itself (1994: 464-93). It is also possible, however, that the holy house 'erected' in Proverbs represented some sort of opposition—whether lay or priestly or both—to the leadership of the Jerusalem temple at the time. At the very least, it suggests an editor whose interests in canon and cult went hand in hand, interests not dissimilar, then, to those that gave Ezra, the purveyor of Holy Writ, a priestly pedigree.

Fifthly and finally, I wish to problematize the sense of apparent resolution, even stasis, that Proverbs seems to offer to the issues just considered. Problems of identity, problems of theodicy, problems of political struggle, problems of purity, problems of authority, all seem

---

34. The articles, originally published in 1947, 1948 and 1967, appear in revised form in Skehan's collected essays (1971). See Chapter 4 for further discusssion.

ameliorated by means of Proverbs's dramatic female imagery, above all by the construction of woman as Other in the figure of the Strange Woman. It will be the project of the rest of my book, however, to argue that this neat package was no more than an ideological cover for persistent if shifting tensions in all these areas, tensions apparent in other parts of the then emerging canon. I shall argue, further, that we find, precisely in the figure of the Strange Woman, an entry into understanding some of the ideological dynamics, if not the entire socio-historical context, of these issues.[35] In the other texts we shall consider we find writers attempting to define 'Israelite' identity over against strangers, and priestly identity over against 'strange' Israelites, all the while wrestling with a God whose ways often seemed strange enough themselves. The degree to which this process of stranger-making was gendered, and the complexity involved therein, is one major preoccupation of this book. We shall find that the effort to construct identity through constructing gender, whether Jewish identity in general or priestly in particular, is in a continual state of slippage. This slippage manifests especially clearly in texts where the image of Woman Stranger is paired in attempted opposition to that of Woman Wisdom. We shall explore the paradoxical relationship between these two figures, first in Proverbs itself (Chapter 2) and then in the stories of Samson (Chapter 3) and Solomon (Chapter 4).

35. This way of thinking about a text's relationship to history represents my adaptation of the approaches in certain works of Jobling (1978) and Clines (1994), though they must be held, of course, blameless for any possible misappropriation by me of their methods and aims.

Chapter 2

WISE AND STRANGE: WOMAN AS TRICKSTER IN PROVERBS

Cross-cultural studies have, in recent years, generated much enthusiasm among biblical scholars. They have been responded to with equally strong and well-taken words of caution about respect for cultural differences and for variations in apparent patterns of social behavior or mythological imagery. Nowhere is such caution better placed than in an attempt to identify elements of the trickster motif in a cultural tradition such as the Bible, which does not have any one character clearly identified as such, unlike the cycles of trickster stories that appear, for example, among many native North American tribes and also among certain African peoples (Thompson 1966; Pelton 1980). The Bible's lack of such a figure is only the first of several methodological difficulties that need at least an acknowledgment before one succumbs to the siren of comparison.

A second difficulty is that, even where comparative mythologists agree on the existence of a trickster, this figure is an extremely elusive and changeable one. What exactly makes a trickster a trickster? The trickster is often portrayed as an enormous buffoon who wanders the earth getting himself and others into trouble, largely because of his outlandish appetite for food and sex. Although he is called the trickster, as often as not he is more the fool, one who gets tricks played on him as well as tricking others. The trickster is a breaker of all social boundaries: not guided by any recognizable sense of good and evil, he flouts religious taboos and conventions of proper sexual behavior, even to the point of changing sex and becoming a man's 'wife' for a period of time in one Winnebago episode (Radin 1956: 22-24). In some folklore traditions, this radical 'outside-the-normness' of the trickster results in his being cast as an animal rather than as a human, although always as an animal who interacts with other characters using the structures of human speech and society (even if only to abuse them).

Oddly, perhaps (though not to aficionados of, say, Bugs Bunny cartoons), trickster stories are not found threatening by their audiences but rather extremely humorous. Even more oddly, antics of this amoral buffoon are sometimes associated with the most serious tasks. Either an actual deity himself, or intimately associated with deity, the trickster regularly participates in the creation or transformation of the world, providing it with its basic cosmic and social structures, cultural knowledge and deepest wisdom.

There does not seem to be any one 'ideal' trickster type. Rather, any given trickster figure may comprise a shifting combination of several, but not necessarily all, characteristics of the general type. We may take some comfort, then, that one may analyze biblical texts under the aegis of the trickster mythologem without making absolute claims about whether a given character is or is not a trickster. The important task is to identify elements of the paradigm and examine how they function in relationship to each other and to other aspects of the culture (Pelton 1980: 14-17). It is with such caution that I hope to treat the female imagery in Proverbs, where there are at least two major objections to finding a trickster. The most critical one is formal. These texts are not oral, folkloric narratives but literary, instructional poems. Secondly and relatedly, they do not exhibit the non-judgmental hilarity that almost always characterizes trickster tales (though not always, as Pelton's presentation of one West African trickster shows [1980: 164-222]). They are, rather, highly moralistic in tone and intent. Nonetheless, I shall try to show that a reading of the female figures in Proverbs 1–9 under the aegis of the trickster paradigm illumines otherwise unnoticed dimensions of the text.

A third methodological problem lies in the fact that the diversity of the trickster is matched by that of his interpreters. Anthropologists' treatments of the significance of the trickster have ranged from the psychic developmentalism of Radin (1956) and Jung (1956) to the structuralism of Lévi-Strauss (1963: 224-30). My own intellectual preference and, hence, the direction of this argument run toward the cultural hermeneutics approach of Robert Pelton. Unlike Radin and Jung, Pelton attempts to explain the often contradictory elements of the trickster myths holistically, rather than explaining them away in an evolutionary scheme that posits a development from animal to human, from amoral buffoon to a savior–transformer. Resisting Lévi-Strauss's tendency toward abstraction, Pelton insists on interpreting the trickster motifs with respect to their native cultural context. One may generalize about the trickster as a combination liar, buffoon and culture-hero, but these traits are always narratively manifest in culturally specific ways that enable a given culture to interpret itself to itself. This concern for cultural specificity built into Pelton's comparative method should, then, provide some desirable nuance in relating a generalized type figure to particular, time-and-place-bound texts and, at best, might enable us to deepen our understanding of the biblical effort to interpret its own situation.

Finally, we must take consideration of the fact that the biblical figures to whom I wish to apply the trickster paradigm are female, rather than male, which makes them unique in any comparative studies with which I am familiar.[1] The significance of this fact is open to question. We must recognize, first of all, that trickster mythology can be applied to male as well as to female characters in the Bible. Jacob, for instance, is a prime candidate, as is Samson (see Chapter 3). Thus, the Bible does not simply reverse the typical expectations. Nonetheless, as others have also argued,[2] the Bible does have a tradition of 'tricky' or deceitful women that should tell us something about Israel's understanding of itself and its women (cf. Camp 1985: 124-40).

While attempting to bear these cautionary notes in mind, it will be my thesis that a comparison of various manifestations of the trickster figure from comparative myth and folklore with the presentations of personified Wisdom and the Strange Woman in the book of Proverbs provides useful interpretive insights into the biblical material. Moreover, this comparison is informative not only at the several points where biblical female imagery fits the typical trickster model, but also where it does not. There are four interrelated characteristics of the trickster that provide categories for analyzing personified Wisdom, the Strange Woman and their relationship to each other: duality, order and disorder, the language of wisdom and deceit, and the intertwining of good and evil (i.e. the problem of theodicy).

Duality

The first and most all-embracing of these characteristics, recognized by virtually all commentators, is the basic duality of the trickster. Reading

---

1. I thank Carole Fontaine for stressing this distinction to me in personal communication.
2. See, for example, the essays in Exum and Bos (1988).

through the collection of any given society's trickster tales, one always finds not only the fooler, but also the fool, both a creator and a disrupter of order. The female imagery in Proverbs also plays upon opposites, personified Wisdom representing creation, love, life, truth, social order and wisdom, while the Strange Woman represents death, falsehood, social disruption and folly. The concern for the proper boundaries of sexual behavior, flaunted so gleefully by the trickster, is also quite evident in Proverbs. Female Wisdom is associated with the wife whom one is to love faithfully (4.6; 5.15-19; 7.4; 8.17), while the Strange Woman allures with provocative descriptions of illicit sex (7.10-20).

The relationship of the positive and negative elements of the trickster has been a subject of debate among anthropologists. Paul Radin argues, for example, based on certain Native American cycles, that the connection of the trickster with cosmogonic activity is a secondary accretion to the trickster mythology, a position that seems to have a fair amount of textual support in the traditions he studied (1956: 124-31; 155-69). Much more speculative, and also suspect because of its evolutionary presupposition, is his assertion that the trickster's 'culture-hero' traits— the various ways he orders or initiates important social structures or useful cultural objects—are later 'developments' from an 'original' conception of a primordial person obsessed by hunger, wanderlust and sexuality, purposeless and little differentiated from the animal world (1956: 165-68). Radin suggests that the elevation of the trickster to divine status with a role in creation was the work of an ancient 'priest–thinker' trying to assimilate the even older myths into an aboriginal theological system (1956: 164).

Unfortunately, this postulated evolution of the trickster literature does not explain the persistent attractiveness of the figure in his dual roles. Pelton takes on this issue with the assumption that members of pre-modern societies sought after a unity of experience in their lives and mythologies and, therefore, that the interpreter 'can best approach the many aspects of pre-modern religious life by searching for the logic that knits diversity together' (1980: 11). Pelton does not imply any particular form of modern logic in this statement. The questions, rather, are those of how any given society structures the diverse and sometimes contradictory elements of the trickster pattern, how these elements work in relation to each other and to other social structures and, thus, how that society uses the trickster to uncover and interpret the meaning of its life and world (Pelton 1980: 16).

Unlike the trickster who unites this duality into a single paradoxical entity, the female characterization in Proverbs divides it into two distinct figures. These opposites nonetheless 'attract'. J.-N. Aletti (1977) has noted astutely the many connecting links between the positive and negative female imagery in chs. 1–9. He argues that the editor of this material has created a very deliberate confusion between Wisdom and the Strange Woman through the ambiguous use of certain vocabulary (Aletti 1977: 132-34). Proverbs 4.8 assures the young man that Wisdom will honor him if he embraces (*hbq*) her, while 5.20 questions why he would embrace (*hbq*) the bosom of the Strange Woman. Even more emphatically, one must grasp (*hzq*) Wisdom and Instruction (3.18; 4.13) and expect to be grasped (*hzq*) by the Strange Woman (7.13). All this grasping and grabbing will take place 'in the street' and 'in the marketplace' where *both* Wisdom and the Strange Woman are to be found (1.20-21; 7.12). After the encounter in the public place, both female figures invite the listener to their respective houses (the Strange Woman or Folly's in 7.15-20 and 9.14-16; Wisdom's in 8.34 and 9.1-6). Both Wisdom and Folly offer bread (*lhm*) at their banquets (9.5, 17). The imagery of water is used to allure the young man to his own wife:

> Drink water from your own cistern,
> flowing water from your own well (5.15)

as well as to seduce him to Folly's house:

> Stolen water is sweet,
> and bread eaten in secret is pleasant (9.17).

With either the Strange Woman or his wife he can fill himself (*rwh*) with love (*dodym*; 7.18) or her breasts (*dadeyha*; 5.19, perhaps a scribal error, but carrying the same implications). Finally, the word used to describe the truthful teaching of the sage (*lqh*) is the same as that employed for the seductive speech of the Strange Woman who is said to be 'wily of heart' (1.5; 4.2; 9.9; 7.21).

Comparison with the trickster invites the interpreter of Proverbs to take seriously the literary unity of the Strange Woman and personified Wisdom before separating them too quickly into 'good' and 'evil'. Other biblical imagery for women points in this same direction. Like the trickster and the Strange Woman—and indeed, by association, like Wisdom herself—Tamar (Gen. 38), Ruth and Judith all break their society's boundaries on sexual behavior in order to accomplish good for themselves, for society and, ultimately, for Yhwh (Camp 1985: 129-33).

Like the trickster also, Tamar and Ruth, in particular, undertake their risky strategies primarily out of their own self-interest. Only secondarily and unintentionally do their actions benefit the larger group (cf. Radin 1956: 125). Yet the biblical authors, like the tricksters' tradents, understand the women's intentions and their effects as of one piece.

This subtle underlying unity of personified Wisdom and the Strange Woman provides a counterweight to the more polemical overtones of ancient instruction ('Understand, my son, that there are two distinct groups of women in the world…') and modern critique ('Look, my daughter, how men have divided us into virgins and whores…'). Such a perspective allows an interpretation of female Wisdom and the Strange Woman not along traditional patriarchal lines of 'virgin versus whore' or 'the ideal woman on a pedestal versus the degraded woman of male experience', but rather as a representation of the necessary complementarity of human experience. If Proverbs, in splitting the typical, paradoxically single, trickster, has to some degree denied rather than affirmed this complementarity, we now at least have a basis for a specific and constructive critique that goes beyond the limitations of a polemic against patriarchy in general (cf. Johanson's [1976] admonition to take on this task). The remaining sections of this chapter will address some of the different aspects of this fundamental feature of duality. In particular, an issue that emerges in the Proverbs material is that of how these sages have structured their experience of the conjunction, as well as the opposition, of good and evil and what role female imagery has played in that structuring.

Order and Disorder

As we have already noted, the trickster represents the forces of creation and destruction, order and disorder, on both the cosmic and social levels. Although the temptation here, once again, is to see two 'originally' distinct characters at work, the structure of many trickster episodes reveals the inherent unity of these two movements. Raven, the North American Haida trickster, for example, begins his creative work by skinning a newborn child and appropriating its skin for himself and then stealing and eating people's eyeballs (Radin 1956: 156-58)! Similarly, the trickster's introduction of valuable tools or social customs to a society often takes place without any intention on his part and, indeed, often as the result of some otherwise unpleasant trick he has played on someone (Radin 1956: 125). Occasionally, this intermixture of ordering and disordering activities results in an ironic double paradox, as in one of Pelton's parade examples, the conflict between Ananse, the trickster of the West African Ashante tribe, and the misanthropic character, Hate-to-be-contradicted (Pelton 1980: 25-27). Hate-to-be-contradicted lives on the outskirts of society; he fools visitors into contradicting him by telling outlandish stories, and then kills them. Hate-to-be-contradicted is outdone by his own contradiction of the even wilder lies told by Ananse, who then takes license to kill him. Having performed this apparent favor for society, however, Ananse cuts his antagonist into bits and 'sows' contradiction among humans.

Contrary, perhaps, to our expectations, the Ashante do not condemn Ananse for his introduction of contradiction into human discourse, but rather delight in this expression of what they know to be their reality. In this, as in other stories, the trickster embraces and embodies the paradox of order and disorder (Pelton 1980: 29).

> Disorder belongs to the totality of life and the spirit of this disorder is the Trickster. His function…is to add disorder to order and so make a whole, to render possible, within the bounds of what is permitted, an experience of what is not permitted (Kerenyi 1956: 185).

The important point is that the forces of disorder are brought inside human territory. Ananse and Hate-to-be-contradicted behave in virtually the same manner, except for the fact that the latter refuses human intercourse while the former insists on it, even in its negativity. 'The true limen', suggests Pelton, 'lies not on or outside the margins of society, but in its midst' (1980: 37).

That personified Wisdom and the Strange Woman represent forces of order and disorder is abundantly clear. Wisdom participates in the ordering process of Yhwh's creation (8.22-30) and is responsible for the governance of society (8.15-16) and the well-being of her followers (8.18, 35-36). The doubled epithet repeatedly applied to the negative female figure—strange woman, foreign woman—captures in its very ambiguity the multileveled nature of the threat she presents to the orders of life and society (Camp 1985: 115-20). Her house is the gateway to death (2.18-19; 9.18), countering Wisdom's offer of life. This death, though imaged in virtually mythological terms, has a concrete social form: being 'cut off from the land' (2.22) and descending to 'the point of utter ruin in the assembled congregation' (5.14). Clearly, the community feels a threat to itself in the actions of the individual.

For all these obvious oppositions between the ordering of Woman Wisdom and the disordering of the Strange Woman, the trickster paradigm invites us to consider the intersections of these forces as well. The Strange Woman, in spite of her 'foreignness', exists very much within the boundaries of society. She appears in the public places of the community and invites people to her house, just as Woman Wisdom does. In portraying the Strange Woman in this manner, the editor(s) of Proverbs have not excluded strangeness, but, in fact, let it 'in'. In so doing, they have acknowledged (whether consciously or not) the reality that a system of order cannot afford to exclude anomaly without ultimately being overwhelmed by it (Pelton 1980: 251). Here the apparently negative Strange Woman enacts one of the paradoxically positive roles of the trickster, symbolizing the manner in which people try to integrate disorder, the anomalous, into their daily lives.

The house and paths of the Strange Woman, moreover, bring within the boundaries of communal apprehension the ultimate disorder, namely, death. Trickster figures are often credited with bringing death into human existence and, thereby, capturing death's 'centripetality' for the center of life and guaranteeing life's 'eternal reirruption' (Pelton 1980: 263; cf. Radin 1956: 147). If this evaluation of death seems a bit *too* positive with respect to Proverbs, we ought nonetheless remember that the 'first woman', Eve, accepted death as the price of a fully human life. The entry of death into human life through the mediation of the woman and the serpent (certainly another trickster figure) goes hand in hand with the acquisition of knowledge of good and evil which, for the sage, means life. At the heart of wisdom thought lies the trickster's paradox: death does yield life.

Death as a metaphor in Proverbs 1–9 is less focused on biological death than on the related connotations of separation from deity, community and progeny, ideas at least as terrifying to persons with a high sense of corporate identity (cf. Bailey 1979: 41). In spite of the danger, the acknowledgment of the Strange Woman within the community's boundaries is quite complete, as witnessed by the poem in Proverbs 7, which paints a shameless picture of her attractions (vv. 13-20) before warning of her consequences. Knowledge of evil must accompany knowledge of good in the search for wisdom and life. Without an appreciation for the strange, a society does not know its own boundaries.

To complete the paradox of order and disorder encompassed by the female imagery in Proverbs, we must recognize not only the Strange

Woman's *inclusion* within Israel's social boundaries, but also personified Wisdom's *transgression* of them. She is, first of all, one of the most universal, non-xenophobic images in the Hebrew Bible, comparable in this respect to Second Isaiah's Servant. She crosses, moreover, the most fundamental line of all, that between creator and created—and in both directions, as is typical of tricksters. She is at one and the same time human wisdom elevated to the word of God (witness the canonical status of Proverbs) and divine wisdom come to reside among humans. But, contrary to expectations, her elevation does not result in death (contrast the king of Tyre, Ezek. 28), nor is her 'descent' from heaven the result of anything other than her own initiative (Prov. 8.30-31). The boundary-crossing that ought to destroy instead becomes a source of life, but we can see the true value of this life only if we also recognize the dangerously disordering process through which it becomes available.

The Language of Wisdom and Deceit

Pelton argues that the bringing of reality to language and the definition of human being as being engaged in discourse, usually accomplished through foolishness or deceit, is one of the hallmarks of the trickster. 'The trickster brings to light all non-sense so that all might become language and therefore human' (Pelton 1980: 242).

The Ashante's Ananse provides a variety of amusing examples. In addition to introducing contradiction into human discourse, Ananse also saves speech for human beings by tricking a monster bird into returning the jaws he stole from human faces (Pelton 1980: 40). He is also associated with the spread of wisdom, which he initially tries to hide by putting it in a gourd at the top of a tree. Aggravated because his son can climb the tree better than he, however, he breaks the gourd and hurls its contents to the earth. In a wonderfully complex episode, Ananse helps the Sun assume his rightful position as High God in the pantheon and settler of human disputes, but again by trickery. He steals a certain word from the Creator God that Sun must know in order to prove his worthiness for the position, and then aids Sun's memory of it by fashioning a drum whose resonance imitates the sound of the word. Pelton comments that the 'light' needed to fashion order out of the tangle of human wills can only be focused through a duplicity that restarts the processes of speech… Ananse rejects truth in favor of lying, but only for the sake of speech… (1980: 50-51).

Furthermore, as a reward for his success in this episode, Ananse's name is given to all the stories—*anansesem*—through which the Ashante remember and shape their culture (Pelton 1980: 27-31, 224).

These Ashante tales represent only a few of the episodes associating various West African tricksters with language. Compare also Pelton's discussions of the Fon's Legba, the 'divine linguist' (1980:72); the Yoruba's Eshu, the introducer of divination (133-48); or the Dogon's Ogo-Yurugu who, with his twin, possesses the 48 categories into which the Dogon divide all speech (188-89).

The connections of personified Wisdom and the Strange Woman to language are numerous and, again, more subtle and complex than might appear at first glance. Woman Wisdom announces herself as a speaker of truth and a hater of perverted speech (Prov. 8.6-9, 13). Her instruction brings happiness and life (8.32-35). The invitations of the Strange Woman (or Woman Folly in 9.13) are, of course, understood as seductions that lead to death. We must, however, consider the underlying currents that partially blur this surface opposition.

Like Ananse, Woman Wisdom presides over and authorizes a tradition that is terribly concerned with language and its proper use (Gilbert 1979: 218; Lang 1975: 170-71). The basic values as represented in the proverb collections are to speak as little as possible (10.19; 13.3; 17.25; 29.20; *passim*), as effectively as possible (15.23; 25.11, 15; *passim*), and to recognize that no matter what one says, Yhwh may have something else in mind (21.1, 2; 20.21; *passim*). Righteous speech is also of great importance (10.11, 20, 21, 31, 32; *passim*), but it shares center stage with words fitly or efficaciously spoken. The moral value of proverbial language is occasionally ambiguous, moreover. The observation that 'a bribe is a magic stone in the eye of him who gives it' (17.8) creates almost as much temptation as the description of the Strange Woman in Proverbs 7. Finally, proverbs that counsel opposite courses of action (presumably depending on the situation; cf. 26.4, 5) indicate an awareness that this form of commonsense truth is to some degree relative and immethodical (cf. Geertz 1975: 23-24). The tradition personified by Woman Wisdom recognizes, then, a complexity in human existence and in the speech that articulates it.

A similar ambiguity exists in the proverb collection with respect to the relationship of folly and wickedness. Although both are evaluated negatively, folly does not entail the dire consequences associated with Woman Folly in 9.13, who opens the same doorway to death, as does the Strange Woman in other poems. R.B.Y. Scott has noted that the contrasted pairs of righteousness and wickedness, on the one hand, and wisdom and folly, on the other, are not interchangeable in the collection (1972: 153-54). The fool can expect poverty and disrepute, but this does not carry an explicitly religious value judgment with it (Scott 1972: 158). Frequently, the actions of fools are simply described (12.15, 23; 13.16; 15.21; 18.2) as if no further comment were necessary, and folly is considered its own reward (16.22). The warnings against the consequences of folly, both to the fool and to others, are sometimes couched in images that border on the amusing and, indeed, remind us of the trickster.

> Like one who binds the stone in the sling
> is the one who gives honor to a fool (26.8).

> Like a dog that returns to his vomit
> is a fool that repeats his folly (26.11).

The sluggard, in particular, is depicted in laughable images (22.13; 26.13, 14, 15), and there is one character who is even worse than the fool:

> Do you see a man who is wise in his own eyes?
> There is more hope for a fool than for him (26.12).

This nuance and complexity found in the tradition is seemingly reduced by the either/or opposition of Woman Wisdom and the Strange Woman in the poems of Proverbs 1–9, yet even here the matter is not quite so simple. As Aletti's analysis pointed out (see above), the one who wishes to distinguish between these two female figures must first contend with their similarities. Aletti argues further that this potential confusion of values was quite intentional on the part of the sage, who used it as one means of emphasizing the crucial importance of language to society as a whole and in the endeavors of the wisdom tradition in particular and, for these very reasons, the dangers of its abuse (1977: 139-40).

The crowning irony in this nexus of language, wisdom and deceit comes in Prov. 18.21, which introduces yet another female image, 'Lady Tongue' (Williams 1982: 91).

Death and life are in the hand of the tongue,
and her lovers will eat of her fruit.

Those who are lovers of language, and the sages are most certainly among them, can expect to taste the fruits of both the Strange Woman's deceit, namely death, and Woman Wisdom's truth, the life that comes from Yhwh (8.35). The fundamental duality that exists in human intercourse is inescapable. Language may, in the abstract, separate truth and deceit, but in experience the two often become one.

This duality is often treated in the Bible with greater appreciation and, sometimes, humor than it is in Proverbs 1–9. Nowhere is this truer than in stories of some of the female characters who are related in theme and imagery to personified Wisdom and the Strange Woman (Camp 1985: 124-40). I have already alluded to the social boundary defying sexual activity of Tamar, Ruth and Judith. In this context, we need also note that the ploys of Tamar and Judith are accompanied by deceit, as is also true in Rebekah's scheme to win the firstborn's blessing for Jacob (Gen. 27). Esther provides another example of cagey locution and circumlocution that, while not quite deceitful, was, at the appropriate moments, less than completely straightforward (cf. Talmon 1963: 437). Finally, in yet another twist on truth, deceit and their anticipated consequences, the wise (but calculating) Abigail kills her husband Nabal (whose name means 'fool') with the absolute, unvarnished truth (1 Sam. 25.37-38).

Theodicy

Although 'theodicy' is not a term typically used by anthropologists in their studies of tricksters, it should be clear from the themes of order and disorder, truth and falsehood already discussed that the question of good and evil, and their relationship to the deity, cannot lurk far in the background. We have seen enough of the trickster to know that, in him, various cultural understandings of good and evil merge in complex ways. What is less obvious and, indeed, varies from culture to culture is the role of the deity in all of this. Sometimes the trickster *is* a deity who represents a primordial blend of power, creativity and destructiveness: for example, the Haida's Raven (see above; Radin 1956: 156-58). Other times, he is a being created by the High God for a special purpose. In an episode of the Winnebago trickster mythology, Earthmaker tells the trickster, Wakdjunkaga:

> Firstborn, you are the oldest of all those I have created. I created you
> good-natured: I made you a sacred person. I sent you to the earth to
> remain there so that human beings would listen to you, honor you and
> obey you and that you might teach them by what means they could
> secure a happy life…(Radin 1956: 150).

Earthmaker goes on to chastise gently Wakdjunkaga for bringing trouble on himself by making light of the deity's creation. Radin notes,
however, that even within one tradition, interpretations of the trickster
can vary. By the early twentieth century, some Winnebagos influenced
by syncretized Christian beliefs had moralized the trickster stories as
examples of inappropriate behavior, or even equated him with Satan
(Radin 1956: 148-50).

The pattern varies again in the case of Ogo-Yurugu, the trickster of
the West African Dogon tribe. In Dogon mythology, Ogo-Yurugu is
one of a set of primordial twins who rebels against the High God,
Amma, his creator, because of his fear that Amma will deny him a
mate. Although Ogo-Yurugu is finally defeated by Amma and banished
from the divine and human domains (he becomes a fox), his attempts to
wrest control from Amma result in the shape of the world as the Dogon
know it.

> [T]he Dogon too must cope with solitude, sexual anxiety and death. They
> do not, however, look at these experiences or the rebellion that caused
> them as unequivocally evil. Without Ogo's search for his female twin
> nothing would be what it is, and even as Yurugu [the fox], he continues
> to reveal and enlarge the boundaries of life. The 'beneficent ferment' of
> Ogo's opposition complements the orderly graciousness of Amma (Pelton
> 1980: 207).

The Western reader of the Wakdjunkaga and Ogo-Yurugu stories is
inevitably tempted to make comparisons with the biblical story of creation and 'fall'. This placement of the trickster in the role of the
archetypal human would not be altogether inaccurate. Over and over his
interpreters comment that the trickster's role is that of making the
human world human. The questions raised by this mythology for the
biblical tradition are: How evil is evil? And what does God have to do
with this dimension of human experience?

According to one interpretive stance, the negative aspects of the
human condition are punishment for the sin of disobedience to God,
enacted out of human free will and thus absolving God of responsibility
in the matter. Although, on one level, such an interpretation seems

comparable to the trickster stories of rebellion against, or at least care-lessness of, the High God's purposes, it does not cope well with their lightness, humor and irony, and their acceptance of human 'evil'. Nor does such a position deal well with certain intrabiblical dilemmas, for example, the terrible logical problem of the existence of evil under the reign of a good and all-powerful God, or the occasional biblical revela-tion of God's maleficence (especially in Job and Qohelet).

The trickster stories represent a different approach to the problem of evil. This approach is more descriptive (being often etiological) than prescriptive, and it is less concerned with explaining evil than it is with interpreting the human condition of which evil is a part. The paradoxi-cal unity of good and evil in the trickster is basically a manifestation of the way human life is. This approach also, then, begs the metaphysical question of the relationship of a good God to evil, but it does recognize the reality of a human experience of evil that is not explicable in the terms of a simplistic theory of retribution. In many respects, I would suggest, the commonsense, human-oriented attitude to this issue found in the trickster stories is most closely akin to that expressed in biblical material associated with wisdom.

We have already noted some of the moral ambiguities in the proverb collection. This ambiguity is coupled with variant evaluations of vocab-ulary associated with wisdom, both within Proverbs itself (McKane 1970: 10-22) and elsewhere, as, for example, in the stories of David and Solomon (Whybray 1968: 57-59). This is nowhere clearer than in the Eden story, where the crafty (*'arum*)[3] serpent leads the way to both human mortality and wisdom. In addition to the traditional interpre-tation of this story as one of sin and punishment, George Mendenhall has also found here a scathing critique of wisdom (1974). I am not con-vinced, however, that either of these perspectives is completely correct.

The simplistic notion of sin and punishment does not deal with the complexities of the text, both in what it does and does not say. First, it does not deal with God's ultimate responsibility for the situation. Who, after all, created the serpent and his intellectual abilities, and provided the temptation of a forbidden tree? The Eden story is really quite like a trickster tale in this respect, concerned not with explaining or rationaliz-ing every logical possibility of a situation but rather with enfolding

3. Compare the positive evaluations of this word in Prov. 12.3; 13.16; 14.14; *passim*.

in an imaginative, narrative embrace the 'way things are' for human beings, in other words, with describing and interpreting the human condition. The text is curiously silent about Yhwh's emotions in reaction to the human deed, especially with regard to any 'wrath' one might expect the deity to feel. Yhwh simply asks what has occurred (Gen. 3.11, 13), describes what every Israelite knows to be the nature of existence (3.14-19), and then makes clothes for the man and woman (3.21).[4] The analyses of several different scholars, working from different methodological perspectives, have all stressed the descriptive, rather than prescriptive, nature of the so-called 'punishments' of the humans, and, thus, the text's concern to bring meaning (not merely condemnation) to the brokenness of human life (Trible 1978: 123-32; Bal 1987: 104-30; Meyers 1988: 72-121).

> The elementary questions about life and its hardships, about the endless and excessive efforts to survive—these are the human enigmas of existence to which this passage speaks. The gnawing WHY—why is life so hard for both men and women, why is there so much to be done for survival alone—is dealt with here (Meyers 1983: 348).

Bal concludes:

> [I]t is not obvious that Yahweh's reaction should be considered as a punishment. It seems more plausible to take it as an explicit spelling out of the consequences of the human action, as another representation of the reality of human life (1987: 125).[5]

Is, then, Genesis 2–3 a condemnation of human wisdom? It is true that wisdom that is 'wise in its own eyes', that does not allow for the disposing of Yhwh as well as the proposing of human beings, is condemned by the sages, not only in the critical books of Job and Qohelet but also in that bastion of human optimism, Proverbs itself. The univer-

---

4.   If God in any sense 'has an attitude' about the actions of the humans, it centers less on the notions that they have disobeyed and thus sinned, and more on the deity-threatening outcome of their eating: they are expelled from the Garden in order to remove them from the tree of life, thus preventing them from becoming gods themselves.

5.   Worth noting, however, are the more complicated readings of Jobling (1986: 17-43) and Fewell and Gunn (1993: 35-36). Jobling retains, in part, a reading of Gen. 3 as a story of the fall, and analyzes the mythic need to blame *someone* (hence, of course, the woman) for the difficulties of the human condition. Fewell and Gunn highlight the deity's need for control in the face of human self-elevation. 'God's rhetoric turns natural consequences into divinely controlled repercussions.'

sality of this critique in the wisdom tradition suggests to me that Mendenhall's interpretation is off-target and that, once again, Genesis's intent is to understand, not condemn, human reality as the author knows it. Yes, the Eden story does associate the acquisition of human wisdom with death, but the rest of the Hebrew Bible makes clear that the mere fact of human mortality is not overly troubling to the ancient Israelites (Bailey 1979: 47-57). Death, too, is part of the 'way life is'. More importantly, I think, Genesis 3 reveals that wisdom, like death—and also like the hard work of farming, the bearing of children, the wearing of clothes and so on—is part of *human* life.

The wisdom tradition was willing both to exalt and criticize itself, but both evaluations were made from the perspective of human beings. Even the God of the whirlwind who appears in Job is a God poetically articulated from a consciously human experience, with no pretense of recording direct divine revelation. The wisdom tradition articulates various facets of the interface between an ambiguous human wisdom and a God who should be good and just, but who is not always so experienced. Wisdom conceives theodicy not as a metaphysical problem, but as part and parcel of life experience.

Woman Wisdom and the Strange Woman in Proverbs also speak to this condition, as always, paradoxically. On the one hand, they represent the idealized conceptualization of good and evil: ever separate, consequences ever inevitable. Under the surface, however, as Aletti's analysis makes clear, lurks the dangerous knowledge that life does not always work so neatly. The Strange Woman is such a horror to the patriarchal order because her words are so close to the truth, not the truth of tidy theological packages, but the truth as humans really experience it. Husbands do go away on business, and strange beds do offer delight. The depth of the paradox becomes visible when we foreground the unity of the female imagery that embraces the duality. In their embodiment, Woman Wisdom and the Strange Woman are one, a fact that their speeches only partially mitigate. As woman, her dual path runs from heaven to Sheol and back, never failing to pass through human territory. The unity of the imagery is important for the same reason the trickster is important. It is a way of representing, and thus encompassing, the anomaly that exists in human life.

The female imagery does not, then, simply mediate between the human and the divine (cf. Camp 1985: 272-81), or only between human life and death, but also unites divinity with death. In the connection of this imagery *both* to Yhwh *and* Sheol, the full range of human experience of anomaly is incorporated, that of the material and social worlds, and of the spirit as well. The ambiguity of the female imagery reflects the moral ambiguity of the deity who stands in the shadows of Eden and bursts forth in the Joban whirlwind. Proverbs thereby acknowledges what its readers would know experientially: one cannot receive good from the hand of Yhwh and not receive evil also.

The unity of this imagery brings a new meaning to death as well. If the woman whose dwelling place is in Sheol is, on one level, the same as she who plays before Yhwh, and if this woman is the human reflection of the nature of God, then God's presence in Sheol is also affirmed. Such a theological perception is typically either denied in the Bible (Job 7.21; Ps. 88.4-6, 11-13 [Eng.: 3-5, 10-12]; Isa. 38.18-19) or, in the case of Job, tantalizingly tasted (15.13; 28.22). In Proverbs, by means of the female imagery, the chaotic anomaly of death is brought fully within the compass not only of human but also of divine experience. The words of Pelton regarding the trickster may be accurately applied to the sisterly embodiment of Wisdom and Strangeness.

> [The trickster] affirms the doubleness of the real and denies every one-dimensional image of it. If he struggles with the High God and causes pain and death to enter the world, spoiling primordial bliss, his quarrel is not with the divine order as such, but with a false human image of the sacred, one that cannot encompass suffering, disorder and the ultimate mess of death (Pelton 1980: 262-63).

No less than Job, though through very different literary means, do the women of Proverbs participate in this struggle.

Conclusion

In the foregoing discussion, I have employed the trickster pattern well known in comparative folklore as a hermeneutical resource for analyzing the female imagery in Proverbs. Although these poems hardly read as trickster narratives, I have argued that significant points of connection afford the trickster paradigm some interpretive value with respect to personified Wisdom and the Strange Woman. To generalize, we might say that reading Proverbs 1–9 through the lens of the trickster produces a form of deconstructive reading of the text, undercutting its most obvious message of absolute opposition between good and evil as represented in these two figures, and highlighting their paradoxical, but experientially validated, unity.

It may well be the case that no author or editor involved with Proverbs consciously 'intended' anything other than straightforward moralism. Evidence exists in other texts, nonetheless, that writers attuned to the kind of issues and conceptualities embedded in Proverbs—to matters of wisdom and strangeness, language and deceit, righteousness and theodicy, male and female—did indeed explore their ideological intersections and contradictions by means of narrative play. It would be my guess that these other texts, two of which we shall examine in the next two chapters, are earlier than Proverbs, that the relatively more rigid articulation of female Wisdom and Strangeness in Proverbs is a fossil, rather than a precursor, of the more complex and nuanced narratives. It is, nonetheless, through the lens of Proverbs's crystallization of Woman Wisdom and the Strange Woman that the women of the Solomon and Samson narratives come to the particular sort of life my readings will offer.

Part II

READING BIBLICAL NARRATIVE AS WISE AND STRANGE

Introduction to Part II

In the preceding chapters I have attempted, first, to construct from the book of Proverbs a paradigm of opposing female images, Woman Wisdom and the Strange Woman, and then, using folklore's trickster as a lens, to problematize the opposition. Although the possibility of this subversion lurks in Proverbs itself, it is most apparent when one considers the figure of the Strange Woman in narrative. Only by undermining the paradigm's polarities can inheritance be established through the foreigners Tamar and Ruth, with their crafty and self-determined use of their own sexuality. Only thus can liars like Rebekah and the Exodus midwives, Shiphrah and Puah, be portrayed as saviors of national heroes. With these characters we have begun to read the Bible with the Strange Woman. Of particular interest to one who begins in the book of Proverbs, however, are narratives dealing with *both* wisdom *and* strangeness, where the dialectic plays out (and plays around!) in all its gendered fullness. Such is the case in the stories of Samson and Solomon.

To approach these texts from the direction of Proverbs is to raise the perennially contentious question of 'wisdom influence' in 'non-wisdom' books.[1] This is not a question I can settle here, although recent commentators are more wont to allow for such 'influence' in the case of Solomon (Gordon 1995; Lemaire 1995) than of Samson. Particularly helpful in this regard is Carole Fontaine's three-layered schema of motifs contributing to wisdom influence (1994: 166): (1) wisdom items (including vocabulary, forms and themes); (2) wisdom characters; and

---

1. Biblical scholars have long regarded certain books—Proverbs, Job, Qohelet, in the Hebrew canon—as the literary products of a so-called 'wisdom tradition' because of their interest in the possibility and significance of human wisdom, whether in daily life or in relationship to the divine. This tradition, no doubt in one sense widespread in oral culture, received its literary expression at the hands of an educated scribal elite (see Introduction). The degree to which these scribes held and articulated a different (usually regarded as more 'secular') view of the world than that evident in the rest of the Bible is a matter of much debate, as is the degree to which they (on the presumption of difference) 'influenced' the rest. As already suggested in the Introduction, I take the view that a more complex model is needed than that of 'wisdom' vs. 'everything else'. I shall attempt here to flesh out some of the observations made in the Introduction, which were mainly of a sociohistorical nature, by means of textual readings.

(3) wisdom functions. While the Samson saga has no 'wisdom vocabulary', it is quite interested in forms, themes and characters important to Proverbs, that is, in riddles, deft use of language, proper relationship to knowledge and, last but hardly least, the Strange Woman in her several guises. Judges 14 contains, moreover, the single canonical instance of riddle performance, while 1 Kings 10 also alludes to the exercise of this communication convention.[2] Although it is not my goal to 'prove' the 'influence of wisdom' on the Samson and Solomon narratives, the combination of motifs and suggested or described performance make the question of the relationship of these narratives to what we call 'wisdom literature' unavoidable. It is hard, I find, not to imagine, at least, a 'wisdom reader' (see Introduction).

Equally interesting, however, especially in combination with the signs of wisdom, are the suggestions of cultic interest in both these narratives. While the notion of 'priestly influence' on the Solomon and Samson texts has even less scholarly currency than that of wisdom, the former is in fact dominated by the account of temple building and the latter by the taking and breaking of the Nazirite vow. The following two chapters, then, while focused on the dynamics of wisdom and strangeness, will consider as well their intersection with these cultic motifs.

---

2. Cf. Fontaine's (1982) definitive study of biblical proverb performance, as well as her more recent study (1997) of proverb use in the later tradition involving the Queen of Sheba and Solomon.

Chapter 3

RIDDLERS, TRICKSTERS AND STRANGE WOMEN
IN THE SAMSON STORY

Let me riddle you a riddle. In this riddle, I give you the answer and you
have to supply the question. It goes like this:

> Out of the eater came something to eat,
> Out of the strong came something sweet.

What is the solution to my riddle? How would you go about figuring it
out? Let me give you the answer.

> What is sweeter than honey?
> What is stronger than a lion?

Could you have guessed? If you are familiar with this part of the
Samson story, were you as fooled in your first reading as the Philistines
of Timnah were when Samson posed this riddle to them? Would you
have felt, as they did, that you'd been tricked, as you realized that the
riddle was based on a very strange experience of the riddler's, which
you could not have known about? Would you have been willing to
resort to death threats to get the answer, as the Philistines did?

Riddles, writ small and large. Writ small is this particular riddle
posed by Samson to the Philistines at his marriage feast to an unnamed
Philistine woman of Timnah. Where did Samson get this riddle? What
did he hope to accomplish with it? Why were the Philistines so upset
with it, and why did Samson become enraged at the discovery of its
solution? Study of this particular riddle leads us to ask the question of
the Samson story's larger riddle: What is the meaning and purpose of
this complex biblical narrative? Does it offer its readers any obvious
'message'? What sort of readers does the story presuppose? What interests and agendas manifest themselves here, and how do these relate to
the identity politics and social and institutional conflicts described thus
far?

Genre and Gender in a Narrative House of Mirrors

The meaning of the riddle in Judges 14 can be considered on three levels: the riddle proper, the riddle performance and the riddle as part of the narrator's art. Neither of the first two levels is the exclusive provenance of an elite intellectual class (often regarded as the main provenance of the biblical wisdom tradition), though both are consistent with it, as well as with the alternative understanding of wisdom as part of the sociocultural shaping and maintenance of the family and tribe (cf. Fontaine 1982; Camp 1985, 1990). Riddling itself is a widely attested folk genre, and riddling at weddings an equally well-attested context of use. The story of Samson's riddle performance may well have originated as a popular folk-hero tale: along with other elements in this cycle it forms a vivid cultural variant of the traditional trickster tale. On the other hand, effective use of language (i.e. performance) is also one of the defining features of the learned sage, according to the book of Proverbs, while understanding riddles is a capacity at the highest level of wisdom, if we are to take seriously the sequence of skills listed in that book's introductory verses.[1] Whatever the folk origins of certain elements in the Samson story, moreover, a case can also be made that, in its present form, it is a relatively late work constructed to epitomize and reflect on themes in the book of Judges (Greenstein 1981: 248). This possibility of a conscious aesthetic–intellectual reflection on emergent written literature also returns us, then, to the ethos of the educated elite, whether or not one labels that 'the wisdom tradition'.

The riddle as genre and performance is, in any case, woven into a larger narrative pattern, extending throughout the Samson story's four chapters, for which it provides a *mise en abyme*, that is, a nutshell rendition—a 'microstructure' (so Bal)—of the larger story in which it occurs.[2] As a metatext that tells its own version of the story, the *mise en abyme* is said to 'reflect'; thus it is metaphorized as a mirror with a

---

1. Proverbs 1.2-4 lists the learning needs of the 'simple', while vv. 5-6, culminating in understanding riddles, addresses 'the wise'.

2. My understanding of the *mise en abyme* comes from Bal (1987: 75-76, 88). Bal's own definition, however, is based on a series of technical narratological distinctions—between narrative text, story and fabula (cf. Bal 1985: 5-6)—that I do not use here. I use the term 'fabula' sparingly; 'story' and 'narrative' are used interchangeably.

'virtually endless regressive potential' that interrupts and 'thus disrupts the version we were reading at the moment it intervened' (Bal 1987: 88). As mirror, Bal argues, the *mise en abyme* presents the paradox of the unique confronting the identical, the (self-)reflection that turns subject into object through confrontation with the symbolic order. This paradox finds its source and means in language, that fundament of human experience of which the riddle, I shall argue, is an exemplar of a particular sort. Bal speaks, finally, of the *mise en abyme par excellence*, 'the *mise en abyme* that, instead of proposing one interpretation, as is usually the case, offers all possibilities' (1987: 76). This, I shall argue, is the appropriate category for Samson's riddle.

Strikingly, the formal *mise en abyme* represented by the riddle is matched and enhanced by another at the level of character, namely, the Strange Woman. Read through the lens of the trickster, this figure forces an infinitely regressing reflection on identity constructed through binary oppositions, challenging neat formulations of us vs. them, good vs. evil, male vs. female, truth vs. deceit. The fact that the Samson narrative is also a strong representative of the trickster tale phenomenon lends yet a third dimension to this perspective. In a story about tricksters and strange women, wisdom will be anything but straightforward. In a trickster tale, we expect to find a character who crosses the boundaries established for the sake of social order, with a special interest in crossing sexual boundaries; we expect to find a concern for language and its confusion between truth and deceit; we expect to discover folly where we sought wisdom and wisdom in the place of folly. Based on our study of Proverbs, moreover, we might expect to find in a biblical trickster tale a concern for theodicy as well.

The collusion of riddle, Strange Woman and trickster, each a transformative figure in its own right, ought to produce a narrative with boundary-shattering potential. Theodicy, I suggest, is the ultimate religious name for shattered boundaries. Taking theodicy together with the riddle-as-exemplar-of-language, we are deep in the heart of the problematic of the wisdom enterprise, as attested not only in Proverbs but also Job and, especially, Qohelet. Like the latter two texts, Samson may, perhaps, be read as wisdom against the tradition.

The Riddle as Mise en Abyme

In an article published several years before Bal introduced the term *mise en abyme* to biblical studies, Edward Greenstein (1981) effectively goes as far as any commentator to apply that concept to the riddle of Samson. Identifying a variety of anomalous aspects of the narrative, he argues that a reading of the story as a riddle integrates the dissonances into a meaningful communication. Six notable oddities, in Greenstein's view, include the following: (1) the character of Samson, who fights personal vendetta rather than leading the Israelite people into battle and 'suffers from an acute weakness for women'; (2) Samson's miraculous birth that yet comes with no expressed desire from his parents; (3) the failure to clearly identify, with a name (in the case of his mother) or parentage (for the father), Samson's parents, and his own ambiguous 'Everyman' sort of name;[3] (4) the anomalous role of the Nazirite vow; (5) Samson's careless religious posture coupled with the narrative's lack of polemic against Philistine religion; and (6) the unique divine fulfillment of Samson's death wish (Greenstein 1981: 239-42).

Greenstein identifies a seventh anomaly that he importantly recognizes as one that straddles the 'fuzzy border from the topic and action of the story to its form and style' (242). This is, of course, the riddle itself, particularly with regard to its inverted form of a statement that produces a question as the 'answer'. Though riddles in the form of statements are not unknown to folklorists, questions as answers—'a complete morphological exchange'—seem to be. Greenstein then broadens the scope of the concept riddle beyond its linguistic formulation to the idea of 'a pattern in which what one is led to suppose to be x turns out—unexpectedly—to be y' (243). Detailing some 15 such reversals of expectation in the Samson narrative, Greenstein goes on to propose that

> just as the narrative unfolds according to a recurrent 'riddle' pattern, so should the interpreter, working in a sense backwards from the manifest to the latent meaning, apply the riddle formula to the story of Samson itself. For by shaping itself in the form of riddles, the text presents itself to us as a virtual riddle to be solved, a code to be cracked. The accumulation of questions, riddles, surprises and gross anomalies prompts us to ask: who strays after foreign women, acts on impulse, and neglects his cultic obligations? (1981:247)

3.   Greenstein (1981:241) observes that the statement that Samson's unnamed mother 'called his name (*shem*) Samson (*Shimshon*)' has the effect of calling his name 'Name'.

Read thus, Samson is Israel, an 'answer' to the riddle of the text that Greenstein argues solves the anomalies identified above (1981: 247-51). I shall not attempt to summarize his points here, but rather address them in the course of my discussion.

To put, then, Greenstein's conclusion in currently favored terms, the riddle of Judges 14 is a *mise en abyme* for the story as a whole, offering a version of the story in which Samson is straying Israel. In identifying the meaning of the sign as singular, however, Greenstein precludes the possibility that the riddle is a *mise en abyme par excellence*, an open-ended figure fraught with many meanings that force reflection on what-ever meaning we thought to tame. Further, although his use of this meaning to solve the text's various mysteries provides a satisfying read-ing on one level—one in which things are neatly packaged, tidied up—textual ambiguities threaten to break in again at virtually every point with other possibilities, subverting this predictable lesson about the Israelite man and the Strange Woman. If riddles presuppose solutions, trickster tales do not! Thus, while I accept Greenstein's characterization of the text as riddle, I shall question whether the model of the solved riddle is most appropriate for the case at hand.

Tricksters and the Breakdown of Binary Oppositions

Tricksters and the Ethics of Reading

Samson is a trickster, and the trickster pattern—involving a character with lusty desires and supreme self-confidence, the wise fool, the tricker who gets tricked—pervades his story.[4] The narrative supplies the broad physical brand of humor that was notably missing from the more cere-bral version of the pattern in Proverbs. Amorality, moreover, sexual and otherwise, goes with the turf.

> Exogamous overtures or sexual connections of a less and less socially
> sanctioned variety combine with deceptions, counter-deceptions, acts of
> superhuman strength, displays of power over fertility, and withdrawal to

4. Any reader of the Samson story must account for the characterization of God's chosen hero as foolhardy rogue. Susan Niditch (1990), more systematically than most, details the links between this narrative and traditional trickster tales, a reading supported by the work of folklorist David Bynum (1990; see also Bynum's *The Daemon in the Wood* [Cambridge, MA: Harvard University Press, 1978]). Margalith compares elements in the Samson narrative to Greek myth and folklore, particularly to Heracles (1985; 1986a; 1986b).

paint a portrait of Samson very much in tune with the tricksters of non-Israelite environments (Niditch 1990: 617-18).

As we have seen from our cross-cultural examples in Chapter 2, however, while the trickster may be an oversexed, overmuscled buffoon, he is never merely that. Not only is he often clever—sometimes too clever by half—he also embodies the paradox of culture creation in the process of culture destruction, and vice versa. Trickster tales are, at least potentially, among the most subversive of cultural genres insofar as they both represent and challenge the most fundamental boundaries of a culture.[5]

Now when cultures tell such tales of the chaos at the heart of their order, and do so in a spirit of high sport, we should not, I think, be too quick to tame them. And tamed has Samson been, as witnessed, for example, in Bal's survey of children's Bibles (1987: 37-67), which either ignore his foibles in order to cast him as the hero of God, or highlight his failings in order to teach a moral lesson. Even a reading as nuanced as Greenstein's ends up assuming that the (male) reader will have learned his lesson: in the name of literary art, everything in the text is finally shown its place.

Feminists have been more subtle in their taming of Samson, and more justified in their will to emasculate. Not driven by conventional moralities or by an abstract aesthetic, readers such as Mieke Bal (1987; 1988a), Susan Niditch (1990) and Cheryl Exum (1993) have given fuller play to the boundary-crossing characteristic that marks the Samson narrative so strongly and which is drawn, I would argue, from its genre as trickster tale. Exum lays out succinctly many of the binaries at work: Israelite–Philistine (the concrete expression of 'own kind/foreign'); male–female; circumcised–uncircumcised; nature–culture; endogamy–exogamy; paternal house–women's houses; clean–unclean; self–other;

5.   As with any cultural expression of liminality, one must take seriously the possibility of trickster stories being coopted to support the status quo (Camp 1988; Bal 1988b: 150; cf. Turner's classic study on liminality, particularly his chapter on status elevation and reversal [1969: 166-203]). The history of interpretation of the Samson narrative certainly bears witness to the reality of such a coopting process. I shall argue here, however, that the use of the riddle and the presence of the Strange Woman contribute to the trickster's narrative, thus increasing its destabilizing potential for any reader with ears to hear.

good woman–evil woman (1993: 72-77). I would add to the list: good–evil; wisdom–folly; life–death; truth–deception; older generation–younger generation; sweet–strong; free will–predestination.

While Niditch focuses on the trickster pattern as such, maintaining a relativized historical perspective on the values of the text, Bal and Exum both challenge what I have called 'high sport' when it comes to the point of the murdered woman. Bal concludes her powerful work by challenging the scholarly convention that the so-called 'judges' of the book of Judges are not 'really' judges, but rather warriors (*gibborim*). 'Denying that the acts of the *gibborim* are acts of judgment, then, is a way to escape the need to judge them in their turn. We must judge such "judgment" and justice and expose its being anchored in power' (Bal 1988a: 245). This is a challenge I wish to vigorously maintain, and with respect to the trickster tale as well. It is hardly enough to say that 'tricksters just want to have fun', or even that 'tricksters empower the weak', when a woman caught between feuding men is burned to death. Yet something pulls at me, something that also does not wish the trickster dead. How might one pass the necessary judgment without flattening the tale's wonderful subversive potential? How might one read for life in the midst of death without devaluing the death?

Predictably, my answer: read with the Strange Woman. Here as elsewhere in the Bible, however, both trickster and Strange Woman come encumbered with the character of God. That so few commentators, especially feminists, give weight to this fact is remarkable.[6] Castigating Samson seems small potatoes in a story where 'what at first seems arbitrary and inappropriate in the hero's character turns out to be perfectly congruent with the theme of deliberate divine deliverance' (Vickery 1981: 66). We might only ask, deliverance for whom? I wish to examine more closely the relationship of the character of God to the binaries identified above, particularly as this relates to readings of the Samson narrative as a tale of binary breakdown.

Binary Breakdown and Blurring Boundaries
Niditch's (1990) analysis of Samson as trickster points to Samson's mediation of nature and culture, 'the raw and the cooked'. A man of

---

6.   Two notable exceptions are David Gunn (1992) and John Vickery (1981). Although my early formulation of this reading was independent of these, the present form of the argument owes them much.

culture, he comes from a conventional family, he creates riddles, displays wit and shapes reality through language. On the other hand, his most notable qualities are in 'the realm of the raw', his exploits in and through nature turned against the culturally superior Philistines. The nature–culture dynamic thus has in this case an Israelite particularity (Niditch 1990: 613-15): with respect to the Philistines, all efforts at mediation, here especially in the form of exogamous marriage, must fail (1990: 617-21). Niditch also notes the gender crossing that is represented by a cluster of images in Judges 16 (1990: 616-17). Samson is womanized by the cutting of his hair, with its sense of 'sexual stripping and subjugation'; by the image of grinding, a euphemism for intercourse (16.21); and by the use of the sexually shaded verb *shq/tshq* ('make sport') to describe his performance before the Philistines (16.25). Finally, the truth–deception binary, with its supposed relationship to good–evil, breaks down as we find that Samson must lie to preserve himself (Niditch 1990: 621). While at least one binary (nature–culture) breaks down rather thoroughly, then, at least one other (Israelite–Philistine) is intractable. Others breakdown partially: Samson is womanized, but no woman is here read as masculinized. Truth–deception dissolves more completely than Niditch, who poses Delilah as a liar pure and simple, allows. For Delilah speaks no untruth and, indeed, her purposes seem strangely bald. The Strange Woman as truth-teller over against the Israelite man as liar is a full inversion of expectation.

Extending Niditch's analysis, Exum points to these and other binaries, and their occasional undoings. The blurring of the male–female boundary gets fuller play in this reading. Samson's association with nature, for example, is more typical of stereotypes about women. Further terms suggesting Samson's womanization also include *pittah* ('seduce'—what the Timnite and Delilah do to Samson to get information from him [14.15; 16.5]) and *'innah* ('sexually humble'—what happens to Samson when his strength departs him [16.5, 6, 19]).[7] This complex of vocabulary reinforces the overall portrayal of Samson as

---

7. See Chapter 7 for a fuller discussion of the meaning of *'innah*, often translated as 'rape'. While the term has a broader connotation than simply the act of abusive sex, it often entails the sexual power of one party over another, often including a sense of shaming. When it is applied here, uniquely, to a woman's action against a man, the implication is one of demasculinizing him.

vulnerable because of his love for women. Acting thus like a woman in love, he surrenders Self to Other, melting this boundary as well (Exum 1993: 76, 79, 83-84). The gender-crossing is yet more complex, in Exum's view. The Philistines also, insofar as they do not bear the distinctive male mark of circumcision, and are dependent on women to gain the knowledge necessary for power, are constructed to some degree as women (Exum 1993: 73, 81, 86). I would note, on the other hand, that the fact that both the Philistine men and Delilah are subjects of '*innah*, the verb for sexual humbling, also masculinizes her. Similarly, to the extent that Samson's pregnant mother takes on the strictures of what will be *his* Nazirite status, a deeper than normal identification is made between male and female.

One other broader observation of Exum's will, with qualifications, be important for our further reflection. She points out that the male–female binary cuts across several others: some Israelites are women; at least one woman is good rather than evil (though only, in Exum's view, because her sexuality is controlled [1993: 76]); the Israelite man seeks out foreign women; both Philistine men and Samson are womanized, which itself perforates the boundaries of circumcised–non-circumcised, nature–culture, self and other (1993: 73-76). In spite of this complexity with respect to gender, Exum maintains a fairly rigorous dichotomy between good woman and bad woman. Likewise, although she sees Samson as a boundary-crosser, a limen, who moves between the Philistine and Israelite worlds without belonging fully to either, she points to the difficulty of maintaining a liminal status. Thus, like Niditch, she concludes that he cannot be a successful mediator between the two 'because the distinctions between them must be rigorously maintained by our story, even if at the price of the hero's life' (Exum 1993: 77). Based in part on the cross-cutting quality of the male–female binary, however, I will argue for a narrative boundary-crossing even more thoroughgoing than Niditch and Exum allow, including the Israelite–Philistine and, not unrelatedly, the good woman–evil woman distinctions, indeed, including life–death itself. This is, after all, a trickster tale, and for the trickster, the limen is all. The difficulty in maintaining it is someone else's problem.

Blaming the Woman, Blaming God
Bal's first foray into interpreting Samson (1987) offers further nuances to a consideration of disintegrating binaries. She is explicit, first of all,

about historical differences in perspective between the text and the modern reader. Instead of framing this as tricksterism, however, as Niditch does, she speaks of different cultural understandings of the hero. There has been a

> shift in the concept of heroism from an [ancient] instrumental view, in which the hero is sent by higher powers to represent their glory through pure physical acts, to a [modern] view wherein individualism and responsibility replace the lack of psychological concerns in the older view...(Bal 1987: 37)

This framework allows Bal to make two important moves: first, to identify God as a force of motivation (a *destinateur*) in the narrative (at least through ch. 15); secondly, to argue that 'blaming the woman' is the recourse of the modern reader, not the ancient one, to a story whose hero-concept no longer satisfies (Bal 1987: 37, 48, 50-51). The ancient was willing to see God at work; the modern needs a human to blame, preferably someone other than the hero. From this historically nuanced position, Bal argues that 'the issues involved in the text...do not require a positive versus a negative distribution of characters' (1987: 38). The possibility of breaking down the good woman–bad woman binary comes, then, with Bal's method, and is worked out in several dimensions.

What she calls the 'own–alien' binary manifests in a complex struggle involving not only sex with the 'wrong' woman, but also the problematic of kinship and affinity. Samson 'involves his parents too much in his sexual relationship' in Judges 14, offering to them the sexually symbolic honey. At the same time, he fails to appreciate the strength of his bride's attachment to her own kin, which results in her mediating to them the answer to her husband's riddle (Bal 1987: 43-44). One could take this analysis further: because even marriage to one's 'own' involves psychosocial separation from one's parents (cf. Gen. 2.24), in this sense, all women are 'alien'. Yet the explicit, if metaphorical, representation of a sexual relationship with parents is also a violation; thus, in the Samson story, kin also become strange. Bal also discusses the related polarities of 'individual–society' or 'personal–general'. These are apparent in Samson's unilateral assumption that marriage requires only his desire, as well as in the lack of logical link between his riddle, drawn from his individual experience, and its answer. Both these attempted mediations fail, in Bal's view, because of Samson's sexual immaturity. He is not yet ready to break from his kin or control the flow of (sexual) information involved in riddling. This readiness gradually emerges in his relationship with Delilah, but then encounters another force, his covenant with the father-god.

Bal's reading of the Delilah sequence is too complex to summarize in all its richness. I shall focus here on aspects of interest to my own argument. On one level, Bal argues, Delilah is the subject of the narrative, but one whose function is only to mediate between the two male forces of Samson and the Philistines, 'to bring those two together' (1987: 56). The Philistines, however, as uncircumcised and thus impure, are linked with women (56), specifically, in the end, with Delilah. With this linkage, Delilah loses her narrative status as a subject in her own right and becomes, with her feminized countrymen whose orders she fulfills, the *destinateur* who puts Samson 'on the trail' leading to the masculine God. Samson himself is a gender paradox: while the focus on his hair links him with the women he pursues, it is also the source of his masculine strength, whose loss womanizes him (58). This is not all it does, however: the haircutting is also the condition of Samson's rebirth into a relationship of filial submission to the father-god, a relationship he had fled in his forays into the houses of strange women. On this level, Delilah serves as 'therapist' to Samson as subject, helping him name and thus work through his anxieties and fears. She mirrors to him the goal of his seeking, which is the submission of love (64-65). Submission to the father-god, however, is a choice for the masculine against women (63). Delilah thus facilitates the loss of her own subject position, reflecting a minimized importance for the woman in the narrative (66-67). She also, however, loses her guilt as 'temptress' and thus her status as the lethal woman of modern male readers (67).

Bal has taken serious account of the character of God as a motivator of the action, specifically of the boundary-crossing action. This perspective also drives the reading of John Vickery, who argues that

> the dominant weight falls on the role of the divine, not the human, figure. Thus Samson's moral dubiety and non-charismatic aura together testify to the power of the Lord and the mysterious ways in which it is exercised (1981: 61).

It is precisely, however, this linkage of the deity and 'moral dubiety' that requires scrutiny. David Gunn offers this harder look at God's character in his reading of 'Samson of sorrows', interlaced with allusions to Second Isaiah's Servant figure (1992). Gunn eschews for Samson some of the tricksterish characteristics I would still assign him, suggesting rather that Yhwh be tarred with the brush usually reserved for the errant hero: a 'reckless and irresponsible practical joker', motivated by 'mere whims and impulses' (Gunn 1992: 248). But a trickster God does not preclude a trickster hero, a unity of character particularly apparent, I shall suggest, when the spirit of Yhwh comes on the scene.

Returning to Bal's work, two final matters: The first concerns her treatment of Delilah and, by extension, the Strange Woman. She has most helpfully historically relativized the sense of evil that modern readers find so 'natural' in this figure and, thus, cut across the good woman–bad woman polarity so common among feminist and non-feminist readers alike. I wonder, however, if she has given away too much of the Strange Woman's strangeness. When one reads this figure in the Samson narrative in light of Proverbs, the possibility that ancient readers also perceived a deadly evil connected with women has to be taken seriously. Nor is the Strange Woman just a tool of Yhwh (as is arguably the case with the Timnite woman), but also, in the reading of Delilah as *destinateur*, a narrative substitute for the deity.[8] Thus, to the extent that Yhwh's justice is in question, the potentially lethal character of the woman again surfaces, though hardly in terms that would make a modern reader comfortable. The character of Samson is, in sum, linked to the character of Yhwh who in turn is linked to the Strange Woman. Such is the substance of my reading.

Finally, I would like to highlight Bal's reference to Lacan to explain Samson's acceptance of Delilah's strategy of extracting his secret from him, a complicity that belies interpretations of the woman as betrayer pure and simple. 'Woman represents in this case the Other who gives access to the symbolic order' (Bal 1987: 60). Hence, Delilah as 'therapist'. Accepting this analysis, I shall, in the course of this chapter, stretch it a bit further. What if Woman *is* the symbolic order?

Samson's Mother and the Riddle of the Vow

Samson's Mother: Wise and Strange

Although the riddle proper does not appear until the next chapter, the annunciation of Samson's birth in Judges 13 already sets the key themes, as well as the subversive tone, of the whole tale. A messenger of Yhwh appears to the unnamed 'wife of Manoah', informing her that

---

8. Cf. Exum's analysis (1993: 61-93) that shows ch. 16 to be a revisiting of chs. 14–15.

she will have a son who will 'begin to deliver Israel from the hand of the Philistines'. Samson's mother is instructed to avoid wine or strong drink and unclean food throughout her pregnancy and is told that, after his birth, a razor will never touch his head. The stipulations on alcohol and haircutting, along with the (here unmentioned) avoidance of corpses, are the terms of the Nazirite vow of separation, as recorded in Numbers 6, and the messenger specifies that the promised son will be 'a separate one of God' (*nezir 'elohim*). The Nazirite status is ultimately formulated for Samson in a particularly radical way: for him it will be a lifelong condition beginning with conception, instead of the typically temporary vow undertaken by an adult.

The focus on Samson's mother foreshadows, as others have noted, the importance of women in Samson's adult life, but it does so in an ambiguous way that adumbrates the breakdown of binaries that will become the story's stock in trade. Samson's mother is, on the most obvious reading, a wise woman: the divine communication is directed to her, and she is courageous and commonsensical in the face of the uncanny. In spite of Manoah's bumbling intervention, it is she who correctly interprets the angel's intentions and implicitly accepts responsibility for the conditions laid down, as well as calming her husband's belated panic at having 'seen God'. Such is Samson's triadic heritage: divine force, wise woman, foolish man. Surely the ingredients of a trickster, by any cross-cultural accounting.

But here already is a reversal of expectation. Like Abigail (1 Sam. 25), this wise woman is married to a fool, hardly the expected match, if Proverbs 31's paean to the woman of worth is any prediction. Proverbs makes one step in breaking down gender polarity by epitomizing wisdom as Woman, but it has difficulty with the male fool. That such as these exist is no surprise; foolish men are both subject and object of much of the sage's instruction. That one of these should attain that rarest of gifts, marriage to a worthy woman, is not, however, envisioned. This particular transformation of the parallelism of wise and foolish is apparently not permitted, though the ideology must work overtime to suppress such an obvious embodiment of its own logic. Hence, Abigail's Nabal ('fool' in Hebrew) is summarily eliminated, that his wise wife might find her proper mate in David. But what of the pairing of foolish Manoah and his wise wife?

Cheryl Exum interprets the problem away through an ideological analysis that shows how 'this positive portrayal of the woman nevertheless serves male interests' (1993: 65). She argues (1) that, as is typical of patriarchy, the absence of sex from Judges 13 'severs the relationship between eroticism and procreation, affirming motherhood but denying the mother's *jouissance*'; (2) that the woman, for all her perceptivity, never challenges her husband's authority; and (3) that her namelessness underscores her cipher quality as one merely fulfilling a role as mother (Exum 1993: 65-67). As an ideological analysis, Exum's makes some astute observations. As a reading of the text, however, it fails to deal with a primary datum, namely, that this patriarchally configured female character is set alongside a male character *of identical origin*. The foolish husband, too, is part of the text's ideology. Also unsatisfying, in my view, is Bal's opinion that the text writes off the mother by writing her out (1988a: 201). It is true that the mother disappears after the first few verses of Judges 14. The father, however, hardly outlasts her: surely the reference to the childless Samson buried in the paternal grave (16.31) does little to establish the father's priority.

Bal offers, however, another line of argument I find more illuminating. She interprets the disappearance of Manoah's wife alongside the role of Delilah as a textual displacement of the avenging mother. Thus, she draws a close identification between these two characters, substantially blurring the good woman–bad woman dichotomy that seems to separate them (1988a: 199-206, 224-26). Whereas Bal draws on the heritage of Greek tragedy (especially Clytemnestra) for this reading, I shall propose a model closer at hand. For the triad of divine force–wise woman–foolish man in Judges 13 evokes the set of relationships found in Proverbs 1–9: the simple student called by Wisdom who offers life from God. This in turn invokes a fourth figure—of course, the Strange Woman. Proverbs, as we have seen, mythicizes the wise woman as divinely endowed Woman Wisdom whom the untutored male must choose over the equally mythic Strange Woman—after first telling them apart! And where is the Stranger in Judges 13 if not embedded in the wise wife? On this reading, Manoah's wife will have to be considered for her attributes both wise and strange. Such a reading will problematize the simple opposition construed by many commentators between Samson's 'good' mother and the 'bad' partners of his adult life, by reading for the contradictions underlying the surface ideology of the text.

As a first move, Proverbs allows us to view the character of Samson's mother not simply as a stereotype of the competent wife and mother,

but also as an avatar of the Woman Wisdom archetype. This understanding is based on the close connection between the exalted, but still
embodied, Woman Wisdom of Proverbs 1–9 and the earthier, but still
idealized, woman of worth in Proverbs 31, of whom Manoah's wife
is surely a manifestation: 'she opens her mouth with wisdom' (Prov.
31.26a). Adele Reinhartz's (1993) analysis of the several links between
Manoah's wife and the heavenly messenger also fits neatly with this
exalted view of the woman. Reinhartz connects the woman and the
angel in terms of their insight, predictive speech and anonymity (1993:
158-65), all traits of Woman Wisdom as well. She points, furthermore,
to the portrayal of their intimate relationship that at least hints at the
sexual (165-68), as does Yhwh's 'acquiring' of Wisdom (Prov. 8.22), a
verb often associated with a man's acquiring of a wife.

It is instructive to see how this analysis interacts with Exum's. Features like anonymity and lack of sexual *jouissance*, when read as part of
the stereotype of a 'good wife', tend, as Exum observes, to detract from
her power and authority. Anonymity functions quite differently for a
divine referent, however, indexing its uncontainability, while sexuality
may be suggested in ways other than a direct statement of husband–
wife intercourse. The issue of sexuality is particularly important to the
present approach, for it lies at the heart of a complex relationship between wisdom and strangeness, a place where easy judgments dividing
good (women) from bad (women) become problematic.

Reinhartz rehearses the textual clues suggesting a sexual encounter
between the angel and the wife of Manoah. Relating her experience
to her husband, the woman says, 'he came to me'—or 'came *into* me'
(*bw' 'l*)—just as Samson 'came into' the Gaza prostitute (16.1). The
'coming' happens in a field, where women are not held accountable for
untoward sexual encounters (cf. Deut. 22.25). The messenger's twice-
stated announcement of pregnancy shifts a key verb from the future
tense in v. 3 ('you will conceive') to the past in v. 5 ('you have conceived'). *Jouissance* after all, perhaps. For Bal, however, the woman's
encounter with the angel, while sexual in one sense, is so on the symbolic level; it is signified by her *knowledge*, both of the messenger's
origin and intent, and of the memory she brings—in the form of her
pregnancy—to her marital relationship (1988a: 74). It is, in effect, by
communicating knowledge of her pregnancy that the angel impregnates
her. For Bal, the Hebrew use of 'to know' to speak of sexual inter-

course is no mere euphemism, but signals a fundamental reality of the sexual experience (1988a: 53).

Did, then, the angel and the woman 'have sex'? The answer is not 'maybe' or 'yes and no', but rather, 'maybe and yes'. The text hints, but is not explicit; thus, 'maybe'. But the text also *constructs* sex most dramatically as the materialization of knowledge. The woman is 'literally' impregnated with what she knows. This construction is utterly consistent with Proverbs's sexualized portrayal of a man's proper love of Wisdom, whom he 'grasps' (Prov. 3.18), calls 'sister' (here, a term of endearment, not kinship) and 'intimate friend' (7.4), and who 'sports with' him (8.31). The last verb is *shq*, used to describe Samson's display before the Philistines, as well as Isaac's intimate activity with Rebekah (Gen. 26.8). The story of Samson's mother, however, presses Proverbs's logic to a surprising conclusion: the wise woman is no virgin; she comes filled with the memory of her encounter with the divine, a wisdom already gone strange.[9] Or is this so surprising? Proverbs does not hesitate to describe Wisdom's activity with Yhwh also as one of *shq* (8.30). The husband, then, foolish or wise, has less of a choice than might be expected. Perhaps, forced to 'choose' a woman both wise *and* strange, he can be naught but a fool.

The suggestion of strangeness in the wise wife's knowledge of her heavenly visitor accords, then, with the underlying coalescence of Woman Wisdom and the Strange Woman in Proverbs. The good mother's association with strangeness—and, more specifically, with the strange women of Samson's adult life—is made even more explicit in her relationship to the Nazirite 'vow', to which we now turn.

When Is a Vow Not a Vow?
There are three peculiarities with respect to Samson's Nazirite status—three things missing, to be exact—that I take as meaningful: a missing vow, a missing corpse and a missing Strange Woman.

First, I use the word 'vow' only in a qualified way because, strikingly, no vow is made. There is only 'everything *commanded*' by the

---

9.   If Judg. 13 materializes knowledge as sex, by the Delilah episode in ch. 16, sex has been sublimated into knowledge. Chapter 14's story of the Timnite woman, with its wise talk about sex, mediates the two extremes. In later wisdom, rabbinic and Christian writings, this slippage comes solidly to rest in sublimation. See Eilberg-Schwartz (1990: 195-234) on this feature in rabbinic and Christian literature.

messenger (13.14) and the woman's implicit acceptance of these words. Even what is 'commanded' comes in two forms: two imperatives to the mother forbidding wine and strong drink and unclean food, and two predictive statements—notably *not imperatives*—that no razor would come upon her son's head,[10] because he would be a Nazirite of God from the womb, and that he would begin to deliver Israel from the Philistines. The relationship of Samson's Nazirite status to the rest of the angel's words, to the Nazirite vow in Numbers 6, and to the story's subsequent events, generates a considerable portion of the debate about this tale. Reading the angel's words about Samson's destiny as predictive, rather than imperative, may shed some light on the matter, while yet casting new shadows.

Three immediate implications may be noted. First, with respect to the prediction about the razor, the angel is simply wrong: a razor *does* come upon Samson's head. Secondly, however, the indicative form of the angel's utterance regarding the connection of razor and Naziritehood leaves the Samson story more in line with the Nazirite text in Numbers than most commentators assume.[11] In Numbers 6 the uncut hair functions more as a *sign* of the vow than a *condition* of it. The hair represents the state of holiness (6.5), and the vow is not broken because the vower cuts the hair, but rather the hair is cut when the vow is uninten-

---

10. My reading contrasts with most if not all English translations, which give some sort of imperative force to the haircutting clause, e.g. the NRSV's 'no razor *is to come* upon his head'. While the verb could be read in that way, on analogy with the imperatives directed toward the mother's food and drink restrictions, there is nothing in the imperfect verb form that demands it. Several points can, on the other hand, be made in favor of a simple future indicative translation. First, the clause occurs in a sequence of indicative clauses: you are pregnant, you will bear a son, a razor will not touch (lit: 'go up upon') his head, the boy will be a Nazirite, he will begin to deliver Israel. It is not set off, as are the two imperatives to the mother, with emphatic particles ('And now, be careful' [*we'atah hishshameri na'*]). Further, as the ensuing discussion will show, the Nazirite's unshorn hair serves more as a sign of the vow than a condition of it.

11. Numbers's restriction on haircutting, like that in Judg. 13, is phrased as an imperfect with the negative, though here in a sequence of similar forms: they shall separate, they shall not drink, they shall not eat, a razor shall not come, they shall not go near. In this case, a list of instructions, there is no escaping the imperative force of the verbs. The matter of haircutting, however, is also distinguished in the larger context from the other prohibitions by its identification as the mark of holiness and by its place in the rituals that purify the corpse-defiled Nazirite or end the time of the vow.

tionally broken by corpse-defilement (6.9) or intentionally ended (6.18). Thus, and thirdly, contrary to the usual understanding of Samson's final moments with Delilah, the rupture of the (non-vow!) vow comes sometime before the cutting of his hair. Does the rupture lie, then, before the unmade vow's beginning, in the angel's false statement about the razor? Has Samson, long hair notwithstanding, never been a Nazirite at all? We could, were it so, make more sense of the rest of his highly *un*separated life. My tendency, however, is to read the narrative as a both/ and: the point (or some point, at any rate) lies in the tension of one who both is and is not separated to God, between a vow broken from the beginning and a vow never made.

What of Samson's mother and the vow? One reading, not out of line with a view of this woman as both wise and strange, comes from Victor Matthews (1989), who interprets the story as a trickster tale, especially insofar as it is marked by the tensive motif of freedom and entrapment. As the trickster, Samson exercises more freedom than any other Israelite hero. He is 'immune to law, morality and dangerous situations'. And yet, Matthews asks, 'who is more tightly fettered from the womb by the vows, the decisions and claims made on him by women...?' (1989: 245). The first woman who entraps Samson, then, is his own mother, the paradigmatic Israelite woman, who mediates the word of Yhwh to her husband. We might intensify the point by returning to the fact that the woman makes no vow. If there is entrapment, its source is the command/prediction of Yhwh. On the other hand, in her response to the messenger, the woman does not simply accept the terms as stated. The angel has said: 'No razor shall come upon his head, for a nazirite of God he will be from the womb, and he will begin to deliver Israel from the hand of the Philistines' (13.5). The woman, on the other hand, omitting the clauses that surround the 'Nazirite' clause in the angel's speech (those dealing with the razor and the Philistines), adds a clause of duration: 'the boy will be a Nazirite of God from the womb *to the day of his death*' (13.7; Alter 1981: 101). Like the messenger, she attributes no causal function to the razor. On the other hand, in substituting 'death' for 'razor' and 'Philistine', she supplies an element necessary to the ultimate logic of the denouement: Samson must die. That death should be on the lips of the Strange Woman comes as no surprise to the reader of Proverbs. That it should compensate for the faulty foreknowledge of the deity might be more surprising. That the utterances of the deity and the Israelite Strange Woman should collude to produce the death of the consecrated one should give us something to ponder further. Binaries are breaking down indeed.

The two other curious features of the Nazirite non-vow in Judges 13 also concern things seemingly missing from it. First, with respect to the Numbers 6 version of the vow, it is surprising that the stipulations given to Samson's mother make no mention of corpse-defilement. Secondly, relative to the rest of the tale, where is the expected warning against the Strange Woman? The elements of danger—sexual knowledge and the word of death—embedded in the character of Samson's mother hint at an answer to the second question, but there is more to be said, for these two curiosities are not unrelated.

A typical approach to the Nazirite vow (I trust the reader to supply her or his own quotation marks from here on) in the Samson story vis-à-vis that in Numbers 6 is to postulate a historical development from the former to the latter. I will leave such speculation to those whom it interests and focus on the fact at hand, namely, a canonical work that, in including both (and, indeed, the postulated 'latter' before the 'former') invites an intertextual reading.[12] We have already begun this task by taking seriously for Samson the relationship of vow to haircutting in Numbers. From an intertextual perspective, the absence of reference to corpse-defilement in Judges 13 is also a meaningful gap, for it is a striking feature of Numbers 6. The Nazirite material in Numbers begins by forbidding 'wine and strong drink' and, indeed, any produce of the vine (6.3-4). Then comes instruction about the hair (v. 5) and—emphatically because belatedly—the stricture on going near a corpse, followed by procedures in case this happens accidentally (vv. 6-12). These procedures further emphasize the matter of corpse-defilement, for there is nothing like them regarding accidental grape-eating! They also connect purification from corpse-defilement to ritual haircutting.

Why, then, is this element missing from the announcement of Samson's presumed vow? Or, is it really missing? I suggest rather a displacement. Numbers 6.7 goes to pains to specify that the Nazirite's avoidance of corpses must extend even to her or his family, to brother and sister, and, most notably for our purposes, to a deceased father or mother. As if to point to this element of the vow, the kinship terminology in Judges 14 shifts from ch. 13's 'Manoah and his wife' to '[Sam-

---

12. Cf. Aichele and Phillips (1995) on this sort of intertextual method.

son's] father and mother' (6 times in 14.2-9; 'brothers' also appears in 14.3). Do Samson's parents, then, serve metonymically as a rather macabre stand-in for corpses? The otherwise surprising association made by Samson's mother between his Nazirite status and his death receives a new twist. As corpse, she does more than speak; she becomes the death that will pollute his untaken vow and necessitate the cutting of his hair. Once again, his 'vow' is finished before it begins. Still in the womb, he is buried before birth in the grave of his father (cf. 16.31). As Freud might say: indeed.

In its concatenation of temporally confusing references to the seven days of Samson's wedding feast, Judges 14 continues, by means of the vow, to reach toward his end at a time of beginnings. The wedding feast lasts seven days (14.12) and Samson apparently tells his riddle on the first; the Philistines then try to guess the answer for three days. But then the 'seventh day' appears several times in a seemingly illogical sequence (14.15-18): the Philistines appeal to Samson's bride on the seventh day;[13] she weeps before him for seven days; he tells her the answer on the seventh day; and the men report it back to him on the seventh day. I would suggest a reason for this confusing repetition, namely, an allusion to the day of haircutting for a Nazirite who has encountered a corpse. 'If someone dies very suddenly right by him and defiles his consecrated head, then he shall shave his head on the day of his purification, on the seventh day he shall shave it' (Num. 6.9). Once again, what looks like a beginning in Samson's life—not his birth, in this case, but his life transition to sexuality and marriage—is already marked by the sign of the end of his Nazirite status. The sign is the haircutting; its meaning is corpse-pollution. If the mother was, strangely, death's harbinger in ch. 13, here, more familiarly, the Philistine woman takes her place.

Whence, then, the narrative? The collapsing space between Samson's conception and his death, the womb of his mother and the grave of his father, is pushed apart by means of another paradox, that between his status as Nazirite and his destiny against the Philistines. The two are mutually exclusive precisely because of the matter of corpse-defilement. How can a warrior avoid corpses? David Gunn notes (1992: 231), but does not elaborate on, the double meaning lurking in the odd phrasing of Samson's vocational assignment: he will 'begin (*yahel*) to

---

13. So the MT. The LXX and the Syriac substitute the more logical 'fourth day' here. But there is, I think, a method in the MT's madness.

deliver Israel from the hand of the Philistines' (13.5). *Hll* in the hiphil, as here, usually means 'begin'; in the niphal, however, it is 'be polluted'.[14] Perhaps not unrelated to the latter meaning is that of a similar-sounding verb, *hwl*, which can mean 'to writhe in childbirth', childbirth itself being a source of pollution. As if asking us to take note of this construction, the narrator uses it thrice more: at the beginning of Samson's adulthood, the spirit of Yhwh 'began to impel' him (13.25); as he slept on Delilah's knees, she 'began to unman him' (16.19); at the end, his hair, after being cut, 'began to grow' (16.22). The first of these instances marks the beginning of Samson's pollution: the spirit's impelling leads to desire for a Philistine woman. The second marks the moment of transition: having shaved his head, Delilah humbles him. The third marks the end of impurity (for the typical Nazirite), but also the beginning of death (for Samson). According to Numbers, the corpse-defiled Nazirite's head is to be shaved on the seventh day, 'the day of his cleansing', eventuating in the offerings that renew the vow on the eighth day (6.9-12). For Samson, of course, the renewal is short-lived. To begin deliverance of Israel, this man—a Nazirite from the womb to the day of his death—must necessarily become polluted. Again, the words of Yhwh collude with those of the Strange Woman: Samson's life will be worked out in the space between deliverance and pollution as much as it is between the womb and the grave. But, like the womb and the grave, deliverance and pollution become one in Samson's story. Like Dagon's temple, the space of the vow collapses once more. It will take a riddle to open it again.[15]

14. The hiphil is also used, less often, in the sense of 'profane, pollute' (Ezek. 39.7; Num. 30.3). This double-entendre may be signaled by another element in the angel's instructions that sets them apart from those in Numbers. Although Num. 6.4 forbids the Nazirite to eat any food produced from the vine, it does not, as does Judg. 13.4, forbid the more general category of 'unclean' food (*'al-to'keli kol-tame'*). The use of *tm'* here, so common in the priestly literature, resonates with the notion of pollution.

15. I will not attempt in this context to unpack fully Bal's rich and difficult analysis of the riddle and vow in Judges as speech acts that kill. If, however, the Samson narrative functions as a comment on the book as a whole (so Greenstein 1981), and if it is significant that the vow with which this story begins is not really a vow, then we might wonder whether the comment, in this case, is a snide one. Similarly, my analysis of the riddle will also focus on the deconstructive qualities that set it counter to the vow.

Tricky Wisdom: The Strange Woman and the God of Tricks

Before turning to the riddle itself, let us consider the larger narrative of Samson's adult exploits, attending particularly to the play of binaries and the problem of theodicy that both thematizes and undermines them, and toys with readers' pious expectations as well.

We know nothing of Samson's youth, for the narrator shifts abruptly from the annunciation of his birth to his adulthood, with only a brief note about his birth, naming and growth in favor with Yhwh. There is just one other sentence of transition between the annunciation story and the next episode, but it is a crucial one: 'and the spirit of the Yhwh began to impel him...' (13.25).[16]

Now, we might expect, given this introduction, some great act of Samson on behalf of the Israelite people. That *is* what the spirit of Yhwh is all about, isn't it? But such conventional expectations are about to be reversed. It is no less than shocking to read the first lines of ch. 14:

> Samson went down to Timnah, and at Timnah he saw one of the daughters of the Philistines. Then he came up and told his father and mother, 'I saw one of the daughters of the Philistines at Timnah; now get her for me as my wife.'

His parents protest the marriage to a foreign woman; Samson is emphatic (belligerent?): 'Get her for me; for she is right in my eyes!'

Our hero! His heroic status not even established—except in the fore-tellings of his mother and his God—and in his first adult act he is ready not to kill Philistine men but to marry a Philistine woman. And uppity to his parents to boot! And what about this spirit of Yhwh? Exactly what kind of impelling is this spirit doing anyway? What has happened to our good God who punishes such hanky panky with death? The nationalistic theology that dots the surface of the narratives from Deuteronomy through 2 Kings would seem to make a clear case that God forbids Israel contact—especially marriage—with foreigners (e.g. Deut.

---

16. Alter (1990: 49-51) discusses the unique use of the piel of *p'm* ('impel') here, in relationship to its three other occurrences in the Samson narrative where it carries its more usual form (*pa'am*), meaning 'time' (16.15, 20, 28). He points to the rather violent root meaning of the verb as 'stamp' or 'pound', as with one's foot. Note also Gunn's potent translation, 'the spirit of Yhwh began to beat on him' (1992: 231).

7.1-5; Judg. 3.1-6). The wisdom morality of Proverbs's father–sage seems equally adamant about avoiding strange women. Thus, when we turn to one of the more extended narratives about an early Israelite hero, we ought to be able to assume that he and his parents will be aligned against such women as the daughters of the Philistines. Should such a woman make advances, as we all know they are wont to do, our hero, deriving strength from his faith in God, will resist these overtures, even at cost to himself. Remember the prototypical wisdom hero, Joseph, and his reaction to the improprieties of 'Ms Potiphar'. Samson's description of the woman as 'right in my eyes' compounds the confusion. The phrase is used later in Judges as an ultimate condemnation of the Israelites for a variety of foul deeds (17.6; 21.25). Is Samson's desire for a bride, even if she is a foreign woman, to be put in the same category as the rape and abduction of women? If he is wrong to want her, why would he appeal to her quality of uprightness?[17]

Thus, the argument between Samson and his parents is mirrored by the competing voices of expectation and discovery in our own heads. We are brought to the point of unbearable confusion, and then…right at this moment the narrator's voice breaks into the arguments with some crucial information:

> [Samson's] mother and father did not know that *she* was from Yhwh, for *he* was seeking opportunity from the Philistines. At that time the Philistines were rulers (*moshelim*) over Israel (14.4).

The Hebrew of the middle clauses is terser:

> from Yhwh, she,
> for opportunity he was-seeking
> from-Philistines

She. He. Both expressed with the emphatic personal pronoun.[18] Also in parallel: from Yhwh, from Philistines. Conflict and difference are articulated in syntax that identifies.

And then there is the important question of who knows what, shared knowledge also establishing alliances. Unexpressed is the fact that Samson, as well as his parents, is excluded from this knowledge of

17. Cf. Gunn (1992: 232), who resists the typical interpretive slippage from Samson's use of a term from moral discourse (*yashar*) to the assumption that he was only interested in the woman's physical beauty.

18. Translators often render 'she' as 'it' (cf. the NRSV's 'this'). This is a grammatical possibility, but it defies the emphatic parallelism of the gendered she/he.

Yhwh's plan, a gap that introduces another central motif from the trickster pattern, namely, the trickster's ambiguous relationship to wisdom. As we shall see, according to one measure, Samson proves himself a master of wisdom. But what he doesn't know about Yhwh and Yhwh's plans, combined with what he doesn't know about women, will become his undoing. Yhwh bonds with the Strange Woman in a manner akin to his election of Samson in the womb: by fiat, each becomes a tool against the Philistines. The alliance is out of balance, for she no more than Samson knows the divine mind. Yet it is in a sense still a closer alliance than that between Yhwh and Samson, for Yhwh allies with the Strange Woman not only against the Philistines—her own people—but also against the hero himself. *She* was from Yhwh. The boundaries assumed normative by the unsuspecting reader have all but disappeared.

Samson and his parents then go down to Timnah. In Timnah's vineyards (and what was a Nazirite doing among the grapes in the first place?), somehow inexplicably separated from them, he encounters a lion. The spirit of Yhwh 'rushes upon him' and he kills the lion, tearing it apart 'as one tears a kid'. Later on, he returns to the lion's carcass, finds a hive of bees and honey inside the corpse, scrapes out the honey and eats it. The narrative voice and Samson's own thoughts intersect at this point in a delightful pun, for the Hebrew of the verb 'scrape out' carries with it a triple entendre. The verb *rdh*, used here as 'scrape out', more frequently means 'make up a proverb or wise saying'. In this latter sense, *rdh* is a synonym for another word for making up proverbs and riddles, indeed the word for 'proverb' itself, *mashal*. But *mshl* also has a second meaning, namely, to 'rule', and in this aspect is precisely the word used to describe the domination of the Philistines in v. 4. They were *moshelim*, rulers, in Israel. So, with one tricky word, the narrator has Samson (1) scrape out his honey, (2) make up a riddle, and (3) begin to enact Yhwh's challenge to the Philistines. Again we note, however, that only the first two actions are part of *Samson's* intention and plan: the prospective groom must feel confident indeed that Yhwh is on his side, empowering him and validating his claim on the honey from his supposedly forbidden bride. *Is* Yhwh on Samson's side? Well, yes and no. On his side, but for the deity's own purposes. Yhwh's intention to have 'an opportunity from the Philistines' is unbeknown to Samson, though the narrator takes the reader into Yhwh's confidence.

Samson takes some honey as a gift to his parents without revealing anything about its source, presumably because both Israelite law in general and his Nazirite status in particular forbid him contact with a corpse. He then goes down again to Timnah to hold his wedding feast. The Philistines, seeing him and perhaps also fearing him (the forms of the Hebrew verbs 'see' and 'fear' are suggestively similar), provide him with a retinue of 30 men. Samson then proposes his riddle, suggesting a wager of 30 of one sort of garment and 30 of another. The Philistines accept. Now we begin to see how the lion-killing, honey-eating Samson conceives the connection of puzzle and solution.

> Out of the eater came something to eat;
> out of the strong came something sweet.

The Philistines have the seven days of the wedding party to answer, but after three days they are angry and suspicious they've been had. They then threaten Samson's bride that they will burn her and her father's house if she does not entice her husband into giving her the answer. With much weeping, she overcomes Samson's resistance and, on the seventh day, the Philistines present him with his answer:

> What is sweeter than honey?
> What is stronger than a lion?

Samson is enraged, and verbally attacks with another two-line verse:

> If you had not plowed with my heifer,
> you would not have found out my riddle!

The spirit of Yhwh then rushes on him again, causing him to go to another Philistine city, Ashkelon, where he kills 30 men, stealing their garments to pay his wager. Yhwh has thus had his occasion against the Philistines. But one occasion doesn't seem to be enough for Yhwh, as one Strange Woman is not enough for Samson. Indeed, there are no less that three more violent encounters between Samson and the Philistines, spiraling out of the cycle of vengeance begun here. Two are attributed to Samson's own initiative (though under provocation) and the last, once more, to the rush of the spirit (15.14).

Although Samson storms back to his father's house after delivering the garments to the Timnite men, he later decides to go and reclaim his bride. As he heads for her bedchamber, however, her father stops him with the information that she had been given to one of his retinue, on the assumption that Samson had rejected her. Furious, Samson makes this telling statement: 'This time I shall be blameless in regard to the Philistines when I do them evil' (15.3).

We should pause and let these words sink in. Samson has experienced the rush of the spirit on three occasions: first, just before his trip to Timnah when he first saw his Strange Woman, again when he met the lion, and thirdly when it sent him on his bloody trip to Ashkelon. The first reference (13.25), coming as it does at the transition between the birth story, with its quick allusion to his adolescence and to the sexuality and violence of his adulthood, may well be understood as a 'prelude' to all three of the hero's sexual encounters. 'In it the rationale for the surge in his sexual drives is seen to be the divine spiritual disposition coordinated with his physical maturation' (Vickery 1981: 65-66). The second occasion leads to violence against the lion, but also to honey and a riddle; intellectual wit is added to sexual desire and physical power. The third time, thwarted wit and desire eventuate in pure mayhem. Never, however, until 15.3, do we find evidence of Samson's consciousness or conscience about his experiences of the spirit. Only now, as he is about to work a new act of destruction on his *own* initiative, do we hear his implicit judgment—as 'evil'—against Yhwh's use of him for the wanton destruction of the 30 Ashkelonites. '*This time* I will be blameless.'[19] Surely, as readers, we are hardpressed not to join Samson in his theodicy.

The 'evil' Samson himself perpetrates at this point is not only small in comparison to the murderous deity's, but also quintessentially trick-

---

19. Translations often obscure the force of Samson's statement, in a couple of different ways. The NRSV's rendering of *ra'ah* as 'mischief' rather than 'evil' weakens Samson's judgment on what has gone before at the behest of God. The clause usually translated 'This time I shall be blameless with regard to the Philistines'—*niqqeyti happa'am mippelishtim*—also suggests deeper meaning. *Nqh* (niphal) can bear a forceful sense, 'be purged, cleaned out'. In other cases where it is followed by the preposition *min* ('from'; here in a contracted form, *mippelishtim*), the next noun refers to that from which one is cleansed or exempt, e.g. transgression (Ps. 19.14); sin (Num. 5.31); oaths (Gen. 24.8, 41); the effects of the bitter water (Num. 5.19). So, is Samson 'blameless with regard to the Philistines' or 'free from the Philistines'? There is another possibility. *Happa'am*, usually taken here as the temporal 'this time' or 'now', is from the same root that, in verbal form, described what the spirit of Yhwh did to Samson in 13.25: *pa'amo*, 'impelled him, beat on him' (see above, n. 16). Though *pa'am* is not preceded by *min* in 15.3, its location in the sentence also allows Samson to fume against the divine impelling by which Yhwh seeks his opportunity 'from the Philistines' (*mippelishtim* appears in both 14.4 and 15.3): 'I shall be free from [God's] impelling with respect to the Philistines.'

sterish: torches tied to foxes' tails set against Philistine grain. It is precisely this action, however, that shines the fieriest light on God's evil. For the trickster God, who had aligned with this Strange Woman, in the end betrays her. His occasion against her people leads inexorably to her death. I have argued that the presence of a trickster God does not preclude a trickster hero. Nor, I think, do Samson's trickster traits preclude another dimension of his character seen by Gunn, namely, his search for a woman who is 'right in his eyes'. 'He is, indeed, a dealer in death, but largely at the dictate of Yhwh while he himself searches for domesticity, attempts vainly to nurture personal connection' (Gunn 1992: 249). Here again expectations are undone: the wild man seeks a wife. But I would go further: it is precisely in the trickster's search for strange domesticity that God's will to evil is disclosed. When all boundaries are transgressed, and the limen collapses into the center, what remains is a death-dealing deity. The death of the Strange Woman is not, however, the end of the story.

As if unable to linger on this moment of bitter irony—a woman burned to death because she sought to protect herself from burning—the narrative turns to boundary-crossing humor. Fun is poked, in the first instance, at the Israelites themselves. The men of Judah prove themselves loyal servants of the Philistines. Recalling both Samson's riddle and Yhwh's opportunity from the preceding chapter, they say to Samson, 'Do you not know that the Philistines are rulers (*moshelim*) over us?' (15.11). Foreshadowing his lies to Delilah in the next chapter, Samson allows them to bind him and turn him over to the Philistines. The spirit of Yhwh and ropes melted like 'flax that has caught fire' take care of the rest. Has the fiery death of his wife been thus avenged? At the least, some boundaries have been melted: in a few short verses, Israelite men have been identified with both foreigners and women.

The fun continues in 16.1-3. While the foreign prostitute represents on one patriarchal level the densest accumulation of negative qualities imaginable, perhaps it is this very extremity that turns her story into farce instead of a lesson in moral censure. Some commentators make the righteous assumption that it was (of course) she who supplied the men of Gaza with information on Samson's whereabouts, but the narrative is curiously silent on this point, to the point of omitting the verb of telling, with its telltale subject. Indeed, if one ignores the Masoretic punctuation, it appears Samson makes his own (sexually laden) announcement.

And Samson went down to Gaza
and saw there a woman, a prostitute,
and came into her,
to the Gazaites saying,
'Samson has come here!' (16.1-2)

Such supreme self-confidence would hardly be put past a trickster, but even if we supply, with the LXX, the passive verb ('*it was told* to the Gazaites'), Samson's pre-emptive maneuver with respect to the men lying in wait also makes clear that someone has told him about them as well. Perhaps, given the mutual embedding of sex and knowledge in this story, it is only to be expected that the free flow of sexuality associated with the prostitute would be linked with the free flow of information, so different from the other two episodes, where sex is problematically attached to a more complex relationship and knowledge is blocked. Again, boundaries are both literally and symbolically broken. Samson pulls up the city gates and doors and carries them to the top of the hill in front of Hebron. The trickster, having breached both sexual and national boundaries with the prostitute, now leaves the foreign city (often personified as female) permanently breached. More than this, however, he plants the symbols of her opening in full view of Hebron, the Strange Woman's sexual tokens in the heart of Judah.[20] The limen stakes once more his (her?) claim to the center.

I think, then, one cannot easily conclude that the narrative leaves impermeable the boundary between Israelite and Philistine. To the contrary, it is breached in a variety of ways, not least in Samson's will toward an otherwise desirable domesticity combined with the presence of the Strange Woman who was 'from Yhwh'. Even Yhwh is thwarted in 16.1-3, however: Samson finds his own Strange Woman, without payment on Yhwh's 'opportunity'. The utter dissolution of boundaries that has occurred by the beginning of the Delilah sequence can, perhaps, only eventuate in death, the ultimate representation of unboundedness, of chaos. Yet death, too, is supposed to be a marker in a moral universe: death to the evil, life to the good. But this boundary also collapses. As Qohelet perceives so clearly, 'the same fate befalls all of them'. The Philistines die. The Philistine-killer dies. Left alive: only

20. It is King David, from out of his stronghold at Hebron, who—after an alliance with the Philistines—completes the deliverance of Israel from these very enemies, the task 'begun' by Samson (2 Sam. 5.25).

Yhwh...and Delilah? If she was present at the fall of the temple, that fact goes unremarked.

Samson's Riddle

The riddle is a *mise en abyme*, reflecting and offering its own interpretation of the larger story. In particular, I shall argue, the combination of the formulation and the form of the riddle, along with its generic function, powerfully reproduce a tension in the larger narrative agenda; the effect is deconstructive. Beyond even this, by means of its metaphors of sweetness and strength, the riddle becomes a *mise en abyme par excellence*, offering not one interpretation, but 'all possibilities' (Bal 1987: 76). This opening up of the interpretive field can be perceived by analyzing the riddle at three different levels, and considering their interaction. The levels are: (1) the riddle as verbal art performance; (2) the links between the riddle and the story in which it is embedded; and (3) the riddle's function as metalanguage, its comment on language itself.

The riddle is a text that has much puzzled interpreters, along with its implications for Samson's character. The question that is regularly asked is whether it was fair.[21] Given the fact that it was based on an extraordinary experience of Samson's, known only to him, were the Philistines not in their rights to go to equally unfair ends to find the answer? The implication for Samson's character would be one of malice. While such a motive for riddling is not unheard of in folklore (recall Rumplestiltskin), it is not consistent with Samson's sense of self-righteousness expressed in 15.3. A second possibility is that Samson is, at best, immature (so Bal), at worst, a dunderhead; either way, one who has not the competence to distinguish between his personal experiences and the social conventions required for effective riddling. To frame this in terms from the wisdom tradition, to which we shall return, Samson is a fool. While the relationship of Samson's wisdom to his folly is an issue, I shall argue that it is not a simple one. As trickster, Samson is the wise fool, always a loaded paradox. It is a paradox embedded, with

---

21. Bal (1987: 45), Soggin (1981: 243) and Moore (1901: 335) call it, respectively, 'not logical', 'unfair' and 'bad'. Crenshaw (1978: 113-14) considers it 'unanswerable', but still a real riddle. Gray (1967: 330), Nel (1985: 540) and Margalith (1986a: 228) all believe it is answerable, but they adduce quite different explanations of the answer. See Nel (1985: 536-39) for a complete review of literature on this text.

others, in the riddle itself, which exhibits, as Fontaine and I have previously shown, manifold competencies. I shall first review relevant portions of this argument, which draws methodologically from the fields of folklore and linguistics.

The Riddle as Verbal Art Performance

Samson, when he enters Philistine territory unaccompanied by any sort of bodyguard, apparently feels he can meet any challenge on his own. The Philistines' action in supplying Samson with a retinue of 30 men is a subtle one.[22] It may be an act of respect to the bridegroom, but is also doubtless a sign of their fear of him and an effort to ward off any preemptive strike from him. What purpose does the riddle serve Samson at precisely this moment?

In their book, *The Language of Riddles* (1984), W.J. Pepicello and Thomas Green argue that the goal of riddles in general is to 'create fictitious problems, competitive events that intensify social disparity' (124). Riddles do this, however, in a playful way that keeps the competition on verbal grounds, rather than physical battle. Riddles also function in such a way as to 'allow reversal of normal power structures, so that in a riddling session it is the riddler who is in authority, whatever [his or her] status outside of [the] session...' (Pepicello and Green 1984: 128). Thus, by propounding the riddle at this moment, Samson—playfully yet seriously—assumes control of a situation whose advantage in that rather carefully balanced setting he may have felt tilting away.

This verbal ploy is remarkably astute. Samson not only takes control of a situation that may have been slipping away from him, but he switches the terms of the contest from a potentially physical one (him vs. the 30 Philistines) to a verbal one. He engineers the situation into more of a game, and the willingness of the Philistines to enter into this specialized ludic performance suggests that they also saw it as a way of gaining prestige points, as it were, without risking excessive loss.

22. The usual translation describing these men as 'companions' is probably misleading. The usual Hebrew word for 'friend, companion' (*rea'*) is bypassed here in favor of *merea'*. *Merea'* is used only four other times in the Hebrew Bible, two of which clearly indicate this person's role to be one of a political and/or military advisor (Gen. 26.26; 2 Sam. 3.8). Although the other two occurrences are ambiguous, they also could easily be construed in the same manner (Prov. 19.6; 12.26). Cf. Boling (1975: 231) and the references to David's '30' in 2 Sam. 23.13; 2 Chron. 11.15.

When the Philistines begin to think they have been presented with a truly unanswerable riddle, however, their umbrage quickly shows. Their angry accusation to Samson's bride that they have been brought to the party to be impoverished demonstrates their belief that Samson has transgressed the boundaries of proper riddle performance. Samson's outrage is also explicable now. He believes—and, as I shall demonstrate in a moment, with much justification—that his riddle is answerable. Not only does he lose both his riddle and his woman, but, from his perspective, it is the Philistines who have 'broken the rules' of the ludic performance context. Thus erupts the physical violence that such verbal art performances are supposed to contain within the structure of the riddle game.

Samson seems to have initiated a legitimate diplomatic maneuver, but one that fails. Did someone, then, break the rules of riddling? Was the riddle fair? Answering this question requires attention to the matter of how riddles work. Pepicello and Green (1984: 21) argue that riddles exploit the 'conventional patterns' existing in a given culture's grammar, metaphorical systems and social settings. Their analysis of the riddle suggests that these conventional patterns or expectations are used to create 'a block element, or what appears to be unsolvable opposition, contained within the riddle'. These blocking devices both provide clues to the solution *and* create the confusion that prevents the hearer from reaching it.

A grammatical analysis of Samson's riddle reveals multileveled linguistic ambiguity in its surface structure, comparable to that discovered elsewhere by Pepicello and Green, 'the result of processes that occur at the phonological, morphological, or syntactic levels of grammar' (1984: 22). Following are three versions of Samson's riddle and its solution: first, a transliteration of the Hebrew; secondly a very literal English translation; and thirdly, a more idiomatic English translation.

a. Verse 14: Samson's riddle

> *meha'okel yatsa' ma'akal*
> *ume'az yatsa' matoq*
>
> From the eater goes out food
> and from the strong goes out sweet
>
> From the eater comes something to eat
> and from the strong comes something sweet

b. Verse 18: The Philistines' answer

> *mah matoq middebash*
> *umeh 'az me'ari*

> What sweet from honey
> and what strong from lion?

> What is sweeter than honey
> and stronger than a lion?

There are two observations to be made here. One is obvious in the Hebrew, namely, the remarkable alliteration of the letter *m*. Pepicello and Green's study makes clear that such a linguistic device is not only a matter of the speaker's art (though it is certainly that; cf. Crenshaw 1978: 55, 111-12); it is also a matter of the speaker's communicative (or communication obstructing) strategy, that is, it has something to do with the block contained in the riddle. This fact leads to the second observation, which is that the alliterated *m* provides *both* a clue *and* a block to Samson's riddle. In Hebrew, the letter *m* sometimes serves as a word that is usually translated into English by the preposition 'from'. That is, the phoneme *m* also functions as the lexeme 'from'. In addition to these two uses, *m* can also serve as a morpheme that generates the participle in certain forms of verbs. In Samson's riddle challenge, *m* is used both as an independent letter and as the word 'from', with a hint at the participle.[23] Thus alliteration of the *m* both signals its importance and, at the same time, introduces ambiguity as to what exactly its importance is.

But the deepest complication lies in the fact that there is yet a fourth use of *m* that does not appear in Samson's challenge statement. This is an idiomatic syntactical usage in the construction of the comparative. As seen in the awkwardly literal translation of the Philistines' answer, if one wants to say 'stronger than' in Hebrew, one must say 'strong from'; 'sweeter than' is 'sweet from'. The use of the comparative 'm'—*in the answer but not in the question*—is, then, the source of deliberate syntactic ambiguity in the riddle. Samson twice uses the phrase *yatsa' m*, 'go out from'. In doing so, he leads (or, rather, misleads) the hearer into thinking that *m* is being used in its usual sense as the preposition

---

23. The word for 'food' or 'something to eat' (*ma'ekal*), is not a participle strictly speaking, but is a noun formed in a manner closely related to the formation of participles (GKC: 236-37, 140).

'from'. The implied question *seems* to be 'under what circumstances does something sweet to eat come forth *from* a strong eater?' The answer suggested by the wedding context seems, then, to have something to do with either love or sex. In order to arrive at the answer, however, the Philistines have to make the syntactical switch to the use of *m* in constructing the comparative. 'What is sweeter *than* honey, stronger *than* a lion?' Such grammatical miscues are one of the standard ploys of riddles.

I alluded a moment ago to the role of social context in analyzing the riddle. This is especially important when trying to interpret its metaphors, another source of the riddle's clues and blocks. Context is a prerequisite for deciding which of the several available meanings of a metaphor are to be emphasized, and how literally or figuratively its terms are to be taken. Riddles, however, with their intention to disrupt, suspend the normal conversational context and thus use their homeless metaphors to confuse rather than to clarify.

Thus, for the Philistines to find the solution, they have to maneuver their way both through the grammatical blocks just mentioned, and through metaphorical ones as well. How are they to interpret Samson's references to eating, strength and sweetness? The wedding context provides two possible routes to a solution. Either route could work but each has its perils. As the reader attempts a solution to the riddle, along with Samson's intended dupes, we discover along each pathway important themes placed by the narrator for our consideration.

The first possible pathway of interpretation opened up by the no doubt bawdy and drunken marriage feast is to 'think sex'. If the implied question is, 'under what circumstances does an eater produce food and a strong one sweetness?', then 'sex' would seem to be the answer. However, the bilinear form of Samson's challenge statement may require a bilinear response.[24] At the very least, it throws the mind to the dyadic relationship involved in sex, changing the question to something more like, 'who is the eater who produces food and the strong one who produces sweetness?'. Now the riddle, our *mise en abyme*, suddenly mirrors the gender confusion we have seen elsewhere in the narrative, likely discomfiting once again the ancient reader along with the Philistines.

---

24. Our paucity of information on ancient riddle performance prohibits anything more than a guess on this score. However, the overwhelming tendency in the book of Proverbs to formulate proverbs in bilinear form suggests this as the aesthetic preference of at least those collectors.

For in sex, either man or woman can eat, and produce something to eat; either can be strong, and either produce sweetness. But how to construct an intelligible and witty response from this? The clue is also a block.

The second metaphorical pathway suggested by the wedding context is to connect sweetness and strength with love. Philip Nel (1985) offers the following train of logic from Samson's riddle challenge, through the Philistines' answer, to the idea of love. Identifying the concepts 'strong' and 'sweet' as the riddle's key metaphors, he proposes that the competent riddle-solver must be able to 'scan through the paradigms of possibly correct equivalents to them' (Nel 1985: 542). Three pieces of 'circumstantial evidence' facilitate the task of choosing among alternatives within the paradigms: the fact that honey is the sweetness par excellence, that the lion is similarly associated with strength,[25] and that in the wedding context 'love enjoys a certain priority' (542). The emphasis on love is most significant, for Nel argues further that the riddle's answer in v. 18, itself in question form, was a 'crystallized riddle', which existed as a popular proverb.[26]

> What is sweeter than honey?
> What is stronger than a lion?

Well, *love*, of course. 'Set me as a seal upon your heart, as a seal upon your arm', says the poet in the Song of Songs, 'for love is strong as death...' (8.6).

Is the riddle then answerable? I believe it is. If Nel is correct about the crystallized riddle in v. 18, and if the Philistines had sufficient cultural wisdom, they might have simply remembered and applied this representative conventional form. Otherwise, given the well-known connections of strength to lions and sweetness to honey, combined with the important grammatical clue in the use of *m*, they presumably could, with sufficient wit, have moved from the sex/love connotations of these words suggested by the wedding context to the more literal answer required by Samson. Thus, in spite of the riddle's origin in Samson's very

25. For honey, see Prov. 16.24; 24.13; 25.16, 27; cf. Song 4.11; 5.1. For lions, see Num. 24.9; Isa. 38.13; Amos 3.8; Prov. 28.15; Lam. 3.10; and *passim*.

26. It is often suggested that numerical sayings such as those in Prov. 30.15-31 are, in effect, crystallized riddles. Nel also calls attention to the gnomic sentences formulated as questions in Prov. 6.27-28; 14.22; 17.16; 26.12; 23.29; 29.20; 30.4; Qoh. 3.21; 4.11.

remarkable and secret experience, he has provided his prospective in-
laws with a multitude of culturally accessible clues. But every clue is
also a miscue! Because of what I see as this logic of wit that connects
the riddle's challenge to its answer, I disagree with Bal's view that
Samson is inept in moving from the particular to the general in formulating his riddle (1988a: 136).[27] In his use of the riddle, Samson demonstrates his mastery over language, as well as his skill at diplomacy, both
of which the Philistines lack.[28] Why, then, does his diplomacy fail? On
this reading, if the riddle leads to violence, it is not because of Samson's intellectual failure in producing a 'bad' riddle, or his immaturity
in proposing it, but because of Yhwh's intentions.

Riddle and Story: The Mirror of Contradiction
In various ways, even at the level of grammar, the riddle *in the story*
points back, not just to human wit, but to the riddler par excellence.
Consider, for example, the multifaceted *m*, which makes its first notable
appearance in 14.4, a verse we have already given some consideration.

ki meyhwh hi'	that from Yhwh she was
ki to'anah hu'	for an opportunity he was
mebaqqesh mippelishtim	seeking from the Philistines
uba'et hahi'	and in that time
pelishtim moshelim	the Philistines were rulers
beyisra'el	in Israel

Here we have two uses of *m* as 'from',[29] one use in the participle
(*mebaqqesh*) and one phonetic use at the beginning of a key word

27. This challenge to Bal's view of the riddle as 'bad' and 'illogical' because of
its failure to generalize from the subject's particular experience has implications for
other significant aspects of her argument, particularly those regarding the status of
the woman. Because she understands the riddle as unanswerable, she sees the character of Samson's bride as necessitated by the narrative logic, the third party who
must provide mediation of knowledge from Samson to the Philistines. As mediator,
however, she becomes 'the object of violence toward which the sequence leads'
(Bal 1988a: 142). If Samson's riddle is not exclusively self-referential, however,
then both the woman's 'opening' of the hero and her death may transcend mere
victimhood (see further below).
28. Clifford Geertz (1976: 1493-97) provides a fascinating description of argu-
mentative poetry 'battles' in Morocco. These are often 'fought' by poets hired by
feuding villagers to settle social conflicts, and style as well as content is crucial to
victory.
29. The emphasis on the *m* is further highlighted here by the odd construction of

(*moshelim*)—the same combination as in Samson's riddle challenge. Like the Strange Woman, then, the riddle is also 'from Yhwh'.

The Trickster has tricked the trickster by means of his own trickery. Samson's intention was that of a diplomatic response to a threatening situation that also allowed his own self-confidence and control to be demonstrated and his right to claim his bride established. Such diplomatic skill is usually judged to be a sign of a wise person indeed: 'a soft tongue can break a bone' (Prov. 25.15b). Thus, along with Samson, a reader who admired such abilities would also experience some cognitive dissonance. For Yhwh's intention, as revealed to the reader but not to Samson, was to use both Strange Woman and riddle as an occasion against the Philistines. By means of the riddle, the narrative plays off one character's intention against the others', creating both drama and humor for readers willing to let their own guards down.

The play on *m* is not the only ludic link between the riddle and the rhetoric of the narrative. We find the same thing in the pun on the verb *rdh* (see above), with its double meaning: in a word, Samson scrapes out his honey from the lion's body and makes up a riddle. *Rdh*'s synonymity with *mshl*, however, implicates Yhwh's plans against the Philistine *moshelim* in Samson's wit. The verbal art of the riddle once again mirrors that of the narrative, while reflecting as well the invisible hand of God.

If forwarding Yhwh's opportunity against the Philistines is part of the narrative agenda, there seems to be another part as well, namely, wisdom's lesson to young men—especially those who would be *moshelim* themselves—against giving up their strength to women. In addition to the adjurations against the Strange Woman in Proverbs 1–9, there is also the instruction of King Lemuel's mother to her son (Prov. 31.1-9), whom she addresses in terms with numerous echoes of the Samson story.

> What, my son! What, son of my womb! What, son of my vows!
> Do not give to women your strength,
> or your ways to (female) obliterators of kings.
> It is not for kings, Lemuel,

the phrase 'an opportunity from' (*to'anah min*). Though '*nh* rarely occurs in the Bible, the prepositions otherwise used with it are *le* (Exod. 21.13; Prov. 12.21; 2 Kgs 5.7) or '*el* (Ps. 91.10), both of which have the root meaning 'to' rather than 'from'.

it is not for kings to drink wine,
or rulers to desire strong drink (Prov. 31.2-4).

While the reference to alcohol recalls Samson's Nazirite status, with its wary constitution between the womb and the vow, this queenly instruction also introduces the motif—missing in Numbers 6—of the lethal woman.[30] Although this motif becomes finally overt only in Delilah's challenge to her strong lover, it is already encapsulated in the riddle's potentially threatening combination of sweetness, strength and eating. To this issue we shall return.

The crucial point for the moment, however, is that of the relationship between Yhwh and the Strange Woman. Just as Judges 13 paints paradoxical portraits of a wise and strange mother and a son whose destiny was to be both warrior and corpse-avoider, so also the doubled narrative agenda of chs. 14–16, encapsulated in the riddle, is inherently contradictory: in order for Yhwh to have his occasion against the Philistines, Samson *must* give up his strength to the Strange Woman.

Sweetness, Strength and the Death of the Tricksters
The narrative's conflictive agendas of Yhwh's occasion against the Philistines and the warning against strange sex are further thematized— and further undermined—by the riddle's metaphors of sweetness and strength. The process of untangling the lines between the riddle's challenge and response has already surfaced at least two issues—sex and love—bubbling underneath the war of words. The interrogative form of that response invites the reader not only to consider the ramifications of these two possibilities, but also to ask whether there are others.

While it is hard to ignore Nel's proposal that 15.18—'what is sweeter than honey and stronger than a lion?'—is a crystallized riddle with the currency of a popular proverb, I question his assumption that its answer is transparently and univocally 'love'. Certainly, the appeal to love by both the Timnite bride and Delilah, in manipulating from Samson answers to their questions, keeps love in view, if not in its most high-minded form. On the other hand, the bawdy wedding feast makes 'sex' at least as obvious, as does Samson's coarse riposte ('If you had not plowed with my heifer, you would not have found out my riddle') to

---

30. This combination of warnings against alcohol and strange women occurs again in Lev. 21. See below for a discussion of the relationship of wisdom and priestly voices in the Samson narrative.

the answered riddle. Even the more edenic vision of the union of lovers in the Song of Songs joins love-talk and sex-talk without a skip, manifest among other means precisely in the image of honey:

> Your lips distill nectar, my bride;
> honey and milk are under your tongue…(4.11)

> I come to my garden, my sister, my bride,
> I gather my myrrh with my spice,
> I eat my honeycomb with my honey,
> I drink my wine with my milk (5.1).

If *both* sex *and* love emerge—whether conjoined or confused—as aspects of the riddle's meaning, we should consider the possibilities found in the narrative's meditation on their relationship. In this, the words 'sweetness' and 'strength' are surely key.

In one typical reading, of which the scholarly literature has many variants, the major issue is strength. Samson sees a woman; she pleases him; he desires her. He violently tears open a lion and scrapes out its honey, as he no doubt anticipates tearing open his bride to claim her honey. The episode culminates in a combination of abusive language against Samson's erstwhile in-laws and physical violence against the Philistines of Ashkelon, and leads quickly to the death of the Timnite bride. At the coarsest, Samson here is no more than a lusty bully who gets what he deserves from the manipulative 'love' of his foreign women, while the 'foreign temptress' also dies an ideologically satisfying death. Bal's analysis, unpacking the illogic in this, offers a more nuanced understanding, arguing that the relationship between sexuality and strength 'is the form "love" takes in this story' (1987: 40). Elsewhere, she proposes the 'formidable woman' herself as the meaning of the riddle, as that which is both sweet and strong. She sees, nonetheless, no possibility except victimage for the woman: the narrative makes clear from the beginning that 'the lion can only yield sweetness when dead' (1988a: 140). These readings join, then, in acknowledging the triumph of male strength.

But what then of sweetness? Gunn's view of Samson as a thwarted seeker of domesticity suggests itself. This hero's vision of the Timnite woman was not that of sex object, but of one 'upright'. And it was not, after all, Samson's own will that led to a lion torn apart 'as one tears a kid'. It was Yhwh's spirit. Left to his own devices, Samson but enjoys the honey. It is Yhwh's spirit that leaves 30 Philistines dead. Samson, on the other hand, clearly regretting his precipitous departure from his wedding, brings an (untorn) kid as peace offering. The spirit chooses strength; Samson looks for sweetness. Even his fiery vengeance for his lost bride resonates with the lost sweetness of desire. Sending foxes against the Philistine plantings echoes the Song of Song's enigmatic love-talk:

> Catch us the foxes,
> the little foxes,
> that ruin the vineyards...(2.15)

Samson seeks sweetness more than strength in his relationships with women, but his search brings about his own death, finally, as well as his bride's. On the one hand, this can be easily read as the wisdom tradition's moral lesson of death to men who mess around with strange women or, from a larger psychological perspective, as a myth concerned with the problems of love:

> fear of the female, the feminine attraction and impurity, fear of initiation, of the first time. Fear of the *vagina dentata*. Fear of emotional surrender, of too strong an attachment. Fear of old age and of the return to the womb, of the powerlessness of the child. Above all, fear caused by the irresistible attraction of all these things. 'Redeem us from love' is the theme of this myth (Bal 1987: 65-66).

But I wonder. Unquestionably, fear is at issue here. But trickster tales are one way fear is faced, one way the chaos at the heart of things is acknowledged and given its place. Samson *chooses* death. It is hard for me to construe this simply as either the 'natural' outcome of liaisons with the Strange Woman or as the wish to be redeemed from love. Has Samson chosen the world of men, or has he, unable to live in the world of women, rejected as well the world of the male god? If the death of the Philistines avenges *one* of his two eyes (16.28), does his own death —the self-chosen death of Yhwh's strong man—avenge the other? Is his final use of his God-given strength an act against God, in the name of sweetness? Does the trickster hero finally even the score with the tricky God? Strength in the name of sweetness may signal a meaning to the riddle that transcends the logic that locks male fear to female victimage.

Love, sex, domesticity, desire—the riddle's meanings are not yet exhausted. It is these that, from the patriarchal point of view, empower woman over man, generating, in the first instance, male fear. It is also these, however, that give emotional force to the male search for wisdom. Sex *is* knowing. One finds wisdom by desiring, seeking, loving Wisdom. Wisdom is a woman. And so is Strangeness. What is sweeter than honey? What is stronger than a lion? Woman—woman, who is the object of love, sex, eros, of the desire to know.

> Riddles have a specific relation to desire. They stage the desire to know, which is, as we have seen, the erotic desire of the Hebrew male. Proposing a question is proposing, for the addressee, the possibility of knowing: knowing the object of the desire to know, enjoying her as the stake of the game. Samson's riddle, caught in the web of the narrative that produced it and was produced by it, was about the desire to know what yields pleasure through violent expropriation, and that is the view of eroticism that the book [of Judges] exclusively represents (Bal 1988a: 144-45).

Again, Woman as victim only? Strange Women do not go down without a fight.

A key word(-play) occurs in 14.15 (cf. 16.5), where the Timnite woman's countrymen call upon her to 'entice' her husband to tell her the riddle's solution. The word 'entice' is in Hebrew *pth*, here in the feminine singular imperative, *patti*. '*Patti* your husband', the Philistine men say. Other forms and variants of this verb, however, can also mean 'to be open' (qal, e.g., Prov. 20.19); 'make open' (hiphil, e.g., Gen. 9.27); or 'be simple' (qal, e.g., Job 5.2; Hos. 7.11). Thus, the word usually translated 'entice him' or seduce him' carries undertones of 'open him up' and 'make a fool of him'. Indeed, the form used in 14.15, *patti*, sounds very similar to the word for simpleton or fool, *peti*. A hardening of the final consonant of *pth* produces a technical term used by the sages, meaning 'to solve (lit.: 'open') a riddle' (Ps. 49.5; Crenshaw 1978: 107-108). Thus we have another triple entendre. With respect to Samson, the woman is to open him, to make a fool of him, and to get a solution to his riddle. All of this is accomplished, of course, by means of love-talk. Because of male desire, Woman controls the talking, masters the master of language. The gender confusion represented in the riddle plays itself out: Samson in love acts like a foolish woman while the woman does a man's job both in opening the Other and in seeking and finding wisdom.

The narrative goes further, however. The Strange Woman dies, but Samson's story does not end. If Bal is correct that 'the force of the speech-act [the riddle] is motivated by the need to undo the woman' (1988a: 140-41), why is there more to say? Is the only message here that of death to sweet female strength? Why then Delilah? Perhaps this trickster tale, this tale of boundary-crossing, is not yet complete. The gender boundary has been broken with the Timnite woman, but other boundaries remain: Samson is still attached to his parents, his bride to hers; Samson tries to break down the national boundary, but she remains loyal to her Philistine kin. In Delilah, however, all boundaries are dissolved. She has no family, and Samson's own parents have left the scene. She dwells in 'the valley of Sorek', on the border of, but not in, Philistine territory. Her own nationality is indeterminate; she has a Hebrew name. She chooses (sells) her loyalty, rather than having it forced on her by either birthright or threats. She completes the trans- formation of Samson into a woman, both emotionally and physically, while enticing from him his wisdom as well. Here is the completion of a tale of crossed boundaries, figured in a woman with no identity, with all identities. Offering 'all possibilities' of interpretation, she is the *mise en abyme par excellence*. In this story, the idea of the *abyme* must be taken literally. As the embodiment of every broken boundary, the Strange Woman figures chaos, the abyss itself. That such chaos leads to death should not be read as a statement that the boundaries are un- breachable, but that they have indeed been breached. Samson joins the Timnite woman in death; the Israelite joins the Philistines. Death is not here a punishment for either wrongdoing or wrong-being. It is the real- ity that comes to all human beings. It marks the falsity of the bound- aries, as well as their necessity.

This collapse of the most fundamental cultural boundaries and reli- gious value claims—of gender, of family, of nationality, of morality, of death as punishment—complicates any effort to read the story of the riddle as simply a binarizing text, although both ancient and contem- porary values often push readers to repolarize what the narrative has dissolved. One can easily imagine, for example, an ancient reader with a conventional wisdom worldview finding it 'natural' that Samson should die as a consequence of intercourse with the Strange Woman. Contemporary feminists, on the other hand, find it equally natural that, in a patriarchal text, a woman should die as the result of male strength. The fact is, however, that Samson as well as the Timnite woman ulti- mately dies, while the Strange Woman—whether embodied as the unnamed prostitute or the named beloved—at least implicitly lives on. Some other model is needed to explain this. The trickster tale, with its inversion of values and acknowledgment of chaos, has provided a point of departure. We turn now to another dimension of that model, namely, the relationship of the trickster to language, where we find a powerful coalescence of tricksters, riddles and (strange) women.

The Riddle as Metalanguage

Bal suggests that in their very trickiness lies the semiotic meaning of tricksters. If a sign is 'anything that can be used in order to lie' (so Umberto Eco), then the ambivalence and deception that characterize the narrative function of trickster figures exemplifies

> semiosis in its central characteristic. Seen in this light, tricksters function as a *mise en abyme* or metasemiotic figure… [T]hey are a sign of the sign. They represent the essence of language, the very language their existence depends on for its representation. This paradoxical status of the trickster may be its most fascinating and culturally valuable aspect (Bal 1988b: 137).

As a *mise en abyme* of language itself, the trickster would seem to be the sort Bal elsewhere designates '*par excellence*', one that reflects not one but all of a story's meanings in the infinite mirror of linguistic possibilities.

The language of riddles also functions, according to Pepicello and Green, as a metalanguage. What is signified by the question–answer unit that constitutes the riddle is mastery of the linguistic code itself (Pepicello and Green 1984: 126-28), such a deep and subtle appreciation for the phonological, morphological and syntactic workings of language that one is able to manipulate these preconditions of linguistic clarity toward the end of confusion. It is the capacity to produce this controlled confusion (the rules are still the rules, though they have been broken) by means of this mastery that gives the riddler a certain degree of social control—at least until the riddle is found out. Like the trickster, then, the riddle represents the essence of language as ambiguity and deception. Samson's riddle goes beyond this generic trait of riddles, significant as it is, to comment on language with even more specificity. For within the wisdom tradition, *language* is one of the most important things that is both sweet and strong. Language itself, then, joins the list of answers to Samson's riddle.

The production of a riddle's answer (and we have now seen that there are several apt answers to this one) to some degree restores clarity, assuming the logic connecting question to answer is finally, if only in hindsight, understood. The social effect of the riddle is, however, longer lasting: one party has won and the other has lost. In the case of the

Samson story, where the riddle's 'answer' is, unusually, framed as a question, the ongoing conflict is highlighted along with the multiplicity of answers. The tension inherent in riddles between the mastery of language and its inherent instability provides, then, both a cultural metaphor for, and a narrative metonym of, this conflict. As a *mise en abyme*, the riddle mirrors in two directions, both encapsulating the already self-contradictory narrative and commenting on the cultural reality of destabilized language that is the narrative's substance and motivation, indeed, turning the two in on each other in doubled self-reflection. Like the trickster who riddles, the riddle too is a *mise en abyme par excellence*.

I agree, then, with Bal that the riddle is the 'motor of the narrative', but, in naming language itself as an answer to the riddle and, thus, a motivation of the narrative, I seek to complicate her assessment that '*the* [my emphasis] force of the speech-act is motivated by the need to undo the woman' (1988a: 140-41). For the gender confusion of both the riddle and the narrative in which it is embedded already undoes the male–female binary this view presupposes, and leaves us still in need of an account of the hero's death.

As I have already noted in discussing the character of Samson's mother, Bal draws from a cross-cultural mythic base to offer the suggestion that Samson dies at the hand of the avenging mother, displaced onto Delilah (1988a: 197-230). Delilah is also, however—in another, Lacanian, reading of Bal's—the midwife to Samson's rebirth into covenant with God. She is 'the Other who gives access to the symbolic order', but who loses her own subjectivity in the process (1987: 60, 64). Once again, as an alternative, I propose to read from a base in the wisdom tradition. This reading will take both 'the woman who brings death' and 'the woman who mediates (patriarchal) life' into account, but will seek to set both of these in a somewhat different frame.

A key image, a *mise en abyme*, for Bal is Judges's allusion to the 'mouth of the sword' as a way of talking about death. Indeed, death-talk, words that produce death, is her primary concern; hence, her regular reference to the 's/word'. To one versed in Proverbs, however, the images of strength and sweetness open up some further associations that I would encapsulate in a Hebrew wordplay between 'word' (*dabar*) and 'honey-bee' (*deborah*; cf. Judg. 14.8). For Bal, the focus is on the killing strength of language. I would like to give equal time to its sweetness, while acknowledging that sweetness can still have a sting.

In Proverbs, sweetness and strength, wisdom and strangeness, weave a complex metaphorical pattern on the warp-strings of Woman and Language. Here it is Woman Wisdom who 'has strength' (*geburah*; Prov. 8.14) and the woman of worth whose strength (*'oz*) is her clothing, and who makes the sort of garments (*sadin*) that Samson must kill to obtain (31.24-25). Samson has removed the foreign city's gates to Hebron, planting there the opening of the Strange Woman's legs. But the city gates are also the representative locus of Woman Wisdom and her earthly counterpart: 'at the opening (again, *pth*) of the city gates' Wisdom speaks (1.21; cf. 8.3); there the wise wife's works speak her praise (31.31). Sex and love are sweet, but so is wisdom.

> Eat, my son, honey, for it is good,
> and dripping honey is sweet upon your palate.
> Know that thus is wisdom to your soul;
> if you find it, there will be a future
> and your hope will not be cut off (Prov. 24.13-14).

Neither the association of wisdom with the mouth or with woman is incidental. It is, in the first place, precisely wise *speech* that is at stake.

> Pleasant words are a honeycomb,
> sweet to the soul and healing to the body (Prov.16.24).

On the other hand, it is this very sweetness in the mouth that marks the Strange Woman who 'cuts off' her followers from the land (2.16-22).

> For the lips of the strange woman drip honey,
> and her palate is smoother than oil (Prov. 5.3).

The fact that two women can 'open' Samson's riddles—and, as a result, bring about his death—accords precisely with the wisdom tradition's identification of Language as Woman. Here is the site of the ultimate merging of Woman Wisdom and the Strange Woman, and the source of the ultimate value of each. The lovers of Woman Language, imaged multisensorially as the tongue, will eat of both her fruits: both death and life.

> Death and life are in the hand of the tongue,
> and her lovers will eat of her fruit (Prov. 18.21).

The Timnite and Delilah, as rulers of language, do precisely what Woman Language is expected to do, opening the speech of human beings. Understanding Woman as Language affirms the mediating role of the Samson story's women, but does so without loss of their subjectivity. For Woman is not simply the Other who gives access to the symbolic order; as Woman Language, she *is* the symbolic order *as* Other. In Woman, in other words, Samson confronts God.

Reading with the Strange Woman, sweetness retains its strength at the metalevel, validating, I would suggest, a perspective on the narrative itself that retains a full dialectic between sweetness and strength, without yielding victory to a patriarchal voice that privileges male strength in the 'undoing' of woman. If Woman is what is sweet and strong, Samson is a strong seeker of sweetness. If his search leads to the death of one Strange Woman, this is mythically balanced by the survival of two others. If his search joins him to the Strange Woman in death, it is only because he has found God, and her sweetness is not necessarily healing to the body.

> If you have found honey, eat only enough for you,
> or else, having too much, you will vomit it (Prov. 25.16).

Samson dies, with his bride, for the love of sweetness. But Delilah bears witness that they do not die, like Romeo and Juliet, caught blindly in the snare of the patriarchal ideology that constructs them, but as tricksters, both eyes avenged, watching their predestined tragedy unfold.

Wisdom and Cult, Riddle and Vow

I have offered a wisdom reading of the Samson narrative. The construction of poetic riddles in bilinear parallelism, the artful application of proverbial metaphors and cultural allusions, appreciation for the sweetness of sex and the attraction of the Strange Woman, facility in the language skills necessary for diplomatic use, the ability to formulate pithy lessons of general application from the particulars of personal experience, the religious sensibility acknowledging the power and will of the deity to redirect the desires and intentions of the human heart—all bespeak an interest in matters of concern to the editors of Proverbs, though perhaps also a challenge to a conventional reading of that literature. Indeed, my reading of Samson is one that exploits the subtle dialectic of wise and strange in Proverbs into a full-blown deconstruction, with its necessary theological outcome, a full-blown theodicy. In this sense, the story is, like the books of Job or Qohelet, wisdom against wisdom, wisdom in the garb of the Strange Woman.

To propose a reading is, of course, to propose a reader, for whom I am the most obvious candidate. I shall, however, dare a bit more. Can we imagine an ancient reader of like mind, a tricky reader, a strange reader, one who would see in the very conventions of Israelite vs. foreigner and the dangers of the Strange Woman the mirror that challenges them? If so, who would it be? My wisdom reading depends on the idea of a 'wisdom tradition', tradents who identify with the conglomeration of skills and interests listed above. But can we further contextualize this movement?

The question of the social location of wisdom is a matter under much debate, whether one considers the monarchic or postmonarchic eras. Without entering into all the dimensions of that debate, I shall here focus on two vectors, both already alluded to in my treatment of Proverbs: the relationship of wisdom to the cult and the place of wisdom thought in the social and religious developments of the postexilic period. In Chapter 1, I proposed a postexilic social setting for Proverbs in which the fundamental us-versus-them act of identity construction is more an internal one (who is the true Israelite?) than external, where the fiction of a foreign enemy is part of the rhetorical battle for internal control, and where the image of the Strange *Woman*, in particular, is a multi-use symbol, both embedded in and transcending the politics of any given moment. The last section of this book will develop a wider picture in which this exclusivist identity politics, usually associated with Ezra and Nehemiah, is itself contested by other segments of Judahite society. Biblical evidence for resistance to exclusivism has long been noted by scholars. Unfortunately, the social provenance of the most obvious examples, Ruth and Jonah in particular, is difficult to determine. The twisted thread of wisdom that a sagacious reader might pull from the Samson story, however, connects this material with the tradition of Proverbs. At the same time, the narrative's toying with the issue of marriage to the Strange Woman is difficult to separate from this postexilic problematic.

As I have argued in Chapter 1, the relationship of wisdom to the Israelite cult is adumbrated in Proverbs 7's allusion to the law on peace offerings and the Strange Woman's violation of it. Although little canonical literature associated with priests is marked by notable wisdom interests, the presence of wisdom psalms in the Psalter cannot be ignored, nor its apparent wisdom editing.[31] Priestly literature also, inter-

---

31. Ceresko 1990: 217 (citing G.H. Wilson, *The Editing of the Hebrew Psalter* [SBLDS, 76; Chico, CA: Scholars Press, 1985]).

estingly enough, manifests a considerable agenda around strangeness and estrangement, as the last section of this book will show. We must, finally, take account of the enormous preoccupation of the later wisdom tradent, Ben Sira (c. 180 BCE), with purity and priests. By virtue of such evidence, I would argue that by some point in the postexilic period wisdom had moved into sufficient proximity to the cult to be in a conversation with it, a conversation of perhaps increasing importance as the years went by.[32] Whether or not this conversation was always a friendly one is debatable. While Ben Sira suggests a coalescence of interests, the Samson narrative shows more tension.

If the Samson story speaks at least to some degree with wisdom's voice, it often does so, and with an equal twist, about matters of cultic interest. We have considered, for example, the Nazirite vow. In itself, the vow replicates, for the layperson, the more rigorous aspects of priestly life: 'wine and strong drink' are only forbidden priests about to enter the tent of meeting (Lev. 10.9), and only the high priest himself is forbidden to attend to the burial of his father or mother (Lev. 21.10-12). In the case of Samson, the terms of the vow are hyperextended and also subverted. Not only is the vow lifelong, rather than temporary, but it begins in the womb, with the instruction to Samson's mother to avoid the alcoholic beverages forbidden the Nazirite. In addition to alcohol, moreover, the narrative also forbids unclean food. This restriction is not found in Numbers 6, but certainly represents a major concern of post-exilic priests. Allusion to the priestly restrictions in Leviticus also fills in another gap between Numbers's Nazirite vow and the Samson story, namely, the concern for strange sex absent in the former, yet so prominent in the latter. Leviticus 21 intersperses its instructions on priests and corpses with others on priests and women, forbidding marriage to prostitutes, defiled women and divorced women, and prescribing death by burning for the prostituted daughter of a priest (shades of the Timnite bride). As we have already seen, Proverbs also joins the motifs of strong drink and dangerous women in the instruction of Lemuel's mother. In terms of his uniquely permanent Nazirite status, then, Samson becomes, in effect, a quasi-priest (indeed, a high priest!); like priesthood, his is a

---

32. My general conclusion about the intersection of wisdom and cult accords with Leo Perdue's (1977) more sweeping study that focuses on statements or allusions to the cult in the full scope of wisdom literature of Egypt, Mesopotamia and Israel. My interest, however, is more historically specific: Do the traces of this intersection in biblical literature cast any light on the situation of its production?

status ascribed from birth. Ascription of priestly status is, however, almost obsessively regarded as determined by paternal inheritance (see further, Chapter 5), hardly, as in Samson's case, a matter of maternal obedience. Is it possible that Lemuel's mother here tweaks a priestly cheek? It is certainly the case that, for all the exaggeration of its terms, the Nazirite vow provides a precise point around which the Samson narrative undoes itself. The 'vow' is, in the first instance, never technically 'taken' and, likewise, broken from the first moment of Samson's independent action. The 'seventh day', the day of haircutting for the corpse-defiled Nazirite, has come to pass before the first day of his wedding feast.

Feminist commentators have understood the haircutting as a sign of castration, with Delilah the embodiment of male fear, either *vagina dentata* or avenging mother. From a priestly point of view, however, other facets of meaning appear. Bear in mind the point made earlier that, contrary to most interpretations, the haircutting can be understood not as an act of disobedience, but as the sign of the vow unintentionally broken by corpse-defilement, a sign enacted on 'the day of purification', in anticipation of a renewed time of consecration. On this understanding, Delilah is the enactor of Samson's purification. That a woman should perform in this capacity is most striking, although the joining of Delilah to Samson in a quasi-priestly status accords with the general boundary-collapsing tendency of the story. The female as agent of cultic purification reminds, moreover, of another case in which a Strange Woman performs a priestly function, namely, Zipporah's circumcision of Moses (Exod. 4.24-26; see further, Chapter 6).[33] Indeed, since circumcision is also often understood as a symbol of castration, these episodes are aligned in more ways than one.[34]

Both haircutting and circumcision are Janus-faced. Both can mean castration, but both also mean purification, and both are a sign of a vow

---

33. This is not the narrative's only allusion to the Moses story. Samson's challenge to Yhwh that produces water from a rock is not incidental (compare Judg. 15.18-19 with Exod. 17.1-7 and Num. 20.2-13).

34. An intertextual reading might also point to the contiguity between Moses' circumcision and his encounter with his brother Aaron, the eventual high priest, and the similar contiguity between Samson's haircutting (Judg. 16) and the story of his brother Danites' acquisition of a priest in Judg. 17–18 (note the reference to Moses' grandson in 18.30).

made and renewed, in the latter case endlessly renewed. Circumcision is particularly powerfully freighted with double meaning; it symbolizes not only castration but also fruitfulness, the opening that allows the flow of the seed (Eilberg-Schwartz 1990: 141-76). Purification is not, in other words, unambiguously aligned with desexualization, though such appears to be the case for the seedless Samson. I wonder, however, whether, in keeping with the narrative's other tricks, circumcision is not also turned on its head and, with it, the exclusivism implied by this quintessential marker of identity. If, in the cutting of his hair, Samson is also symbolically circumcised, then the Strange Woman's is the hand by which he enters not just manhood, but *Israelite* manhood. Only now does he leave the ranks of the uncircumcised, the Philistines; only now is he truly separated, a Nazirite. The vow is finally taken, but to what end? Not the life and seed promised the circumcised ones, but death, death alongside the uncircumcised.

And death, finally, by what means? The circumcised one falls under the weight of an unholy temple. Does this tragic end to the trickster hero express a simple moral on the keeping of necessary boundaries? Thus it has always been read. But the story's tricks and turns suggest to me another possibility. Could this ending rather be a comment on the keepers of a different temple, a temple for insiders only, perhaps perceived as unjust and self-satisfied in their very policy of exclusivism? Is it *Judah's* priests who narratively receive their just deserts for their part in the death of the free-thinking Samson?

Such an interpretive suggestion about a text requires a hypothesis as to the circumstances of the text's production. For this I turn to two of Philip Davies's (1998) observations about the scribal production of what would become biblical literature. He argues, on the one hand, that 'it will be among the scribes of the postexilic Jerusalem temple...that the impetus for a literature of national ideology is likely to have developed' (Davies 1998: 68-69). This would certainly account for a Samson narrative conventionally read. On the other hand, however, when considering scribal activity more generally, he notes that

> written texts, though overwhelmingly the produce of the scribal *hand*, are not necessarily all products of the scribal *mind*. And the necessity of serving rulers to whom they may have regarded themselves as intellectually superior no doubt instilled in the scribes the techniques of satire and ambiguity: the ability to inscribe on the surface of a political text their own traces (1998: 19).

Herein lies a possibility of scribal resistance to a dominant ideology, a Samson narrative read as subversion. I can imagine two possible contexts for the production of the text as I have read it: either a group of scribes outside the temple elite, commenting on their more powerful peers, or an upstart (younger?) group of temple scribes resisting the politics of their elders. The latter, of course, would be the nemesis confronted by the editor of Proverbs.

Chapter 4

READING SOLOMON AS A WOMAN

Solomon was a woman. There you have it, a thought I have been enter-
taining for the last ten or fifteen years. Mostly, however, we have dined
alone, my thought and I, for I have found no way of introducing her in
polite company; which is to say, I have had (until, perhaps, now) no
proper intellectual clothes in which to garb her. The clothes I've found
are a bit makeshift, but I shall let her try them on and, thus, you her as
well.

I have, as you can well imagine, not a thread of data with which to
make a historical claim about Solomon's gender, although the image of
Hatshepsut in her beard certainly comes to mind when dealing with a
king so fond of things Egyptian. Do I intend, then, a literary argument,
suggesting that the author or editor or narrator, actual or implied, constructs Solomon as a woman? This is closer, but 'construction' is too
strong a term. At most, there are what amount to breathy intimations:
the lack of sex in the narrative of a reign about a king who elsewhere,
as in the Song of Songs, appears as the lover par excellence (Jobling
1991b: 63-64); Rehoboam's comparison of his little finger to his father's
genitals; the various women (all strange) who drift through this narrative in some relationship to Solomon, but sometimes also, arguably,
representing some aspect of his character.

More than this, however, what I mean by 'Solomon is a woman' is an
approach to reading the narrative that emphasizes the relationship of
Wisdom, personified here in Solomon, and Woman, the form of wisdom's personification in the tradition's definitive text, the book of Proverbs, which is, completing the circle, ascribed to Solomon. Even at this
point I would not be so bold as to call Solomon 'woman' were it not for
the pervasive strangeness of both women and wisdom throughout this
narrative, an ambiguity in terms of the values associated with them, a
sense of crossed boundaries: Solomon is the quintessential wise man

and also the embodiment of Israel's most fundamental estrangement. It is this ambiguity I have chosen to encapsulate in an expression of crossed gender.

The wise Solomon came to be regarded as the patron and ideal of the biblical 'wisdom tradition', having ascribed to him the books of Proverbs, Qohelet, the Song of Songs and the apocryphal Wisdom of Solomon.[1] It is not surprising, then, that the story of his reign is laced with vocabulary, themes and images from the wisdom literature, especially Proverbs. Of particular importance is Proverbs's use of female images to personify two central ideas—wisdom and strangeness, or folly. The Solomon narrative in 1 Kings 1–11 draws on these symbolic portrayals of Woman Wisdom (love of whom leads to life) and Woman

---

1.   Considerable scholarly ink has been spilled on the question of how Solomon came to be connected with the wisdom tradition, often in the effort to historically reconstruct the reign and capabilities of the 'real' Solomon in such a way as to assign or deny him one or more of the several varieties of 'wisdom' apparent in the narrative (e.g. judicial, administrative, architectural, natural, intellectual). The tendency in scholarship until recently was to assume some degree of historicity to the tradition of Solomon's wisdom (see Scott's review of literature [1955: 262-63]), with von Rad's formulation of a period of 'Solomonic enlightenment' often accepted with little question (1962: 48-56; 1966b: 293). Although he accepts von Rad's reconstruction of the tenth-century ethos, Scott's literary analysis of the extravagant notices of Solomon's wisdom in 1 Kgs 5.9-14 (Eng.: 4.29-34) and 10.1-29 gives ample reason to date the texts themselves to the postexilic period. More recently, scholars have focused on the work of the Deuteronomistic Historian in configuring Kings's picture of Solomon's wisdom (Kenik 1983, Gerbrandt 1986, McCarter 1990, Parker 1991; 1992, and Fox 1995). Brueggemann (1990) has nonetheless recently reconsidered von Rad's reconstruction, analyzing the relationship of Solomonic wisdom to a 'broadly based social transformation' (121) in the tenth century, which he takes to explain the variegated canonical memory of Solomon as a patron of wisdom. Despite the greater sophistication of his historical methodology, there remains in Brueggemann's work, as in von Rad's, too much uncritical acceptance of the Bible's depiction of tenth-century history. I doubt there is much that can be said about the 'historical Solomon', including, unfortunately, any assessment of the nature or quantity of his wisdom; how that connection got made is lost to us. It is not surprising, however, in a mythic sense, for a story of origins to move from a successful warrior–hero like David to a builder–king who oversees a time of peace. Babylonian mythology combines these traits, successively, in one character, the god Marduk. To take a more recent example, American mythology glorifies the warrior–president George Washington succeeded by the philosopher–architect Thomas Jefferson, the historical interstice of John Adams largely ignored by any but professional historians.

Stranger/Folly (whose embrace brings death), not only to construct its female characters, but to structure and thematize the narrative as a whole. Moreover, given the density of occurrences of the root *hkm* ('wise')—21 times in chs. 2–11—it is hard not to imagine some comment being made on wisdom itself. The next few pages will sketch out the issues and problems that emerge when one reads the Solomon narrative through the triple lens of Woman, Wisdom and Strangeness. The rest of the chapter will then work through their complexities and interconnections by means of a reading of the text.

Issues in the Interpretation of the Solomon Narrative

The Evaluation of Wisdom

This narrative is surely in some sense 'about' wisdom. But what exactly is being said? The idea of wisdom is variously defined in these 11 chapters. There is, on the one hand, the political wisdom that leads to assassinations (2.5-9). On another, there is the God-given wisdom (3.4-15) that defines one ideal, typically royal, of the divine–human relationship. Royal wisdom eventuates in the judicial wisdom that 'executes justice', particularly for the marginalized (3.16-28; 10.9), as well as in the diplomatic and commercial wisdom that produces peace and a flow of wealth to the nation's coffers (5.21-26 [Eng.: 7-12]; ch. 10). There is also wisdom in the form of intelligence, especially manifest in wise speech (5.9-14 [Eng.: 4:29-34]; 10.1-3), and wisdom that plans a house for Yhwh (5.15-21 [Eng.: 1-7]), as well as that which dresses it magnificently in bronze (7.13-14).

Most of this sounds quite glorious, but all is not quite as it seems. By the end of the narrative, the wise Solomon has succumbed to the gods of foreign women, and his son will pay the price, losing most of the kingdom. Even in the course of the story itself, fissures appear in wisdom's façade. One we have already noted: the rather nasty beginning to Solomon's reign in 1 Kings 2, involving the two assassinations recommended by David as 'wisdom' and yet another death involving twowomen, Abishag and Bathsheba.[2] A second fissure lies in the fact

---

2.   1 Kgs 2 is a chapter that looks both forward in the narrative and backward. On the one hand, it raises a question about the perspective on wisdom in 1 Kgs 3– 11; on the other, its representation of wisdom from the dying David's mouth also marks this chapter as the conclusion of the story of David's reign in 2 Sam.9–20.

that wisdom's apparent glories in 1 Kings 3–10 are shadowed by constant reference to strangeness. Although, on one level, the recognition of Solomon's wisdom by foreigners may suggest an openness and internationalism to be celebrated, his final demise casts a backward shadow on that aspect of his reign.

How can this failure of wisdom be accounted for? A number of scholars interpret it in light of an assumed deuteronomistic redaction of the story. Michael Fox (1995) is representative of this approach (cf. Parker 1992; Kenik 1993). In a critical response to Lasine's argument (1995) that 1 Kings 3–10 is a text rife with indeterminacy, Fox argues that the ambiguities in Solomon's character are not true indeterminacies, ones that would leave open textual meaning, but rather the 'subtle and credible' incongruities that contribute to a 'picture of a great and flawed monarch' (Fox 1995: 185). Solomon

> is a model of all Deuteronomic virtues but two: avoidance of foreign
> women and strict adherence to centralized worship. No nuancing of char-
> acter is allowed to blur the thematic clash between Solomon's wisdom
> and his two failings (1995: 186).

For the Deuteronomist, Fox argues, it is precisely a critique of the king's wisdom that is at issue; wisdom is by this editor subordinated to divine law.

> Had Solomon followed the charge in 2.1-4 (also Dtr) and elsewhere to
> walk in God's way and obey his laws 'as is written in the law of Moses',
> he would have kept his kingdom whole. Solomon's fate proves it is not
> enough to be wise (190).

This sort of reading by Fox and others is important for my purposes in that it highlights a textual conversation between wisdom and Torah, thus implicitly pointing to larger issues in canonical development. Who engages in such a literary conversation and to what end? To such questions we shall return. More immediately, however, it is not clear to me that the Solomon narrative frames the relationship of wisdom and Torah in the simple terms of subordination seen by these interpreters.

(This is a literary judgment that has become commonplace in biblical studies for
other reasons as well.) The relationship of these two larger bodies of material—the
narrative of David's reign and that of Solomon's—will bear consideration with
respect to both women and wisdom.

Ambiguating Strangeness[3]

To interpret the Solomon narrative as a case of 'Torah over wisdom' does not require that wisdom be seen as bad, only that its relative goodness be less than that of Torah. Torah, however, must then be understood as an unambiguous good. I would argue, on the other hand, that both wisdom and Torah bear the marks of strangeness, encumbering with them both the deity and his temple as well.

The strangeness of wisdom is obvious, first, in the narrative's female characters. The Queen of Sheba embodies the ambiguity (10.1-13). She is, on the one hand, a wise woman, capable of testing Solomon with riddles, the wisdom tradition's ultimate skill (cf. Prov. 1.6). She is also, on the other hand, a foreign woman. Her narrative role, moreover—precisely this riddle testing—is similar to that of the two harlots whose riddle Solomon solves with a sword. These two episodes, one near the beginning of the Solomon narrative and the other near its end, subtly link one sort of strangeness (that of the foreigner) to another (that of the sexual outsider). That such a woman makes the ultimate pronouncement of divine purpose and royal achievement cannot but give pause, particularly when the foreign women who lead Solomon into apostasy appear in the next chapter, their very numbers representing sexual excess as well as forbidden origin. What would motivate an editor to put side by side such diametrically opposed portraits of foreign women in the story of the wisest of kings? Their contiguity certainly recalls Proverbs's depiction of Woman Wise and Strange. But what are we to make of this textured juxtaposition in Kings? The strangeness of women is multifold: sexual as well as national and religious. And strangeness and wisdom intersect as well as oppose each other. These complications of strangeness are not accounted for by a simple 'wisdom versus Torah' reading of the narrative.

The ambiguating interfoldings of wisdom, women and strangeness in the Solomon narrative affect other crucial elements in the story: Torah, temple and, by implication, the divine author of the former and inhabitant of the latter.

Wisdom, although already tinged with violence in 1 Kings 2, receives strong theological approbation in ch. 3, where Solomon in his dream

---

3.   This discussion suggests a reading of the Solomon narrative that will be developed in detail in the next major section of the chapter.

chooses it instead of wealth and honor. Fox assumes that God's insistence on following his statutes and commandments at the end of the dream theophany (3.14) already qualifies the gift of wisdom with reference to the law. But the qualification is itself qualified: God offers *David* as a model of obedience! Can another Bathsheba be far from the picture? The legal requirements regarding foreign wives are also fuzzy. Egyptians are not on the deuteronomistic exclusion list. Does this omission authorize Solomon's Egyptian wife? Such approbation is suggested by 3.1-3, where the report of his marriage is followed by commendation for walking in God's statutes (though, again, as his father walked). On the other hand, the Egyptian wife appears in the list of condemnable marriages in ch. 11. Where does this author draw the line on illicit marriage? Further, if deuteronomic law is the definitive criterion of goodness, why are Solomon's Egyptian horses and acquisition of gold and silver not explicitly condemned, as in Deut. 17.16-17 (cf. Jobling 1991b: 68)? Finally, if foreign wives are such a problem, why are foreign relations in general not regarded with more suspicion? In particular, the report of the planning and construction of the temple, authorized by Yhwh as the definitive work of David's heir (2 Sam. 7.13) is laced with the motif of strangeness—financed by a foreign king and built with foreign material and labor—in a way that undermines any simple reading of obedience to the prime directives of Deuteronomy regarding centralized worship.

The end of Solomon's story, then, seems to resolve the relationship of wisdom and Torah—and thus theologically rationalize the division of the kingdom—more neatly than the rest of the narrative allows. The purpose and actions of the deity do not shine with moral clarity. If wisdom is introduced only to be subordinated to Torah, why is such theological emphasis placed on it in ch. 3 and what are we to make of the reference to David as the model of Torah-piety? God, moreover, is the giver of wisdom to Solomon, but also the provider of unasked-for wealth and honor (3.13). Although wisdom and wealth make a happy marriage in, for example, the book of Proverbs, wealth in Kings arguably becomes part of the judgment against Solomon. If Lasine is correct that the genre expectations of ancient readers would have associated a large royal harem with a divine promise of wealth and honor, then Solomon's many wives may also have been seen as part of God's doing (1995: 87-94). What are we to make, then, of the character and motives of the deity? Must Yhwh be seen, in at least certain respects, as the tempter of

Solomon (so Lasine [1995: 106-10] and Eslinger [1989: 137-38])?[4]

Sexuality and Ideology

The ambiguities discussed in the preceding section could in large measure be framed in terms of David Jobling's mythic–ideological analysis of the Solomon narrative. Jobling sees chs. 3–10 as a myth of a Solomonic Golden Age, 'someone's (not untroubled) dream of national glory' (1991b: 59), while 2.12-46 and ch. 11 function as a frame to which all the negativity has been consigned. His analysis of the two major semantic fields of economics and sexuality, however, reveals a complexity that the myth works to conceal. There are both an ideal and a real economics at work in 3–10.[5] The former proposes a natural abundance enabled, in effect, by the 'surplus value' of wisdom. The latter acknowledges a process of 'fair exchange or trade, any acquisition by one party diminishing another's store' (Jobling 1991b: 61), witness, for example, the imposition of forced labor and apparently unfavorable trade deals with King Hiram of Tyre.

---

4.   Scholars are not incapable of generating answers to these questions, but the fact that different scholars make such different decisions as to which questions require answers, and the degree to which any presumed 'answer' suits the rest of a given scholar's reading, is enough to make anyone a believer in reader-response theory. Fox's argument against the indeterminacy of wisdom is especially striking in this regard. He assumes a dissociation of the concept of wisdom in Proverbs from its use elsewhere. In Proverbs the term signifies 'sound and temperate judgment, together with a knowledge of human nature, applied to the conduct of life', as well as 'an ethical quality'; in other texts it is 'an all-embracing faculty for analysis and problem-solving', 'not necessarily moral or even far-sighted' (Fox 1995: 188). While the latter meaning would relieve the tension around wisdom in the Solomon narrative, I find this too neat a solution. The narrative is in fact closely tied to Proverbs, not only in its obvious interest in the wisdom of Solomon, but also in its emphasis on strange women and on wisdom as a divine gift. It is hard to imagine ancient readers interpreting these two texts independently of each other.

5.   As I read Jobling, 'real economics' is for him a structuralist category (i.e. one member of the real–ideal binary), not a materialist one. It represents an economy of exchange as opposed to one of limitless abundance. It is, in other words, unlikely that this report on Solomon's economic policies represents a transparent window into a tenth-century reality. On the other hand, the text is not utterly detached from real life: centralized government and taxation were certainly facts of life under any king, whether a native or a foreign imperial. The assumption of this text, that the king's wealth and the people's happiness went hand in hand, may be either that of a propagandist or an ironist.

There is also a real and an ideal sexuality at work. Jobling, summarizing his 1986 analysis of Genesis 2–3, points to that narrative's 'attempt to depict the ideal of the past as the opposite of present reality', but also to the failure of that attempt, 'because the real was "always already" there in the supposed ideal' (1991b: 59). The implicit ideal of sexuality in Genesis is, on the one hand, 'humanity without sexuality or sexual difference', yet at the same time *male*, 'since this was the "default value" of "human" in the mindset at work' (59). The ideal was, however, both obfuscated and tainted by the intrusion of the real into the Garden, humanity in two sexes, leading inevitably to the 'fall'. Akin to Genesis's ideal of human asexuality, 1 Kings 3–10 also 'excludes, in a remarkable way, any sexual activity on Solomon's part' (63), a fiction turned on its head in ch. 11, where his relationship with his wives leads to the aged Solomon's 'fall'. Wisdom, Jobling argues, serves this agenda as a sex-substitute, a point to which we shall return.

This rendering of sex serves the textual logic in a couple of related ways. First, it relieves the economic sphere of 'guilt' for the failure of the united kingdom, a displacement all the more obvious for 1 Kings 12's open blame of Solomon's real economics. Secondly, it resolves the textual wavering between the conditional or unconditional nature of divine blessing, which is the major point of indeterminacy in Jobling's reading. The Golden Age ideology of chs. 3–11 keeps conditionality marginalized, though hardly absent. 'When we reach ch. 11, though, we find that everything was conditional after all; conditional on something repressed to that point—sexuality' (Jobling 1991b: 69).

Like Fox, then, Jobling focuses on Solomon's wives in ch. 11 as a crucial meaning-determining point, although his analysis in other respects aligns more with Lasine's appreciation for indeterminacy. Jobling and Lasine agree, for example, that, in contrast to chs. 3–11, Solomon's murderous 'wisdom' in ch. 2 is depicted negatively, while Fox, given his assumption that Solomon has only two faults, is necessarily sanguine about it. Further, while Jobling acknowledges the narrative effort to blame the women in ch. 11, he finds it far less satisfying than does Fox; for Jobling, both the mythically suppressed problem of real economics and the ambivalence about the conditionality of the divine blessing are too close to the surface to ignore.

By reading for textual ideology (rather than, like Fox, authorial intent), Jobling also produces a more nuanced understanding of the role of wisdom in the narrative. While wisdom may on one level be *repre-*

sented as 'a virtue but an insufficient one', on another level it *functions* powerfully as an ideological cover for unresolved issues surrounding economics, sexuality and divine intention. The tension between these two levels of interpretation itself introduces an ambiguity of meaning worth further attention.

By foregrounding sexuality, Jobling's analysis also forces the issue of the multivalence of the concept of 'strangeness', which is my particular concern. As I have argued in Chapter 1, interpreters must be sensitive to the logic by which any given writer uses and combines the different rhetorics that construct the Strange, with special attention paid to the intersections of strange sex, strange religion and national/ethnic strangeness. For Fox, however, the textual perspective on foreignness in 1 Kings is unproblematic: foreign women, with their gods, are the cause of deadly folly, even for the wisest of men. Solomon's 'discretion and good sense were undermined by his relationships with women, whom he followed befuddled to the gravest of sins' (Fox 1995: 188). Fox thus, to a surprising degree, accepts uncritically the narrative's ideological confusion of foreignness, sexuality and idolatry. To a neutral observer, the strangeness of female sexuality that leads to male 'befuddlement' should be easy to distinguish from the religious strangeness that marks 'their' gods from 'ours'. In 1 Kings 11 it is not easy to make this distinction, in spite of the fact that sex lies only between its lines. Although Fox notably elides the middle term, as does the narrator, the logic of the quoted sentence is clear: foreign women generate sexual befuddlement (i.e. illicit sexual behavior), which both leads to and is identifiable with idolatry.

Jobling, on the other hand, puts the burden entirely on sexuality, finding foreignness incidental to the narrative logic.

> Though the text makes an effort to insist that *foreign* women were the problem, it is hard to make mere foreignness into a negative, after all the positive treatment of foreigners in chaps. 3–10, and the specific problem—the power of female wiles over an aging man—is a problem of sexuality as such (1991b: 64).

If Fox accepts too readily the ideological connection of sex and foreign worship, Jobling seems to me to ignore the latter's real rhetorical force. He assumes that, because foreignness was not an apparent problem in chs. 3–10, it is not in 11 either. I would suggest that ch. 11's combination of sexual and national strangeness can easily be seen to color what precedes, calling into question the apparently sanguine perspective up to that point.

Dating the Solomon Narrative

These questions regarding the narrative evaluation of wisdom—wisdom's relationship to Torah, foreignness, gender, sexuality and the temple—are necessarily connected to questions concerning the era, social location and ideology of the author or redactor, as well as any presumed audiences. Identifying these factors, however, is hardly a precise science.

Although it had once been a scholarly commonplace to find in this material a more or less transparent window onto the 'historical Solomon', with only occasional and clearly discernible editorial intrusions, more recent scholarship has typically found such vision blocked by the hand of the redactor, usually identified as the Deuteronomistic Historian (DH).[6] Accompanying this scholarly shift has been another, marked by a lowered assessment of the text's view of wisdom. Gerhard von Rad, stylizer of the tenth-century 'Solomonic enlightenment', saw wisdom as part and parcel of this laudable intellectual awakening. In contrast, scholars who have focused on DH (see above, n. 1) temper this glorification of wisdom by emphasizing, as does Fox, its juxtaposition with Solomon's ultimate failure to follow the law.[7]

While this reading has a degree of plausibility, I find the Solomon narrative, as I have already begun to indicate, more complex than this. It is not just about wisdom and law, but also about women and strangeness and wealth and the temple. And, for all its apparent clarity about the worship of foreign gods, it takes its fine old ambiguous time getting to that point. I am interested in the logic that connects all these narrative threads. One analytic move, I propose, may be to reframe the question from one of editorial motivation, which seems only ever able to deal with a couple of thematic parameters at a time, to an ideological analysis that seeks the likely-less-conscious logic connecting them all. The path has been blazed by David Jobling's Jamesonian materialism. 'What the text represents is *the historical necessity of its production*

---

6. Brueggemann (1990) is one recent exception to this generalization.

7. Interestingly, no one takes up Scott's suggestion (1955) that the passages in 1 Kings that glorify Solomon's wisdom (1 Kgs 5.9-14 [Eng.: 4.29-34] and 10.1-29) are the latest additions, post-dating the DH. I shall return to consideration of a variant of this proposal.

(and, especially in the case of an ancient canonical text, its subsequent *reproduction*)' (Jobling 1991b: 59; emphasis in original).

For Jobling, as for most others, however, the (re)production that matters is identified by the heavily baggaged siglum 'DH'.[8] The literary, historical and sociological debates that rage around this concept are well known to biblical scholars and will be incomprehensible to others. I shall, therefore, avoid these issues as much as possible. For the necessitating circumstances that I find particularly interesting are those necessitating the (re)production of the text as one of a group of (sometimes competing) canons and canonical institutions in the postexilic period.[9] This historical point of entry serves my purposes in two respects. First, the discussion in preceding chapters has already laid the groundwork for the view that the postexilic period provides the most likely context for the conglomeration of themes and uncertainties found in 1 Kings 1–11. Secondly, as a relatively late date, it both allows for and compels intertextual analysis between the Solomon narrative, with all its ambiguities, and other texts also seeking and offering the authority of canon. It is in this process, I shall argue, that we shall find the historical necessity for the production of the Solomon narrative in its present configuration.

Given the paucity of direct information about the production of what would become the biblical canon, any judgments made about the (re)production of the Solomon narrative *as* canon will be necessarily tentative. There is no access to this process except through the textual images I seek to explicate as part of the process. Thus, the argument will be not only tentative but also to some degree circular. There are, however, two

8. A recent book by James Linville (1998) moves away from this scholarly convention toward a more complex and uncertain view of the group(s) that produced Kings (he refers to the 'Deuteronomistic Mystery'!). I encountered Linville's work after this chapter was complete, but have reached some similar conclusions independently, both with respect to a postexilic provenance for Kings and to the need for a light hand in speculating about precise dates of authorship, given how little we know about what must have been the complex and shifting power structures of this period and the fact that different readers may have read different things in the same text.

9. Cf. Davies (1998: 56): 'To an appreciable extent, Jewish literary canons can be readily associated with the canonization of such institutions [e.g. the Davidic dynasty, one or another of the priestly groups, or prophecy], linking the canonical books with real or ideal political institutions.' I might substitute the word 'circumspectly' where Davies has 'readily' (see Introduction), but my approach substantially agrees with his.

points of canonical reference, datable to the postexilic period, that link closely with the images and themes of the Solomon narrative. The first is Ezra–Nehemiah, with its combined concern for rejecting foreign women and promulgating the book of the law. The second is Proverbs, which includes my central thematic of female wisdom and strangeness, while offering as well a literary lens on the sociohistorical considerations and processes that produced a *book* with those concerns (Camp 1985).[10] Important in this regard is another network of imagery in Proverbs that links up with Woman Wisdom and Woman Stranger, as well as back to the Solomon narrative, namely, that encapsulated in the notion of the 'house'. The connections between Wisdom's house, Folly's house, the construction of the book of Proverbs as a house modeled on Yhwh's house, the houses of Solomon's wives, and the house of David remain to be drawn out. We turn, then, to a reading of the text as wise and strange.

The Solomon Narrative: Wise and Strange[11]

1 Kings 1–2

Surrounding and mediating the transition from the reign of David to that of Solomon are two female characters, one passive and one active.

10. As I have indicated in Chapter 1, I would no longer argue, as I did in 1985, that the redaction of Proverbs was the work of the *early* postexilic period. I would still affirm, nonetheless, the importance of the ideological impulses I identified in Proverbs in my earlier work: particularly that the use of female imagery to craft Proverbs as a book was a response to the struggle to define and control 'Israelite' identity in a postmonarchic setting. The crucial change I would make to my earlier argument regards my assumption there that from the 'temple-structure' of the book of Proverbs (Skehan 1971; and see below) one should infer a temple-substitute for a *yet to be rebuilt* holy place. The rest of this book will develop a more complex scenario of a time of struggle over who would *control* the temple, a struggle that began as early as the late sixth century, that certainly continued in the time of Nehemiah (if we assume him to be fifth century), and whose winners were still creating the ideological means to consolidate their control at least a century after that. Proverbs, then, should be seen as part of a conversation about the meaning of the temple and the form of its leadership. And see now Linville (1998), who theorizes what I have drawn only inductively from the texts, namely, that the issue of *golah* identity was likely one that persisted for centuries after the presumed 'return from Exile'. This means that texts cannot necessarily be dated to the fifth century just because they apparently deal with the interests of returned exiles. Linville uses the term 'exilicist' to refer to this longer-term ideological picture.

11. Elements of the discussion in this section appeared in Camp 1992.

Abishag the Shunammite is 'a beautiful maiden' sought 'throughout all the territory of Israel' to lie in the aging David's bosom and be his nurse. If this fairy-tale-like characterization implied that Abishag was expected to work a revitalizing miracle, those who sought her were disappointed, for 'the king knew her not'. This report of the final failure of David's sexual energy leads immediately to the self-exaltation of Adonijah, David's eldest son by his wife Haggith, as the man who will be king.

Although joined by David's general Joab, Adonijah does not have the support of the prophet Nathan. Nathan counsels Bathsheba to 'save [her] own life and the life of [her] son Solomon' by challenging the apparently beclouded David to resist Adonijah's power play and remember his oath that Solomon would succeed him. The reader is left curiously (purposefully?) in the dark, however, as to whether David had ever made such an oath. Bowed to the floor, using both Nathan's words and harsher ones of her own, Bathsheba presents the alternatives to David: either designate Solomon king or ensure both his and her deaths. As she speaks, Nathan enters with a similar message. David then recalls Bathsheba to his presence (another textual oddity: when had she left?). As she stands before him, he affirms Solomon's reign.

Although King Solomon initially shows mercy to Adonijah, his approach changes after David's death. Indeed, his father's final words (2.1-9) counsel a deadly 'wisdom' (vv. 6, 9), the executions of general Joab and one Shimei of Benjamin. Though Solomon finds ways to rationalize these killings (2.28-46), they bear the mark of political assassination, as does the murder of Adonijah after another curious episode involving Abishag and Bathsheba (2.13-25). Adonijah approaches Bathsheba with the request that she speak to Solomon on his behalf, asking that Abishag become his wife and expressing confidence that Solomon will heed his mother. Solomon greets Bathsheba with honor and agrees to grant her 'small request'. He reacts violently, however, to the message from Adonijah, equating his request for Abishag with a request for the kingdom itself. Immediately, he orders Adonijah executed.

Indeterminacy governs the first two chapters of 1 Kings, both internally and with respect to its larger literary setting. I shall discuss four interwoven aspects of indeterminacy: (1) the moral evaluation of Solomon's violence in 'establishing the kingdom' (2.12, 46); (2) the moral evaluation of the 'wisdom' to which this violence is ascribed (2.6, 9); (3) questions regarding God's nature and intentions: whether Yhwh intended Solomon to succeed David as king, the divine view of the 'wisdom' required of the new king to secure the throne, and the relationship of this wisdom to the divine gift in ch. 3; (4) the ambiguities surrounding the presentation of the women, Abishag and Bathsheba.

1. The phrase 'establish the kingdom [or throne]' is introduced in 2 Sam. 7.12-16, as part of the classic statement of the so-called Davidic covenant.

> When your days are fulfilled and you lie down with your ancestors, I will raise up your offspring after you, who shall come forth from your body, and I will establish his kingdom. He shall build a house for my name, and I will establish the throne of his kingdom forever... Your house and your kingdom shall be made sure forever before me; your throne shall be established forever (7.12, 13, 16).

This intention of Yhwh's seems quite clear in one important respect and is implied in a second: first, that it is the deity who will do the work of 'establishing'; secondly, that it will be Solomon who is to be established following David. The latter point is suggested by phrases that foreshadow the later events in Solomon's life—that David's issue will build Yhwh's house and that he may be 'punished', but never forsaken (vv. 13-15)—though Solomon is never named.

Clarity quickly departs, however. The events of David's reign that eventuate in Solomon's succession seem undirected by any plan, much less a divine one, unless one imagines a deity of extraordinary and random maleficence. The sequence of adultery, murder, rape and rebellion in 2 Samuel 11–20 culminates in the three political assassinations ordered by Solomon in 1 Kings 2. There is a perverse echo of Yhwh's promise in the king's pronouncement of *self*-blessing as he addresses the last of these targets.

> The king also said to Shimei, '...King Solomon shall be blessed, and the throne of David shall be established before Yhwh forever.' Then the king commanded Benaiah, son of Jehoida, and he went out and struck him down, and he died. And the kingdom was established in the hand of Solomon (1 Kgs 2.44-46).

2. King Solomon seems well and truly to have done his own establishing, though not without the urging of his father David, who, as already noted, counsels two of these deaths as 'wisdom'.[12] If this is

---

12. See Gunn (1978: 94-108) on the tension between the 'giving and grasping' of David's kingdom that culminates in Solomon's accession.

wisdom, it is a sort related, as others have pointed out, to the political wisdom exhibited by different characters in the story of David's reign, for example 'wise' Jonadab, who set up Amnon's rape of Tamar (2 Sam. 13.3). Jonadab's advice is not dissimilar in content or mendacity to that of Ahitophel, whose counsel (*'etsah*) 'was as if one consulted the word of God' (2 Sam. 16.23). Ahitophel coached David's rebel son Absalom to rape his father's concubines on the palace roof 'in the sight of all Israel' (16.21-22). Gordon comments: 'If "counsel" is a wisdom term within a wisdom-influenced "Succession Narrative" then "deconstructionism" would scarcely provide a term strong enough to describe what the narrative is doing to itself' in the Ahitophel material (1995: 97). Whether or not one sees the narrative evaluation of wisdom in 2 Samuel 13–1 Kings 2 as entirely negative,[13] this political connotation surely connects the Kings narrative of Solomon's accession with Samuel's account of his father's reign. Like Solomon's ruthless establishing of his own throne, the moral value of his wisdom is at best, by the end of 1 Kings 2, in question.

3. Also very much in question, however, by dint of the theological ambiguity throughout the David story, as well as the murky relationship of the two 'establishment' texts, is the intention and role of Yhwh in the wisdom of this king. The literary connection of 1 Kings 1–2 to the story of David's reign in 2 Samuel has long been a scholarly commonplace. The problem of theodicy raised by this material, however—was it Yhwh's will that Bathsheba be taken in adultery, Uriah killed, Tamar raped, all to allow for the succession of Solomon?—is often ignored (though see Gunn 1978: 110; Eslinger 1989; Linafelt 1992: 106-108; Fewell and Gunn 1993: 158-60). The presence of this problem, as well as its scholarly suppression, is quite germane to the evaluation of Solomon's wisdom, for it calls into question analyses like those of Fox (1995) and McCarter (1990). Fox in essence puts the wisdom of Solomon in ch. 2 on a continuum with that attained later. Solomon at the outset has 'native good sense', he is 'smart and cunning'; later he comes to a 'higher level of discernment and judiciousness', able to select bene-

---

13. Differences of scholarly opinion on this point result in part from whether one includes 'counsel' like Ahitophel's as part of the wisdom topos, and in part from how one evaluates the wisdom of the wise women of Tekoa (2 Sam. 14) and Abel (2 Sam. 20). On the latter point, contrast, e.g. Crenshaw (1976: 491-92) and Camp (1981).

ficial goals for all the people, as well as achieving his own immediate ones (1995: 186 and note). Like Fox and others, McCarter hears a presumed DH voice that subordinates wisdom to Torah, but he makes a stronger source-critical distinction between DH and an ethically neutral pre-deuteronomistic view of wisdom, which he finds in 1 Kings 2 (1990: 292-93). Neither interpreter, however, acknowledges the *theological* implication of Solomon's deadly and self-directed 'wise' establishing of the kingdom promised by God or its relationship to the unholy events of David's reign.

4. These themes—the question of God's work in establishing Solomon's kingdom, with its attendant theodicy, and that of the moral and theological status of wisdom—find expression in 1 Kings 1–2 in the subplot involving Bathsheba and Abishag. Both the character of Bathsheba and her narrative role are crucial elements in the transition from David to Solomon and, thus, from the 'Succession Narrative', so-called, to the narrative of Solomon's reign. This is evident, as Carole Fontaine (1986) has shown, in the connection of the Bathsheba episode in 2 Samuel 11–12 to that of Yhwh's gift of wisdom to Solomon in 1 Kings 3.

The presence of two women in a story so concerned with wisdom immediately raises for the student of Proverbs the specters of Woman Wisdom and the Strange Woman. Yet the characterizations of Bathsheba and Abishag, especially when set in the larger context of the story of the united monarchy, seem to play with these archetypes rather than simply reproduce them. The interweaving of the paradigms of wise and strange begins with the introduction of Bathsheba in 2 Sam. 11.3. Bathsheba's very name carries a potentially negative connotation (though see below for different possible meanings). Understood as 'daughter (*bat*) of seven (*sheba'*)', it could be taken as a reference to uncertain parentage. She is, on the other hand, explicitly called the 'daughter of Eliam', whom 23.34 identifies as the son of Ahitophel, the advisor whose counsel is likened to 'the word of God' (16.23). As Fontaine comments, Bathsheba is 'wisdom's own granddaughter' (1986: 63). The narrative judgment on the two cases where Ahitophel's counsel is actually given, however, makes irony of 16.23. In the first instance, immediately preceding this seemingly adulatory comment, Ahitophel gives the rebelling Absalom the shocking advice to have public intercourse with his father's concubines (16.20-21).[14] The dishonoring of one's father in

---

14. Her wise grandfather's association with a rebellion may suggest another

this particularly sexual way could hardly be more offensive to the tradents who produced Proverbs, but is not without resonance with the illicit affair of Bathsheba and David (cf. 2 Sam. 12.11). It finally requires, on the other hand, precisely the will of Yhwh to circumvent Ahitophel's more truly godlike advice in Absalom's battle against David (17.14), just as it required divine intervention to uncover David's perfidy. Given this portrait of Ahitophel's wisdom, it may be no surprise that 'wisdom's granddaughter' is also the 'woman who brings death' (in an immediate sense, to her husband; indirectly, to all the children of David's house felled as the result of his folly) by means of her sexual appeal.[15] This element of sexual strangeness is accentuated by the marriage of Bathsheba to Uriah the Hittite. She comes to her affair with David already tainted by the sexual identity of a man whose national heritage should preclude his marriage to an Israelite woman (Deut. 7.1-3).[16]

In a variety of hues, then—birthright, nationality, sexuality—2 Samuel 11 paints Bathsheba as a liminal figure, a Strange Woman, while at the same time—if her relationship to Ahitophel is taken seriously—subtly sullying wisdom as well. She is, on the other hand, a curiously innocent 'temptress', her own wishes or intentions indicated directly by neither word nor deed.[17] Here then we have, as is the case with Samson's foreign liaisons, the strangest thing of all, that is, Yhwh's alliance with the Strange Woman. For without the so-called folly of David's relationship with Bathsheba, there would be no wise Solomon to establish the kingdom or build the temple. She is, therefore, the medium

inference from Bathsheba's name. Sheba is also the name of another rebel against David's throne, whose fate is negotiated by a wise woman (2 Sam. 20). The introduction of the rebel resonates verbally with that of rebellion's daughter. 2 Sam. 11.3 refers to 'Bathsheba, daughter (*bat*) of Eliam, woman (*'eshet*) of Uriah the Hittite'; 20.1 to Sheba, son (*ben*) of Bichri, man (*'ish*) of Yemin'.

15. The gender ideology behind this typological characterization of Bathsheba certainly demands critique (cf. Fontaine's reflection on her own work in this regard [1994: 163-65]). In the present context, however, it is precisely the function of this patriarchal construction that I am concerned with.

16. Cf. Niditch's discussion of how sex marks a woman with the man's identity (1993a: 85-86).

17. Randall Bailey's exegesis (1990: 84-90), which makes Bathsheba very much the mistress of her own fate, is not to be taken lightly. In my view, however, the possibility of such a reading remains at best implicit.

through which God's promises of royal house and holy house are ful-filled.

Although Bathsheba produces the heir to David's throne without indi-cation of volition on her part, her passivity is transformed in 1 Kings 1–2, where the old king's wife becomes the new king's mother. Another notable change in these two chapters, especially given Jobling's obser-vations about the non-role of sex in 1 Kings 3–10, is the suppression of the sexuality of this erstwhile object of desire. The suppression of Bathsheba's sexuality is, perhaps, not surprising, given her impending shift in status from king's wife to queen mother. It is, nonetheless, literarily significant that not only Bathsheba's, but *all* sexuality, is sup-pressed in the first two chapters of Kings (suppressed, but hardly elimi-nated: I shall remark below on its latent presence), making them a suitable introduction to the desexualized narrative that follows. The suppression of Bathsheba's sexuality also opens the characterization of this figure to reassessment. How do the shifty attributes of wisdom and strangeness manifest in a sex object become queen mother?

The relationship of David and Abishag sets the stage for the narrative suppression of sexuality. What was expected of this beautiful woman when she was brought to David? Although many commentators seem to suppose an effort to sexually 'jump-start' the aged king, a sexual test may be more to the point. The narrative's abrupt shift from David's impotence to Adonijah's self-aggrandizement may suggest that Adoni-jah's supporters had devised a symbolic test of potency, in which the sexual equals the kingly, or, at least, that the narrative's ideology pre-supposes such an equation. Repetition of key words supports this read-ing: in 1 Kgs 1.4, the narrator reports that David 'did not know' Abishag; in 1.11, Nathan informs Bathsheba that David 'does not know' of Adonijah's presumption; in 1.18, Bathsheba repeats to David's face that he 'does not know' what is going on. The king's sexual impotence is mirrored in his political blindness. If chs. 3–10 idealize the sup-pression of sex in favor of wisdom (so Jobling 1991b), one could argue that, as in other respects, ch. 1 retains a more pragmatic political per-spective on both: 'to know' is 'to have sex' is 'to have power'. When one fails, so do the others.

The interchange between Adonijah and Bathsheba, and between Bathsheba and Solomon, regarding Adonijah's request to marry Abishag, also functions narratively to suppress sexuality or, to be more precise, to continue the suppression begun in David's failure to know

Abishag.[18] Whatever unexpressed motivation is hidden in Adonijah's move to marry this woman, one of the effects his success would have had would have been the renewal of sexuality in the story of Solomon's ascent to the throne. Likewise, whatever the reasons for Solomon's refusal, it functions to maintain the (perhaps unwished for) continence of David. The fact that the woman in question, Abishag, is the same in each case heightens the likelihood that this suppression of sexuality was an intended effect of the narrative. Here we may see a perspective on sex and wisdom in transition from that of ch. 1 to that of 3–10. Another way to put Jobling's suggestion regarding the ideal 'Golden Age' suppression of sex is to say that the ideal *king* is one who does not have sex. If a statement about ideal kingship is the (at least one) point of the narrative, then Solomon proves himself worthy by refusing to allow his half-brother to reintroduce sexual activity to the scene of the throne.

Perhaps even more pointedly Solomon's action redresses a dynamic relating to royal aspirants and their father's concubines. During Absalom's rebellion, David had unconscionably abandoned his concubines in Jerusalem to the mercy of his son and the pragmatic counsel of Ahitophel (2 Sam. 16). Ken Stone argues that the major issue at stake here is not some supposed 'custom' that assigns royal legitimacy to a man who takes over the royal harem, but rather a matter of prestige and power calculated in the currency of honor and shame.

> By having sexual relations with ten concubines of David, Absalom has demonstrated David's inability to fulfill a crucial part of a culturally inscribed view of masculinity. As all Israel can see, David has been unable to maintain control over sexual access to the women of his house, and so has failed with regard to what is, in many cultures, a critical criterion for the assessment of manhood (1996: 121).

In the larger narrative picture, however, this episode marks both David and Absalom as failures: David is sexually shamed, but, in dishonoring his father in this manner, so is his son Absalom. From a wisdom reader's point of view, Absalom is a fool, in the sense of one who throws

---

18. The interpretation of this exchange, which leads to Adonijah's death, has rested for almost all commentators on a presumed custom according to which a claimant to the throne asserts symbolic power by having sex with the previous king's women (cf. 2 Sam. 3.6-11; 16.20-22). Ken Stone (1996) has recently helpfully reframed the issue as one of honor, and I shall take up his argument below. My point in the immediate context does not, however, ride on this debate.

off patriarchal constraint in the matter of sexuality. When Adonijah moves to narratively replicate Absalom's shame, wise Solomon appears as doubly honorable: not only does he *not* take his father's concubine himself, he prevents yet another upstart (foolish) son of David from doing so. Thus is one man proved fit for kingship and the other discredited.

If the ideal new regime replaces sex with wisdom, what then of the Strange Woman? The shift in Bathsheba's character from sex object to queen mother would seem to parallel this displacement rather nicely. But is the transformation complete? Does Bathsheba become a wise woman like King Lemuel's mother, who counsels her royal son on the dangers of strong drink and giving his strength to women (Prov. 31.1-9)?

Bathsheba has two related functions in 1 Kings 1–2: first, the successful mediation of kingship from her husband to her son; secondly, the failed mediation of sexuality from her husband/son to a royal contender. With respect to the first, debate among interpreters often centers on the relationship of Bathsheba to Nathan: did she act on her own motivation or was she simply the prophet's pawn? Though the initiative for her action appears to come from Nathan, there is evidence enough that Bathsheba possesses her own power, skills and motives for her role. At stake for her is the position of supreme female power in the land, that of queen mother. She stands to lose more than power, however, for Adonijah would suffer his opponents to live no more than did Solomon. Moreover, with Abishag in place as David's companion, if not his sexual partner, Bathsheba faces another potential rival, especially if Abishag herself is a pawn of the Adonijah faction. The narrator explicitly includes Abishag in the scene when Bathsheba confronts David, suggesting the underlying reality of this woman versus woman conflict. As we have seen, however, the potentially sexual character of this rivalry is suppressed. Nor does Bathsheba speak so as to curry favor. Despite her humble obeisance, her words are direct and demanding, repeating to David's face that he 'does not know' what is going on (1 Kgs 1.18). Nathan then enters to provide back-up, but it is for Bathsheba that David calls when he renders his decision.

At this moment (1.28), there is an apparent gap in the story's unfolding. Having heard Nathan's words, David calls for Bathsheba's presence, though there is no indication of her prior withdrawal. While one might suspect an editorial glitch, the textual gap may rather be a means for emphasizing a point, namely, the significance of Bathsheba's name, here with quite a different connotation from those noted above. In this context, the root *shb'* takes its alternate meaning of 'oath'. In an unusually emphatic phrasing, David says, 'Call for me to Bathsheba'. When she arrives, the king swears (*yishshaba'*) his oath. The call to Bathsheba, when one expects her to be already at the king's side, focuses attention on her name. This woman is identified as 'daughter of an oath' at the moment the oath is taken.

The characterization of Bathsheba has shifted, then, from that of a woman constituted by male desire to a woman constituted by words, an analog to her change in status from lover/wife to queen mother. The equating and sometimes displacing of sexuality with language is also a favorite move of Proverbs, whose editors perceive that 'death and life are in the hand of the tongue, and her lovers shall eat of her fruit' (Prov. 18.21). The essential distinguishing feature of Woman Wisdom and of the Strange Woman is found in the words each uses, one speaking truth and offering life, the other tempting with honeyed words that lead to death. So what, then, of Bathsheba's words and the oath that identifies her? Wisdom and strangeness work together here in mysterious ways. Even the most cursory reader of the story of David's reign notices that this is the first mention of his supposed oath promising Solomon the throne. The problem is not simply that Bathsheba's words about some earlier oath are deceitful, however, but that the *reader* 'does not know' one way or the other the intentions of these human minds, much less those of the deity. These words encode, that is to say, the fundamental theo-epistemological dilemma of wisdom. In Bathsheba, however, divine inscrutability meets its gendered narrative match, for it is a strange combination of a woman's desired body and her untestable words that engender the prototypical wise king. Like Woman Wisdom, Bathsheba might say, 'By me kings reign' (Prov. 8.15).

A final element in the strange wisdom of Bathsheba emerges in concert with the character of Abishag.[19] Just as, in their separate ways, they

19. Abishag's only other mark of identification, her home in Shunem, is itself an interesting study in wisdom and strangeness. Shunem otherwise appears only twice in the Bible. It is the home of a 'great woman' who might be considered quintessentially wise, one who recognizes, supports and testifies to the power of the prophet Elisha (2 Kgs 4.8-37; 8.1-6); it is also in the vicinity of the medium of Endor, with her house that opens to death (1 Sam. 28.3-25; cf. Prov. 2.18; 9.14, 18).

helped deprive Adonijah of the throne, now, together, they constitute 'the woman who brings death' to this fool who fails to understand his own desire in relation to female mediators of power. Stone may be correct that the issue in Adonijah's request for Abishag has more to do with attempting to regain prestige than a completely irrational symbolic assault on his half-brother's throne (1996: 127-33). If what I have argued above is correct, however, the text constructs this interchange as a comment on kingly wisdom, as well as on prestige. And Adonijah is twice foolish. Not only does his reach exceed his grasp, but both the object of his desire (his father's untouched woman) and his means to reach it (his brother's desexed mother) are, to use Qohelet's term, *hebel*, 'vapor': they mark a space absent of the sexuality that gives even wrong-headed desire its reason for being.

The character of Bathsheba, then, at this point in the story, has taken on that quality of asexual embodiment that also marks the figure of personified Wisdom in Proverbs. Yet in this transformation lies a deadly twist. For the death of Adonijah is narratively linked to Solomon's two other political assassinations, both of which were ascribed by his father to his 'wisdom'. The quick narrative movement from these last words of David (2.1-9), to his own death (2.10-12), to Adonijah's conversation with Bathsheba (2.13-25) construes her, I would suggest, as wisdom's new transmitter. Bathsheba replaces the dead king as advisor to Solomon and sends Adonijah to his death. It is not surprising that David's deadly definition of wisdom would come to rest in the hand of his erstwhile Strange Woman, now functioning as wise mother of their son.

1 Kings 3

The bloodshed ended, the first two verses of this chapter point to two crucial themes in the Solomon narrative: his foreign marriages and the building of the temple. The tale then turns to a third theme, that of wisdom. In language redolent of Proverbs, 1 Kgs 3.3-15 relates Solomon's choice for wisdom, and Yhwh's promise of riches, honor and long life as well. This wisdom is immediately tested (3.16-28) with the dilemma posed by two prostitutes, prototypical strange women.

In the latter episode, one woman speaks, describing a situation in which each of the two, who share a house (a brothel?), had borne a child within the space of three days. She claims that the other woman had lain on her son, killing him, and then traded the dead child for the living one in her own bosom. The second woman, however, claims that the living child is hers. Solomon proposes dividing the living child with a sword in order to apportion him equitably, an order resisted by, and thus marking, the child's true mother.

This story reveals both the social reality and the literary manipulation of the role of prostitute. The prostitute is the tolerated outsider to patriarchal urban culture, both despised by society and enjoyed by the men who run it. As a woman whose sexuality is uncontrolled by either father or husband, she represents on one level a threat to the very fabric of society. Yet she is also one of its underpinnings, insofar as she allows men the sexual outlet that restriction on *all* women would preclude. The prostitute embodies, then, the patriarchal big lie. The liminal position of this social role, combined with its part in the ideological cover-up, generates the social expectation that all one would hear from such a woman would be lies (cf. Bird 1989a: 133). As Bird suggests, however, this stereotype is confronted with another one, namely, the mother who loves her child so much as to surrender him rather than have him harmed. Solomon's wisdom is manifest in his ability to uncover one stereotype hidden beneath another.

Considered from the perspective of wisdom thought, these female characters yield another reading as well. In Proverbs, the task of the sage is to discern one female figure, Woman Wisdom who brings social order, from another who is portrayed in often similar terms, Woman Stranger or Folly, the promiscuous purveyor of social chaos. Significantly, these 'women' are known by their speech: Wisdom's 'mouth will utter truth' (Prov. 8.7), while the seductive Stranger's 'lips drip honey and her speech is smoother than oil' (Prov. 5.3). Female sexuality that exists outside of male control functions as a metaphor for deceitful speech, and vice versa; the character of the 'harlot' thus poses the ultimate riddle to kingly wisdom. Solomon demonstrates his ability to bring social order by dividing from the chaos of female sexuality before him the 'true speech' of the mother, the woman whose sexuality is (stereotypically, if not actually) controlled, and thus acceptable. Turning the sex–language metaphor back on itself, one could say that Solomon's discernment makes him father to the child, the one who provides it with (new) life and symbolically rehabilitates its mother from harlotry as well (Reinhartz 1994: 54). By discriminating between these sexually defined women, Solomon resolves the thematic tension and seems to absolve the lineage of David's sexual folly: the foolish father is redeemed in the wise son (Fontaine 1986: 72). Neither resolution nor absolution, however, will last the generation.

Chapter 3 is crucial to the larger narrative structure. It begins a new unit while also connecting the story of Solomon's reign back to that of David. Carole Fontaine (1986) has detailed how wisdom vocabulary, theme and structure link the authorization of Solomon's rule in 1 Kings 3 to 2 Samuel 11–12, the affair of Bathsheba and David that culminated in his birth. David made a choice definitive of folly, the choice for adultery, resulting in an illicit pregnancy, deceit and murder (cf. Prov. 6.24-35). 'And the thing that David had done was evil in Yhwh's eyes' (2 Sam. 11.27b). Solomon, of course, chooses wisdom, bringing him riches, honor and long life as well. The narrative comment parallels that of 2 Sam. 11.27, to make one of wisdom's favorite antitheses: 'And it was good in Yhwh's eyes that Solomon had asked this thing' (1 Kgs 3.10). The foolish father is brought to judgment with the death of Bathsheba's first child and the pronouncing of a curse upon his house, while the outcome of the wise son's judgment is a living child restored to its mother. By wisdom, 'rulers decree what is just' (Prov. 8.15b). Solomon's redemption of David's folly may, then, redeem the wisdom of the David narrative as well, setting this positively valued judicial wisdom over against the at best ambiguous political craft of 2 Samuel 13–1 Kings 2.[20]

Jobling adds another dimension to the wisdom of ch. 3, in keeping with his perspective on the suppression of sexuality in the myth of the Golden Age. Wisdom, he argues, correlates negatively with sexuality. On this reading, one would say not simply that Solomon chose 'right sex' over David's 'wrong sex', but that, in choosing wisdom, Solomon chose *against* sex.

> Wisdom as a sex-substitute may also be in play at the very beginning of the account of the Golden Age. It is Dame Wisdom who in 3.5-14 [the dream at Gibeon] has Solomon's nocturnal attention, not his new bride (the 'foreign woman'); the early introduction of Pharaoh's daughter (3.1) functions to establish such a contrast (Jobling 1991b: 66).

Although in pursuing his agenda Jobling resists attaching as much importance to foreignness as to sexuality, both of these factors seem to

---

20. Gordon (1995: 103) sees God's statement in 3.11 that Solomon 'did not ask for the death of [his] enemies' as 'an oblique commentary on his previous actions'. Why should he have to request their death when he has already accomplished it!

me very much in play in this case, as the quoted statement reveals.[21] In terms of my own argument, sexuality (at least, 'wrong sex') and foreignness are to a significant degree metaphorical substitutes, each evoking the other. The textual strategy in ch. 3 strikes me as one of 'management' of sexuality by means of these qualifiers, rather than outright rejection. Wisdom is indeed a sex-substitute, but her rival in 1 Kgs 3.1 is not 'all women' but rather a *foreign* woman. As in Proverbs, moreover, so also in 1 Kings 3: foreignness is itself only one aspect of the more complex paradigm of strangeness. Its figuring as 'wrong sex' comes quickly to the fore in the persons of the prostitutes, whose sexuality is also, *mutatis mutandis*, 'managed' by wisdom, the proper distinctions made and socially acceptable relationships symbolically established.

It is not impossible that this narrative management of sexuality expresses on one level a desire to be rid of sex altogether. There is, however, yet another issue at stake in this narrative manipulation and sublimation of sexuality, namely, the continuation of the Davidic covenant—which is to say, in practical terms, lineage. 'One can hardly fail to be struck by the absence [in chs. 3–10] of the theme of royal succession, so central to chaps. 1, 2 and 11 (and of course to the whole David narrative)' (Jobling 1991b: 63). Because sex is necessary precisely to the patriarchal values of lineage and inheritance, its suppression is an operation that requires considerable ideological finesse, a finesse evident, I would suggest, in 1 Kings 3. The question of who would use these particular rhetorical means is a question still to be considered. To conclude that wisdom sublimates sex in the Solomon narrative, however, raises another question that may help direct this inquiry: what is the relationship between the issue of Solomon's mouth and the (non)issue of his body?

1 Kings 3 not only looks backward to 2 Samuel; it also turns forward to the ensuing chapters of the Solomon narrative, where the themes from 3.1-2 of foreign women and house-building, along with the theme of wisdom from 3.3-28, play key roles.

---

21. That Jobling pushes his point too far is evident, I think, in his statement that the text 'simply expel[s] the foreign women from the narrative space of chaps. 3–10' (1991b: 63). This ignores the several references to Pharaoh's daughter and the Queen of Sheba, as well as the strange (though perhaps Israelite) harlot mothers.

1 Kings 4–9
In 4.1-19, having divided the women with the threat to divide the child, Solomon turns to dividing the kingdom into 12 districts, not conforming to old tribal boundaries, and assigning them (along with two of his daughters) to his officers. Each administrative district is charged with supplying food for the king and his household for one month out of the year. For the peasant women and men of Israel, the combination of divide-and-control districting with the centralization of planning and taxes to support the king must have had deleterious effects, in spite of the editor's saccharine comment that 'Judah and Israel...ate and drank and were happy' (4.20). Here we have Jobling's ideal Golden Age economics, an economics driven by the motor of wisdom, the ' "surplus value" which, residing in Solomon, enables him to accomplish his "economic miracle"' (1991b: 64; cf. 1 Kgs 5.1-8 [Eng.: 4.21-28]). In accordance with the formula in Proverbs (e.g. 8.15-21), the establishment of social control and the abundance it brings to the king is narratively linked to Solomon's God-given wisdom and understanding. This wisdom also produces a lot of good wisdom-speech (3000 proverbs and 1005 songs) and an international reputation (5.9-14 [Eng.: 4.29-34]).

1 Kings 5–9 detail Solomon's building of the house of Yhwh (5.15–6.38 [Eng.: 5.1–6.38]), his own house (7.1-12), and the bronze and other metalwork for the temple (7.13-51), followed by his ceremony of consecration (8.1-66) and Yhwh's response (9.1-9). Just as the temple-building narrative provides a literary-structural center to the Solomon story,[22] the image of the house is also at the center of a web of associated images and concepts. Fundamental to this network is the intimate linkage of Yhwh's house to the promise of a dynastic house to David (Savran 1987: 159) and to the houses of women. Although it is often assumed that the material on the temple comes from the hand of a 'Deuteronomist' who is the temple's chief ideologue, not all of these associations are entirely positive.

The temple-building sequence is surrounded and interlaced with allusions to Solomon's other competing loves: the daughter of Pharaoh, for whom he builds a house like his own (3.1; 7.8; 9.16, 24); his other building projects, including his own house, which are twice described as 'all that he desired' (9.1, 19); the other foreign wives whom he 'loves' and for whom he builds high places (11.1-2, 7); and the wisdom

22. So Frisch (1991a: 10-12). Though his structural analysis is disputed by Parker (1991), it is one, though perhaps not the only, intelligible reading of the text.

of God, which he will forsake at his own peril (3.3-28; 5.9-14 [4.29-34]; 5.21 [5.7]; 5.26 [5.12]; 9.2). Overlapping these allusions to women and wisdom are also references to Solomon's international relations, reflecting the ambivalence Israel will feel toward foreigners. Solomon's widespread reputation for wisdom (5.9-14 [4.29-34]) and his avuncular relationship with King Hiram of Tyre, who supplies Solomon with both encouragement and timber for the temple (5.5-15 [1-11]), are noted with apparent approval: Solomon's dealings and treaty with Hiram are designated as part of the wisdom Yhwh gave Solomon (5.26 [12]). The same passage, however, records without comment the enormous cost of this treaty to Israel in food (5.25 [11]) and forced labor (5.27-31 [13-17]). And how are we to evaluate the parallel witness to Solomon's wisdom by both the omniscient narrator (speaking on Yhwh's behalf?) and a foreign king?

> And men came from all peoples to hear the wisdom of Solomon, and from all the kings of the earth, who had heard of his wisdom (5.14 [4.34]).

> When Hiram heard the words of Solomon, he rejoiced greatly, and said, 'Blessed be Yhwh this day, who has given to David a wise son to be over this great people' (5.21 [5.7]).

The metalwork for the temple is done by an artisan of Tyre, also named Hiram, of whom two notable things are said (7.13-14). First, he is 'filled with wisdom, understanding and knowledge' to do any work in bronze. While 'wisdom' often refers to a person's intellectual and moral capacity, it appears here in its most concrete sense, as the consummate skill of a craftsperson worthy to do the temple's work. Secondly, Hiram is the son of an Israelite widow and a man of Tyre. This characterization of mixed ancestry may suggest the writer's perspective on the temple itself: it is the product of Solomon's treaty with the foreign king and will bear the burden of foreign worship within it. Indeed, the material of Hiram's craft, bronze (*nehoshet*), intersecting with the word for serpent (*nehash*), provides the name for a temple icon, Nehushtan. This bronze serpent bears a notable theological ambiguity (2 Kgs 18.4; cf. Num. 21.9).

A further moment of tension connecting the themes of women, foreignness and the temple occurs in 1 Kgs 8.41-43 and 9.24. The first passage appears in the middle of Solomon's dedicatory prayer, where he asks Yhwh, quite remarkably, to hear the prayer of 'a foreigner, who is not of your people Israel' who will come and 'pray *toward this house*'. The second (ironically?) notes that the quintessential foreigner, Pharaoh's daughter, 'went up from the city of David *toward her own house*', a movement that, in contrast to Solomon's prayer, foreshadows the turning of his heart *away* from Yhwh's house by the strange women in ch. 11. Just as the first mention of Yhwh's house comes in the same sentence as the notice of Solomon's marriage to Pharaoh's daughter (3.1), so also its completion is tied to her house.

What is the rhetorical effect of this interweaving of Solomon's temple-building with his wisdom, his foreign women, other foreigners, and other buildings? It points, I would suggest, to a flaw in the lovingly described temple construction, a fault-line also traceable in Jobling's analysis of the tensive interplay of conditionality and unconditionality of divine blessing (1991b: 68-69). The temple, a fundamental component of Yhwh's unconditional dynastic promise to David (2 Sam. 7.13), is marked in 1 Kings with the conditions of its destruction, so powerfully described in 9.6-9: '[T]he house that I have consecrated to my name I will cast out from before me, and Israel will be a proverb (*mashal*) and a taunt among all the peoples. This house will become a ruin…' (vv. 7b-8a).[23] There is no small irony in the fact that this baleful warning places in parallel the notion that 'Israel will become a proverb (*mashal*)' with the image of the house as ruin. Proverbs are the hallmark of Solomon's wisdom, that which 'people came from all the nations to hear' (5.12, 14 [4.32, 34]), just as the temple, to which foreigners will come, is its material manifestation. In spite of Solomon's ardent prayer for those who turn toward and pray in 'this house', however, this structure marked by foreign wisdom will not save them; its ruin is foreseen.

What then would have saved them? Many interpreters, as already noted, have argued that the point of this narrative, as far as wisdom is concerned, is to make it subordinate to the Torah. Wisdom is good, but not good enough; obedience to the law is paramount. Conditionality, moreover, is presumably the name of the deuteronomic game, however much the spell of unconditionality, 'the charm of the Golden Age' (Jobling 1991b: 69), may hover over things. Conditionality hinges in this story on one thing and one alone: the Strange Woman in her

---

23. Reading, with many translators, the Syriac and Old Latin, *le'iyyin*, for MT's *'elyon*.

multiple aspects of sexuality, foreignness and idolatry, her essential-
izing of disobedience to the Torah. But does not the fault-line of foreignness in the construction of Yhwh's house suggest already a kind of
fatalism, a prediction of the foreignness that will subvert Solomon's
wisdom? The strange building that Solomon 'desires' foreshadows the
strange women he will 'love'. To put things in Proverbs's terms, does
not this wise and strange house for Israel's god embody the paradoxical
insight that the Wisdom who builds her house and the Stranger who
tears it down (Prov. 14.1) are one and the same?

What engenders this paradox and its fatalism? On one reading, at
least, the answer is sex. The sex that is required for the building of
David's dynastic house, for the Davidic covenant (and its ideological
predecessor, the Abraham covenant) to perpetuate itself. The sex that is
nonetheless found by the editor of the Solomon narrative (who? why?)
so in need of management, to the point of suppression. The sex, once
qualified by the ideological tautology of '*foreign* sex', that is so convenient to blame for the fall. Sex is necessary for the covenant to continue, yet sex is strange and thus must be narratized as 'foreign'. The
logic of the paradox, and its inexorability, is well marked in the text.
Jobling notes (1991b: 64) the 'quantification' of wisdom in 5.9 (4.29):
'And God gave Solomon wisdom and understanding beyond measure,
and largeness of mind like the sand on the seashore', a metaphor used a
few verses earlier for the abundant population of Judah and Israel in
Solomon's time (4.20). This metaphor, found verbatim in Gen. 22.17,
also expresses the fulfillment of God's promise to Abraham to make his
'seed as numerous as the stars of the heaven and as the sand that is on
the seashore'. Somehow, then, in the narrator's ideal world, wisdom is
to be Solomon's seed, replacing the more materially substantial seed of
Abraham.[24] Biology cannot be so easily done away with in the real
world, however. If quantified wisdom stands for quantified seed in chs.
4–5, quantified sex returns with a vengeance in 11.3 (Jobling 1991b:
66), matching with its enormity (700 princesses and 300 concubines)
the virulence of its foreignness.

Wisdom is sex, sex is Strangeness. The house will be built, the house
must fall: David's house, erected on strange sex; Yhwh's house, erected
with strange wisdom; Solomon, caught in the vise.

---

24. Cf. Eilberg-Schwartz's (1990: 229-34) analysis of the rabbis and their
replacement of the seed of the body with the seed of the mind.

1 Kings 10–11

I began this chapter by proposing an image of 'Woman Solomon'. The point at which 'Woman Solomon' as a reading strategy most clearly intersects with what happens in the text is in the Queen of Sheba episode (10.1-13). Sheba is characterized as a woman who is both wise and strange, and thus set in complementary relationship to the king.

The Sheba episode has had a roller coaster history in recent interpretation, some readers finding it pro-Solomon (Scott [1955], Jobling [1991b], Frisch [1991a], Fox [1995]) and others anti-Solomon (Lasine [1995], Parker [1992]). Brettler (1991) proposes that it was originally pro-Solomon, but has been become part of DH's critique of Solomon. The pro-Solomon readers focus on the story's glorification of the king's wisdom, while the antis stress its representation of Solomon's accumulated wealth, which is narratively linked to his horses from Egypt (10.28) and many wives (11.1-8), three things forbidden the king in Deut. 17.16-17. To the extent that these assessments of the episode base themselves on analysis of literary structure (as do all but Scott and Lasine), the arguments tend to be circular: it is determined on some other grounds that the narrative shifts from a positive view of Solomon to a negative one at this or that point (9.1, or 9.26, or 11.1), and thus 10.1-13 is judged pro or anti to suit. Scott's approach is source-critical rather than structural, but has a similar problem of circularity. What, then, can be said of 10.1-13?

Brettler's statement strikes me as prima facie correct. 'The texts between 9.26 and 10.29 were not written as anti-Solomonic texts, and were probably originally positive illustrations of his wisdom' (Brettler 1991: 96).[25] The question then becomes: when did they become negative, if that is indeed what has happened, or, alternatively, what is such apparently positive material doing in a narrative about to go bad? As I have noted, arguments based on literary-structural data alone are quite inconclusive: each of the scholars just mentioned can support his reading in a reasonable way. Clearly, then, a sense of what is structurally

---

25. It is, of course, possible to assume this material was intended ironically from the start, on analogy to the saccharine perspective in 1 Kgs 4 on the people's comfort and pleasure in the face of centralization and taxation. There is a difference, however, in 9.26–10.29, in that Solomon's wealth here comes from foreign trade, rather than out of the blood of his own people. It is well within reason, therefore, to imagine a straightforward reading of this passage, however much the present context may temper that with irony.

important (or, in Lasine's case, the unimportance of structure) depends to some degree on the reader. My own interest in the representation of female wisdom and strangeness inclines me, in the case of the Queen of Sheba, to conversation with Jobling and Brettler, both of whom, despite their different understandings of the episode's role in the narrative structure, take up issues of importance to my argument.

In Jobling's analysis, as we have seen, ch. 10 provides the concluding moment in the tale of the Solomonic Golden Age begun in ch. 3. These chapters depict, he argues, an era marked by a sexuality sublimated in wisdom, an economics that has repressed its egalitarian heritage in favor of celebrating royal wealth, and a theology of unconditional blessing in tension with one of conditionality. Sex provides the resolution to the tensions, explaining how unconditionality became conditioned, while shifting the blame from wealth. The fact that sex is absent from the relationship of Solomon and Sheba keeps this episode in the Golden Age. Brettler, on the other hand, places heavy weight on the strong verbal linkage between 3.1-2, with its references to Pharaoh's daughter and Solomon's sacred and secular building projects, and 9.24-25, with its similar vocabulary and concerns:

> And Solomon made a marriage alliance with Pharaoh, king of Egypt, and he took as wife the daughter of Pharaoh and brought her to the city of David, until he had finished building his house, and the house of Yhwh and the wall around Jerusalem. But the people were sacrificing on the high places because a house for the name of Yhwh was not built until those days (3.1-2).

> But the daughter of Pharaoh went up from the city of David to her house which he had built her. (Then he built the Millo.) Three times a year, Solomon offered up burnt offerings and peace offerings upon the altar that he built for Yhwh, and incense with it, before Yhwh. And he completed the house (9.24-25).

Having thus, by means of this inclusio, sealed off 3.1–9.25 from what follows, Brettler finds a deuteronomistic thematizing of the remainder of the narrative in terms of wealth (including the Queen of Sheba passage, 9.26–10.25), horses from Egypt (10.26-29) and foreign wives (11.1-10). Thus, Brettler argues, while the Sheba episode may have been composed as part of a celebration of Solomon's wisdom, it must now, per Deut. 17.16-17, be *read* as an indictment of his wealth. Each of these analyses, contradictory as they are with respect to 10.1-13, strikes me as having merit. I shall begin by extending Jobling's Golden

Age analysis, and then consider it in relationship to Brettler's alternative.

In 1 Kings 3, Solomon chooses wisdom (implicitly construed as a female personification, in contrast to his foreign wife) over riches and honor, though God then promises the latter as well. The following scene confirms the king's wisdom by his ability to order with justice the chaos represented by the two prostitutes, 'strange women' within their own society. The riddle presented by (indeed, embodied in) the prostitutes is thematically matched in the final scene by the Queen of Sheba, who comes to test Solomon with riddles (Reinhartz 1994: 53), a form of speech that is crucial to the wisdom tradition (Prov. 1.6). Just as 'all Israel' perceived Solomon's God-given wisdom to 'do justice' in the case of the prostitutes (3.28), so also the queen acknowledges Yhwh's love for Israel in making Solomon king 'to do justice and righteousness' (10.9). The vocabulary is again akin to Proverbs, where Woman Wisdom says of herself:

> By me kings reign,
> and rulers decree rightness;
> by me rulers rule,
> and nobles, all the judges of rightness...
> I walk in the way of righteousness,
> along the paths of justice,
> endowing with wealth those who love me,
> and filling their treasuries (Prov. 8.15-16, 20-21).

Although the Queen of Sheba acknowledges Yhwh as the lover of Solomon and the source of his rule, it is difficult not to see her own character as a narrative transmutation of Proverbs's Woman Wisdom. True to this role, she fulfills Yahweh's earlier promise by bringing the riches and honor that should accompany Solomon's choice for wisdom.

Sheba is also, paradoxically, a Strange Woman, a characterization highlighted most obviously by her foreign nationality, but also subtly by the structural relationship of her story to ch. 3. First, the 'justice' she recognizes in Solomon is linked both verbally ('do justice') and thematically (the solving of riddles) to the story of the prostitutes, with their estranged sexuality. It is not just *women* who test Solomon (so Jobling 1991b: 66), but *strange women*. Secondly, by appearing as, in effect, Woman Wisdom in the flesh, this foreign queen re-embodies the disembodied wisdom chosen by Solomon in ch. 3. In so doing, she also forges the missing link between this wisdom and the real sexuality of the foreign princess (3.1), which were narratively divided in Solomon's 'ideal' choice. It is no accident that Sheba's story follows closely the narrative's final mention of Pharaoh's daughter in 9.24. Whereas ch. 3 divided male wisdom from female strangeness, however, the Queen of Sheba unites wisdom and strangeness in one female persona.

Sexuality remains undercover in 1 Kings 10, but barely. As is typical in wisdom rhetoric, this tale of verbal sparring only partly conceals an erotic subtext. The contest between Solomon and the Queen is framed as a language game, a riddle match that Solomon wins, as he had solved the prostitutes' dilemma, by discerning the truth amid trickery: 'there was nothing hidden from the king' (10.3). While the narrative speaks of Solomon's victory of wits, however, later tradition will elaborate on its unspoken possibility of sexual relationship between the wise king and the foreign queen: 'King Solomon gave to the Queen of Sheba every desire she expressed' (10.13).[26] In the foreground is the power of wisdom; in the background, a seductive strangeness that can be suppressed but not eliminated.

Commentators sometimes suggest that Solomon's relationship to Sheba, especially its end in her departure, epitomizes the wise man's relationship to women. According to Jobling, it represents the appropriate Golden Age suppression of sexuality in favor of wisdom. Reinhartz puts a feminist slant on the relationship.

> It is worth noting that the only relationship of equality portrayed between Solomon and a woman is one which does not end in marriage; she is the queen whom he does not marry. Indeed, to have married her would have been to destroy the parity of their relationship. To demote her from her unique position, turning her merely into another foreign woman in Solomon's massive harem is a transformation which would have run completely counter to her characterization in 1 Kgs 10 (1994: 51 n.).

Without denying the validity of either of these perspectives, I wonder whether the story of the departed queen does not also suggest a wish unfulfilled. On one level, we might imagine a glimmer of a sustainable egalitarian relationship, of the union of a wise Israelite king and a wise foreign queen who, fulfilling each others' desires, resolve the fundamental polarities that constitute the many facets of 'us' and 'them'.

In a somewhat different spin, I suggested in Chapter 2's discussion of the trickster that this character represents the mythic perception that

---

26. See Fontaine (1997: 219) for a survey of texts from the later Jewish and Islamic traditions.

chaos must be embraced as part of the dynamic of sustaining order. Though 1 Kings 10 is not a trickster tale as such, the trickster's shadow rests on the wise strangeness of the riddling Queen. In this mythic sense, she embodies in her own person the balance of order and chaos. She is an ideal figure, not, notably, in her absolute purity, but in her divine confluence of all that is both wise and strange. That Solomon lets her slip through his fingers may be both tragic and necessary. Ideals are unattainable; a fall is unavoidable. Or, to sharpen the point, perhaps we must once again follow Jobling and concede that, from the biblical point of view, the sexuality necessarily implied in an ongoing relationship is finally unable to be apprehended as part of the ideal. The queen may embody it, but Solomon cannot claim it. Nonetheless, the seeds of resistance produce their own fruit: Solomon stumbles on what he cannot name.

If her combined wisdom and strangeness ambiguate the character of the Queen of Sheba, further complications appear when the characters of the king and queen are triangulated with Woman Wisdom of Proverbs. The net effect is the melding of personae, with Solomon's becoming dominant. We have already called attention to the connections between the queen and Wisdom. There are, in addition, certain parallels in the speech and action of Solomon and the queen. In 2.45, Solomon blesses himself (!) for establishing David's throne, while in 3.7, he more properly acknowledges Yhwh for making him king. Sheba resolves this tension, blessing Yhwh for making Solomon king (10.9). Similarly, the queen's gifts to Solomon (10.10) are matched by his to her (10.13). The wise king whose own desires have been fulfilled (9.1, 19) fulfills in turn the wise queen's desires (10.13). Reading this episode intertextually with Proverbs, we find the figures of Solomon and Woman Wisdom also linked. Important for our purposes is the representation of Wisdom, like Solomon, as the builder of a house (Prov. 9.1). No one, moreover, has ever been like Solomon with respect to wisdom and no one ever will be (1 Kgs 3.12); likewise, nothing one desires can compare with Woman Wisdom (Prov. 3.15). In a standard wisdom form, Woman Wisdom declares 'happy' one who listens to her (Prov. 8.34). Using the same form, Sheba declares 'happy' those who hear Solomon's wisdom (1 Kgs 10.8).[27] Finally, Kings's narrative of the riddle-master is epito-

27. And who are the happy ones? In Proverbs, it is the lover who waits and watches at Wisdom's gates and door (8.34). In Kings, 'servants' are named, along with another group whose identity is clouded by textual uncertainty: the MT says

mized by Proverbs's presentation of Solomon as authorial sage par excellence, the one who understands 'the words of the wise and their riddles' (1.1, 6).

What has happened here? Woman Wisdom, in the form of Sheba, has confronted the king. Unlike Wisdom, however, who powerfully 'pours out her spirit' (Prov. 1.23), Sheba's encounter with Solomon leaves her without 'spirit' (10.5). The narrative thus seems to resolve one of the oddities of Proverbs, namely, the mirrored femininity of Wisdom and Strangeness. While patriarchy teaches us to expect a Strange Woman, it also leaves us surprised to find her countered by a Wise Woman, rather than a Wise Man. By the end of the Queen of Sheba episode, however, conventional expectations have been fulfilled. On one level, Woman Wisdom has lost her spirit to, been absorbed into, the Royal Man. On the narrative surface, the woman departs (10.13) and the man remains, but the effect is the same. This analysis leaves us not far, then, from Jobling's observations about the depiction of sexuality in mythic narratives (1991b: 59), where the male is the 'real human' or, in this case, the 'truly wise'. On the other hand, the spirit taken by this man was not only that of Wisdom, but also of a Strange Woman. In this way, as well as in the sublimated sexuality of their wise discourse, Solomon's fall is anticipated in his relationship with the Queen of Sheba, at the same time that his ideal kingship is celebrated.

What, then, of Brettler's view that 9.24-25, understood in relationship to 3.1-2, marks a distinct structural transition from a positive to a negative view of Solomon? There are two points here that, in my view, must be given serious attention. The first is the thematic connection of 9.26–11.9 to the law on the king in Deut. 17.16-17. The second is the odd, intimate contiguity, to which I have already directed attention, of the Strange Woman and the temple in the two structuring passages. I shall address the first of these issues here, and return to the second in the next section.

Jobling's article plays down the influence of the law of the king on 1 Kings 10–11. He observes that, while the foreign wives are portrayed

---

'men'; the Greek and Syriac presuppose the Hebrew for 'women'. English translators usually render the latter choice as 'wives', which is fair enough, given the numbers of those registered in ch. 11. On the other hand, I have found no translator of the MT suggesting 'husbands' as an alternative to 'men'. To the extent that Solomon becomes (Woman) Wisdom, however, this textual duplicity seems to give the reader a quick wink.

in strongly negative terms, Solomon's abundant wealth and Egyptian horses are simply noted in 10.14-29, without evaluative comment; indeed, the Queen of Sheba episode actually puts a positive spin on his wealth. Thus, as we have seen, Jobling views sexuality as the real narrative issue. Brettler in effect counters this argument by appeal to redactional activity. The wealth and horses material was originally positive, he argues, while the material castigating the foreign wives is from the later hand of the Deuteronomist, thus explicitly negative. The completed text, however, must be read through the lens of Deuteronomy 17, with its negative assessm§ent controlling the whole unit.

Although I find it hard to resist seeing the influence of the deuteronomic kingship law in this material, I think Brettler's reading needs nuancing. It is not impossible, as he argues, that a final redactor intended to provide a negative lens on originally positive material. This possibility does not, however, erase the disproportionately negative weight put on the foreign wives. Jobling's perception here seems apropos: sex is made to shoulder the blame for what is at worst a mixed opinion on Solomon's wealth. Jobling may go too far, however, in asserting the absolutely positive tone of ch. 10. Like the Queen of Sheba episode at the beginning of the chapter, the references to wealth and horses at the end take on an uneasy quality when read as part of the text's final form and in relation to the law on the king. The chapter as a whole seems transitional in this regard. Chapters 10 and 11 together *interpret* Deut. 17.16-17, however, rather than simply reproducing it. This is true in two senses. First, as Jobling notes, the problem with women is rhetorically stressed. Secondly, and crucially, however, these chapters emphatically add the element of *foreignness* to what in Deut. 17.17 is only a limitation on the *number* of the king's wives.

There are two other questions to be put to Brettler's final form reading of the Queen of Sheba episode as anti-Solomonic. First the history of interpretation demonstrates the ease with which the episode can be read, even in its present context, as a glorification of Solomon, his wisdom *and* his wealth. The happy confluence of wisdom and wealth in Proverbs and in traditional narrative generally (so Lasine) suggests that some ancient readers may also have missed whatever irony may play in the narrative's redactional shadows. A final redactor who wanted to criticize Solomon's wealth would have had ample, neutrally described evidence for this in 9.26-28 and 10.11-12, 14-25, without incorporating the fairy-tale-like story of the Queen of Sheba. Why, then, was it included, and by whom? The second, and related, question that must be raised about Brettler's work concerns his assumption that, while the original, pro-Solomon meaning of the text would have focused on his *wisdom*, a final form reading would be interested exclusively in its contextually negative comment on his *wealth*. Again, however, it seems to me it would take an extraordinarily blind eye to block out the wisdom theme, especially given its prominence in the narrative as a whole. Wisdom may be criticized in some way, but it is hardly ignorable. And so, again, we return to the question of who would have had an interest in maintaining or including a vibrant, though foreign, female embodiment of Wisdom in a narrative about to founder on the Strange Woman.

We return, in other words, to the question of a sociohistorical contextualization of the Solomon narrative in its final form.

Solomon and Proverbs: Canon and Authority

In spite of their reflections on the intent and/or ideology of the 'Deuteronomist', neither Brettler (1991) nor Jobling (1991b) (at first) addresses the question of the sociohistorical location of this narrator/redactor. In a recent reprinting of Jobling's essay (1997), however, he includes a new paragraph indicating his inclination toward a postexilic dating, pushing it closer to the time when the book of Proverbs took shape. The Solomon narrative, with its similar thematics of women, wisdom and strangeness, can certainly be read as tightly interwoven with Proverbs. The connections in vocabulary and images point, moreover, to similarities in terms of a larger agenda. Let me make three points in this regard.

First, the words of Solomon in Proverbs are surrounded by female images and voices: Woman Wisdom and Woman Stranger in the opening chapters and the queen mother of Lemuel and the woman of worth at the end. The character of Solomon in Kings is likewise surrounded by women wise and strange: his queen-mother Bathsheba, Abishag, two prostitutes, and his Egyptian wife at the beginning; the Queen of Sheba and the multitude of his (foreign) wives and concubines at the end. Like Proverbs, Kings plays with variations on the notion of strangeness. Taken together, Solomon's female companions and interlocutors comprise a remarkable set of variations on the Strange Woman, spotlighting at different moments her attributes of uncontrolled sexuality, duplicitous speech, foreign nationality and strange gods, as well as the downfall—loss of inheritance—threatened to her lover. These female characters also represent the range of the Strange Woman's relationship to Woman Wisdom. At the opposite extremes of the spectrum stand disembodied Wisdom, chosen by Solomon in his dream, in contrast to the multifold Strangeness of his multiple wives. The story of the prostitute mothers depicts (male) wisdom's victory over (female) strangeness. Sheba and Bathsheba, however, one at either end of the narrative, cloud the picture. Each in her own way embodies a wisdom and a strangeness that cannot be separated. Herein lies a fourth connotation of Bathsheba's name: she is, curiously, daughter of Sheba. Each stands, moreover, in important relationship to the will of God. While Bathsheba brings a king to the throne when God's will is narratively in doubt, Sheba proclaims that state of affairs to be not simply God's will, but the result of God's love. More overtly than in Proverbs, then, Kings plays with the tensive relationships embodied in Woman Wise and Strange, refusing to reduce her into polar opposition.

Secondly, Proverbs seems concerned to purify the (e)strange(d) wisdom of Solomon represented in Kings. Like David's acts of adultery and murder, Solomon's ultimate sin against his wisdom and his God should be, to the text's moral logic, beyond redemption. The irrational willfulness of the canon with respect to the heroic stature of both father and son depends on readers willing to leap this moral chasm. Chronicles solves the problem by cutting out the offending texts. Proverbs, however, takes another tack, accomplishing the feat by, in effect, throwing invisible ink on Solomon's traitorous body and redeeming him by his mouth. In Proverbs, Solomon is all words. The *content* of these words—women, wisdom and strangeness—makes abundantly clear the problematic connection of their speaker to the narrative, but the problem is covered up by the absence of his body. The narrative has moved in this direction, but not without ambiguity: the tension between the absence and the presence of Solomon's body is narratized in the desexualization of his strange mother, in his remothering of the prostitute, and in his (apparently!) exclusively verbal relationship with the Queen of Sheba. Even his ultimate sin is cast as much in theological as in sexual terms. But always sex lurks under the surface of the words. Proverbs in effect completes what Kings has begun, though with no small irony in return, for Solomon's disembodied voice there gives body to both Woman Wisdom and the Strange Woman.

Thirdly, between the pious wisdom of Solomon's words and the sinful strangeness of his body lies another fractured image, that of the temple. Commended by a foreign king, built of foreign materials, decorated by a mixed-blood craftsman, literarily bound in its conception and its completion to a foreign wife and her own house, the temple is at best a tarnished crown to Solomon's wisdom. If a 'Deuteronomist' tells this tale, it is one whose purported protemple theology has been chastened by history. The line between the temple and all Solomon's other building projects—including high places for foreign gods—is blurred. All are the products of Solomon's 'desire' (9.1, 19).

What might a reader understand from this picture? Does the limning of the temple with the language of foreignness and desire suggest a context of contention? It would not be impossible to read the Solomon narrative as a text of resistance to *re*building—or, more likely, to the rebuilt—temple. I will take up in Chapters 5 and 7 some of the dynamics of what was likely a multifaceted intra-Israelite struggle over leadership and identity in the postexilic period that certainly involved the rhetoric of foreignness as an invective against other Israelites. The emphasis on illicit foreign unions in 1 Kings 11 fits, to a certain degree, the picture of Ezra–Nehemiah's rejection of 'foreign' wives (whatever they may have meant by that characterization, and whenever these books were written), and Neh. 13.26-29 styles Solomon as the paradigmatic sinner in an attack on a defiled priesthood. Yet there are, as Chapter 1 has suggested, differences in the rhetorical logics of these texts.

Proverbs seems to strike the balance a bit differently. For one thing, as in Kings, there is an inherent interest in preserving a more positive sense of Solomon, as well as of a woman who is wise while appearing strange. If Patrick Skehan's analysis of the literary structure of Proverbs is correct, moreover, then one might argue that the problematized temple of Kings also receives a rereading here. In a series of three articles Skehan (1971) argued that the literary structure of Proverbs 1–9 can be visualized as seven columns, thus embodying the 'seven pillars' with which Woman Wisdom is said to build her house (Prov. 9.1). This seven-pillar edifice 'fronts' a book that, in its entirety, is also structured to accord with the measurements of an architectural entity, namely, the temple of Solomon, as described in 1 Kings 6.[28] Kings's temple, in

28. Skehan's argument is detailed to the point of estericism, and difficult to summarize. His basic procedure, however, is straightforward. He envisions a

other words, has been 'read' as the book of Proverbs, which is also understood as Wisdom's house. The connection between Kings and Proverbs is drawn all the tighter by the fact that the Strange Woman also has a 'house' in both books (1 Kgs 9.24; Prov. 2.16; 5.8; 7.27; cf. Dame Folly's house in 9.14). Like the narrated Solomon, the reader of Proverbs is faced with a choice of houses: houses constructed, in the first instance, on Solomon's orders, in the second, by his wise words. Proverbs, then, while retaining an interest in the temple, shifts the emphasis from the temple-as-building to the temple-as-book. The wisdom and the strangeness that were inextricably bound together in the material structure are separated in the literary one—as separated, that is, as the houses of two women can be.

What sociohistorical sense can be made of this intertextual reading of the book of Proverbs with Kings's story of a wise king, his women and his houses? In his interpretation of Solomon's 'exotic wives', John Burns (1991) draws together this narrative with DH's stories of Jezebel and Athaliah and Ezra–Nehemiah's condemnation of foreign marriages to construct a picture of postexilic resistance to the foreign wife. Al-

---

Proverbs manuscript written in literary 'columns' made up of certain numbers of verse lines, with each line construed as a cubit; the 'heights' of the columns match in significant measure the height dimensions of the temple and its three-story outer structure described in 1 Kgs 6. Some rearrangement of the MT of Proverbs is necessary to produce the overall 'temple' picture, though one would hardly call it wholesale: indeed, much fits Skehan's scheme neatly. The LXX is already different at points from the MT, moreover, and in no case does Skehan's arrangement violate otherwise discernable textual units (see Camp 1985: 237-38, 319 n. for a summary of the textual variations). In a footnote to one of his articles (1971: 27 n.), Skehan rather plaintively notes the skepticism of his colleagues to the sort of process of book-formation he imagines for Proverbs. I myself wonder whether my fascination with the possibility Skehan *could* be right outweighs my own skepticism about some of the admittedly more stretched points in his argument. To these scholarly qualms, I would make two observations. First, I would urge scholars interested either in the book of Proverbs or in ancient literary production to take up a thorough-going evaluation of the plausibility of Skehan's proposal. I fear the challenge of sorting through the details of these articles has been its own dissuasion. But at this point we need, I would say, a close analysis of the argument's strengths and weaknesses, both of which exist in some measure. Secondly, in defense of my own present argument, while it would be all the stronger for Skehan's being right, it does not completely depend on that. The close association of Solomon with both temple and Proverbs, as well as the interlacing imagery of house(s) and women wise and strange, provides sufficient justification for my intertextual reading.

though I agree with Burns's inclination to read this material intertextually, I find his univocal identification of Proverbs's Strange Woman with literal and literally foreign women too one-dimensional. 1 Kings 11 connects exogamy with idolatry in a way Ezra–Nehemiah does not. Solomon's wives, moreover (except perhaps the Hittites?), are from 'really' foreign countries; in this the narrative fits with Nehemiah 13, but not with Ezra and elsewhere in Nehemiah, where the problem seems to be with the 'peoples of the land', that is, non-*golah* Judahites (though the list of forbidden unions in Ezra 9.1 includes both sorts of 'foreigners'). These differences, along with the uncertainties in dating either the persons or the books of Ezra and Nehemiah, prohibit a definitive connection of the production of the Solomon narrative with that of either of those books or the events (if such they were) they describe. 'Nehemiah' (the person? the character?) knows some version of Solomon's story, but may be as much the creator as the reader of this text.

Burns's conclusion thus ignores, on the one hand, the possibility (already present in the foreign coloration of the temple in 1 Kings) that the rhetoric of foreignness was used by 'Israelites' against other 'Israelites', and, on the other, the metaphorical quality of the idea of strangeness that combines with foreignness connotations of illicit sexuality and deceitful speech. The latter entailments appear not only in Proverbs but also in one of Burns's key intertexts, the Jezebel story, which, indeed, is itself more than likely of postexilic origin (Rofé 1988).

I suggest, then, that while a problem with foreignness as such may be one historical factor embedded in the rhetoric of strangeness in Kings and Proverbs, it is not the only one. It must be understood in relationship to other ideological forces that are also working themselves out in these texts. Jobling has pointed to the structurally submerged connection between the ideology of sexuality and the ideology of monarchy in the Solomon narrative. We can now, I think, expand his analysis in two other related directions, to the temple and the book. Reading from Kings to Proverbs, we can trace several dovetailing shifts of emphasis that seem to begin in the narrative and find completion in the wisdom poems. Proverbs, I have argued, moves from a primary understanding of the temple-as-building to the temple-as-book, the literary description of an architectural structure becoming an architecture of literary structure. Analogously, Proverbs's interest in the temple-builder shifts from his embodied existence to his words. The latter point is already anticipated in the displacement of sex for wisdom in 1 Kings 3–10, and the utter lack of interest throughout the Solomon narrative in his successor. I suggested earlier that, in the narrative's ideal world, Solomon's 'seed' is found in his wisdom, in his words, rather than in his sons. The narrative cannot sustain this ideal, however. In the real world, not to mention the theological world of the Davidic covenant, the king must have a son. This contradiction manifests itself in the rocky transition from the notice of Solomon's strange women in ch. 11 to the previously unmentioned Rehoboam in ch. 12, whose mother is identified only in his death notice in 14.31. She was Naamah, a woman from Ammon. Thus Solomon's Strange Woman produces an heir with the same ethnic/religious/sexual gesture that costs this very son most of his inheritance. What the narrative cannot manage, however, poetry can. Just as the temple is perfected in the book of Proverbs, the book also realizes the ideal of Solomon's seed as wise words.

Let me make one further move. I have argued elsewhere (Camp 1985: 272-82) that, in the kingless social configuration of the postexilic period, the figure of Woman Wisdom in Proverbs can be understood to replace the monarch as a fundamental symbol of God's ordering presence in the world. 'Replacement' may be too strong a term, however, for Proverbs certainly retains the presence of Solomon. With more nuance, I might say that Woman Wisdom gives body to the king's voice, a gender merging perhaps hinting at another of the mythic ideals noted by Jobling, namely, the androgynous human. Solomon is never more a woman than in Proverbs. This shift is both analogous to and reinforced by the shift in interest from the temple to the book or, more precisely, to the temple *as* the book that, in turn, is Wisdom's house.

In considering the intersection of the book of Proverbs and the Solomon narrative, then, I propose we are seeing something both much more complex and much more elusive than a simple straightforward representation of the rejection of foreign wives, however much such an issue may, at some point, have been in play. What we see, rather, is the literary fossil of a process of shifting and without doubt conflicting authorities. What is at stake, surely, is in some sense the authority of a book, not altogether over against king and temple, yet in uneasy relationship to them. Indeed, over a period as long as that which scholars call 'the postexilic', the understanding by any given reader of the power relations embedded in these texts may well itself have shifted. What we have remaining is, finally, no more than a fossil; we can but guess at the fullness of the circumstances that produced it and that it in turn engendered.

If, however, understanding turns to some significant degree on the authority of a book, then we have found ourselves in the stream flowing toward the promulgation of authoritative literary canons. Yet the canon of whose authority I speak is not the one scholars usually refer to when discussing the beginnings of 'holy Scripture'. That book is the book purportedly brought to Judah by Ezra, some version or part of the Torah; the book I speak of is Proverbs.[29] What, then, is the relationship of one to the other, and of the proponents of one to those of the other? And what is the relationship of any of these to that other bastion of authority, the temple? I will not claim to offer answers to these questions; the following chapters will but accumulate some hints from other textual fossils.

---

29. Cf. Davies (1998: 40, 136), who also discusses Proverbs as an independent canon.

Part III

SISTER, BROTHER, OTHER: THE ISRAELITE WOMAN ESTRANGED

Introduction to Part III

Beginning from the perception that the dialectic of wise and strange in Proverbs is just that, a dialectic and not a polarity, I have argued in the last two chapters both for its surprisingly deconstructive literary effect in the Solomon and Samson narratives, as well as for its possible expression of a subtle and witty anti-priestly polemic. Our study of Proverbs also showed that the image of the Strange Woman may function in largely symbolic ways. Real ethnic foreign women are less a concern than all the metaphoric implications associated with them, and the purported concern with 'foreignness' is, more than likely, a displacement of the need to establish 'true Israeliteness' by defining differences between different (= right vs. wrong) kinds of Israelites, combined with a nascent moral ontology evident in the Strange Woman as cosmic symbol of evil.[1]

The awareness of this intra-Israelite conflict—especially the perception that rhetoric about foreign women may have been applied to women who were not foreign at all—combined with the breakdown of apparent opposition in our already imperfect wise–strange binary, leads me to approach the issue of female strangeness in another sort of way. In Part III, we shall consider the case of clearly identified Israelite women, Miriam and Dinah, who are 'made strange' in the narratives about them. Dinah is raped by (or, at least, has illicit sex with) a strange man while out visiting strange women; Miriam is struck with the uncleanness of what for convenience's sake we'll call leprosy, and finally dies in the wilderness where there is no water for purification. In each case, the woman is a sister of an Israelite man or men, and this sister status is, I suggest, crucial to understanding the stories' underlying ideology as well as the surface narrative. There is, of course, a third important sister story, that of Tamar in 2 Samuel 13, and it is not uncommon to find the stories of Dinah and Tamar analyzed as a pair, as both deal with rape and its ensuing violence between men.[2] Less obvious is the fit of Miriam into a pattern with the rape stories. There are, however, striking ideo-

1.   Cf. Pardes's observation (1992: 96) of the connection in monotheistic culture between the continued longings for 'a maternal representative in the divine sphere' and longings for 'other repressed pagan realms, such as the demonic and the underworld'.

2.   Judges's story of the Levite's concubine is a third example of the rape-and-war pattern, though she is not (obviously, at any rate) a sister.

logical resonances between the Miriam and Dinah narratives that are missing in Tamar's story. This is so, I shall argue, because of common priestly interests at work in the transmission (even if not the origin) of the Torah tales, but missing in 2 Samuel. Notably, these estranged women are sisters of the two major forebears of the priestly lineage(s?), Levi and Aaron figuring prominently as characters in their respective stories.[3]

Consideration of the concept of strangeness in the priestly literature has, moreover, its own rewards, and will serve in Chapter 5 as a prelude to my studies of the women's tales in 6 and 7. Here we shall find that, without wisdom as its ideological partner, the attempt to establish identity by drawing boundaries against the strange leads, paradoxically, to self-immolation. The dialectic of wisdom and strangeness, though undermining of settled and singular meanings, in effect keeps a narrative space open in which meaning-making can take place. In the priestly ideology we are about to consider, however, the imperfect binary of strangeness and wisdom shifts to the more perfect one of strangeness and holiness. More perfect, that is, in certain senses: to the extent that holiness involves standing at the center, purity with respect to improper mixing, separation from sexual activity, and maleness; while strangeness involves standing at the outside edge, boundary-crossing, sexual activity and femaleness. On the other hand, the root meaning of *qadosh*,

---

3.   My analysis in the following chapters takes the term 'priestly' in a broad institutional sense, a portmanteau for what may have been cultic functionaries of different sorts. This means I shall not engage the scholarly debate about whether the Levites were or were not 'really' priests—i.e. in direct charge of sacrificial ritual— at any particular point in time. Whatever that case may be, the biblical texts consistently use the terms 'Levite' and 'levitical' to refer to persons with significant cultic presence (though perhaps not of the same sort at all times), who were at least sometimes engaged in struggles for cultic control. It is in this sense that I shall refer to Levi as a 'priestly' brother and, subsequently, to Levites as a 'priestly' group. (I am tempted to compare the relationship of Levites and priests—assuming they were not always the same—to that of college administrators and faculty. The faculty may fulfill the ritual function of the college environment, but that hardly means administrators are powerless to shape the academic setting; administrators may, indeed, be drawn from faculty ranks.) Equally important for my analysis is my perception, for which I shall try to provide argument, that the Bible depicts what might be thought of as a cultic ideology regarding gender and genealogy, shared by priests and Levites, in spite of other sorts of differences between Levites and specifically *Aaronite* priests.

the Hebrew word for holy, is 'separated'. To be separate is, by one logic at least, to be strange. In this sense, the binary does not deconstruct itself in an endless push and pull of tensive meaning and opposition, but collapses into self-identification: the Holy is the Strange. To analysis of this effect in the priestly literature, particularly the book of Numbers, we now turn.

Chapter 5

OF LINEAGES AND LEVITES, SISTERS AND STRANGERS:
CONSTRUCTING PRIESTLY BOUNDARIES IN THE POSTEXILIC PERIOD

This chapter sets the ideological stage for the two that follow through three moves:

1. An introduction of two conceptual frameworks from recent scholarship that will guide my attempt to read Miriam and Dinah intertextually. The first concerns the structure of priestly thought; the second, a larger structure, arguably pervading the entire biblical mythos, that puts special focus on sisters. These constructs will be brought into conversation with each other, as well as with my own interest in women and the variations of their strangeness.
2. An analysis of the concept *zar* ('strange/r') in the priestly writings, a major locus where it appears without 'wisdom' as a counter.
3. An attempt, using Mary Douglas's (1993) anthropological analysis of the book of Numbers as a foil, to place the priestly rhetoric of descent and strangeness into the discourse of the postexilic period, with its emphasis on 'pure seed' and its antipathy to foreign women.

Here is the argument in a nutshell. The postexilic priests (at least that faction dominant in our present canon), were a group preoccupied with male lineage as the key to identity. For them, sisters represent an unbearable contradiction: they are, by birth, of the 'right' lineage and yet, by gender, 'not-Us'. As the strangers-within-the-family, the sisters of priests must thus be narratively transformed into outsiders. In this sense the sisters' stories function as part of a myth that both mediates and suppresses the contradiction of a group of people that considers itself genealogically to be both part of and separate from a larger group.

Often the myth operates in terms of the contradiction of 'Israel's' relationship with 'foreigners', all of whom, of course, 'descended' from Adam, and many from Abraham or his father. In this study, however, the focus will be on the 'priests'' relationship with 'the people'—these laity also, somewhat surprisingly, referred to as *zar*—although, as we shall see, the rhetoric of national/ethnic 'foreignness' lies not far under the surface. The problem becomes evident through a study of the concept *zar* in priestly ideology, which reveals an infinite regression in boundary-line drawing: the *zar* is the outsider to the chosen priestly lineage, but the line between inside and outside proves unstable, and the circle of insiders tends to shrink. This is the problem of the stranger-within writ large, for which the sister narratives provide both icon and displacement. In the texts I shall focus on here, however, we will find the Levites on the line.

The Ideology of Purity and the Myth of Descent: Two Models

Priests and Purity

In his provocative book, *The Savage in Judaism*, Howard Eilberg-Schwartz contrasts priestly and later rabbinic concepts of impurity, suggesting that each was related in turn to distinctive views on *cosmogony*, *human will*, *genealogy* and *status* (1990: 195-234, my italics). Priests, he argues, understood impurity to be based on categories established by God at creation, suggesting already the propensity for a *cosmogony* like that of Genesis 1 rather than Genesis 2. In contrast to rabbinic thought, priestly impurity focused on 'events and processes over which a person exercised little or no control' (195), such as death, skin disease and uncontrollable bodily emissions, and was understood as a property of objects, intrinsic and unchangeable, thus limiting the significance of *human will*. Eilberg-Schwartz also argues for a logical link in priestly ideology between this view of impurity and a larger sense of lack of control, as evident in the priests' emphasis on *genealogy and descent*. This connection

> is particularly plausible to the priests as a community in which genealogy played a fundamental role in ideology and social relations. The emphasis on [arbitrary, biological] descent is precisely what differentiated the priestly community from those that came afterwards. As descent lost its importance in defining the boundaries of a community and as an idiom for communal self-understanding, the connection between contamination and lack of control weakened. Increasingly for the groups that

followed, contamination could be controlled by human action and will
(Eilberg-Schwartz 1990: 195-96).

This symbolic matrix of impurity was, for the priests, related to their
structure of social relations, specifically *the assignment of status by
ascription* rather than achievement. Ascribed status is derived from the
arbitrary and uncontrollable fact of birth into a particular lineage rather
than from hard work or commitment to goals. Eilberg-Schwartz draws
all these elements together with this reasoning:

> Status assignation has a critical impact on shaping individuals' experi-
> ences of social life, and those experiences are expressed in symbolic pro-
> cesses. The more ascription plays a role in defining status, the less con-
> trol individuals have in determining who they ultimately are or will be...
>
> When status depends primarily on ascription, the idea of contamina-
> tion takes a corresponding form in the religious system. Just as an as-
> cribed status is something over which one has little or no say and which
> is experienced as imposed from the outside, impurity is something which
> is 'out there', an intrinsic property of objects... Individuals are thus
> powerless to avoid impurity, and becoming contaminated is an inevitable
> consequence of living. In short, impurity has the same 'objective' quality
> that status does (Eilberg-Schwartz 1990: 197).

Eilberg-Schwartz's analysis of the priests' affinity for a concept of
uncontrollable impurity depends on their self-understanding of their
own difference due to the arbitrary fact of lineage. He demonstrates
how this interest in descent is manifest in the priests' concern for procreation and detailed genealogies, and notes the lack of any narrative
justification for their divinely privileged status, even in a text like Numbers 16, which deals with challenges to priestly authority (1990: 199).

Important for my purposes is what I take to be the reverse side of this
ideology of descent, evident in the distinctive use, in the priestly writings, of a term germane to our present study, namely, *zar* ('strange/
stranger'). Before undertaking a study of the priests' use of this term, I
turn to a second theoretical framework that will inform our consideration of biblical sisters.

Sisters and Other Women in Israelite Ideology
In *The Logic of Incest: A Structural Analysis of Hebrew Mythology*
(1995), Seth Daniel Kunin argues that, at the level of deep structure, the
biblical ideology of Israel as the chosen lineage generates a preference
for endogamy that manifests itself in narratives about incest. Both
mythologically and sociologically, wives are 'other', outside the lineage

and therefore dangerous. The Genesis narratives, he suggests, mythologically redress this concern by transforming wives into sisters, by
devices such as the wife–sister stories or, in the case of Jacob, through
his marriage to his wife's sister who is, structurally, his own sister. It is
only after these mythic incorporations of the outsider-wife into the
patriarchs' own lineage that the divine seed can be passed on to the next
generation.

Kunin's analysis shows, however, that even after the wives have become (structural) sisters, the sense of danger produced by these women
persists at the sociological level, in terms of their apparent tendency to
introduce disharmony into the family: Sarah feuds with Hagar, and
Rachel with Leah, while Rebekah masterminds the theft of Esau's blessing. The wife's presence can, furthermore, leave an 'opening' for the
invasion of her alien family, as witnessed by Rachel's theft of Laban's
teraphim. Kunin's analysis of the rape of Dinah suggests that the
sister/daughter presents a similar threat. 'This text reveals that the position of sister and daughter is also structurally dangerous. The sister must
be given away in marriage and thus breaks the cohesion of the family
and creates an opening to the outside' (Kunin 1995: 138).

Kunin's work is highly explanatory with respect to the often unortho-
dox family relationships portrayed in Genesis. Part of his argument
hinges on the fascinating paradox of a mythology that is so trapped in
its structure of dividing insiders from outsiders that it cannot stop doing
so, even when all the parties involved should be regarded as insiders.
Thus, in Genesis, it makes sense to have a story that divides Abraham
from Lot and his offspring; Isaac from Ishmael; Jacob from Esau and
from Laban. It makes much less sense to divide Joseph from his brothers, for all of these become forebears of the Israelite tribes. While
Kunin's treatment of the mythic structure behind this narrative makes
mythological sense of narrative paradox, he fails to account fully for
Dinah, the thirteenth of Israel's 'sons' (taken, as in Hebrew, generically), in whose case he does not, I believe, take his own theory to its
logical conclusion. Rather than leave the analysis hanging at the level
of the sociological danger of the sister, I shall argue that Genesis 34,
and Numbers 12 as well, work through *mythologically* the problem of
the sister in a patrilineal system with greater complexity than he suggests. The problem or danger of the sister is not simply the sociological
one of marriage, but the mythological one of the relationship of a
female to an ideology of identity defined by maleness.

Priests and their Sisters

A theoretical side-step is necessary to put the issue in proper perspective. Eilberg-Schwartz and Kunin need to be brought into conversation with each other on the matter of fertility, which is brother to the ideology of descent. Both stress its importance, but with different emphases. Kunin stresses the mythological need to create the perfect insider-marriage of brother and sister as the channel of the chosen seed. Until the wife becomes sister, the true son cannot be born. Ultimately, however, the myth requires the removal of human agency altogether. The seed is a divine seed, and in each generation its carrier must be narratively reborn, of God alone.[1]

Although I will adopt Kunin's general understanding of the mythic requirements for fertility, it has three related ramifications that in my view receive helpful nuancing from Eilberg-Schwartz. The first has to do with the social location of this mythic logic, its tradents and receptors. Kunin takes a 'final form' approach to the text, locating its 'editorial present' in the fifth century, at the time of Ezra–Nehemiah, with their concerns to resist marriage to foreign women. Agreeing with other recent commentators, Kunin sees this as an effort not, paradoxically, to combat demonstrable foreigners, but rather to divide the 'true Israel' from those closest to them, in particular, the Samaritans. In this context of identity contest, Kunin argues that the myth responds to a fundamental question posed by Israel's theology of chosenness: How is it that we Israelites are members with all people in one human family while, at the same time, different from the rest? The myth replies with the notion of divine rebirth, a strategy that pervades all levels and strands of the biblical tradition (Kunin 1995: 91). What, though, we must ask, is the institutional basis for the promulgation of the myth? Besides 'Ezra and Nehemiah', whose myth is this?[2] A second aspect of Kunin's reading that needs nuancing is the fact that it is a non-gendered one. Since the

---

1.   To take one example, Kunin argues that the birth of Isaac to the aged Abraham and Sarah, miraculous though it may be, still involved human fertility. This explains the need for the Akeda: Isaac must be symbolically killed and saved by the action of Yhwh (1995: 94-100).

2.   This question becomes further complicated if, as I have discussed in the Introduction, the books of Ezra and Nehemiah are not a transparent window on events of the fifth century, but are from later (and probably different) times. My concern in this chapter, however, will not be dating as such, but rather an understanding of the particular priestly variant of this myth apparent in Numbers. This

myth requires the removal of all human agency to produce the new heir, the roles of both mother and father are, in his view, equally discounted in the process. Thirdly, Kunin articulates the significance of circumcision in terms of his understanding of this gender balance. Circumcision in his reading is a symbol of castration, equivalent then to the mytheme of the mother's barrenness. Neither of these latter two points is altogether wrong, but neither tells a whole story.

Eilberg-Schwartz's method is both more widely comparative and more interested in institutional contexts than is Kunin's study of mythic structure. His slant on circumcision as 'the fruitful cut' is drawn from comparative studies, and emphasizes not castration, but rather the connotations of 'fertility, procreation, and intergenerational continuity' (1990: 173). While these interests were to some degree general among Israelites, Eilberg-Schwartz argues that they were of particular concern to the priests with their ideology of descent and need to distinguish themselves by lineage not just from *non*-Israelites, but from *other* Israelites.

> Circumcision solved several vexing problems that, from the priests' perspective, would face anyone founding a new lineage. As the progenitor of a new lineage, Abraham had to be distinguished from all humans who had come before. But he also had to be connected to all his descendants. Circumcision solved both of these problems simultaneously (Eilberg-Schwartz 1990: 167).

While the connection of the penis with both kinship (descent) and fertility makes it a doubly appropriate locus for the symbol of God's covenant, it also represents a 'set-apartness' in two different ways: from other men and also from women.

> [C]ircumcision symbolizes and helps create intergenerational continuity between men. It graphically represents patrilineal descent by giving men of this line a distinctive mark that binds them together.
>
> Since circumcision binds together men within and across generations, it also establishes an opposition between men and women. Women cannot bear the symbol of the covenant (Eilberg-Schwartz 1990: 171).

Thus, by socially locating the practice of circumcision among the priests, Eilberg-Schwartz's analysis contrasts with Kunin's, insofar as

---

may have been associated with some (which?) 'time of Ezra and Nehemiah', but is more likely one component of a complex and extended (though probably all post-exilic) development of the myth as it now appears in the Pentateuch.

the priestly emphasis on patrilineal descent led them 'to stress the connection of males to one another and to devalue and minimize women's roles in reproduction' (Eilberg-Schwartz 1990: 232-33). In spite of their differences, both agree that there is a tension about the mythological and social status of women: both necessary for reproduction and dangerous (Kunin) if not devalued (Eilberg-Schwartz), women presented a case of 'can't live with them and can't live without them'. Eilberg-Schwartz's interest in institutional context and the political ramifications of ideological stances are more in line with my own. Nonetheless, each approach will offer important gateways as we seek to enter our texts, texts about sisters and their brothers.

My analysis of Miriam and Dinah—sisters not just of any brothers, but of priestly ones—will take up on two fronts where Kunin leaves off, offering further considerations of both sisters and social context. I shall suggest, in the first instance, that the transformation of wives into sisters still leaves a mythological problem as well as a sociological one. Women are not only dangerous because of the openings they create for one family's (culture's) intrusion into another; they are also problematic precisely because they are not men, not 'us', at least from a priestly point of view. Women's Otherness has to be mythologically confronted in the same way as that of ethnic foreigners, which, indeed, it comes to represent. Far from solving the problem, sisters raise it all the more acutely, since they are the closest thing to 'us' without being that. All that Kunin says about genealogical closeness requiring ideological distancing (1995: 58-59) applies, magnified, to sisters. At this point, I shall suggest, Eilberg-Schwartz's analysis of priestly interests sharpens the problem further, particularly in stories whose subjects are priests' sisters. Where descent from males is all, sisters are an anomaly that cannot be encompassed by the system: apparently of the 'right' lineage, they must be mythically disclosed as the outsiders they are.

We find in the exclusion of sisters from the descent group an infinite regress of identity-boundary drawing that is analogous to that in the story of Joseph divided from his brothers. This matter of myth run amok on the synchronic level must be mediated, according to Kunin, by a diachronic level found in the narrative of the reunion of the sons of Israel at the end of Genesis (1995: 140-46, 160-61). This tale of the division and reunion of Joseph, father of the primary northern tribes, and his brothers is not without political import in the postexilic period, when the question of Judah's relationship with the people and leadership of Samaria repeatedly created tension. And it is not without parallel to another postexilic case of tensions—in this case an overt power struggle—that was 'settled' (by the winners, of course, and well after the fact) by appeal to descent from the proper forebear. The claim to authorized priesthood by the 'descendants' of Miriam's brother Aaron over against the other 'descendants' of Dinah's brother Levi is yet another example of the problem of infinite regress presented by the effort to establish identity through genealogy. The relationship of estranged sisters to this dynamic in the stories of priestly brothers will be the topic of the next two chapters. Before turning in that direction, however, we must first consider more generally the role of the concept *zar*—strangeness—in the priestly writings.

Zar *Texts (I): Of Line(age)s and Levites*

As we have noted, *zar* has a wide range of meanings: the *zar* is the other, sometimes in a general sense, sometimes with specifically national, familial or religious force. In the priestly literature, however, *zar* occurs some 15 times,[3] always with the connotation—either direct or indirect—of those not belonging to the priestly clan, especially the family of Aaron. No *zar* can eat the food of atonement, used to consecrate Aaron and his sons (Exod. 29.33) or the sacred donations brought to Yhwh (3 times in Lev. 22.10-13). Only Aaron and his ritually clean sons can eat the former, though slaves and childless daughters of the lineage may also partake of the latter (this is a distinction to which we shall return). Nor may any *zar* make or use the priestly anointing oil, a restriction also implied for incense (Exod. 30.33, 38).[4]

In these passages, the concern seems to be to distinguish the priests (Aaron and his lineage) from all other Israelites (see Fig. 1a).

---

3.   Twelve of these occurrences are in the material usually designated P, while three (those in Lev. 22) are part of the Holiness Code.

4.   Note, however, the work of the divinely gifted 'wise' (*hkm*) craftsmen, Bezalel of Judah and Oholiab of Dan, in Exod. 31.1-11, who make all the accouterments of the cultic place, including the anointing oil and fragrant incense (v. 11). The call of Bezalel and Oholiab is repeated in Exod. 35.3-35, but expanded (36.1) to include all the 'skillful ones' (again, *hkm*) of Israel. To this larger group is then attributed the making of the oil and incense (39.38). The substitution of wise men for priests in this process is interesting.

Relationships of Aaronites, Levites, Israelites (Fig. 1)

Aaronites vs. all other Israelites (1a)

Exod. 29.33	no *zar* [non-Aaronite] may eat the food of atonement, used to consecrate Aaron and his sons, who are holy
Exod. 30.33	no *zar* may use or make the holy anointing oil, used to anoint Aaron and his sons and the sanctuary utensils
Exod. 30.38	the holy incense must be reserved as 'holy to Yhwh', never made for common use (cf. 30.9: no 'strange incense')
Lev. 22.10-13	no *zar*, only the priest's (Aaron's) family, may eat of the sacred donations

Levites vs. other Israelites (1b)

Num. 1.51	Levites will attend to the tabernacle, and the *zar* who approaches will be put to death

Aaronites vs. other Israelites, with Levites as the line (1c)

Num. 3.6-10	Levites are made to approach the tabernacle to perform duties for Aaron and the whole congregation; (only) Aaron and his sons are to be registered and perform the duties of the priesthood; and the *zar* who approaches will be put to death
Num. 3.38	Moses(!) and Aaron and his sons perform the duties of the sanctuary, with respect to the duties of the sons of Israel; and the *zar* who approaches will be put to death
Num. 18.2-5 per-	Levites are made to approach the tent of meeting to form duties for Aaron and the whole tent; but they must not approach the sanctuary utensils or altar lest 'both they and you' die; Levites will perform the duties of the tent; No *zar* may approach Aaron and his sons; Aaron and sons will perform the duties of the sanctuary and altar
Num. 18.6-7	Both Levites and priesthood given as 'gift' to Aaron and sons to perform the service of the tent of meeting; Aaron and sons perform as priests regarding the altar and area behind curtain; the *zar* who approaches will be put to death

Elsewhere, particularly in Numbers, the pie is sliced thinner yet; the Aaronite priests must be distinguished not only from the people in general, but even from other members of the levitical ancestral group. The five *zar* passages in Numbers all concern the question of who may approach (*qrb*, translated more pointedly by Milgrom as 'encroach upon' [1990: 342]) the tabernacle. The word always occurs in a variant of the phrase: 'any *zar* who approaches shall be put to death'. In Num. 1.51, *zar* draws a line between the Levites, who may approach the tabernacle, and other Israelites who may not. The clarity of this line is notable because it seems to put the *Levites* on the same side of the line as the Aaronites, that is, over against the *zar* (Fig. 1b). The clarity is also notable, however, because the other passages in Numbers are more ambiguous as to which side of the line the Levites are on: are they or are they not classified with the *zarim*? I shall suggest that Numbers struggles with this issue, the narrative slipping from one side to the other as it attempts to keep the Levites on the line between priests and *zarim*. An initial distinction between Aaronites and Levites (3.5-10) leads to a further effort to distinguish Aaronites from a sub-group of Levites, the Kohathites (3.27-32; 4.1-20). The problem of infinite regression manifest here necessitates an episode of dramatic rupture (the rebellion in Num. 16), which concludes with an attempted reinstitution of the Levites' line (18.1-7).

Aaronites and Levites

Using the technical 'approach/encroach' term (*qrb*, here in the hiphil), Yhwh tells Moses to 'bring the tribe of Levi near' to minister (*shrt*) to Aaron and to perform duties (*shmr mishmeret*) for Aaron and for the 'whole congregation' before the tent of meeting.

> Bring the tribe of Levi near and have him stand before Aaron the priest and minister (*shrt*) to him. They will perform his duties (*shmr mishmeret*) and the duties (*mishmeret*) of the whole congregation before the tent of meeting, to perform the service (*'bd 'et-'ebodat*) of the tabernacle. And they shall attend to (*shmr*) all the vessels/utensils (*keley*) of the tent of meeting and the duties (*mishmeret*) of the sons of Israel, to perform the service (*'bd 'et-'abodat*) of the tabernacle (Num. 3.6-8).[5]

5.   It is difficult to maintain consistency in translating the terms used to describe the work of the cultic personnel. This is due in part to the extraordinary degree of repetitiveness, but mostly to the often hard to specify, sometimes overlapping, but not always identical, meanings of the three main Hebrew roots: *shmr*

The position of the Levites is, then, in-between Aaron and the rest of Israel. If Milgrom (1990: 16, 341-42) is correct that *shmr mishmeret* (usually translated something like 'perform duties') in fact refers to the duty of boundary-guarding, this in-between position is sharply emphasized: the Levites guard Aaron from the whole congregation and the whole congregation from Aaron.[6] Numbers 1.51 had drawn the line between the Levites who may approach the tabernacle and any other Israelite—called *zar*—who may not. Numbers 3, however, after giving the Levites to Aaron, returns to Exodus's distinction between Aaron's family, who may perform (guard for themselves?) the priestly functions, and the *zar* who may not 'approach'.

Yhwh goes on to say to Moses,

> You shall give the Levites to Aaron and his sons; they are unreservedly given to him from among the Israelites. And you shall make a register of Aaron and his sons; and they shall attend to their priesthood, and the *zar* who comes near shall be put to death (Num. 3.9-10).

(used 46 times in its technical cultic sense in Numbers), *'bd* (65 times), and *shrt* (11 times). Milgrom argues (1990: 315, 343-44) that *'bd* always refers to the physical labor of the Levites (or their sub-clans) in taking down and carrying the parts of the tent/tabernacle. This is certainly the term that dominates those instructions in Num. 3 and 4, but Milgrom cannot account for the exception in 18.7, where, though the text is corrupt, the priestly duties of Aaron and his sons are described as *'bd*. *Shmr* and *shrt* cause further problems because the subjects and objects of these roots vary wildly. The Levites can 'perform duties' (or 'guard boundaries'; so Milgrom) for the tabernacle (= tent of meeting), for Aaron, for the whole congregation (= the sons of Israel), or for the holy vessels (or utensils). The Aaronites perform duties for (or of) the priesthood, the sanctuary, the sons of Israel, or the altar. Even Israel is said to perform the duties (or, perhaps less technically, 'keep the charge'?) of Yhwh by not setting out while the cloud rests over the tabernacle (9.19, 23). The work of the Levites is also described as 'ministering' (*shrt*) to the tabernacle, to Aaron (and his sons), to their brother Levites, or to the congregation. A significant ambiguity enters the picture when both the Kohathites and the Aaronites seem to be described as 'ministering' with the sanctuary objects (3.31; 4.12, 14). My point is not, in the end, to sort these things out, but rather the contrary, to read the confusion.

6.   Milgrom argues, in fact, that the phrase always and only means boundary-guarding. Levine (1993: 141-42) disputes this, allowing that this is *sometimes* the meaning, but arguing for the more general sense of 'maintaining' the tabernacle in this case (cf. Num. 1.53). One does not have to be as definitive as Milgrom, I would suggest, to find the boundary-guarding sense in play here; Levine seems to go too far in the other direction.

But into which category do the Levites now fall? In v. 6 they have been 'brought near' (lit., 'caused to approach'), but in v. 10 they are clearly excluded from the register of Aaron's sons, the only ones who may approach without pain of death (Fig. 1c).

Betwixt and between, the Levites in Numbers 3 are on the line: neither fully *zar* nor fully priest, they constitute the line between. This representation occurs, however, in the context of a chapter where distinguishing the Aaronites from the rest of the Levites emerges as a problem because of their common ancestry. Numbers 3 enumerates the three major clans ('father's houses') of the tribe of Levi, and assigns them their duties and encampment locations with respect to the tabernacle: Gershon to the west, Kohath to the south and Merari to the north (Fig. 2a). Moses, Aaron and Aaron's sons encamp on the east and perform the duties (*shmr mishmeret*) of the sanctuary on behalf of the Israelites. These instructions close (3.38) as they began (3.10) with the admonition that any *zar* who comes near be put to death.

> Those who encamp before the tabernacle to the east, before the tent of meeting toward the sunrise, are Moses and Aaron and his sons, performing the duties of the sanctuary, on behalf of the duties of the sons of Israel; and the *zar* who comes near shall be put to death (3.38).

The encampment locations seem to distinguish clearly between the Aaronites and the Levites, as does the final allusion to the Aaronites 'performing duties' on behalf of the Israelites. Contrast 3.7-8, where the Levites seem to have that role (Fig. 1c), though the locus of their duty is 'before the tent of meeting' rather than the sanctuary. Have the Levites disappeared into the *zarim*? Not quite: the discussion of the location and duties of the Kohathites, Aaron's own father's house, in Numbers 3 and 4 pushes the issue of genealogical boundary-line drawing back one step.

Aaronites and Kohathites

The son of Amram, Aaron is a member of the clan of Kohath (Exod. 6.18, 20), one of the three Levite clans. What then is the relationship of this sub-group of Levites to the family of priests? The question in effect shifts the burden of line-drawing to a yet narrower, presumably even more difficult, purview. The Kohathites take up the position of limen between the Aaronites and the other Levites.

The tension involved in dividing up what should have been a unity is expressed in a couple of ways (Fig. 2). First, the Kohathites' responsibilities (*mishmeret*) include 'the ark, the table, the lampstand, the altars, the vessels of the sanctuary with which they minister, and the screen—all its service (*'abodah*)' (3.31; Fig. 2b). This clan's work, in other words, brings them into contact with all the holy objects inside the sanctuary, in contrast to that of the other two clans, which involves only the frames and hangings of the tabernacle structure itself. Whether the Kohathites were understood to 'minister' (*shrt*) themselves, or whether they merely carried (so Milgrom) the holy objects with which the (real) priests ministered is ambiguous in 3.31. The subject of the verb *shrt* is not specified, though the context suggests 'ministry' by the Kohathites themselves (cf. the Aaronites' 'ministering' with these same objects in 4.12, 14). The NRSV supplies the subject 'priests' in 3.31, an indication of the discomfort of the translator about this ambiguity.

Aaronites vs. Levites, with Kohathites on the Line (Fig. 2)

Encampment locations and duties of Levite houses (Num. 3.14-39) (2a)

West:	Gershonites	Tabernacle tent, hangings, screens
South:	Kohathites	Sanctuary objects/duties (*keley/mishmeret haqqodesh*), overseen by **Eleazar**
North:	Merarites	Frames and hardware of the tabernacle
East:	Moses, Aaron, Aaron's sons (includes **Eleazar**)	Performance of sanctuary duties (*mishmeret hammiqdash*)

Duties of Aaronites vs. Kohathites (2b)

Numbers 3

Kohathites Duty (*mishmeret*), service (*'abodah*) with respect to the sanctuary objects—ark, table, lampstand, altars, vessels (3.31)

Aaronites Eleazar has oversight over those who perform the sanctuary duty (3.32);
(Moses), Aaron and his sons perform the duty of the sanctuary (3.38)

Numbers 4

Kohathites Carry, but may not touch (4.15) or look at (4.20) the most holy things

Aaronites Cover the sanctuary objects—ark, table and everything on it, lampstand and everything associated with it, altar, vessels (4.5-15); Eleazar has oversight over oils, incense, grain offering (4.16)

A second expression of tension in dividing Aaronites from Kohath-ites (or, alternatively, an expression of this group's position at the limen between Aaronites and other Levites) appears at the end of the section describing their encampment location south of the tabernacle and duties (3.27-32). Here, anomalously, 'Eleazar, son of Aaron the priest' is named as 'chief of the chiefs of the Levites, overseer of those who per-form the duties of the sanctuary' (or, 'the holy duties [*mishmeret haq-qodesh*]'; Fig. 2a). The introduction at this point of a character and func-tion that 'belong' six verses later on the east side with Moses and Aaron and his sons makes manifest the difficulty in drawing the line between who is in and who is out of the priestly circle. *Mishmeret haqqodesh* itself, moreover, is an ambiguous phrase, possibly referring narrowly to duties involving sanctuary objects, but also potentially more broadly to duties in the sanctuary, thus seeming to connect these residents of the south side with those on the favored east. As we shall see, the 'duties of holiness' are finally assigned to Aaron and his sons alone (18.5).

The confusion as to the exact duties of the Aaronites vis-à-vis the Kohathites continues in Numbers 4 (Fig. 2b). The 'service of (*'abodat*) the Kohathites' is first connected with 'the most holy things' (4.4). Then, however, Aaron and his sons are depicted as actually dealing with those things (4.5-14). Only after the most holy things are covered by the Aa-ronites, the Kohathites may 'carry' them, but not 'touch' them (4.15; do the covers allow carrying without touching?). Parallel to ch. 3, Eleazar's work is suddenly introduced into the discussion of the Kohathites (4.16), reserving several items as his responsibility, notably including the in-cense and anointing oil that Exod. 30.33, 38 forbids the *zar*. Finally, a concern to protect the Kohathites from death is expressed, which in-volves keeping them from even looking on the holy things (4.17-20). Their service with regard to the most holy things is, in other words, both steadfastly maintained and impossibly circumscribed.

The Kohathites mark the impossible line between the Aaronites and the rest of the Levites. When the existence of the Kohathites is fore-grounded, as it is in Numbers 3 and 4, the Aaronite–Levite difference seems obvious because the mediating group puts the need to actually define it at one remove. We might quibble about how to distinguish an Aaronite from another Kohathite, but the line between the Aaronites and the rest of the Levites is as clear as, well, as the difference between the east side of the tent and the rest. By 'being there', by being material entities, the Kohathites fill the line in, make it a space. That the problem will not go away, however, is evident in the messy separation embodied by Eleazar, who moves between his father's house and his father's house's house, as well as in the blurred duties of the Aaronites, the Kohathites and the Levites.

Aaronites and Levites Revisited

The Aaronite versus Levite problematic re-emerges explicitly in Numbers 18, a chapter covering some of the same ground as ch. 3, but without the cover of the Kohathites. When, following the rebellion of Korah (Num. 16), the people of Israel express fear that *everyone* who approaches the tabernacle will die (17.28 [Eng.: 17.12]), Yhwh assigns the Levites to serve Aaron and his sons while they perform their priestly functions, within certain limitations.

> They shall perform duties for you [Aaron] and for the whole tent.[7] But they must not approach either the vessels of the sanctuary or the altar, otherwise both they and you will die. They are attached to you in order to perform the duties of the tent of meeting, for the service of the tent; no *zar* shall approach you. You yourselves will perform the duties of the sanctuary and the duties of the altar, so that wrath may never again come upon the Israelites (Num. 18.3-5).

The Levites are on one level, as in ch. 3, bound closely to the Aaronites; much, however, in 18.1-7 conspires to ambiguate the relationship, cutting off with one hand what seems joined by the other.

The unity of Aaronites and Levites is expressed here not only in the nature of their service, but also by the family relations highlighted in 18.1-2. Yhwh speaks first to Aaron regarding 'you and your sons and your father's house' (v. 1), and then alludes to 'your brothers of the tribe of Levi, the tribe of your father' (v. 2). On the other hand, unexpected distinctions are made in what would seem to be primal bonds. The anticipated indissolubility of a man, his sons and his father's house (v. 1a) suddenly dissolves in the next clause, where responsibility for the priests is assigned only to Aaron and his sons (v. 1b). Similarly, the brothers of the father's tribe require, surprisingly, to be 'joined' to Aaron in order to minister to him[8]. The verb here is *shrt* (piel), as in

---

7.   The phrasing shifts here from 3.7's 'perform duties for [Aaron] and *for the whole congregation*' to '[Aaron] and *the whole tent*'.

8.   There is a wordplay here: the brothers of the tribe of Levi (*lewi*) must be joined (*yillawu*) to Aaron. Cf. the poignant origin of Levi's name in Leah's excla-

Num. 3.31. In ch. 3, the subject of the ministering was ambiguous, though context suggested, contrary to expectation, that the Kohathites ministered with the sanctuary vessels. In 18.2 it is clearly the Levites who minister. Here, however, there is a direct object—it is the Aaronite priests who are to be ministered to—that gives *shrt* a hierarchical force (so also in 3.6).

The Aaronites thus both are and are not kin to the other Levites, a relational ambiguity expressed also in this passage in the use of the technical term, 'approach' (*qrb*). Aaron is instructed to have the Levites 'approach' (v. 2) in order to serve him. They may not, however, 'approach' the vessels of the sanctuary or altar, lest all die (v. 3). With this instruction, the duties of the Kohathites, assigned in Numbers 3 and constrained in Numbers 4, are effectively shifted to Aaron and his sons. The narrative and mythic space held by this clan in chs. 3–4, unmentioned in ch. 18, also disappears. Thus, when v. 4 makes the dramatic announcement (repeated in v. 7), 'As for the *zar*, he shall not approach you', it appears that the Levites who serve the tent are, like the Kohathites in chs. 3–4, walking a dangerous line. The unformulaic use of the pronoun 'you' in v. 4 as a direct object of 'approach' heightens the tension. How can the Levites be 'joined' to those they cannot 'approach'?

Perhaps one may approach in a different way, and say that, just as the Kohathites in ch. 3 constituted a line that made the Levites *zarim*, in ch. 18, the Levites have become the line. Focusing on the muddle between the Aaronites and the Kohathites in chs. 3–4 creates a space, a comfort zone, between the Aaronites and the Levites; analogously, ch. 18's attention to the muddle at the next larger ring of these concentric circles seems (however speciously) to clarify the distinction between the Aaronites and the other Israelites. 'Are we all to perish?' they ask. The answer: no, the Levites—those who may approach, but not too close— will mediate. Neither fully one nor completely the other, they are the line, they fill the line and thus make the space between the true priests who may approach Yhwh and the *zarim* who will be forever separated off.

Although Numbers 18 apparently succeeds in securing the Levites on/as the line, this position is inherently unstable, as we have already seen in the case of the disappearing Kohathites from chs. 3–4. Numbers

mation at his birth: 'Surely this time my husband will be joined to me!' (Gen. 29.34). The joining remained at best partial in each instance.

18.1-7, moreover, not only repeats the dynamics of those earlier *zar* texts, it also completes another narrative sequence that begins with another *zar* text in ch. 16, the story of Korah's rebellion. Here again we shall see the Levites walk the line(age).

The surface of Numbers 16 is generally agreed to resemble the poorly stitched visage of Frankenstein's monster. Expanding on Alter's analysis (1981: 133-37), however, I will assume that the seams are there to be read along with the rest. The seam that interests me here is the one joining Korah to other parties in the dispute and how it informs the status of the Levites as liminals and strangers. It is typical for scholars to divide up Numbers 16 into two sources, one involving a secular power struggle between Moses and some of the Israelite chieftains (16.12-15, 27b-32a), and the other involving a contest for cultic leadership between Aaron and 250 Levites led by Korah (16.5-10, 16-18, 35-40).[9] While the text supports this division, it also complicates the matter (and thus the position of the Levites as well) by associating Korah with the '250' chieftains (*not* at first described as only Levites; 16.1-2) and, indeed, with the 'whole congregation' (16.3, 19, 41-50). Watch the boundary lines move.

Korah purports to represent the view that 'all the congregation are holy' (16.3), a position implying no line whatsoever between priest and *zar*, indeed, no such thing as a *zar*, at least among the Israelites. Moses' angry response, however, reasserts the existence of a line between priest and people, constituted by the Levites.

> Is it too little for you that the God of Israel has separated you from the congregation of Israel, to allow you to approach him in order to perform the duties of Yhwh's tabernacle, and to stand before the congregation and minister to them? He has allowed you to approach him, and all your brother Levites with you; yet you seek the priesthood as well! (16.9-10)

At the same time that Moses redraws the levitical line (separation from/service to the congregation but exclusion from the priesthood), we note also his skillful rhetoric, especially the twofold use of 'approach', that suggests the line is somehow closer to the inside than the outside: God himself is here approached! But Moses' exaggeration of the Levites' honor serves only to justify the horror of their punishment. By 16.16, the '250 Israelite men' from 16.2 have been transformed, through a series of narrative leaps (16.7, 8, 10, 16), into the 250 (ostensibly

---

9.   See Milgrom (1988) for a more complicated developmental analysis.

Levite) followers of Korah who are burned with fire by Yhwh while offering incense (16.35). Their censers are then hammered into plates as a covering for the altar, to be forever 'a reminder to the Israelites that no *zar*, who is not of the descendants of Aaron, shall approach to offer incense before Yhwh...' (17.5 [Eng.: 16.40]). The Levites are herewith cast into the outer darkness.

If the Levites are *zarim*, then the line between the Aaronites and the rest of the congregation has been made utterly clear, the blurring embodied in the tribal kindred eliminated in a narrative tour de force. On the other hand, if the Levites are *zarim*, then the line is but a conceptual abstraction, unfilled, thus infinitely fine, and also a gulf, incapable of transversal. A kind of line too dangerous (impossible?) to be maintained. Numbers 17 expresses both the fruitfulness of the clean cut and its danger. Yhwh tells Moses to gather 12 staffs, representing the 12 tribes (here, 'father's houses'). The name of 'each man' (presumably each tribal father) is to be written on his staff, but Aaron's name is to be written on Levi's. This brazen overwriting of the father by the son has two results: Aaron's staff sprouts, blossoms and bears almonds, but the people of Israel react with terror at the prospect of having no mediator between themselves and the tabernacle. Aaron has gone too far (cf. the mutual accusations of Moses and the Levites in 16.3 and 7). His overreaching thus culminates in 18.1-7 with the renewed assignment of the Levites to perform duties for the Aaronites and the congregation. The (muddy) line, in touch with both priest and *zar*, has been of necessity reconstituted. Myth prefers mess to clear contradiction.

Zar *Texts (II): Sparks, Scents, Seed, Sex*

Our discussion of the priestly *zar* texts in Numbers has shown the function of this term as a point of leverage between the Aaronites and the rest of the Israelites, with the Levites as a variably substantial boundary line between. In what follows, attention turns to the ultimate biblical act of line(age) drawing, that within the family of Aaron itself: two of Aaron's sons are struck down for no apparent reason, while two, equally arbitrarily, are spared (Lev. 10). An intertextual reading of this material with the *zar* texts in Numbers will suggest (we might note with some relief) that the tradition has some problem in maintaining such a bald narrative expression of anti-evolutionary self-mutilation—the last stage in the cutting off of family members. It requires a variety of metonymic and metaphoric displacements.

To preview my argument in this section: I shall suggest that the related images of fire and incense play a role in this process of displacement. This role is reinforced by the projection of the irredeemable-because-unmediatable division at the level of the nuclear family's males onto that (ideologically speaking) absolute line between (male) Israelite and (female) foreigner. In other words, when the ever-regressing drawing of genealogically based identity-boundary lines reaches the point of no return, the myth moves to the opposite, and easiest, extreme: the Strange Woman is sacrificed (we note with a return of despair) in place of the pure seed. This move is not without theological import: in Leviticus 10, the blessing of Yhwh's arbitrary choosing becomes a curse, one removed only by the Strange Woman.

Aaronites and (other) Aaronites (see Fig. 3)
Exodus 30.9 specifies that, while Aaron must make a daily offering of fragrant incense (*qetoret sassim*) on a special altar built for that purpose, he must not offer any 'strange incense' (*qetoret zarah*). This precise terminology does not occur again; here, it seems to refer to the use of a specific recipe for the incense, which is given in 30.34-38 and which, like the anointing oil, is reserved for priestly use. Offenders in both cases are 'cut off' from the people, a phrase implying lack of offspring (cf. Gen. 17.14; Eilberg-Schwartz 1990: 148). These passages on incense are immediately preceded by the instructions, in Exodus 29, for the ordination of Aaron and his sons. A similar sequence occurs in Leviticus where the actual enactment of this ordination is narrated in ch. 8. In ch. 10, however, as the new priests begin to practice their office, two of Aaron's sons, Nadab and Abihu, offer with their censers not 'strange incense' but 'strange fire' (*'esh zarah*) to Yhwh, and are immediately themselves consumed with fire that 'came out from the presence of Yhwh' in order that Yhwh might 'show [him]self holy' (10.1-3). This incident is alluded to twice more (Num. 3.4 and 26.61), with little further comment except, significantly, that Nadab and Abihu die heirless.

The terminological shift from the law's 'strange incense' to the narrative's 'strange fire' is highly significant for our present study, for the otherwise unattested Hebrew phrase *'esh zarah*, 'strange fire', sounds too much like *'ishshah zarah*, 'strange woman', to be coincidental. On some level, whether consciously or not, the offense of Aaron's sons has been mnemonically related to the image of the Strange Woman.

Priestly Line(age)s: Holy and Strange (Fig. 3)

Exodus 30 (separation of strange from holy, under penalty of loss of lineage)

No strange incense (30.9)
Holy oil applied to *zar* → cut off from the people (30.33)
Secular use of holy incense → cut off from the people (30.38)

Leviticus 10 (collapse of strange and holy; half of Aaron's lineage lost)

Nadab and Abihu use strange fire to burn incense, and are burned by
Yhwh's fire (10.1-7)
Explanation: 'Through those who are near me (*qrb*), I will show myself
holy' (10.3)

Numbers 3 (Levites established as line between holy and strange; lineage problem ameliorated)

'And this is the lineage of Aaron and Moses...' (3.1)
Deaths of Nadab and Abihu for strange fire are recalled; 'and they died
childless' (3.4)
Levites brought near and given to Aaron (3.5-9)
Aaron and descendants registered to distinguish them from *zar* who may
not draw near (3.10)
Levites accepted by Yhwh as substitutes for firstborn of Israel (3.11-13)

Numbers 16–18 (Line[age] problem revisited: Levites step out of line and are
brought back in; Aaron's lineage reconfirmed)

Levites burned while burning incense (16.1–17.5; Eng.: 16.1-40)
'No *zar* who is not of Aaron's seed shall approach to offer incense'
(17.5; Eng.: 16.40)
Aaron's staff sprouts and bears nuts (17.16-26; Eng.: 17.1-11)
People express fear at approaching tabernacle (17.27-28; Eng.: 17.12-13)
Levites (re)joined to Aaron as barrier against *zar* (18.1-7)

As Tod Linafelt and Timothy Beal point out (1995: 27-28), moreover,
zarah itself can be read in either of two ways. The usual translation is
as a feminine participle of *zwr*, 'be strange'. The verb *zrh* can also,
though, mean 'winnow, scatter'. There is thus a further connection in
sound and semantic field between *zrh* and *zr'*, whose verbal and nominal forms mean 'to sow' and 'seed/offspring'.[10] Linafelt and Beal's Der-

10. There was a printer's error in setting the Hebrew font of the Linafelt and
Beal article (Tim Beal, personal communication). The relevant sentences should
read: '*Zr'* as a verb...is synonymous with *zrh*, and is typically rendered as "to sow"

ridean analysis finds traces of child sacrifice in Leviticus 10. Thus, they suggest a translation of *'esh zarah* as 'seed fire', and propose as suppressed referents either Nadab and Abihu's sacrifice of their own children or Aaron's sacrifice of these two sons as punishment for his sin with the golden calf. Notably, however, just as the Strange Woman is not explicitly named or blamed, neither of these warrants for punishment is cited. The text leaves us with Yhwh's fire and strange fire, in Greenstein's words, a punishment in search of a crime (1989: 56). On one level, this is an implicit indictment of Yhwh for an irrational act of murder: Yhwh's fire *is* the strange fire. On the other hand, the odd term *'esh zarah*, with its homophones, invites intertextual considerations that reduce this ultimate theological tension.

Of particular importance is the story of Korah's rebellion, discussed above, that culminates in the (re-)investiture of the Levites as ministers between Aaron and the congregation (Num. 16.1–18.7). In each case, priestly claimants—with apparent legitimacy based on lineage criteria—are burned by Yhwh's fire while making an incense offering, and a smaller segment of the lineage is established as the true priesthood. As we have already seen, the outcome in Num. 18.1-7 essentially repeats the notice of the Levites' special status from Num. 3.5-10. To that we can now add the further observation that Num. 3.5-10 is itself immediately preceded by what seems to be an out-of-place reminder of Nadab and Abihu's offering of the strange fire (3.4). The anomaly is explained, however, if we see Nadab and Abihu as analogous to Korah. Both in Numbers 3 and in 16–18, the unit on the selection of the Levites is then preceded by one describing cultic officiation—specifically, incense burning—by inappropriate persons. The fate of Nadab and Abihu is

---

or "scatter seed". The noun form of *zr'*, in turn, means "seed" or "offspring" (also "semen")'. I would nuance this statement somewhat. While *zrh* as a verb does mean 'scatter', it is used only once in reference to sowing seed. Almost always, the connotation is harsher: scattering as winnowing, separating wheat from chaff, and, with respect to humans, as punishment (*Dictionary of Classical Hebrew*, III, 134-35). It is used with this sense in Num. 17.2 (Eng.: 16.37), where Aaron's son Eleazar is told to scatter (*zrh*) the fire from the censers of the immolated followers of Korah. This connection is quite relevant for our larger discussion. *Zr'*, then, is not synonymous with *zrh*; it is, however, a near homophone, as well as related in terms of the agricultural activities of sowing and winnowing. Thus, the essence of Linafelt and Beal's argument is quite on target. Important for my purposes, furthermore, will be the homophonic relationship of both these verbs to *zarah* (the feminine participle of *zwr*, 'be strange').

also alluded to (and also ameliorated) in Num. 3.11-13 (cf. 3.40-41), where the Levites are designated as 'substitutes for all the firstborn' consecrated to Yhwh. In sum, Numbers 3 practically requires we read Leviticus 10 and Numbers 16 in light of each other. Likewise, describing Nadab and Abihu's fire with the adjective *zar* categorizes them with Korah's Levites, whose incineration is a warning to all *zarim* against cultic encroachment (Num. 17.5 [Eng.: 16.40]).

Both Leviticus and Numbers confront the same issue: the lineage basis of a distinctive priesthood—that is, the equation of ritual correctness with genealogical correctness—in a society that features itself as all from one lineage. Numbers, however, deals with the issue writ large and multidimensional: Aaronites from Levites, Aaronites from Kohathites, Levites from people, people from Aaronites. As I have tried to show, when the contradiction gets too much at one level, the narrative slips to another. The problem of the arbitrary choosing of one family within The Family is not solved, but it is masked by the mediation of the Levites who also, when we start to squirm under the narrative illogic, have the grace to 'rebel' against Yhwh's chosen leaders. We can, the text informs us, equate ritual and genealogical correctness, with a bit of moral rectitude for good measure; all we have to do is make sure we are looking at the right branch of The Family. Reading Leviticus 10 in light of Numbers helps throw this mediating cloak back over the situation of Nadab and Abihu, where—because the division occurs within the nuclear family—there can be no structural mediator, and where there is no obvious rebellion against authority. The problem with such intertextuality, of course, is that it works both ways, illuminating with its strange fire the dirt under the rug in Numbers. As if realizing that this route offers no final satisfaction, Numbers provides another masking alternative, this time invoking the Strange Woman herself.

Aaronites and the Strange Woman
If the problem we face is Yhwh's arbitrary choosing of one branch of Israel to be priests, the story of the deity's inexplicable rejection of two of Aaron's sons takes us as far as possible out on that limb. One way to avoid sawing oneself off is to do a narrative flip from the end of the branch back to the trunk; to turn the story, that is to say, from one about priestly brothers, men of the same seed whose arbitrary death must provoke some sense of horror, to one about (all) Israelites and strange women, where the boundary is as wide as the Jordan and where death

can be righteously cheered. How convenient the trace of the Strange Woman in the strange/seed fire. Again, what cannot be faced in Leviticus 10 finds more ideologically palatable form in juxtaposition with Numbers. In the story of Israel's entanglements with foreign women at Shittim (Num. 25), the other metaphorical entailments of strangeness—wrong sex = wrong nationality = wrong god—are marshaled in support of the right (lineage within the) lineage.

We have just read Leviticus 10 alongside Numbers 16. In each case, the Strange Woman is present only by suggestion. In Leviticus 10 it is by wordplay, the *'ishshah zarah* in the shadow of the *'esh zarah*. The wordplay takes another turn in Num. 17.2 (Eng.: 16.37), where the homophone *zrh*, 'scatter' (see above, n. 10), appears. After Korah and his men are immolated by fire from Yhwh, the deity says to Moses: 'Tell Eleazar, son of Aaron the priest, to take up the censers out of the flame and scatter the fire (*ha'esh zereh*) far and wide...' Strange fire, strange seed, strange woman; scattered fire, scattered seed...scattered woman? In Num. 16.31-33, scattered women and scattered seed join the scattered fire: the wives and children of Korah and his colleagues are, tragically, made strange by virtue of their relationship to strange men. They are swallowed up with their men into Sheol during an earthquake, a rather literal, though ironically twisted, fulfillment of the fate promised men who associate with the Strange Woman.

> Her house is the way to Sheol,
> going down to the chambers of death (Prov. 7.27; cf. 9.18).

Numbers 16–18 is, moreover, narratively linked in several ways with the events of Numbers 25, which deals overtly with foreign women. In both cases, there is a rebellion resulting in a plague that is ended by the action of an Aaronite priest. Both units also culminate in the reiteration of Yhwh's covenant of priesthood with the Aaronite lineage. Numbers 25 reprises the problem of drawing identity boundaries, but now under circumstances where, given the apparent clarity of the distinctions to be made, there should be a high level of narrative comfort: the Strange Woman makes an easy target.[11] Two thematically similar events are

11. In the larger context of Numbers, however, this comfort is not complete, for the violent rejection of marriage to foreign women in ch. 25 is undercut by Moses' marriage to a Cushite in ch. 12. Indeed, if we go back to Exodus, we find Moses married to a *Midianite* woman, the very nationality of the rejected wife in Num. 25. This tension will be further explored in Chapter 6.

linked in this chapter. In vv. 1-5, Israel 'yokes itself' to Baal of Peor by 'playing the harlot with Moabite women', an episode whose telling itself inextricably combines language about wrong worship, wrong nationality and wrong sex. Then, in vv. 6-18, Phineas, the son of Eleazar, kills with one thrust of his spear the Simeonite man Zimri and his Midianite wife Cozbi, whom Zimri has 'brought near' (*qrb*) to his brothers at the entrance of the tent of meeting.

Three moves are made here simultaneously. First, the winner of the battle for the priesthood is announced: not simply Aaron, but, from among the purported 'sons' of Aaron, Eleazar, the scatterer of the Levites' strange seed fire. Secondly, the fact that there has been a battle is covered up by substituting narrative about the cutting off of family members with narrative about the cutting off of Israel from national/ ethnic strangers, or, to capture the mythic point, of Israelite men from strange women. That there has been a battle is evident in its remaining narrative traces. Who else besides Cozbi has been 'brought near' the tent of meeting, only to be killed for approaching *too* near? Who else, if not the Levites; who else, if not the two sons of Aaron? But liminal men are now displaced by the Strange Woman. This trace of the Levites is repeated in the tribal affiliation of Zimri. As a Simeonite, Zimri would seem to be a clear outsider with no priestly claims, as *zar* as his wife is *zarah*. On the other hand, the traditional association of Simeon and Levi in Genesis 34 and 49 may make this one more concealed slap at the Levites (see Chapter 7 for further discussion of the connection of Simeon and Levi). The text hints, finally, at ritual violation on a couple of levels. Phineas's dispatching of the couple with one thrust of his spear suggests, both by metaphor and by the physical image evoked, that they were caught in the middle of sexual intercourse, and this possibly in the tent of meeting itself.[12] The man who may not approach

---

12. The passage is ambiguous on this point. It locates the scene with the whole congregation weeping at the entrance of the tent of meeting, and says an Israelite man (later identified as Zimri) 'brought near to his brothers' a Midianite woman in the sight of Moses and everyone else. Phineas, however, is described as 'arising from the midst of the congregation' to do his killing, suggesting movement apart. Confusing the issue once more, however, Phineas goes after Zimri and Cozbi 'to the *qubbah*', the latter a hapax that may mean 'tent'. There is, then, at least a hint in the text that the non-Aaronite *zar* and the Midianite *zarah* transgressed sacred space.

approaches as one flesh with the unapproachable woman: *zar*-ness in all its glory.

The third move made by the narrative is to further warrant the victory of Eleazar's line on its own presumed merits and through confirmation by Yhwh. Phineas re-enacts his father's ending of a plague, this time with direct action against the epitome of evil, the Strange Woman, without the cover of strange/scattered fire. Phineas, the ultimate refinement in pure seed, is no longer merely a bystander to the death of his brothers, as is Eleazar in Leviticus 10, but is set victorious against the worst of impure mixing. Genealogical correctness is thus confirmed on the principles of national/ethnic correctness and right worship, and what seemed arbitrary is assuaged with a sense of moral satisfaction. The lineage of true priests and the identity of an Israel separate from 'foreigners' are established in a stroke. Phineas's initiative both ends the plague and, notably, earns 'for him and his descendants after him a covenant of perpetual priesthood' (25.13), reiterating in the third generation what Numbers 18 had established for 'Aaron and his sons'. Right family + right nationality + right ritual practice + right sex → established priestly lineage.

Theologically, there is even more at stake, for the presence of the Strange Woman is required to make moral and theological sense of the seed fire. Her absence in Leviticus 10—her absence from the altar, that is to say—makes the seed fire not only theologically inexplicable but apparently uncontrollable. In an infinite regress of lines drawn between the holy and the strange, the priestly lineage seems about to end, the chosen priest impotent, Yhwh's fire gone strange. With her presence in the holy place in Numbers 25, reason returns to the slaughter of one Israelite by another in the name of God: it is punishment for illicit consorting with the wrong people and wrong gods she represents. The presence of the Strange Woman may not bridge the theological abyss, but she shields its true depth from the eyes. The cult of Yhwh could not survive without her.

Priest and Zar(ah) *in the Postexilic Context*

Our consideration of the use of *zar* in priestly literature has, among other things, brought the issue of 'right cult/wrong cult' into the purview of the paradigm of strangeness, highlighting in particular the rightness and wrongness of given cultic practitioners. While 'right and wrong' in this case tends to get formulated in terms of genealogy, there are at least two problems that enter in. One we have examined: the problem of how to draw distinguishing genealogical lines in a group that purports to be 'one family'. But this problem has a sociohistorical grounding as well in the obvious but little understood tensions between rivals for cultic control in the postexilic period and the relationships of these rivals to various and equally rivalrous secular powers.

The tension apparent in Numbers (and cf. Exod. 32) between the Aaronites and the other Levites has long been understood as representing conflict between different claimants to cultic leadership; the deaths of Nadab and Abihu, and the victory of Phineas, must as well be the winners' version of the demise of other ostensibly legitimate priestly voices. But is Numbers simply a tale of priests versus priests, or does it shed light on the larger social, political and economic conflicts of postexilic Judah? Mary Douglas has recently added her anthropologist's perspective to the analysis of Numbers in this historical context. Her work in *In the Wilderness: The Doctrine of Defilement in the Book of Numbers* (1993) deserves attention at this point.

In the Wilderness is a study of the rhetorical structure of the book of Numbers, combined with an analysis, drawn from culture theory, of the power relations expressed in this book. She discerns in the complex and artful literary structure of Numbers's final form the work of a member or members of an elite hereditary priestly hierarchy working in the sociohistorical context of what she terms an 'egalitarian enclave culture' at the time of Ezra and Nehemiah.[13] The two sociocultural forms (in Douglas's terminology, the 'cultural biases') of *hierarchy* and *enclave* meet, argue and compromise in Numbers, as they (purportedly) did in fifth-century Judah. I find her analysis imprecise in formulating an overall picture of how these elements mix and match—what the

---

13. I leave it to the reader to investigate Douglas's complex argument regarding literary structure. While perhaps stretched at points, I find it over all a viable, even compelling, reading. Thus, my point will not be to critique her literary analysis. I shall, rather, suggest the presence of elements within the structure that, by allowing for alternative readings, undermine it even as they constitute it. It is also worth noting the considerable doubt that scholars have cast in the last few years on a 'fifth-century' Ezra and Nehemiah (see Introduction). I shall not press this point here, for to the extent Douglas's arguments are valid at all, they could as well be applied to a later date. Likewise, although she assumes a much more historical 'Ezra' than I do, one could follow her argument by substituting the notion of an 'Ezra group' who identified itself with this narrative.

effect finally is of combining these particular bits of enclave and hierarchical thought—but this critique will come as we consider her contributions to our understanding of the postexilic period. Most important
for our purposes is her thesis that the final editor of Numbers resisted
the exclusionary enclave policies of Ezra and Nehemiah, policies likely
supported by other priests whose power was served by emphasis on
pure genealogy and its concomitant in-marrying. If I do not finally completely agree with this assessment, its articulation nonetheless provides
an important sounding board for issues I wish to raise.

The enclave mentality is that of a dissident minority with a sense of
strong boundaries (like the hierarchy), but (unlike the hierarchy) a weak
authority structure and few offices or titles. Its overriding fear is leak-
age of members and it is thus obsessed with the issue of mixed marriages. Enclaves are egalitarian, resisting discrimination among members, but often rent with jealous suspicion over power- and resource-
grabbing within. These conditions make for factionalism that takes the
form of moral accusations against the enclave's own members. Outsiders are not the real problem, but are typically vilified as a means of
group cohesion and preventing defection (Douglas 1993: 51-57). In the
enclave, the main source of pollution is the evil of the outside world
(49). 'The holy war is a welcome distraction from internal strife' (60).
This cultural system, Douglas suggests, typifies Ezra, Nehemiah and
the so-called children of the exile (*beney haggolah*), with their exclusionary policies both to the residents of the former northern kingdom
(Samaritans) and to the 'people of the land' (identified by Douglas as
'the immigrants, refugees and displaced persons who now inhabited
Judah' [36]). With such high-premium items as land claims and access
to imperial authority at stake, the *golah* engages in a effective and coer-
cive insider–outsider maneuver, accusing other members of the community of intermarrying with the peoples of the lands (9.1-4, 11; 10.11),
specifically, foreign women (10.2-3, 10-11, 14, 17-18, 44).[14] Self-satis-

---

14. Who is accusing whom is surprisingly ambiguous. 'Officials', presumably
Ezra's own men, accuse 'the people of Israel, the priests and the Levites' (9.1). But
are the accused ones people who had never been exiled, those who had returned in
previous generations, or those who had just come back with Ezra? Practically
speaking, members of the first two groups would seem the most likely perpetrators.
It now seems clear, however, that the first group, those who had not been exiled,
were in fact among the now-proscribed 'peoples of the land(s)'. Ezra, moreover,
describes himself as appalled at 'the faithlessness of the *golah*' (v. 4), a term else-

fied with their own genealogical purity, they feel free to exclude from membership and confiscate the property of any who do not toe the marital line.

It is in its purity laws, Douglas argues, that the priestly voice of Numbers both shows its debt to the enclave culture, in and to which it speaks, and its resistance to certain aspects of it. Unexpected, both from a hierarchist's point of view and from the comparative anthropologist's knowledge of other religions' taboo systems, is the fact that these laws do not make distinctions between persons and thereby shore up the social distinctions that are a defining feature of hierarchy (Douglas 1993: 48, *passim*). This egalitarianism is matched, however, by a typical hierarchical stance of assimilating the outsider, rather than 'separating the pure faithful from the impure outsiders'. In Numbers, 'contact with the foreigner is not defiling, only idolatry' (49, *passim*). Repeatedly, the reader is informed that the same law should apply to the resident alien (*ger*)[15] as to the Israelite, including access to purification and to cities of refuge (Num. 9.14; 15.14-16, 26, 29-30; 19.10; 35.15; cf. Exod. 12.48-49; Lev. 24.22). Indeed, Leviticus features the Israelite as a *ger* in Egypt become *ger* in Yhwh's land (19.34; 25.23). If, then, all are obligated under the law, all are protected under the law, a crucial political statement 'in a community about to divide itself on the basis of pure descent' (Douglas 1993: 152).

It is in terms of this presumed fifth-century political statement that Douglas explains the odd mixture of hierarchical inclusiveness and egalitarian (lack of) social structure in the purity laws.

where used for those who returned *with him* (8.35). Thus, even the identity of the *golah* is not clearcut. The flow of the narrative from ch. 8, which describes Ezra's arrival in Jerusalem with 'the sons of the *golah*' (8.35), to the accusations at the beginning of ch. 9, either confuses an older generation with a younger, or transposes a situation from late in Ezra's tenure, when 'his' *golah* would have had time to intermarry, to a much earlier moment. On the other hand, the intermarriage of the (early?) *golah* with the people of the land suggests a porous boundary between these groups, a 'boundary' perhaps non-existent until Ezra defined it. One wonders what any of these distinctions amounts to. Perhaps all that counted was willingness to sign on with Ezra.

15. Douglas translates *ger* as 'stranger', thus eliding the priestly literature's distinction between the *ger* ('resident alien'), the *nekar* ('foreigner' [used rarely in priestly literature; Exod. 12.43; Lev. 22.25; Ezek. 44.7, 9]) and the *zar* ('outsider to the priesthood'). This is a point of confusion I shall discuss below.

> Let us suppose, as very easily happens, that there was a populist theory of ritual contagion; that the people were hostile to immigrants, foreign settlers, itinerant journeymen and landless labourers of no local tribe. Some priests would cite old sources to condone the populist discrimination against foreigners; some politicians would be tempted to fan popular anger and direct pollution ideas to political purposes. But other priests would deplore harnessing the idea of God's purity to mundane and unacceptable ends. What could they do? They could write a Bible which provided a non-discriminatory theory of defilement.
>
> The central idea is that the redactor, a hierarchist, and a brilliant poet, is also a person of his times, with strong political concerns, with anti-xenophobic and anti-government views (1993: 159).[16]

Douglas's work points in an important way to some of the complexity in assessing the power dynamics of postexilic Judah. Although she is not alone in biblical scholarship in stressing the inclusiveness of Numbers with respect to the resident alien, she puts a striking political face on the book by tying this policy to a program opposing Ezra–Nehemiah's limitation of the identity of 'Israel' to the tribes of Judah and Benjamin. Further, against the common scholarly view, she insists that the priests of Numbers (and Leviticus) were not the self-interested winners in a power struggle against the righteous egalitarians represented by, say, Korah (Num. 16), but the losers against the 'pure seed' party of Ezra and Nehemiah (Douglas 1993: 40-41).[17] To see Douglas's point one has to gain a critical perspective on the tendency of the mod-

---

16. To take one example, the story of Balaam becomes, in her reading, a political satire, with Nehemiah as the ridiculed prophet, Israel as the beleaguered but insightful ass, and the king of Persia as Balak (Douglas 1993: 216-34). We shall consider in Chapter 7 Eilberg-Schwartz's proposal that the ass is a metaphor not for Israel but for the *ger*, the person whose status is in-between that of native and foreigner (1990: 126-28). This results for Eilberg-Schwartz in a reading of Balaam quite different from that of Douglas: here he is 'the paradigmatic outsider who becomes a lover of Israel' (127). Despite this difference, the role of the ass as the vehicle of mediation between insider and outsider is similar in both readings.

17. Eskenazi (1988: 30-33), following Japhet and Williamson, makes a similar sort of case for distinguishing Ezra–Nehemiah from Chronicles, based on the exclusionary policy of the former vs. the openness of the latter not only to 'Samaritans' but also in recognizing the children of mixed marriages as members of Israel. Indeed, 'Samaritans' do not effectively exist in Chronicles because the territory of the former northern kingdom is there regarded as of a piece with 'Israel'. Chronicles's construction of 'Israel' as the 12 tribes—as opposed to Ezra–Nehemiah's 'Judah and Benjamin'—is also in line with Numbers (cf. Douglas 1993: 172-84).

ern democratic West to see the tradition-preserving interests of hierarchy as always and only self-serving and the egalitarian instincts of the
enclave as entirely, nobly self-sacrificing. Hierarchy depends on communal well-being, and populism can be deadly to those not regarded as
'of the people'.

Although I have been intrigued by Douglas's work, I find it in need
of nuancing, on a number of levels. For a start, even if one accepts the
biblical chronology as history, there is considerable oversimplification
in setting off 'those who remained in the land' against 'those who returned from exile' with no attention to the earlier and later phases of the
return: 80 years had passed from the beginning of the 'restoration' to the
time of Ezra. In different ways, the work of Jon Berquist (1995) on the
historical changes over this time period and the adaptations by Daniel
Smith(-Christopher) (1989; 1991) and Joseph Blenkinsopp (1991b) of
Weinberg's 'citizen–temple community' construction offer important
(though different) thickenings of sociohistorical description. In Blenkinsopp's view, it was the early returnees who had power in Judah when
Ezra and Nehemiah arrived, having adopted the dual strategy of controlling the Temple and (re-?)claiming what they considered their land
from those who had taken it over in the interim (cf. Camp 1985: 239-
42). Intermarriage for political purposes was obviously not condemned.
Ezra and Nehemiah indeed had problems with the priests they encountered, but hardly because of the latter's theology of inclusiveness or
their pastoral concern for the marginalized. In Smith-Christopher's reconstruction, on the other hand, the early returnees divided between the
few who prospered, partly by means of intermarriage, and the majority
(still a minority of the population), who separated themselves as a form
of survival strategy, and who later were supported by the separationist
policy of Ezra and Nehemiah. This sounds quite compatible with Douglas's view until Smith-Christopher ties this line of thought to (who
else but?) the priests responsible for Leviticus and Numbers (1991: 85-
86). Not only do these reconstructions differ from each other, but it is,
in the end, quite likely that all give too much historical credibility to the
books of Ezra and Nehemiah, which may, perhaps, be best regarded as
based on founder myths (so Grabbe 1998a; see Introduction).

Where does all this leave us? I have not found for myself a satisfying
sociohistorical reconstruction that precludes all others. My guess is that,
had we but a time machine, we would discover a set of shifting alliances
and animosities—sometimes predictable and sometimes not—through-

out the entire postexilic period. Nonetheless, Mary Douglas's question remains. How shall we account for the (at least relatively) inclusive perspective of Numbers—its insistence on the same law for the Israelite and the *ger*, its embrace of all the tribes of Israel, and its non-hierarchical pollution system—expressed in what she perceives as an arcane but beautiful literary structure? In what follows I shall attempt to address these issues through a threefold critique of *In the Wilderness*. I shall point, first, to a certain confusion in her enclave/hierarchy model; secondly, to a failure to account for the significance of the intrapriestly power politics in Numbers; and, thirdly, to certain undermining elements embedded in her tightly conceived literary structure, specifically, the presence of the *zar* and the Strange Woman.

(1) I find throughout Douglas's book a rather jumbled application of the categories of enclave and hierarchy to Numbers. It is clear she wants to present the book as the work of a hierarchist who has adapted certain enclave elements, but there is no explanation of how the enclavist and hierarchist aspects of Numbers fit into a functional synthesis, either socially or literarily. Given the enormous degree of coherence she attributes to the book, one would expect its enclavist and hierarchist aspects not to appear an entirely random aggregate. On the social front, one would like to see some proposal for how a group of hierarchists integrated enclave elements into their praxis. If hierarchy is defined by institutionalized distinctions among its members, how would it continue to operate when it ignored or denied these, as the Numbers poet purportedly does? But does Numbers in fact deny all distinctions? Put another way, what happens when the cultural form or 'bias' of hierarchy gives up its desire to classify persons? According to the model, it should become an enclave. Yet an enclave is defined in (another) part by an anti-foreigner rhetoric absent, as Douglas would have it, from Numbers. Or is this rhetoric completely absent?

These questions move already into the second and third parts of my critique. I shall argue that Douglas tends to mask these problems by constant appeal to what is, in my view, an idealized facade provided by the Numbers hierarchist that allows her to read past some serious tensions. Underneath her account of order, inclusiveness, an unconcern with matters of control, and an attitude of forgiveness, I perceive a constant attention to bulwarking certain boundaries against a threat of imminent collapse and a deep concern for who is in control—the enclavist's nightmare. The effects of combining the hopes of a hierarchist with the *fears* as well as the forms of an enclavist—two sides of one coin in the book of Numbers—deserve some attention.

(2) Part of what troubles me about *In the Wilderness* is that, while Douglas develops a rather convincing scenario of conflict between a traditional priestly caste with a catholic view of community member-ship and a dissident but power-hungry minority shaping its identity through vilification of outsiders, her analysis would seem to suggest that this power struggle was resolved without residue. The 'good' priests, having made a generally understated literary-theological response to a pressing sociopolitical problem, nonetheless lose to their opponents. Having fought the good fight, they...what? Ride off into the sunset? What does a hierarchy do when it finds its power challenged by the sur-rounding political forces? Perhaps it does, as Douglas argues, issue an idealistic political tract asserting old values of tradition, while shaping itself to new realities. The book of Numbers also suggests, however, that it finds a way to entrench itself for the long haul.

Not at issue here is Douglas's claim that the system of defilement we find in Numbers is, in its refusal to use defilement to delineate social groups, significantly different from the taboo systems of other cultures. Her further conclusion, however, that Numbers exhibits no interest at all in social control, is inherently dubious for any ideological literature; it is also contradicted every time she mentions (though only to dismiss) the one dividing line of such concern in the book. This is the line between sanctuary and camp and, hence, between priests and laity, the marking of which generates so much tension between priests and priests (cf., e.g., Douglas 1993: 155). Dismissing the Levites' challenge in Numbers 16 as merely 'a matter of priestly families squabbling to be first' (134) misses the rather important point that control of the cult always constitutes a significant social power base. Her failure to take account of the power issue at stake here is all the more surprising in the context of her discussion of Numbers 16–17, where she makes the bril-liant point that the submission of Judah's rod, along with those of the other tribes, to the rod of Aaron represents a contest between 'church and state', resolved in the direction of theocracy. If she is correct that this victory marks 'the theocratic political solutions of the enclave' (134), then we are watching the practical working out of the position of a still-viable priesthood in an enclave environment. It appears as some-thing like a round table with the biggest chair reserved for the priest.

There is, however, some amount of confusion here regarding who has lost and who has won and on what terms. By 'theocratic political solutions of the enclave', does Douglas mean that the priestly editor of Numbers has given up his bias toward hierarchy in favor of enclavism, or that the 'Ezra'-associated enclavists have taken over the priesthood? The latter formulation is more typical of biblical scholarship's view of history, but I think, as an interpretation of Numbers, Douglas intends the former. A round table with a big chair is a good description of the enclave political style, which does not lack leaders, but only structure. The only question is who sits in that chair: Numbers insists it will be Aaron, or to be more precise, Aaron's 'grandson' Phineas.

According to this vision, however, our Numbers poet has no intention of losing to anyone. Naturally not, but this sort of power politics does not get much play in Douglas's reconstruction of the voice behind Numbers. 'Inclusivism' gets a bit tainted on my reading. If the Numbers priests were willing to adopt as much of an enclave style as it seems, how far removed from the ways and means of an Ezra-style group were they? To sit in the big chair requires supporters around the table. Douglas's assumption that 'the people of the land' were all poor immigrants or landless tribesmen seems naive. It is far more likely that many of these families (especially those married into by the priests and other leaders) had acquired (whether in the nearer or more distant past) land holdings of some interest to a priestly group under siege.[18] Open arms toward the northerner, the *ger* and others who had not gone into exile (or had come back early) is a good investment as well as nicer theology.

My point is not finally to reduce Numbers's inclusive vision of Israel to mere political manipulation of tradition. But I find the power struggles behind Numbers more complex and the literature itself less sanitized of them than Douglas suggests, especially in terms of her unwillingness to factor in what seem to be clear indications of a battle for the priesthood. I suspect that the priestly interest in those not of the tribes of Judah and Benjamin (the latter, presumably, Ezra's and Nehemiah's constituency) is no less self-interested (if functionally still more admirable) than the exclusionist policy of Ezra–Nehemiah. This suspicion

18. Douglas acknowledges this at points (e.g. in her discussion of Ezra), but does not factor it into her power analysis. In contrast, compare van Houten (1991: 129-30, 151-57), whose analysis of the priestly laws on the alien (*ger*) shows that the law presupposes the alien to be 'economically secure, even wealthy' (129).

derives from a linkage of two other dimensions of Numbers's rhetoric to which Douglas pays little or no attention: first, the concept of strangeness tokened by the word *zar*; secondly, the matter of gender. We return, then, to these ideological flashpoints in the literature.

(3) In terms of our conversation with Douglas's work, what is important about *zar*-ness and femaleness is that they mark the breaking points of the ideological coherence she finds in Numbers or, put otherwise, they point to a more problematic ideo-logic disruptive of its irenic surface structure. The repeated yet contested distinction between priest and *zar* is the one exception to Douglas's crucial point that the purity laws make no distinctions between persons. Not only is this distinction regularly at issue in the book, its violation results in death, which is, in Douglas's formulation, the single, essential meaning of the defilement system: 'The biblical idea of purity is simple and coherent. The nature of the living God is in opposition to dead bodies' (Douglas 1993: 24). Femaleness, on the other hand, marks the outer boundary of Numbers's inclusiveness. A hierarchy is, in Douglas's model, a cultural form marked by strong boundaries. Though it may have a wide-reaching catholicity—anyone who wishes can find a place—it must in some way establish a line between inside and outside. Douglas argues that, for Numbers, the line is defined by idolatry. The gender rhetoric is, however, tied to this concept in telling ways.

With respect to *zar*, our study has revealed in Numbers (and its priestly companion material in Exodus and Leviticus) an interesting split between this lexical item and the concept of foreignness it often renders. The priests build on one of *zar*'s common connotations, as 'outside [any given person's] family', specifying this as 'outside *Aaron*'s family', apparently without implicating its possible meaning of 'national/ethnic foreigner'. Could this be taken to indicate a lack of ideological energy against the latter? Douglas does not make this argument, but it certainly coheres with her overall perspective. The problem with such a conclusion, as with her emphasis on Numbers's inclusiveness, is that it fails to account for some very xenophobic portions of Numbers, in particular, the stories of the Moabite and Midianite women (Num. 25; 31) and Yhwh's command to commit genocide against the Canaanites (33.50-56; cf. 21.1-3; 31.1-12). It may well be true, as Douglas theorizes, that an enclave culture vilifies an enemy outsider not because the outsider is a problem, but rather to induce group cohesiveness. Foreigners, in the form of strange women, are nonetheless vilified in Numbers in a manner not alien to Ezra and Nehemiah. Strange women, along with the non-priestly *zar* who approaches, bring death. This choice of rhetorical strategy has consequences, perhaps especially so when it is done not by a group of pure enclavists, but one with a strong hierarchical bent. Who are represented by these foreigners? What is the significance of tying rhetoric against them so closely to the figure of the Strange Woman? What is the relationship of death at this outer boundary to the *zar* who is threatened with death inside?

There are two noteworthy points in all this. One is that Numbers's almost technical use of but one of *zar*'s several connotations has in fact added to its semantic range. If *zar* refers to one outside Aaron's family, and if Aaron's family controls the cult, then *zar* has come to connote 'strange cult', that is, cult unacceptable to Yhwh. Second is that the failure to use *zar* to refer to national/ethnic foreigners has not eliminated anti-foreign rhetoric and, most especially, has not eliminated the figure of the *zarah*, the Strange Woman, as the embodiment of the dangers of foreign people and their gods. Our previous discussion has already raised the possibility that the concern for strange cult in Leviticus 10 and Numbers 16–18 is not without allusion to the Strange Woman. The narrative dramas involving Midianite and Moabite women in chs. 25 and 31 offer an invitation to refill the connotative gap in Numbers's use of *zar* and thereby to align the one crucial social-theological distinction wrought by its defilement system—that between priest and *zar*—with its rhetoric of exclusion of foreigners. Thus is the ideology of the enclave woven into the fabric of hierarchy with the Strange Woman as the thread.

The ideological unity of the *zar*-just-outside-the-inside and the *zarah*-on-the-periphery is marked in two important ways. We have already noted how crossing either line results in death. The role of Phineas the priest in Numbers 25 is also important. By slaying both the Strange Woman and the Israelite man who brought her near the sanctuary, Phineas establishes his priestly credentials and receives the renewal of Yhwh's covenant with Aaron's house. Victory over the threat at the outer boundary is thus construed as justification of one's claim to the center. And idolatry is thus construed as resistance to the victor's claim. Let no *zar(ah)* approach.

Before turning to an extended analysis of the texts about women in Numbers, we might take a glance back to our point of departure in this chapter and place in conversation the work of Douglas (1993) with that of Eilberg-Schwartz (1990). What we have seen in the priestly literature is an inversion of the word *zar* from a typical use as a marker of boundaries at the furthest reach of strangeness—what is altogether outside the community and its framework of values—to a marker of what is most deeply inside, but separate from all else. I would argue that the semantic reversal in the priestly use of *zar* is predictable given Eilberg-Schwartz's description of priestly ideology. In either case, one of the strongest metaphorical entailments of *zar*-ness is that of birthright (or birth-wrong, as the case may be). Thus, to be a priest one must be born a priest; the priests' references to *zar* inform us by negation that biological descent is the ruling principle. More surprising is the implication that other Israelites—even other Levites, and even certain Aaronites!—can be regarded as 'strange', subject to divine fire not for claiming to be holy as Yhwh is holy, but simply for claiming to be holy as Aaron is holy. For no apparent reason, though with obvious political force, the vast majority of Israelites have been made strange by reason of birth.

Eilberg-Schwartz focuses on what he takes to be the embrace of the arbitrary in the priestly ideology, embodied in its principle of descent. In contrast, Douglas emphasizes the element of intentionality in the laws of Numbers as peculiarly definitive of *these* priests' worldview (1993: 157, *passim*).[19] Given our analysis of the interaction of hierarchical and enclavist elements in the book, we should not, I think, be surprised to see both these perspectives at work, but the emphasis on descent surely disallows the thoroughgoing intentionality perceived by Douglas. Numbers shares with Ezra–Nehemiah, furthermore, the rhetoric of lineage in combination with resistance to the Strange Women and with the fear of polluting holy space. These may have been applied, in the course of things, against or on behalf of different groups, but the ideologic—the logic of sex, seed and strangeness—is the same. It is not as clear to me as it is to Douglas that the ideology of Numbers stands completely opposed to Ezra–Nehemiah; in both cases, the binary of strangeness and holiness is at work. In the following chapter, we shall consider the other ways, in addition to or in combination with lineage, that Numbers overrides its intentionalist strands. What choices were offered to Miriam, to Aaron, to 'the Canaanites', to the women of Midian?

---

19.   This is a perspective Eilberg-Schwartz associates with the later rabbis, as over against the priests (1990: 195-216).

Chapter 6

THE (E)STRANGE(D) WOMAN IN THE WILDERNESS:
MIRIAM AMONG THE PRIESTS

In this chapter we shall consider the construction of the character of Miriam in Numbers in terms of the priestly ideology and struggles discussed in Chapter 5. Though an Israelite—indeed, sister to the quintessential Israelites, Moses and Aaron—she is twice 'made strange' in classic priestly modes: first, impurity by leprosy and exclusion from the congregation (Num. 12); later, by death where there is no water for purification (Num. 20). This tale of the sister estranged is marked by doubling, a device Kunin associates with ideological masking. 'This double structure is one of several patterns found in the biblical text which serve to cloud or obscure the underlying structure' (Kunin 1995: 133). In Numbers 12, the impetus for Miriam's crime is apparently twofold: Moses has married a Cushite woman, a Strange Woman in the most obvious of our senses of the term, and he is perceived to have claimed an authority from Yhwh exceeding that of his co-leaders. The accusers are also doubled: Miriam is joined by Aaron in her complaint. In each case, however, the doubling is not overtly maintained. The issue of marriage is immediately dropped in favor of the dispute over authority, and Miriam is ultimately singled out for punishment while Aaron joins Moses as her intercessor with Yhwh.

The doubling leaves its mark in Numbers nonetheless,[1] masking an

---

1. This sort of doubling, with one episode or version of an event intercut with another, is rampant in the rebellion chapters of Numbers: Num. 11 interweaves the people's demand for meat with Moses' complaint to Yhwh; Num. 16 presents a confused mix of rebellion leaders (Korah, Reubenites, leaders of the congregation); Num. 20 patches together the deaths of Miriam and Aaron with the people's wish for death. If Kunin is correct about doubling as a device of concealment, then each of these chapters needs to be read with an eye to unmasking the ideological tensions at play. See further Chapter 7's discussion of Levi and Simeon in Gen. 34.

'underlying structure' similar to that discerned by Kunin in Genesis, particularly in the Joseph story. The tension in the latter case is between, on the one hand, the affirmation that 'Israel' is comprised of the 12 sons of Jacob and, on the other, the mythic drive to select one son as carrier of the divine seed. We have already observed in the preceding chapter how Numbers manifests an analogous tension of identifying a chosen lineage within a chosen lineage, here, with respect to priests.

Kunin's work also introduces another element in the myth of descent, what he calls a preference for incest, which works itself out in Genesis by means of narratives in which wives must become sisters before the chosen seed can be passed on. As I have suggested, however, and must now argue, priestly ideology turns this logic of incest back on itself. It is, on the one hand, terribly concerned with fertility and descent, yet marks itself though circumcision as set apart from women (so Eilberg-Schwartz). Sisters are a dangerous anomaly in a system of male descent —both closest kin in the 'right' lineage, yet, as not-male, altogether Other. Priestly narrative[2] must, then, as complication to the wife–sister transformation, also disclose the sister as the Stranger within. This is, as we shall see, no simple task; indeed, we are working with a paradox that is fundamentally self-deconstructive.

In what follows, I shall argue that the relationship of sister and priestly brother functions in Numbers as a cipher for the problem of infinite regress in the marking of identity boundaries, and this on several levels:

2.   Scholarship informed by the Documentary Hypothesis would dispute assignment of the Miriam narrative to the so-called Priestly source (P), though its composite form resists easy categorization in one of the other sources. See, e.g., Noth (1968: 93-94), who regards Num. 12 as 'one of the secondary additions to J'. He insists, nonetheless, that it is a relatively 'early' addition because it shows no awareness of the brother–helper relationship between Moses and Aaron established in Exod. 4 and 6, the brother–sister relationship between Aaron and Miriam in Exod. 15.20, or the sibling relationship of all three recorded in 1 Chron. 6.3. My interest, however, is not in the origin of independent units in Numbers, but in a final form reading. There is indisputable P material at the beginning and end of Numbers (chs. 1–10 and 26–36) that encourages a priestly reading of the text now in-between in the interest of a larger agenda. It is in these terms that I cast the Miriam narrative as 'priestly'. I am, further, interested in a canonical reading that puts the relationships depicted in Numbers in conversation with those in Exodus. This sort of reading assumes necessarily a 'late' text.

the political problem of dividing priest from non-priest when both are of the same lineage plays out in the more intimate terms of acknowledging and resisting the unities of brother and sister, and brother and brother, as well as in the theo-national terms of dividing one son of Abraham/Isaac from another, and in the ultimate theological terms of dividing God from human. In each case, strange women, and especially the estranged sister, bring into focus the often suppressed narrative effort to delineate boundaries both impossible and essential. Through the Strange Woman paradigm, the symbolic components of 'true Israelite' identity—right nationality, right deity, right sex—are brought into relationship with the construction of 'true (= priestly) leadership'—right lineage, right cult, right gender. Also through this figure, however, these clear lines of identity are undermined, only to be recast at her demise.

Woven into this troubled fabric of boundaries and identity are related concerns about power and authority. Some of these we have examined in Chapter 5's discussion of the conflicts between groups of priests narratized in Numbers. In the present chapter we turn to the narratives' expression of a priestly epistemology. How is the claim to know God's will made? Here, as in the wisdom texts already studied, we find concern for the forms and transmission of language, often parsed with body parts—lips, tongue, penis—but finally embraced as a body of writing in which priestly flesh is made one with the Torah. The chapter will conclude by arguing that the union of priest and lawgiver, established through the narrative bonding of Aaron and Moses over against the (e)strange(d) Woman, reflects alliances made in the books of Ezra and Nehemiah, but alludes as well to intergenerational power struggles: Moses' and Aaron's 'first generation' leadership, based in orality, remains tainted by strangeness and is subtly effaced in favor of the written word associated with the new generation of leaders.

Miriam among the Priests

In several different ways, Numbers 12 connects the story of Miriam's rebellion against the authority of Moses with issues we have otherwise identified as priestly: ascribed status, fertility, impurity and holiness. At the surface level, of course, is the linkage of Aaron to Miriam in this episode, first as co-rebel, then as intercessor. The shifting characterization of Aaron raises its own questions, however. Why was Miriam so afflicted while Aaron seems only to gain in stature following their rebellion? In this section, I shall address this question through an anal-

ysis centered precisely on the priestly concerns underlying the narrative
surface.

Status and Fertility

I suggested at the beginning of Chapter 5 that a combination of the
theories of Eilberg-Schwartz (1990) on priestly ideology and Kunin
(1995) on the Bible's mythological preference for incest could provide
a framework for interpreting the stories of estranged priestly sisters.
Beginning with Eilberg-Schwartz, one might consider the narrative's
odd disparity of treatment of Miriam and Aaron in terms of the priests'
embrace of their own ascribed status, alongside their phallicly based
ideology of fertility and descent. Numbers 12 falls amid of a series of
episodes in chs. 11–16 and 20 relating the congregation of Israel's
repeated complaints about their current lot and various levels of resistance to the authority of Moses and one or another of his co-leaders. (In
Num. 11, the challenge is to God's ability to provide tasty food; in 12,
to Moses' exclusivity as a spokesperson for God; in 13–14, to Joshua's
and Caleb's [surrogates for Moses and Aaron] capabilities as military
strategists; in 16, to Aaron's claim to the priesthood; and in 20 against
Moses and Aaron due to lack of water.) Eilberg-Schwartz observes,
with respect to Korah's rebellion in ch. 16, that 'the priestly writer
never justified the privileged status of [Aaronite] priests vis-à-vis other
Israelites in terms of performance… [T]he priestly writer offers no
explanation as to why God preferred [Aaron's] genealogical line over
others' (1990: 199). On one level, the same level of (non)reasoning
seems to apply in Numbers 12. Why was Miriam punished and not
Aaron? Because. Just as God makes an arbitrarily fine distinction not
just between one tribe of Israelites (the Levites) and the others, but between lineages within that tribe (Aaron, not Korah), so also God picks
and chooses within that lineage: Aaron, not Miriam. (And here we
might also remember Nadab and Abihu.) Ascribed status—a matter of
birthright—is by definition arbitrary; it is just as arbitrary as the punishment of Miriam and not Aaron, and is, in fact, modeled by the fates
of those two characters.

The fact that Miriam is female is hardly irrelevant, however. The
priestly editors of Numbers construct Woman as part of and in further-
ance of their larger agenda, a key component of which is that *patri*lineage is the order of the day.[3] In the sequence of rebellions in Numbers

3.   I take issue here with Douglas's dismissive view of the importance of gen-

11–16 that culminate in the validation of God's choice of Aaron, Miriam's gender serves this larger, but still manifestly gendered, symbolic purpose. Female gender signifies the Other. But, as Kunin would argue, the Other most difficult to deal with is the one closest to the Self. The sister–brother relationship of Miriam and Aaron represents this dynamic. On one level, she is one of his two closest living relatives; then again, by virtue of her femaleness, she is everything he is not. Her affliction with leprosy, a form of impurity, merely dramatizes the point; her various structural associations with strange women (including, but not limited to, Moses' foreign wife; see below) intensifies it. Aaron is clean no matter what he does—his status is ascribed, not achieved—and the primary importance of his relationship with his brother is established. Miriam's (female) impurity, her irrevocable difference, is simply made manifest, the reality of her strangeness to the patrilineage exposing the illusion of her insider blood.

As Eilberg-Schwartz points out, however, the priests know, regarding women, that if they cannot live with them, they still cannot live without them. Women have a part to play, as necessary as it is unfortunate, in the production of the descendants that structures a major part of the priestly worldview and system of self-justification: 'These are the generations' sounds the priestly chorus throughout the Torah. There is thus a logic to the fact that Miriam's brother, the quintessential priest, must be the one to beg for her restoration. In this, he seems to be aligned with 'the people' who are presumably also aware they cannot live without them, and who delay the march to the promised land until Miriam is brought in again (12.15-16). The sister is first estranged, then recuperated. That her restoration 'bears fruit' is evident in the result of the Israelite spies' initial incursion into Canaan in the immediately following episode (13.1-24). They return from the Wadi Eshcol, carrying a single cluster of grapes so large it had to be borne on a pole between two men. To this image of two men bearing a single rod we shall return.

The connection of priest and people, established by the common need for procreation, must also, paradoxically, be denied, even as it is ac-

der in this story. With a slap to feminist interpretation, she contends that the priests had more important things on their minds ('a large-scale philosophical agenda') than putting down women. Douglas misses an important ideological point about the role of gender in the priestly construction of reality.

knowledged. Thus, in Numbers 17.6-15 (Eng.: 16.41-50), in the last episode before a pause in the rebellion sequence, the 'whole congregation'
rebels against Moses and Aaron, and Yhwh threatens to kill them all.
However, just as men need women, priests need a congregation: comparable to his plea for Miriam, Aaron makes a ritual atonement for
his rebellious flock, an atonement that immediately eventuates in the
blossoming and bearing of almonds by his proverbial 'staff' (17.16-26
[Eng.: 1-11]). Though in tension, both fertility and separation are assured when the proper priest performs his proper duty. Both stories,
then, tell the same story. As brother is to sister so priest is to people.

This analysis of Numbers 12 reveals the same concern for priestly
boundaries that we have seen elsewhere in this book. The episodes involving the Levites in Numbers 1–4 and 18 deal mainly with the synchronic issue of kinship; they address the problem of impossible lines
between brothers without overt narrative tension. Tension overflows,
however, in Korah's rebellion and its aftermath in chs. 16–17, as well
as in the story of Miriam and Aaron. Both of the latter sequences also
deal with brotherly relations, but now tied symbolically (via grapes on
a pole and a seed-bearing staff) to diachronic issues of fertility and
descent. In Numbers 12, then, the irresolvable paradox of brothers separate yet joined is transformed into an equally irresolvable paradox of a
sister who is both Israelite and strange. Miriam takes up the position of
the Levites on the line.

Miriam as Israel
Mary Douglas (1993: 196-215; cf. 160-71) offers a bold interpretation
of Miriam as a symbol for idolatrous Israel.[4] Also important for our
purposes is the way in which her analysis draws in the concern for the
holiness of the sanctuary. As we have seen in Chapter 1, the figuring of
foreignness and impurity in female form is characteristic of the exilic
and postexilic rhetoric of Ezekiel, Malachi and Ezra–Nehemiah. Douglas bases her reading of Miriam on her analysis of Numbers's literary
structure, which connects Miriam's story to stories of foreign women:
to Cozbi, the daughter of a Midian clan chieftain, taken as wife and

---

4.   I shall treat here the first and last of Douglas's three major points regarding
Miriam as Israel. The second, which connects Miriam to Dinah, will be taken up in
the next chapter.

brought near[5] the door of the tent of meeting by the Simeonite Zimri (Num. 25); and, further, to the non-virgin Midianite women ritually slain by the victorious Israelites after a battle (Num. 31). 'Miriam and Cozbi are paired, two conspicuously well-connected women, encroaching on holy things' (Douglas 1993: 199). The slaughter of the Midianite women who had previously known a man was also justified by the concern for cultic purity. It is structurally paired, in Douglas's analysis, with the material on the sanctity of the tabernacle in Numbers 7–9, which is notable for its absence of all women, and certainly defiling ones. Thus, all three women's stories have to do with desecration of the tabernacle (201).

Douglas regards Miriam's leprosy, moreover, as more than ordinarily defiling: leprosy is 'the ultimate defilement, the figure of idolatry and betrayal', as attested by its presence in Num. 5.1-4, at the beginning of a section on broken faith (199; cf. 209, 212). Douglas also relates the concern for idolatry, particularly what she takes to be a then current syncretistic goddess worship, to Miriam's status as Moses' sister.

> Being Moses' sister would cast Miriam in one of these roles pre-set for vilification. Numbers, by putting on record God's rejection of Miriam's claim to be as good as Moses, would empower the denunciation of women's fertility cults. For the women of Israel were continually succumbing to the temptation to pay cult to Ashtoreth. Why else should they be continually being rebuked for it?... By ensuring that the reader knows Miriam is the leader's own sister, the poet marked her out as a major symbol of Israel's broken faith (202-203).

Douglas's analysis offers a useful point of departure. The prophetic metaphor of idolatrous Israel as faithless wife of Yhwh was certainly available to the editors of Numbers as a mold for casting the character of Miriam. To stop at this point, however, is to stop too soon. The ramifications of the text are more complex than this, as I shall argue in a variety of ways throughout the rest of this chapter. At this point, I would like to consider particularly the implications of reading this symbolic statement in the context of mid-to-late-fifth-century Judah, the context Douglas posits for the final redaction of Numbers.

We have already raised the question (see Introduction) of whether the books of Ezra and Nehemiah represent actual persons and events of that time. Even granting some degree of historicity, we must still ask whether

5. The verb is *qrb*, usually in Numbers a technical priestly term indicating proximity for cultic service; see Chapter 5.

worship of foreign gods was, by this time, a major issue. It is not clear, when Douglas cites Jeremiah 44's reference to worship of the queen of heaven, whether she understands this (already ideological) early-sixth-century text as a transparent window on religious practice 150 years later. Perhaps things had not changed so much; on the other hand, the failure of Ezra and Nehemiah to address idol worship explicitly raises a question. I have argued for the likelihood that the figure of the Strange Woman in Proverbs operates a metaphorical step away from the actual practice of goddess worship. She thereby becomes a symbolic locus for a variety of entailments of Otherness—including cultic transgression—that is further complicated by her tensive relationship of opposition and identity to Woman Wisdom. The question must be raised with respect to Miriam, then, whether the figuring of Woman as Strange always refers to idolatry or whether the accusation of idolatry is itself a piece of adversarial rhetoric. In Numbers's context of cultic conflict it may, I propose, have as much to do with who may rightfully approach the holy space.

Numbers in fact speaks only once of foreign gods, in the brief episode of Israel's sin with the Moabite women and Baal Peor (25.1-4). This is a passage so replete with the rhetoric of strange sex, gender and nationality as to be of dubious historical value. Even if the text recalls the prophetic rhetoric, with Miriam understood in some sense as a figure for idolatrous Israel, 'idolatrous Israel' could itself be a figure for those challenging the leadership group. Douglas is quite clear elsewhere (e.g. 1993: 78-82) that Numbers expresses a controversy over leadership and asserts the exclusive right of priests to the top of the hierarchy. It is thus surprising that she does not frame the supposed concern with idolatry underlying the characterization of Miriam in terms of these struggles. Numbers 12, I would argue, a priestly adaptation, not a simple reiteration, of the prophetic figure of the straying and repentant wife of Yhwh.

Miriam as Strange Woman
Douglas is hardly unaware of the priestly concerns at work in Numbers. Indeed, as discussed in the preceding chapter, her thesis depends on it, as does her reading of the female offense in Numbers 12, 25 and 31 as 'desecrating the tabernacle'. The differences between her perspective and mine depend in part on what I take to be her too simple and too sanguine view of these priests' universalism and intentionalism—their

offer of inclusion to any who repent and accept Israel's god. Not surprisingly, this interpretation of priestly interests is coupled in Douglas's analysis with an unproblematized reading of gender and national/ethnic identity: the disjunction goes unremarked between, on the one hand, Numbers's purported offer of easy forgiveness through the sacrificial system and, on the other, its treatment of women who defile the tabernacle and its invocation of the ban.

What is at stake here is the question raised at the end of the preceding chapter: granted that intentionality is a strand in Numbers's anthropology, does it apply equally to all? Clearly the answer is no. There is, in fact, notable arbitrariness in some quarters. What could be more arbitrary than the right of Moses to marry a foreign woman coupled with the estrangement of his sister for resisting this forbidden union? Equally contrary to any apparent moral logic (including, typically, Israel's own) is the required massacre of women who had had sex with their husbands, as happens to the Midianite women in Numbers 31. Of course, just as Miriam's punishment can be 'explained' in terms of her revolt against God's chosen leader, so the case of the Midianite women can be 'explained' by reference to a system of thought that posits what amounts to identity contagion passed on by sex: a woman who has had sex with a man 'can transmit the man's essence to another man who lies with her, while for his part, he absorbs her essence' (Niditch 1993a: 85). Nonetheless, in both cases the stories of (e)strange(d) women embody a fundamental moral contradiction: women who do the 'right' thing, whether challenge a leader's foreign marriage or have sex within prescribed social boundaries, are so constructed by the text as to produce in readers the judgment of their wrongness. This evidence contradicts Douglas's assertion that 'in the biblical creed defilement is not caused by other people', but only by what comes out of the body or by moral failure (1993: 25). Two things have happened here. First, the text ratifies a particular social construction of 'right birth'—collapsed first into an image of right gender, then into one of right nationality—as the basis for purity and, thus, community membership. Secondly and contrarily, however, the possibility of a sustained community is undermined by the denial of status to (a necessary) half of its members and by the denial of its fundamental moral norms. Such a rowdy play of values is, I have tried to show, endemic in the figure of the Strange Woman.

Ambiguous Relations:
Blurred Boundaries in Exodus 2, 4 and Numbers 12, 20

The narratives about Miriam and her brothers in Numbers and Exodus present a series of characters with overlapping identities that both generate the need, and provide the means of execution, for drawing identity boundary lines. Numbers 12 and 20, with their emphasis on sibling rivalries and relationships, stand in close connection to Exodus 2 and 4. In Exodus 2 we first meet Moses' sister and his wife, Zipporah, daughter of a Midianite priest; in Exodus 4, the brother–brother relationship of Moses and Aaron is introduced, in close narrative association with this foreign wife. The strange wife also enters Miriam's story directly in the form of Moses' Cushite wife, whom she and brother Aaron oppose (Num. 12.1). These intertwining relations suggest that Zipporah, Miriam and the Cushite can and should be read together, as three characters with overlapping identities. The wife must become a sister in order to produce acceptable fruit of the lineage, while the sister must be exposed as Other. These are not, however, the only three characters in these chapters whose identities overlap. Indeed, overlapping identities, with the attendant need for boundary drawing, seem to be the order of the day: father and daughter, brother and brother, sister and brother, deity and human—all these relationships, in their multiple facets, require the narrative's attention to produce, in the end, Yhwh's true priest.

The Wife–Sister Motif in Numbers 12 and Exodus 2 and 4

'My sister, my bride', exclaims the lover in the Song of Songs (4.10). Kunin's (1995) analysis suggests that the wedding of these terms of endearment is not accidental. The matter of Moses' Cushite wife, which opens and then disappears from his sister's story in Numbers 12, occasions an inquiry into the connection of this chapter to Exodus 2 and 4, which also deal with a sister and a wife of Moses. Noting anthropologist Edmund Leach's question, 'why did Moses have a sister?', Kunin rejects Leach's answer—that Miriam is both sister and *mother*—on methodological grounds (1995: 66-67 n.). Kunin responds that the role of mother is 'structurally insignificant' in the biblical myth and proposes instead that 'Moses has a sister because mytho-logic requires that his wife be his sister'. Because Kunin limits his work to Genesis, however, he spells out no details for Numbers. How exactly, then, might this logic play out?

The argument hinges on a certain level of narrative identification between Zipporah, Moses' Midianite wife in Exodus, and the Cushite wife of Numbers.[6] Although the textual reticence to equate clearly the two women cannot be ignored, there are, as we shall see, a number of connections embedded in the depiction of family relationships in Exodus and Numbers that allow these segments to be read intertextually, foregrounding identification rather than difference. Most obvious, of course, is the fact that both these women are foreigners. It may be that failure to make an explicit identification is a mythic masking device, occluding while also facilitating the wife–sister transformation. The failure to name Moses' wife in Numbers 12 would thus correspond structurally to the failure to name Moses' sister, who saves her infant brother from the pharaoh in Exodus 2, a chapter in which the wife Zipporah later is named.

At the same time, the relationship between the Cushite wife and Miriam, while oppositional on one level, also involves a transformational identification, signaled by the problematic disappearance of the strange wife after her brief mention in Num. 12.1, coupled with the subsequent estrangement of the Israelite sister.[7] Positing an identification between the Cushite wife and Miriam, the negativity associated with Miriam's punishment could be turned completely inside out and read as symbolic

6.   The different geographical origins of the wives is the most obvious impediment to identifying them with each other. Some identify Cush with Midian (cf. Hab. 3.7), but this seems to eliminate the possibility of the wife's blackness, which depends on locating Cush in Africa (cf. the LXX's translation 'Ethiopia'), and on which, in turn, the meaningfulness of Miriam's punishment—leprosy that makes her white as snow—depends. It is possible that the narrator was aware of, and played with, two ancient understandings for the location of Cush. It is also possible that the traditions regarding Zipporah and the Cushite were originally independent, brought together only by means of editorial art. One way or the other, my argument will be that we are indeed dealing with art, and not accident.

7.   Worth noting in this context is Randall Bailey's argument (1991: 179-80) regarding the relationship of the Cushite and Miriam. He suggests that Miriam's complaint against her brother lies in an attempt by Moses to achieve status through marriage to a black woman rather than, as is proper in Miriam's eyes, through being addressed by Yhwh. Hence, Miriam's own status is lowered by being made white. As do I, Bailey sees Num. 12.1 as essential, rather than incidental, to the story of Miriam's rebellion. While acknowledging the force of this argument on its own terms, my own interest lies elsewhere, in analysis of the logic of kinship; from this perspective, the matter of skin color appears as just one element in the construction and deconstruction of binaries, rather than the central point of the narrative.

of death and rebirth, precisely the process each Genesis ancestor must undergo (Kunin 1995: 91, *passim*). Her leprosy changes her from black like the Cushite to white, while her placement outside the camp is a classic liminal locus of a rite of passage before her restoration. Aaron's comparison of her to a child being born is, then, not a rejection of her newborn status, but only a plea that she not be stillborn (12.12).

On one level, then, the foreign wife has become the Israelite sister in a manner structurally analogous to the narrative assignment of sister status to the wives of Abraham, Isaac and Jacob. The larger narrative, however, contains a more complex and less resolved web of familial identifications and dissociations than is suggested by this analysis. Unraveling the web requires further consideration of Numbers 12 alongside the early chapters of Exodus, where we are introduced to Moses' relations as well as to the deity who will become his god. In both contexts, the interaction of priests and the Strange Woman produces some surprising results.

Strange Woman, Strange Priest, Strange God

Let us examine, then, the family relationships in Exodus, under the signs of priest and Strange Woman. In the wilderness, Moses meets four significant characters: Jethro and Zipporah, Yhwh and Aaron. While the first two represent quintessential outsiderness, the latter two embody the ultimate inside. All four also intertwine, especially in terms of the question of priestly status and the related practice of circumcision. As we shall see, curious hybrids will thus appear. The *strange priest* will appear repeatedly in this chapter's readings, raising the question of the purpose his presence serves in the Exodus and Numbers narratives. We shall finally take up this question at the end of the chapter. Relatedly, the Strange Woman will perform a priestly act (circumcision) to provide salvation from a malevolent act by Israel's deity. The combination of shocking plot and anti-typed characters inverts expectations about insider and outsider status, as well as their attendant moral evaluations. These are challenges to orderly categories and identities that Numbers 12 will attempt to resolve.

Jethro (elsewhere Reuel or Hobab) is Zipporah's father and a priest. Despite historical-critical speculation that Moses may have learned worship of Yhwh from Jethro, there is little way to understand his status in the text except as a foreign priest, 'a priest of Midian'. The potential tension inherent in the scene of a strange priest offering a sacrifice is on one level mitigated by a sort of structural neutrality. Although Jethro is a foreign priest, his deity is unnamed; in the presence of Aaron, the not-yet priest of Yhwh, he offers his sacrifice 'to God' (Exod. 18.12). Jethro as the priest of no-god-in-particular leaves a structural blank that Aaron's ordination to Yhwh (Lev. 8–9) will only later fill. As the father of Moses' foreign wife, on the other hand, Jethro and his daughter highlight what should be a dangerous nexus of strange cult and Strange Woman.

Outsider and insider status also collapse, moreover, in the character of Zipporah: she is a foreign wife, but one who performs the definitively Israelite priestly task of circumcising her son/husband.[8] I shall suggest below that the recollection of the wife who circumcises at the beginning of Numbers 12 is not incidental to a priestly reading of that text. For the moment, there are two other points of interest. First is the way in which Exodus identifies Zipporah with her father Jethro through the use of the root *htn*. *Htn* is used regularly, in the form of an active participle (*hoten*), to designate Jethro's relationship to Moses, in these cases most often translated 'father-in-law'. It is also used, in what can be construed as a passive form, by Zipporah to describe the effect of her circumcising: 'you are a bridegroom of blood (*hatan damim*) to me...a bridegroom of blood by circumcision', she says to Moses after 'touching his feet' with the bloody foreskin. As Propp argues, however, 'it seems likely that in Hebrew as well as in Arabic *htn* formerly connoted both circumcision and marriage' (1993: 508). In other words, *hoten* and *hatan*—'father-in-law' and 'bridegroom'—also imply 'circumciser' and 'circumcised'. Thus, in creating a *hatan*, Zipporah adopts her father's role as *hoten* (1993: 514).

The circumstances of the circumcision are also noteworthy to say the least, indeed, incomprehensible in terms of the surface logic of the narrative. Yhwh has just appointed Moses his hero, then, on Moses' journey to Egypt to carry out the divine plan, tries to kill him (Exod. 4.24).

---

8.   There is debate as to who is 'really' circumcised by Zipporah. We are told that Yhwh tries to kill 'him'. Zipporah then cuts off her son's foreskin, touches 'his' feet (presumably a euphemism for genitals) with it, and says, 'you are a bridegroom of blood to me'. The text creates, it seems, deliberate intergenerational confusion that, I would suggest, is part of its larger ideological agenda in which the son will play a part in the father's redemption. For our present purposes, however, we can safely speak, I think, of at least a symbolic circumcision of Moses by his wife.

Moses is saved only by Zipporah's timely act with the flint, which causes Yhwh to 'let him alone'. As with the other characters we have examined, however, Yhwh and Zipporah stand not simply in antithetical but also dialectical relationship to each other: the Strange Woman plays the role of a savior who overcomes the deadliness of Yhwh, as dramatic a reversal of expected roles as ever there was.

The priestly identity narratively offered to Zipporah as the circumcising daughter of a priestly father takes on further substance when her connection with Aaron is also considered. Exodus 4–6 establishes a relationship between Moses' wife and Moses' brother, again by means of the motif of circumcision, understood both literally and as a metaphor for language. Examination of this relationship will, in turn, shed light on the shifting relational boundaries in Numbers 12, where the relationship between sex and language also plays out.

In Exodus, Moses requires circumcision of two sorts: that by Zipporah of his penis (4.24-26) is narratively sandwiched between two versions of the circumcising of his tongue, both involving Aaron (4.10-17, 27-30 and 6.10-13, 28-30; 7.1-2). The sequence begins in Exod. 4.10, where, having been commissioned by Yhwh to speak to Pharaoh, Moses complains of being 'heavy of mouth and heavy of tongue'. Although the explicit sexual metaphor, 'uncircumcised of lips', will not appear until Moses' second protest in 6.12, sexual wordplay is already present here. 'Heaviness' (*kabod*) can connote sexual 'weight'.[9] Further, Moses' convoluted protest includes the notion that his lack of eloquence is evident both in the past and now (*gam mitmol...gam me'az*). *Mitmol* is aurally reminiscent of *mul*, meaning 'to circumcise'; compare *mulah*, which appears in Zipporah's 'bridegroom of blood' speech (4.26). Yhwh responds with the offer of a verbal assistant, brother Aaron, into whose mouth Moses will put Yhwh's words (4.15). Moses' circumcision by Zipporah follows, after which he meets Aaron in the wilderness, appropriately, with a kiss (4.27). Moses' protest about his inability to speak is repeated in ch. 6; here he uses the explicit metaphor, 'uncircumcised of lips' (*'aral sephatayim*; 6.12). Again, Aaron is the solution; he will be Moses' 'prophet' (7.1-2).

9.   I suggest this connotation based in part on the ideology of honor and shame in which male honor (also *kabod*) is closely linked to sexual control. The same play of ideas also occurs in Gen. 34.19, where Shechem is described as the most *kabod* ('honored, weighty') in his family just at the point when he is circumcised (see below, Chapter 7), as well as in 2 Sam. 6.20 (see Fewell and Gunn 1993: 154).

To summarize, then, the relationship between Aaron and Zipporah is tightly drawn in three ways:

1. First, by the movement of the narrative. In the narrative flow, Yhwh's introduction of Aaron (4.14-16) is followed by the reintroduction of Zipporah (4.20), while her priestly act (4.24-26) is followed by the first meeting of Moses and the man who will be priest (4.27).

2. The second form of narrative linkage between Aaron and Zipporah appears in the thematic envelope created by the circumcision metaphor. The repetition of Moses' complaint about speaking in ch. 6, with its reference to 'uncircumcised' lips, completes the circle of mouth–penis–mouth begun in ch. 4: Moses has complained to Yhwh about his heavy mouth and tongue; Zipporah has circumcised Moses' penis in defense against Yhwh; now Yhwh uses Aaron to operate on Moses' lips. While the language moves in a direction from less to more sexually explicit ('heavy' → 'uncircumcised'), the gaze returns in ch. 6 from the embodied danger of the penis to the more abstract matter of the tongue, as well as from the Strange Woman to the Israelite brother.

3. Thirdly, Zipporah and Aaron, along with Jethro, are drawn together through their successive fulfillments of the role of priest. As the second generation, Zipporah and Aaron are, in effect, daughter and son to father Jethro, and thus sister and brother to each other through this priestly connection, as well as through their shared relationship with Moses.

What light, then, does this analysis of collapsing relational, gender and priestly identities in Exodus shed on the difficult dynamics in Numbers 12 involving Moses, his strange wife, his estranged sister, and his about-to-be-priestly brother?

Assuming Moses' Cushite wife can reasonably be read as Zipporah, the brief and apparently anomalous appearance of this character in Num. 12.1 in fact draws with it a wagonload of significance: she is the nodal link between the wife–brother identification established in Exodus 4–6 and the wife–sister conflation that will occur in Numbers 12. Two things have happened at the mythological level. First, as Kunin would have it, the wife is narratively transformed into a sister: the black Cushite disappears and re-emerges as the whitened, newborn Miriam. In the process, however, the sister herself is revealed as Other, leprous and thus cultically polluted: identification with a strange wife makes the sister strange. This second move, not predicted by Kunin's model, is, I suggest, a function of the paradox of infinite regression in genealogical boundary-line drawing associated with a priestly ideology. It begins with a need to separate the 'true' priestly family from otherwise related families in the tribe and nation. But this process has no logical conclusion, as the deaths of Aaron's two sons makes clear (see Chapter 5); lineage exclusivism becomes lineage annihilation. The mythic solution lies with the sister. Because this ideology constructs identity as much in terms of gender as of lineage, the estrangement of the sister, the stranger within, displaces the implacable mythic cutting off of brothers onto the relative who can be named as Other.

Numbers 12 works out this agenda in a very precise way, undoing the intimate relationship generated in Exodus between Aaron and the priestly wife–sister, there Zipporah, now the Cushite wife. The Cushite evokes the blurred relational boundaries in Exodus: the strange wife who circumcises the penis and the brother who both kisses and circumcises the lips. Circumcision, metaphorically and metonymically considered, has, in effect, joined the brother and the wife–sister at the sites of sex and speech. Thus, as Siamese twins Miriam and Aaron approach the cloud alongside Moses in Numbers 12 to face Yhwh's wrath at their rebellion. There Yhwh first distinguishes Moses as the only one with whom he speaks 'mouth to mouth'. Then the cloud departs, leaving Miriam leprous, unclean, thus set apart from her untouched brother. Aaron speaks, first in confession of sin, then in intercession for Miriam, joining his speaking mouth with that of Moses, as he had with his kiss on their first meeting (Exod. 4.27). Severed now from Miriam at the lips, so also at the genitals, Aaron is transformed into a fully male-identified self, the true priest. Miriam is multiply-polluted, barely human, her death in Numbers 20 prefigured.

In sum, then, Exodus 4 collapses a remarkable number of binaries, all in a broad sense definable as 'foreigner versus Israelite', but expressed in several permutations: between another-god/no-god and Yhwh, between *zar*-priest and Aaronite priest, between male and female, between older and younger generation, between life and death as assumed attributes of, respectively, Yhwh and the Strange Woman. Numbers 12 redraws that line most crucial to a priestly self-understanding, the line between male and female. But will this line hold?

Homosexual Relations

I have argued that once the wife becomes the sister, the sister must herself be estranged. Estranged, perhaps reborn; estranged, and then recuperated, perhaps creating the conditions for fertility (Num. 13; 17), perhaps merely an unpurifiable corpse (Num. 20). The sister plays another role as well. She stands between the brothers, both preventing and enabling their physical relationship with each other. At her death the boundary collapses, and with dire results.

In our discussion of Exodus 4, we have already observed the narrative intertwining of the man who will be priest and the wife who will be sister. That narrative contains further adumbrations of things to come through further linkages of sister and brothers. The chapter begins with Moses' protest, following Yhwh's commission, that the people might not believe Yhwh had appeared to him. Yhwh in turn gives him three signs (vv. 2-9). The first is the staff that becomes a snake and, when seized by the tail, stiffens again. Next is the sign of the hand that, when put inside his cloak, becomes leprous and is restored in the same manner. Finally Moses is given the ability to turn Nile water to blood when it is poured out on dry ground. The combination of sexual and purity imagery in these three signs is dense, to say the least. Leprosy and blood connect the passage with Numbers 12, and thus Moses with Miriam, though his impurity is more easily overcome than hers! Moses' erect staff, moreover, foreshadows the staff/snake of Aaron, swallowing those of the Egyptians (Exod. 7.8-13), as well as his producing staff that defeats the sterile staves of his tribal peers (Num. 17.16-26 [Eng.: 17.1-11]). Sister and brothers, impurity and fertility: relationships conceived in the substance of bodies.

And language. It will not surprise us that the verses immediately following the three signs deal with Moses' heavy mouth and tongue. The remedy, of course, is Aaron, and the relationship of the brothers and God is then described as one of great intimacy, even identity. Moses will put the words in Aaron's mouth, and Yhwh will be with both their mouths.

> You shall speak to him and put the words in his mouth; and I will be with your mouth and with his mouth... He will be to you as a mouth, and you will be to him as God. Take in your hand this staff... (4.16-17).

Carrying his staff, 'the staff of God' (4.20), in his hand, Moses goes to get the wife who will circumcise him (4.20, 25-26). Only then does he go to the wilderness to meet, with a kiss, his brother (4.27).

In terms of the narrative flow, then, Zipporah has been interposed at the point of most explicit embodiment of this brotherly relationship. Just when we expect Aaron to come on the scene, Zipporah takes, as it were, the staff from Moses' hand. At the crucial moment, she handles the penis. Not only does this save Moses from Yhwh, it also means that, when Moses meets Aaron, who might have been expected to perform the circumcision, they touch no more than mouth to mouth.[10] On the other hand, as we have seen, Zipporah's status as daughter of the priest Jethro, and her performance of the priestly act of circumcision, bind her ineluctably to Aaron. Through the brothers' mutual surrogate, one brother does not avoid the other's flesh.

I have spelled out in the preceding section the ways Exodus 4 identifies Aaron with the circumcising wife and thus, indirectly, with the wife–sister Miriam. Numbers 12 makes the Aaron–Miriam identification explicit under the sign of language, through the initial unification of Aaron's voice with Miriam's, speaking against Moses. It seems, however, that this identification is here foregrounded only in order to provide the vehicle for their separation. The flesh of the sister who both joined and separated brotherly flesh must be consumed, her mouth closed, that the union of the brothers' mouths may be consummated.[11]

Eilberg-Schwartz (1994) also raises the problem of shifting gender in Exodus 4 and Numbers 12. Although his reading is different from mine, the two intersect in an interesting way. Eilberg-Schwartz brings to bear a point we have examined elsewhere, namely, that the metaphor of God's marriage to Israel requires the feminization of Israel. In our pre-

10. This scenario may remind us of the law in which a woman seeks to help her husband in a fight by grabbing his opponent's genitals (Deut. 25.11-12). Her hand is to be cut off; 'no pity' shall be shown. An echo of Miriam's fate?

11. If Exod. 4 hints at the law of the genitals-grabber, is it no more than coincidence that Num. 12 echoes the immediately preceding law in Deut. 25.5-10? I refer to Yhwh's scathing question regarding Miriam's plight: 'If her father had but spit in her face, would she not bear her shame for seven days?' (Num. 12.14). The only other biblical reference to someone spitting in someone else's face occurs in the aforementioned Deuteronomy text, only here the spitter and spittee are not father and daughter, but widowed wife and brother-in-law. The case, of course, is that of the refused levirate obligation. Though in Numbers Yhwh turns the family relationships in odd ways, the (subconscious?) allusion to a law dealing with a woman's sexual relationships to two brothers is striking. Equally striking is that Deuteronomy, unlike Numbers, sides with the sister/wife: the spittle and the shame fall on the brother who refuses union.

sent texts, Moses stands for Israel, and Eilberg-Schwartz shows how the texts both acknowledge and resist the feminization of Moses, who becomes God's wife. The women involved, Zipporah and Miriam, are dangerous to men because, as the more natural partners of the male deity, they pose 'a threat to men's intimacy with the divine' (1994: 150). On the other hand, Zipporah's action shows that women can save these expendable men through the act of circumcision, the sacrifice of their masculinity to God.

The implication of this reading for my own is this: if Moses is to be as God to Aaron (so Exod. 4.16), then, following this logic, Aaron should become as a wife to Moses. Seen thus, Kunin's theory of the mythologic of the wife–sister either fails or transcends itself. The wife of Moses has indeed become his sister in Miriam, but this has not eventuated in the predicted transmission of the holy seed. For, in the ultimate priestly regression of genealogical boundaries, the sister must not merely be made *zarah*; she must become the brother–wife. This transgressive logic reaches its climax in Numbers 20, where, following the death of the sister, the brothers' rods are narratively confused beyond recovery.

> So Moses took the staff from before Yhwh [i.e. the nut-bearing staff of Aaron; cf. 17.23-25], as he had commanded him... Then Moses lifted up his hand and struck the rock twice with his staff; water came out abundantly... (20.9-11)

The many scholarly efforts to decide whose staff is taken in Moses' hand and struck against the rock to bring forth the water—Is it Moses' (20.11)? Is it Aaron's (20.9)?—miss this point: with the death of the mediating, strange wife–sister, the brothers achieve full genital union—one rod, struck twice—and lose the land of Canaan. Contrast the single, fruit-bearing rod carried between two men in 13.23, after Miriam's return from the death of leprosy. Yhwh's accusation that Moses and Aaron did not 'show his holiness' (20.12, 13) may mean several things, but surely among them is an allusion to the laws restricting sexual contact, including that between two men, in Leviticus 18 and 20.[12] These are laws by which Israel demonstrates its own holiness as comparable to Yhwh's (Lev. 20.26), and on which possession of the land depends (Lev. 18.24-30; 20.22-24). The land's previous inhabitants, who pur-

---

12. 'Showing himself holy' was also Yhwh's stated purpose in destroying the priestly brothers Nadab and Abihu (Lev. 10.1-3).

portedly defiled themselves with such practices, were 'vomited out'.

One further point is worth our notice with respect to the (e)strange(d) wife–sister and her brothers, and that is the degree to which her narrative role as both boundary and mediator between them replicates that of the Strange Woman assassinated in Numbers 25 (see Chapter 5). Whereas Moses' Midianite wife Zipporah circumcised her husband in preparation for his meeting with Aaron, Aaron's grandson runs through with his spear an Israelite man, Zimri, and *his* Midianite wife, Cozbi, who draw near the tabernacle. I have argued that the Cozbi and Zimri episode provides a narrative resolution to Numbers's larger, conflictive agenda of establishing the true priestly lineage by dividing brothers from brothers. It does so by displacing the disturbing death of priestly brothers by divine fire (Lev. 10) onto the satisfying death of a foreign women by priestly spear. The Strange Woman of Numbers 25, while alive, marks a definitive boundary between 'us' and 'them' at the periphery of Israelite identity and, in her death, provides the sign that divides the true priest at the center from all other Israelites. In the intimate tale of a sister and her brothers, the dynamics are similar, yet more subtle. The Estranged Woman, while alive, provides the impossible but necessary line that divides the (male) center from itself. The logic of priestly desire drives toward male intercourse, a consummation sublimated in the presence of the Estranged Woman. At her death, center and periphery collapse upon themselves in the central brothers' forbidden (that is, definitively foreign) union. The desire to absolutize categories ends up destroying them.

Brothers, Bodies, Boundaries

The motif of water appears again in the passage following Miriam's death (Num. 20.14-21), along with even more explicit, though metaphorical, reflection on the problem of boundaries. Here we discover that the transgression of brotherly boundaries is not confined to the body of Israel but marks also Israel's relationship with his brother Esau/ Edom.[13] Moses sends messengers to the king of Edom asking safe passage for 'brother Israel' through his land, and promising to stay on the King's Highway, 'not turning aside to the right hand or to the left', and

13. The use of kinship terminology in Num. 20 ('brother Israel') alludes to the eponymous ancestors of the nations of Israel and Edom, viz. Jacob (whose name was changed to Israel) and his twin brother Esau (later, 'Edom'; Gen. 25.24-26; 36.1).

not to 'drink water from any well'. Denied this, 'the Israelites' press
their request, again promising to stay on the highway, but this time
saying they would pay for any water they drank (was the first promise
not to drink so insincere?). Edom sends out an armed force, however,
and the Israelites turn away. Numbers 20, which began with the death
of Miriam, then concludes with that of Aaron (vv. 22-29), an event that
takes place on Mount Hor, 'on the border of the land of Edom'.

Water and boundaries, foreigners and (subtly) women mark the terrain of Israel's conversation with Edom in 20.14-29. The presence of
sister Miriam hovers still, first in the allusion to 'brother' Israel and
then in the ongoing quest for water, a problem since her death. Pollution now threatens from another quarter, however, for Israel needs to
enter Edom's space. Edom, his brother. Edom, his foreign enemy. The
metaphor shifts: (wrong) brother replaces sister; foreigner substitutes
for (estranged) woman. Israel hopes to walk a highway, a boundary, but
still a fine line. 'If we stay on the line, turning neither left nor right,
won't you consider your body still intact?' (Beg your pardon, that's not
what we meant to say at all.) 'The point is, we won't even touch your
women'. (Sorry, we mean, of course, drink from your wells.[14]) Edom,
the brother, the foreigner, seems to understand the need for separation
better than does Israel: 'No.' 'Well, of course, we'd *pay* for the wom—,
er, the water'. 'Get the hell out; we will not allow the boundary to be
breached.'

Numbers 20 is a study in the metonymic conjunction of kinship and
(national) boundaries. It begins with the death of a sister and ends with
the death of a brother, the sibling relationship mythically embodying
the issue of boundaries in a variety of ways, some of which we have
touched on, others to be discussed. Important for our present purposes
are the locations of these events. Miriam dies after the people encamp
at Kadesh (20.1), a name derived from *qdsh*, having to do with what is
holy. But to be holy in the biblical worldview is to be separate. Thus
Kadesh is the place of holiness, the place of separating.[15] The significance of the name becomes clear later in the chapter: first in Yhwh's
accusation regarding Moses' and Aaron's failure to 'show his holiness',

14. See Prov. 5.15 for the sexual side of the metaphor, and Exod. 2 for Moses'
previous sexual success with foreign women at a well.

15. Jobling (1978: 48) observes a similar connotation in the place of Miriam's
and Aaron's rebellion (Num. 11.35; 12.1; 12.16): Hazeroth can mean 'enclosures'.

then in Moses' subsequent message to the king of Edom. He describes the people's location as 'in Kadesh, a city on the edge of your boundary' (*qetseh gebul*; 20.16). The people then leave Kadesh and go to Mount Hor, which is also described as 'on the boundary of the land of Edom' (*'al-gebul 'erets-'edom*; 20.23). Here on this second boundary line Aaron dies.

The deaths of Moses' sister and brother surround two other sub-units that deal with brothers and boundaries. In 20.2-13, Yhwh responds to the thirsty people's wish that they had 'died with their *brothers*' (v. 3) by providing 'many waters' (*mayim rabbim*; v. 11). The use of *mayim rabbim* is not accidental, nor does it connote in Hebrew the easy sense of divine grace conveyed, for example by the NRSV paraphrase, 'water came out abundantly'. *Mayim rabbim* signifies distress and danger, the threat of the return of primordial chaos. 'Many waters' means, in other words, loss of boundaries. The fact that the quarreling people and their animals are sustained thereby may indeed be an act of grace! Immediately, though, a new and severe line is drawn by Yhwh: the boundary of the promised land will be closed to the water-drawing brothers (v. 12). Whereas Moses and Aaron failed to 'show [the deity's] holiness' (v. 12)—that is, his separation—Yhwh 'shows his own holiness', draws his own boundaries, by means of the very waters of chaos (v. 13):

> These are the waters of Meribah
> where the sons of Israel quarreled with Yhwh
> and through which he showed his holiness.

The next sub-unit (20.14-29) takes up the same themes. 'Brother Israel' addresses the king of Edom, who stands in for brother Esau. Mary Douglas (1993: 207-208) argues that the resulting stand-off, with Israel turning aside rather than fighting (contrast the bellicose response to a similar refusal of passage by Sihon of the Amorites in Num. 21.21-32), reflects the undeservedly peaceful response of Esau to Jacob on the latter's return to Canaan (Gen. 33.1-11). Just as Esau had once let his brother be in the face of provocation, so now Israel returns the favor. In Douglas's view, the message of the Numbers text is that of a postexilic priestly call to peaceful coexistence among all the sons of Abraham. I would argue, however, that while the message of peace may be there, so also is the message of boundaries between these brothers. One brother may not penetrate the other, even with the promise to stay on the line. Esau understands the meaning of Kadesh.

Miriam dies at Kadesh, the place of holiness and separation. Her death in the holy place causes pollution, which requires unavailable water to cleanse. The need for water, in turn, causes contention that brings holiness into question, requiring God to overcome the human failure to 'show holiness'. The confusion begun in this sequence by the polluting sister in the holy place continues, moreover, as the king who is both stranger and brother must then help Israel maintain the holiness of separation. Perhaps most poignant is the final vision of Aaron in 20.24-29. The erstwhile guardian of the ultimate boundary, the one who lives inside the finest of lines (see Chapter 5), here dissolves into the line.

In terms reminiscent of Exod. 19.24, Yhwh instructs Moses to take Aaron up the mountain. This time, however, Aaron's son Eleazar is instructed to accompany them, in contrast to Exod. 19.24, where 'the priests' except for Aaron are commanded to remain with the people. Aaron's death foretold (vv. 24, 25), they go up 'in the sight of the whole congregation'. What a reversal from the hidden work of the priest inside the tent. The exposure intensifies as Moses, on Yhwh's command, strips his brother naked. As if for emphasis, the action of stripping Aaron of his vestments—which include, quite specifically, undergarments (Exod. 28.42-43)—is repeated: God gives the order (v. 25) and then Moses carries it out (v. 28). Indeed, this whole sequence is dense with repetition. Aaron's death is announced twice in advance (vv. 24, 25), as well as described when it happens (v. 28); the going up is both commanded and enacted (vv. 25, 27), as is the stripping of Aaron and the vesting of Eleazar (vv. 26, 28). It is as if the reader is invited to watch these events in slow motion, along with 'the whole congregation'.

Once a priest, once the drawer and preserver of boundary lines, this naked man dies on the top of Mount Hor, on the border of the land, between Israel and Esau, his body to rest forever alongside his strange brother's. Recalling our discussion in the preceding chapter of the infinite regression of priestly genealogical boundaries, one might say that here the priest becomes the boundary with/against his brother, the *zar*. Gender difference, lineage difference, national difference—with all the separation, all the holiness they signify—end in the union of death.

Between a Rock and a Hard Place:
Locating God's Rod in Numbers

What does God really want? Freud's (suitably modified) question provides a point of departure for adding the divine ingredient to the ambiguous relational mix we have been considering. How God understands
Israel's boundaries, and where he is in relationship to them; how God
understands the Strange Woman, and his relationship to her; how God
understands his chosen leaders, and their relationship to his phallic
power—lines drawn and dissolved mark the divine–human relationship
embodied in Miriam's story.

Inside the Camp, Outside the Camp
The understanding of God's location, as embodied in the tent/taber-
nacle, floats in the book of Numbers, and with it, the relative valuation
of centrality and liminality. Although the notion of boundaries could be
drawn in any number of configurations, the priestly worldview is that of
concentric circles, with the elements of the Israelite spatial arrangements in the wilderness matching that of the later temple and its setting.
The ark is the center in each case, circumscribed by the tent of meeting
(= holy of holies), then by the enclosure (= the temple itself), the camp
(= Jerusalem), and the outside world (Kunin 1995: 274-75; cf. Jenson
1992: 89-114). This conception is, however, in tension with other texts
(those source critics would call earlier) that depict the tent on the outside of the camp.[16]

In his study of Numbers 11–12, Jobling argues that there are actually
three locations at work: the tent, the camp and outside the camp (1978:
50-51). These are configured in pairs: tent–camp and inside–outside the
camp. While recognizing the ambiguity in the movement of the tent
between inside and outside the camp, Jobling accepts the logic of the
larger pentateuchal narrative which requires a tent inside the camp (cf.
Num. 2.2). Thus, in his view, Numbers 11–12 operates with the priestly
system of concentric spaces. I would urge, to the contrary, that the still
more-than-evident confusion about the location of the tent not be thus
suppressed. There remains a textual dialectic about where to locate the

---

16. Of particular note is Exod. 33.7-11, with its 'strong traditional links' to
Num. 11–12 (Jobling 1978: 50). Here Moses is described as speaking to Yhwh 'face
to face', as to a friend. Compare their 'mouth-to-mouth' relationship in Num. 12.8.

presence of Yhwh—in the center or on/outside the limen—that is not far removed from a similar tension about where women belong relative to the true Israel, as our study of Woman Wisdom and the Strange Woman has suggested. The fact that Miriam is the one character in Numbers 11–12 who occupies all three locations—tent, camp and outside the camp—identifies her with the god whose presence drifts back and forth across the boundaries, calling them into question.

Numbers 11, the episode of the sharing of Moses' spirit, is notably ambiguous about the location of the tent. For example, the verb *'sp* ('to gather') is used in both v. 16 and v. 30 to describe the movement of the 70 elders, first, from camp to tent, then from tent to camp. *'sp* typically implies 'centripetal movement' (Jobling 1978: 50), which might in turn imply in the first occurrence a 'gathering' to a tent inside the camp but, contrarily, in the second, a 'gathering' into the camp from an outside tent. The tent's outside location is indeed presupposed in 11.26-27, where we are told that two elders who did not 'go out to the tent' are found prophesying 'in the camp'. Contextually, then, the latter verses qualify v. 16, but only after reading most of the unit under a possible misconception.

In Numbers 12, the location is again ambiguous. If we assume some continuity in the narrative from the last mention of the tent–camp pair in 11.26-30, then the tent remains outside. God's call to Moses, Miriam and Aaron to 'come out' to the tent confirms this impression (12.4, twice). However, when God ordains Miriam's seven-day quarantine, he instructs that she be shut outside the camp (12.14), a location corresponding to the place the quails fell at the end of ch. 11 (vv. 31-32). The most obvious meanings to be attached to 'outside the camp' in these latter two instances are punishment and (reading also with the purification procedures in Numbers 19) impurity. There is no doubt here about the concentric priestly topography or its valuations with respect to boundaries and purity—except, perhaps, for the doubt wrought by the context. It is precisely the clarity of the inside–outside value structure in 11.31-32 and 12.14-15 that makes the utter contradiction in the tent's outside location in 11.26-30 and 12.4 so striking. The problem is not simply one of conflicting locations, easily assigned to variant traditions, but of a fundamental moral contradiction in the edited text: if 'good' is inside, what do we make of an outside tent? If we can assume that the tent has suddenly and without notice moved inside the camp by the time of Miriam's exclusion from it in 12.14, all is well. Otherwise, taking the text at face value, we must imagine something else, namely, that Miriam was in the divine presence during her ordeal.

The presence of Yhwh outside the boundary with the Strange Woman appears as a recurrent possibility in the tale of Moses's wife and sister, as it has in other Strange Women stories we have examined. One cannot, however, settle into a simple liberationist reading of the text, with Yhwh identified with the marginalized resister of the powerful.[17] This message is here, but it is complicated by other considerations. For the text does not merely set Yhwh on the unexpected side of a boundary. Boundary contradiction creates boundary dissolution while, paradoxically, helping to maintain those very boundaries.

Jobling expresses certain aspects of this textual dynamic in terms of a 'main program' of Yhwh, which is met by rebellious human 'counter-programs', resulting in the deity's 'counter-counterprograms'. The semantic field ('isotopy') of 'unity and diversity' that underlies this narrative requires that Israel must be one, without foreign admixture, led by one leader (Moses) and true to one god. At the same time it establishes internal separations, between Miriam and Aaron and between Israel and Moses, 'a hierarchy of unmixed entities' (1978: 41, 47-48). This program of separation is accomplished, however, by some roundabout means. Jobling suggests, for example, that the separation of Moses is attested in part by God's implicit defense of his marriage to a foreign woman (47, 48). On this reading, Numbers 12 thus begins and ends in the same peculiar way, with the deity aligned with the (e)Strange(d) Woman.

Or perhaps we should say, as in the case of Samson's women, that the deity merely makes use of the Strange Woman for his own purposes. This would be the implication of Jobling's notion that Yhwh's counter-counterprograms involve a partial cooperation with the rebellious counterprograms. Thus, the people's request for meat is both met and turned against them, as is Moses' demand for assistance in leading the people. Similarly, God joins Miriam and Aaron to Moses at the

---

17. The geography of holiness carries with it social implications. When the tent is outside, all Israelites are equally removed from it, with the exception of those few who are called to its entrance, usually Moses, but in Num. 12, Aaron and Miriam as well. When the tent moves inside the camp, and is then enhanced by the tabernacle with its different concentric areas, divisions are made among the people based on who may come how close to the center.

locus of leadership, the tent of meeting, before separating them (1978: 35, 39-40, 42-46).

This separation of Miriam and Aaron, and the establishing of Moses' authority over both, only happens, however, in and through Yhwh's manipulation of strange women, specifically, in the resistance of Moses' strange sister to his strange wife. But the character of the deity does not go unmarked by such machinations. For Yhwh's cooperation with the counterprograms, limited though it may be, involves a 'counter-deceit' on his part, a disjunction between what is Yhwh's will and what it appears to be (Jobling 1978: 43). Though Jobling suggests (35) that it is only the rebels in each case who are affected by the divine deceit, this seemingly minor moral two-step (it is acceptable for God to tell a lie in order to forward the divine plan) explodes into multiple contradictions when Yhwh aligns with the foreign woman married to the hero against the Israelite sister. The separate and superior identity of the ultimate Israelite has been created through denial of the marriage law that (on some accounts, at any rate) defines the true Israelite. God has become as smooth-tongued and hellbent as the Strange Woman herself; the deception undermines Israelite identity while passing itself off as inconsequential in the name of a greater good.

I have pointed here to an elusive union between Yhwh and the Strange Woman, worked out in terms of the ambiguous location of the tent of meeting, the adoption by the deity of the Strange Woman's deceptive form of communication, and the realization of divine intent through (e)strange(d) women. The next section continues this exploration of moral, theological and identity boundaries by adding the congregation to the relational dynamic between Miriam and God. Here, in place of the moving tent that delineates purity boundaries at one moment and dissolves them at the next, we will follow another figure: the defiling corpse.

Over her Dead Body

One feature of Numbers 12 that would hardly escape the notice of a priestly reader is the multiple pollutions that are associated with Miriam. Not only does her leprosy introduce the issue of purity; it is coupled in Aaron's simile of the stillborn child with the further pollutions of death and childbirth: 'Do not let [Miriam] be like one stillborn, whose flesh is half consumed when it comes out of its mother's womb' (12.12). Douglas contends that relative to other pollution systems the Bible's is extraordinarily simple and coherent, centered on the contrast between life and death.

> The nature of the living God is in opposition to dead bodies. Total incompatibility holds between God's presence and bodily corruption... Humans are subject to normal processes of physiological decay, but woe to the human person who does not take immediate steps to be purified after contact with death... Defilement is lethally contagious (Douglas 1993: 24).

Corpse-defilement receives significant attention in two other contexts in Numbers, in chs. 9 and 19, each of which resonates with the death and rebellion motifs of chs. 11–12 and 20. Again, underneath the ideological clarity articulated by Douglas, we shall encounter as much confusion as certainty regarding what side of the line God is on, a confusion also expressed as a question about God's justice.

Numbers 9.6-10 raises the question of whether a corpse-defiled person can eat the Passover meal. The language of eating and corruption connects this passage to Aaron's visceral description of Miriam's half-consumed skin, as well as to the horrifying vision of half-consumed quails in ch. 11. The affirmative answer, moreover, includes a further, unanticipated, affirmation that a *traveler* may also eat the Passover meal (9.10). Chapter 9 concludes with a description, repetitive of the last few verses of Exodus (40.36-38), of the dependence of Israelite travel plans on the movement of the Yhwh's cloud over the tabernacle: when the cloud was settled, the Israelites remained encamped; when it lifted, they set out (9.15-23).

Traveling is also at issue with respect to Miriam's corpse-like defilement in Numbers 12. Here, however, reliance on the cloud is not articulated; the people make their own decision: 'So Miriam was shut up out of the camp for seven days; and the people did not set out on the march until Miriam had been brought back in again' (12.15). Trible has noted the positive significance for modern readers of the people's self-identification with Miriam, their refusal to abandon or forget her (1989: 23). One might also find here the possibility of a narrative fusion of God's will with the people's will. If the action of Yhwh's cloud is inferred, based on Exodus 40 and Numbers 9, then the text can be read as a divine affirmation of Miriam's inclusion. An opposite reading is also possible, however. Failure to mention the cloud could as easily imply the people's self-identification with a rebellious woman. The latter phrase is to some degree tautological. Women, as outsiders, 'naturally' represent rebellion, and the people's choice to feminize their identity is perversion of the worst sort. Does God, then, join the people in their identification with the Estranged Woman, the one like a corpse, outside the camp? With an ambiguity we have grown accustomed to associating with this figure, the text answers, 'maybe, maybe not'.

Jobling has taken a clearer position, arguing that travel is a crucial motif in the narrative, with movement towards Canaan representing alignment with Yhwh's 'main program', and delay the rebellious counterprogram (1978: 34, 47, 54). Thus the people's tarrying on Miriam's behalf would be judged as negatively as—indeed, of a piece with—her resistance to the true leadership of Moses. One can appreciate the strength of this position and still notice some complicating textual eddies remaining from our discussion of inside–outside above, here in collusion with the matter of corpses.

The first suggestion of corpses in Numbers 11–12 comes in the brief episode (11.1-3) that sets the pattern for these two chapters. Here 'the people' complain, but Yhwh responds with a fire that consumes only the 'edge' (*qetseh*) of the camp, calling to mind both the importance and the danger of the boundary, though without reference to persons. In the second episode (11.4-34), the request for meat results in the mixed blessing of quails. Here 'the sons of Israel' are distinguished from 'the rabble' (*'asapsup*) who had a craving for meat (11.4) and who were apparently the only ones killed by the subsequent plague: 'they buried those who had the craving' (11.34).

The word for 'rabble', however, comes from the root *'sp*, 'to gather'. The ambiguities noted earlier regarding this term surface again. Who is gathered and where to? Some commentators assume these 'riffraff' (so JPS) are identical with the 'mixed multitude' (*'ereb rab*) who joined Israel in the escape from Egypt (Exod. 12.38; cf. the LXX, which uses the same Greek word in each place). 'Rabble' would thus refer to 'the foreigners gathered around Israel's boundary' (Jobling 1978: 51; cf. Milgrom 1990: 83). The parallel between the first and second episodes certainly has the effect of placing the rabble 'on the edge' with those burned after the first complaint, but the assumption that these persons are foreigners rather than 'true Israelites' grants too much to an ideological text. Precisely because of its tendency to label as 'foreign' any who do not agree with 'us', this subtle allusion to Exodus's 'mixed multitude', if that is what it is, must be resisted.

The choice of terms in Numbers is not insignificant. For *'sp*, as we have noted, has a centripetal force. Why use an unusual word with this 'insider' connotation, when Exod. 12.38's *'ereb rab* was at hand and would have expressed 'foreignness/mixedness' so much better? Is it because, as Numbers 12 makes clear, Israelite insiders could also become rebels? When Miriam is given the appearance of a corpse, and shut up outside in the place of corpses, we recognize, against the ideological cover-up, that she has been *made* strange. As if resisting itself, moreover, the text makes a further identification. Not only do 'the people' identify with Miriam by delaying travel until the end of her quarantine, but both Yhwh and the narrator identify her with ch. 11's rebellious 'gathered ones': at the end of the seven days, she too is 'gathered' (12.14, 15; *'sp*, niphal). Naming Miriam as a rebel is no surprise; the ingathering of the rebel surely is. The boundary of the camp may be in flames, but the Strange Woman lives inside.

Numbers 19 details the process of purification after contact with corpses. Given the pollution and death imagery associated with Miriam in ch. 12, it seems hardly accidental that her death is reported in 20.1, immediately after these instructions. The purification process involves the burning of a red heifer outside the camp, and then the storage of its ashes, also outside the camp. While the location of the ritual points back to ch. 12, its enactment anticipates the circumstances following Miriam's death in ch. 20. Purification requires that the ashes be mixed with water to be sprinkled on the unclean persons. Those who do not purify themselves 'defile the tabernacle of Yhwh; such persons shall be cut off from Israel' (19.13, 20). As Douglas points out, defilement of the tabernacle is a problem particularly associated with strange women in Numbers, and to be cut off is, as we have seen, phrasing associated both with the priestly concern for fertility and with the problem of strangeness. It is not surprising, then, that the episode immediately following Miriam's death begins with the notice that 'there was no water for the congregation' and that this lack leads the Miriam-identified people to quarrel with Moses once more (20.2-13; cf. Exod. 17.1-7). Although the complaint is framed in terms of lack of sustenance, the metonymic link with the need for water for purification from corpses and Miriam's death is noteworthy.

Again, multiple readings are possible. The association of Miriam's death with lack of water suggests the possibility that her life was equally connected to having water. If so, the text affirms her as a life-giver, aligned thus with the deity, and confirms the rightness of the people's decision not to abandon her in her leprosy. In Trible's evocative phrasing,

> [n]ature's response to Miriam's death is immediate and severe. It mourns, and the community suffers. Miriam, protector of her brother at the river's bank and leader in the victory at the sea, symbolized life. How appropriate, then, that waters of life should reverence her death. Like the people of Israel, nature honors Miriam (1989: 23).

On the other hand, Miriam can be perceived as a corpse whose defilement cannot be exorcised, generating defilement of the holy place and exclusion/infertility for any who might perform the necessary burial rites.

The episode that follows continues this unnerving undecidability: whose side is God on? Yhwh's response to Moses' and Aaron's prostration before the entrance to the tent of meeting after being confronted by the assembly seems reassuring. Moses is told to take the staff, assemble the congregation, and, with his brother Aaron, command water from a rock. When all are gathered, however, Moses (presumably, though the text just says 'he') addresses the people angrily, as 'rebels', before striking the rock with his staff to bring forth the 'many waters'. Yhwh then accuses Moses and Aaron of lack of trust for 'failure to show my holiness before the eyes of Israel', and condemns them to death before entering the promised land.

I have already offered one reading of this passage, and shall explore other nuances below. Here I want to focus on the corpse of the Strange Woman and the relational boundaries that come to expression in its presence. By ch. 20, it is a real corpse, completing what was begun in the death imagery on Aaron's lips in ch. 12, and requiring that we read these chapters together. As in chs. 11–12, ch. 20 involves the rebellion of God's leaders against the deity. Shifts have occurred, however, in the relationships of those rebelling. In ch. 11, both Moses and the people rebelled, but the leader stood against his flock as much as against God. Chapter 12 began with a close identification of Miriam and Aaron, but ended with Aaron's identity transferred to Moses and Miriam's to the (dead, rebellious, but still 'gathered'[!]) people. Her death in ch. 20 marks other changes. For the first time, a rebellion of the people does not end in their death (compare 11.3; 11.33; 14.28-29, 37; 16.31-35, 45-50). Has Miriam died, sacrificially, in their place? Or has the final exorcism of the Strange Woman finally removed the real evil from their midst?

One way or the other, her death affects not only the people with whom she was identified, but also the two leaders from whom she was separated. 'Miriam's death has initiated their demise' (Trible 1989: 25). But Yhwh's reaction to Moses' and Aaron's 'sin' has struck most commentators as extreme, especially given much more obvious offenses by each in other contexts. Indeed, there is much debate about exactly in what sense they did sin in Numbers 20. Propp offers a useful point of departure. He proposes a felt need on the part of the priestly writer to maintain the purity at least of Aaron. 'Ironically, P found it easier to show Yahweh acting unjustly (at least from our perspective) than have Aaron commit even a peccadillo' (1988: 24).[18] I will not speculate on authorial motivation, but only observe that Yhwh's injustice comes into play with the death of the Strange Woman, a fact in keeping with the comparison of Proverbs and Isaiah 28 in Chapter 1. The Strange Woman mediates the terrible theodicy of monotheism by providing a source of evil apart from both God and men. At her death only these two are left to blame. Enter the promised land? Over her dead body.

Face to Face, Mouth to Mouth

Neither Moses nor Aaron escapes the wilderness alive. Why not? There are the textually obvious answers: they did not trust in Yhwh to show his holiness through the waters of Meribah (Num. 20.12-13; cf. Deut. 32.51); they rebelled against Yhwh's command at the waters of Meribah (Num. 20.24); they broke faith with Yhwh at the waters of Meribah-Kadesh (Deut. 32.51). Our readings with the Strange Woman have suggested other layers of signification: the failure to maintain brotherly boundaries and the flare of divine injustice, both on the occasion of her death. Here we shall turn again to the bodily signs of mouth and rod (as male penis), considered in relationship to the divine word and God's rod (as divine Phallus). What are the terms of their conflation and separation?

The analysis that follows is deeply indebted to that of Ilona Rashkow (1996), who establishes the theoretical groundwork for thinking about Moses' and God's rod in terms of Freudian oedipal theory and the Lacanian theory of the Phallus. I cannot accept her uncritical historiciz-

---

18. Propp in this way separates Aaron from Moses, who did sin in striking the rock, an interpretation not all commentators agree with (e.g. Sakenfeld 1985). Even Moses' 'sin', however, requires explaining for Propp (1988).

ing of the Exodus text in its own ostensible time and place: an Egypt in which Moses would have seen the parades of Isis-worshippers carrying the symbolic Phallus of Osiris. If, however, the thirteenth century is not the time, and Egypt not the place, if Isis is not the desired and suppressed Mother of Exodus, when, where and who, then, is it? In keeping with my overall thesis, we shall turn to the Strange Woman in postexilic Judah.

In perhaps the most remarkable description of a human being in the Bible, Moses is (twice!) compared to God by God. The first time describes Moses' relationship to Aaron.

> You shall speak to him and put the words in his mouth, and I will be with your mouth and with his mouth, and I will teach you [pl.] what you will do. *He* [emphatic *hu'*] will speak for you to the people and it will happen that *he* will be for you as a mouth and *you* will be for him as god (Exod. 4.15-16).

The second instance includes Pharaoh.

> Yhwh said to Moses, 'See, I have given you as god to Pharaoh and Aaron your brother will be your prophet' (Exod. 7.1).

Aaron's mouth, as we have already observed, is often joined to Moses': with a kiss, as a mouthpiece, as a prophet. The latter two joinings also suggest Aaron's subordination to Moses; indeed, who could not be subordinate to a god? It is only in Numbers 12, however, that Aaron explicitly accepts the priority of Moses' mouth, and that through the mediation of the Strange Woman. The rods of Aaron and Moses track an alternate but related course. Initially they are separate: Moses has his in Exod. 4.2 and Aaron his own in 7.9, though both become snakes. Aaron's rod comes to fruit after his subordination to Moses and under Moses' instruction (Num. 17). With the death of Miriam, however, the brothers' rods achieve a deadly union in Numbers 20. This tensive linkage of rod and mouth in the relationship of Aaron and Moses begs our attention to their connection in that of Moses and Yhwh.

The rod is first introduced as belonging to Moses (Exod. 4.2). It is next referred to neutrally as 'the' rod (4.17), but is then transformed into 'God's rod', carried in Moses' hand, as he departs from Jethro's house for the last time (4.20). For Rashkow, 'God's rod represents the ultimate power of a sacred Phallus' (1996: 75). In this sense, it denotes not the anatomical male organ, but power itself, especially in terms of what we want, but do not have, desire, but lack. Seen from the perspective of Freudian oedipal theory, however, the meaning is not divorced from the concrete shape of the symbol. As the male child's desire for his mother confronts his father's right to her, 'the Father's penis, the anatomical organ, becomes the Father's Phallus—the symbol of the Father's power' (Rashkow 1996: 79). God's rod is the symbol of divine authority that Moses, for a moment at least, grasps in his hand. That this is an authorized grasping, and that it involves power as much as sex, is attested, I would suggest, by the immediately preceding passage that identifies Moses as God, and joins the mouth of one to the other ('I will be with your mouth'). That it *also* involves sex and fertility, however, is equally well confirmed by the closely following passage in which Zipporah circumcises their son (Rashkow 1996: 78).

The oedipal conflict is ideally resolved by the male child's 'transcending the familial oedipal triangle, and replacing it with the father-dominated super-ego, a process that for Freud is "designed to make the individual find a place in the cultural community"' (Rashkow 1996: 79, citing Freud, *The Interpretation of Dreams* [1900] and 'Female Sexuality' [1931]). It does not always work; in Rashkow's words, 'Oedipus wrecks'. For Rashkow, this wreckage happens in two related ways. First, Moses abandons/suppresses his desire for the Mother (conceived by Rashkow as polytheism in general and Isis in particular) and 'accepts Yhwh as *the* supreme Law—the will of the Father' (79-80). Secondly, this acceptance is marked on the circumcised penis, representing a partial and thus ongoing threat of castration by the Father (80-82). God thus retains the true power of the Phallus: 'Moses may wield God's rod, but never its power' (83).

I would like both to accept and to complicate Rashkow's reading by weaving into it the motif she omits, namely, the mouth. Importantly, Moses not only holds God's rod, but also speaks with God's mouth. He meets God 'face to face', conversing as if with a friend (Exod. 33.11). The very process of subordinating Aaron's mouth to Moses' is accomplished through affirming that Moses and God are, uniquely, 'mouth to mouth' (Num. 12.8). One could argue that the mouth, representing the Word, explicitly embodies the paternal super-ego, the cultural law into which the (male) individual must integrate himself in order to finally take the Father's place. If so, then the message that Moses is joined to God's mouth, and will therefore be as God to both priest (Aaron) and king (Pharaoh), represents a *successful* oedipal transformation of son into (cultural) Father. The importance of the fact that Moses in part (though only in part) completes his pilgrim's progress will become apparent in a moment. We must first consider further the partial failure of the transformation.

Rashkow locates this failure in the circumcised penis as symbol of castration, an interpretation that can, however, be balanced by Eilberg-Schwartz's comparative data that prove it equally a symbol of fertility (1990: 144-46). The crucial point is that even the fertility meaning is placed in the biblical covenant relationship under divine control: 'off-spring are possible only with the assistance of *this* male god' (Rashkow 1996: 80). While Rashkow reads this as a rejection of the goddess, however, I would argue that, in the postexilic priestly context, it is rather *a rejection of human women and their role in reproduction*. Rashkow's intimation that acceptance of divine law makes Israel 'a kingdom of priests' should be read quite literally, priests being those who do not require women for the transmission of seed.

Now, with Moses' mouth to God's mouth and his hand on God's rod, what can go wrong? It is indeed in the matter of the rod that Moses' oedipal transformation, his full identification with the divine, fails. What is it that Moses and Aaron do wrong in the matter of the waters of Meribah? As others have argued, though for different reasons,[19] they rely not on God's mouth, but on their own rod(s), to bring forth water from a rock. Why, though, did God tell them to bring the rod to the rock? Were they to bring it, but not use it? Just so, a Kunin-style reader might say. The rod, understood as the human male sexual organ, must be present, but only so that its efficacy can be denied in favor of divine causation, a denial that also denies the necessity of human women for fertility. The Strange Woman dead, the time had arrived for the full transformation of penis to Phallus, of male physical potency to supremely authoritative divine word.

The text does not say why Moses used his rod on the rock. Perhaps this silence implicitly acknowledges that he could do no other, that, as human male, he was constitutionally unable to meet God's impossible requirement that human fertility be divorced from the relational activity of human bodies. Having gone so far, in uniting with his brother rather than his sister, as to deny women a role in fertility, he could not give up desire for the already obviated necessity of his—of their—own ejacula-

19. See Milgrom 1990: 456; Sakenfeld 1985; Propp 1988.

tion; of their embodied humanity; perhaps even of their relationship to sister, bride, Strange Woman, with whom they will reunite in death in the wilderness.

There may be more yet to the failure of the text to complete the transformation of penis to Phallus, a failure of the entire male heterosexual power structure to achieve full domination of the symbol system. That Moses' final rupture from God is represented in an allegory of his sexual union with his brother already suggests such an ideological breakdown. The extraordinarily tactile image from Numbers 12 of Moses mouth to mouth with Yhwh complements this picture of ancient ideological failure and offers as well a challenge to an absolutizing theoretical identification of Word and Phallus. If Yhwh in ch. 20 rejects the union of Moses' rod with his brother's, is this because their coming together was itself a denial of Moses' fidelity to Yhwh's mouth, that site of spoken word...and of female pleasure? The picture of the conjoined mouths of the goddess and the woman Moses stands in some tension with that of the gushing rods of brothers. And yet both stand together against the totalizing rule of the Phallus in and through the language system. Numbers 20 distinguishes male penis from symbolic Phallus by naming the latter as heterosexual, thus pointing to the limits of its assumed universal domain. In Numbers 12, on the other hand, the image of the divine mouth seeking a human one to come to expression holds something of language in reserve from the totalizing Phallus. Here, the divine Word is embodied as a woman's Word. The image thus challenges as well any reductive theoretical identification of the Word with the paternal super-ego.

Who now is half-consumed? Picture Moses: in a lip-lock with God, cock cut off—half-consumed, half-apotheosized. Does this sound like Ezekiel, whose deity is but fire below the waist and who offers a scroll as a gustatory delicacy? The relationship of Moses and Aaron to a transcendent Word awaits our further consideration.

After (the) Word

I have spent considerable time on readings of the Miriam texts divorced from any sociohistorical concerns apart from a generalized nod to 'the priests'. Without departing from a discourse-oriented approach, it is now time to draw the lines of social context more clearly. My argument is this: that the Miriam narratives in their present context reflect an interest in authorizing a priesthood in particular terms. To its genealogical concerns I have already drawn attention. Here I shall do two things: first, point to evidence that this priestly handiwork comes from those who consider themselves a new generation, 'sons', not (or perhaps not yet) 'fathers', seeking to establish themselves as the new leadership. They must thus find a way both to honor and to authoritatively replace 'Moses' and 'Aaron'. Secondly, and relatedly, I shall try to show that this priesthood is marked by a particular relationship to God's word, identifying themselves with (their understanding of) its written form and working this out in their narrative construals of Moses and Aaron. If we think of this in Douglas's terms, these are the enclavists, associated with Ezra/Nehemiah, setting their hard boundaries against dissent and ambiguity. Where Douglas and I disagree is in the fact that I hear Ezra's voice in Numbers.

Renewing the Line(age)s

Aaron's death in the wilderness, blamed on his 'rebellion against Yhwh's command' (Num. 20.24), has often been seen as a denigration of Aaron's (or Aaronite) authority. This is not necessarily the case. As Kunin understands the basic structure of the Israelite myth, it is always necessary for God's exclusive intimacy with one man to come to an end before it can be transferred to that man's seed. It is, thus, significant that when Aaron's vestments are stripped from him at death, Moses clothes Eleazar with them, Aaron's son. Aaron, then, is not dishonored, nor his lineage cut off; indeed, precisely the opposite is true. As we have noted, moreover, the up-the-mountain, down-the-mountain sequence in Numbers 20 is quite reminiscent of that in Exod. 19.20-25; 32.15; 34.29. Whereas in Exodus, Moses came back down the mountain with the tablets of the law, however, in Numbers 20 he returns with the new priest.[20]

---

20. It is worth noting the variant in Exod. 24.9-11. Here, the following persons go up the mountain and actually see God without harm: Moses, Aaron, Nadab, Abihu and 70 elders (also referred to, in the next verse, as 'chief men of the people of Israel'). Aaron, however, is almost immediately distanced from this group by the conflicting note in 24.12-15, which, in a disjunctive new sequence, sends Moses up the mountain with Joshua and leaves Aaron below to make the golden calf. The others are all textually cut off in various ways. Nadab and Abihu are, as we have discussed, burned as the result of their strange fire in Lev. 10. The 70 elders receive a rather useless spirit of prophecy in Num. 11 (see further below), and some group

There are several important ideas embedded in these few verses regarding the priesthood and the written law. They are, at the most obvious level, narratively identified as that which is brought down the mountain by Moses. Numbers also brings resolution to Exodus's disjunction between lawgiver and priest. The character of Aaron is divided there: he is both presumably up the mountain with Moses receiving the law (Exod. 19.24) and down below breaking it with the golden calf (Exod. 32). Although he goes up in Exodus, he does not come down. Numbers completes the topographical process as a part of its integration of priest and lawgiver. Moses is established, moreover, as mediator in both cases: Moses gives the law; Moses gives the priesthood. At a deeper level, Moses may be seen as midwife or even mother in the birth of new priest from his father's line (a role he earlier refused with respect to Israel [Num. 11.12]); he is, in any event, the guarantor of the priestly seed.

We shall return in the next section to the relationship of priest and lawgiver. My interest here is to examine the narrative's representation of the transfer of power to the next generation.[21] This shift is clearly depicted in the account of Aaron's death and Eleazar's garbing, and further elaborated in the episodes of violence that follow it: the massacre of Arad (21.1-3) and the execution of Zimri and Cozbi by Eleazar's son Phineas (25.6-15). I shall argue that this intergenerational power transfer is narratized in such a way as to clarify and harden, for the generation of the land, lines left blurry and ambiguous by the generation of the wilderness.

The carefully nuanced recovery of Aaron's character after the golden calf debacle begins in Numbers 12, with the identification/ subordination of his mouth to Moses' mouth, though this chapter looks both backward and forward. Douglas argues for reading several episodes in Numbers as 'fulfillments' of Jacob's prophecies in Genesis 49. She reads Aaron's initial complicity with Miriam with reference to Jacob's curse on Levi and Simeon, that they will be 'scattered in Israel' (49.7). The Levite Aaron's rebellion is paralleled in Numbers's literary structure with the Simeonite Zimri's sin with Cozbi (25.6-15; Douglas 1993:

or other of leading men is destroyed in Num. 16. Seeing God in Exod. 24 seems to have been a dangerous experience after all.

21. Cf. Olson (1996: 4), who argues that 'the transition from the old generation of the wilderness to the new generation of hope and promise on the edge of the promised land forms the primary structure and theme of the book of Numbers'.

194). Thus, Douglas finds it appropriate that Miriam and Aaron die together in ch. 20. While I, too, have suggested a number of resonances of chs. 12 and 20, particularly in terms of the linkage of priest and Strange Woman, it is also true that Aaron is dramatically vindicated in Numbers 16–17, precisely *over against* the Levites, just as Numbers 12 placed him over against the estranged woman. Unlike the Levites (or their cinders [17.2]), then, and in contrast to Jacob's curse, Aaron is *not* 'scattered in Israel'. On the other hand, Douglas is quite right that the pairing of his death with that of his strange sister and, as I have argued, his final resting place alongside his strange brother, insist on a liminal dimension to this central character.

This liminality is eradicated from the priesthood in two steps, over the next two generations. In Numbers 16, Eleazar, Aaron's son, is both identified with his father and depicted as the agent of a fundamental boundary-line drawing between Aaron and the Levites. Although the text slips and slides in identifying its actors (see Chapter 5), on one reading, the '250 men' burned alive by Yhwh while offering incense are Levites (16.35; cf. vv. 6-7). Somewhat surprisingly, it is Eleazar, not Aaron, who is then told to take up the censers, scatter the fire, and hammer the now holy censers into a covering for the altar, all this as 'a reminder to the Israelites that no *zar* who is not of the seed of Aaron shall draw near to offer incense before Yhwh' (17.2-5 [Eng.: 16.37-40]). Only subsequently, 'the next day', during the plague caused by the ensuing rebellion of 'the whole congregation', is Aaron called to duty, putting fire from the altar and incense into his censer, running to the middle of the congregation, and, standing between the living and the dead, making an atonement that stops the plague.

Why this repetition of action and why in this order: first son, then father? The repetition serves to identify Aaron and Eleazar: these are indeed the same seed. That continuity stands in contrast to the Levite-consuming fire that is 'scattered'. The latter word in Hebrew is *zrh*, and the sentence's word order places the object first in the command—*'et-ha'esh zerah* ('the fire scatter')—calling to mind once more the word-play on *'ishshah zarah* ('strange woman') and *'esh zera'* ('seed fire'; see Chapter 5). Eleazar, the proper seed, thus scatters the strange seed. But who is this strange seed if not, as Levites, his own ancestral house? The son has thus drawn the crucial (and impossible) genealogical bound-ary-line between a house and its seed. He thereby establishes his father as the primal father, without forebears or kin, except for his line-drawing son. As Eleazar makes the holy cover for the altar, right seed makes right cult. Only with this boundary firmly marked can the primal father then draw the line between the living and the dead.

Purity at last! The line is clearly drawn...or is it? As Linafelt and Beal recall traces of Aaron's own burned sons in Leviticus 10, here, too, it is hard, or maybe easy, to overlook the fact that the altar cover, hammered from the Levites' censers, arises from the cinders of (e)strange(d) seed. Perhaps some sense of these remaining traces leads the narrative to supply yet another episode of separation in the next generation. In Numbers 25, Phineas, son of Eleazar, runs through with his spear Zimri the Simeonite and his Midianite wife Cozbi in or near the tent of meeting,[22] thus ending another plague. Two things are different here, however. First, this is the first occasion when a priest acts on his own initiative to achieve separation, without being given an instruction by Yhwh through Moses. In Phineas's spear, then, we find a fully realized identification of priestly penis with divine Phallus. Yhwh clearly recognizes the multiple meanings in the event. He states that Phineas has 'turned back his [Yhwh's] wrath', suggesting Phineas's power is equivalent (at least) to the deity's. And he renews the covenant of perpetual priesthood to Phineas and 'his seed' (Num. 25.11, 13).

The second difference between this and earlier line-drawing episodes is that Numbers 25 involves dividing Israelite from foreigner, rather than reiterating the infinite regression of intra-Israelite and intra-Levite boundaries we have encountered so far. There are several mutually inclusive explanations for this shift. We have reached the point in the story where Israel is about to leave the wilderness and enter the land. Thus, the shift away from internal struggles to the need to separate from foreigners makes narrative sense. As Douglas argues, however, it is typical of enclavist rhetoric to cast internal enemies as outsiders. Thus, at one important level, we can assume that the shift in rhetoric after Numbers 20 still masks a struggle of 'Israelite' versus 'Israelite' for control of 'Israelite' identity. It is notable that the rhetorical shift to foreigners only occurs in Numbers 21, after the deaths of Miriam and Aaron and after the encounter with the Edomites, they of liminal status with respect to Israelite/Other. By the end of Numbers 20, the infinite regression of genealogical boundary drawing had reached the point of no return, every permutation of kinship relation and union examined

---

22. See Chapter 5 n. 12, on the problems with the exact location.

and cut off. The mediation supplied by the Israelite woman-estranged is at an end; there is nothing to do but shift all the identity tension she sublimated onto those 'we' can all agree are 'real outsiders'.

The shift in Numbers 21 is violent, a preview of the ban against the 'Canaanites' in the book of Joshua; Israel 'utterly destroys' the people of Arad and their towns. This episode previews both the events of the 'book' we today call 'Joshua' as well as the leadership of the character Joshua. Though he is not named in Numbers 21, Joshua is identified as the war leader against Amalek in the parallel story in Exodus 17, which also follows that book's version of the Meribah incident. Just as the leadership of Aaron's seed begins before his death, with Eleazar's scattering of the strange seed and creating of the altar plate, so too Moses' successor Joshua begins his task as war-leader while Moses still lives. And, just as the next priestly generation takes a harder (boundary) line, so too the political leaders. Moses had acquiesced to the king of Edom in Numbers 20; not so the allusive/elusive 'Joshua' in ch. 21.[23]

Moreover, just as the investiture of Aaron's son by mother Moses brings to full (re)union the identities of priest and lawgiver that were partly severed by Aaron's idol-making in Exodus, so also the contiguity of this investiture with the victory over Arad heals the breach in another way. In Exodus, Aaron's aborted accompaniment of Moses up and down the mountain had been, albeit partially, played out by Joshua, who, in fact, raised the alarm against Aaron's golden calf (Exod. 24.13; 32.17). Indeed, Joshua seems more at home with Moses in what would be Aaron's domain, the tent of meeting, than Aaron himself (Exod. 33.11). In Numbers, however, the completion of the priestly mountain journey by Aaron's seed immediately precedes the military victory by an unnamed Joshua, thus suggesting a full integration (or at least a firm pact) between the priestly and political leadership of the young Turks.

It is not, finally, surprising that Numbers 25 requires the death, at a priest's hand, of a Midianite woman married to an Israelite man—of a surrogate, that is, of Moses' wife–sister. The (e)Strange(d) Woman, the woman of the wilderness, ambiguates the heroic status of her brothers. With her death at the hand of Aaron's seed, they can be redeemed. More than this, as we shall see, Moses and Aaron can now be appropriated as mouthpieces by those who will claim to speak in their name

---

23. Jobling notes the older generation–younger generation opposition, as it relates to the topographical code, by observing that 'Joshua is cognate with Canaan', while 'Moses is cognate with the desert' (1978: 49).

while exceeding them in perfect purity: those who will cut off the Strange Woman from the midst of Israel, those who will cut off the sisters from the family tree.

Moreover, if Douglas is correct that Zimri's death is a kind of ful-fillment of Jacob's prophecy regarding Simeon, then Phineas, son of the house of Levi, puts a horrifyingly ironic twist to the tale. For he repli-cates the violence of Jacob's sons against the non-Israelite who seeks marriage inside the line (Gen. 34; see Chapter 7). Just as the Israelites broke a treaty with Shechem, so too does the murder of Cozbi and Zimri violate the presumed peaceful relations entailed with a marriage cove-nant. But here again, as at the death of Miriam, the demise of the Strange Woman places brothers in unmediated relationship: this time Simeon, Levi's twin in violence in Genesis, 'gets what's coming to him' at the hand of this very brother.

I have argued in this section that Aaron is redeemed from past folly in the book of Numbers, but only in order to transmit the authority of his priesthood to succeeding generations. Indeed, it is only in these later generations that full purity is narratively achieved—from the *zar(ah)* within and the *zar(ah)* without—a reflection, one must suspect, of a self-authorizing agenda carried out by latter-generation priests in post-exilic Judah. There was, however, yet another issue involved in this intergenerational transfer of authority, namely the establishment of priesthood itself as the divinely authorized form of sociopolitical lead-ership in a context where the Mosaic Torah in its written form was gaining a credibility of its own to mediate knowledge of the divine will. We turn next, then, to an examination of Numbers's narrative merging of the voice of the lawgiver with the office of the priest.

Kinship, Knowledge and the Distribution of Authority in Numbers 11– 12 and Exodus 18

David Jobling has argued that the semantic field ('isotopy') of 'commu-nication and knowledge' is a major thematic component of Numbers 11–12. It is manifest both in terms of awareness of Yhwh's will (the 'main program', in Jobling's terminology) and of establishing Moses as the permanent channel for communicating that awareness (Jobling 1978: 42-45). In ch. 11, Moses complains to Yhwh about his burden-some responsibility for a discontented people, and Yhwh responds by distributing Moses' spirit of prophecy to 70 elders, who prophesy briefly and then, curiously, 'did not do so again' (11.25). In ch. 12, Miriam and

Aaron challenge (in addition to Moses' Cushite wife) his exclusive right to speak for Yhwh, and are rebuked with divine words about Moses' special status, 'mouth to mouth' with Yhwh. Accepting, then, Jobling's basic point, I shall consider the question of communicating knowledge in terms of the genres and the institutional matrices involved, with an eye toward articulating the relationship of cultic authority to the written word in postexilic Judah. As before in this analysis, I shall argue that these issues find narrative expression in terms of gender relations; that there is a relationship, to use Jobling's terms, between the communication and knowledge isotopy and another semantic field he identifies, that of 'kinship and sexual relationships' (1978: 49). It is in and through manipulation of these narrative themes that the 'proper' authority arrangement is achieved, one derived from Moses, but embedded in the priesthood.

Scholarly interpretation of the authority roles in Numbers 11–12 tends to take one of two tacks, either (à la Deut. 34.10) focusing on Moses as the supreme prophet among prophets, or construing Numbers 12, in particular, as an account of prophet over priest. While the first option makes sense of the conflict between Moses and Miriam (who is called a prophet in Exod. 15.20), the second explains better the presence of Aaron. Neither interpretation accounts well for the doubled opposition to Moses which, I have argued, is as much about Aaron's and Miriam's relationship to each other as that of either to Moses. The narrative, in finally severing Aaron from Miriam, actually serves as a point of departure for validating the Aaronite priesthood through the ever-increasing narrative identification of Moses and Aaron over the course of chs. 12 to 20.

Beginning from this analysis, I would prefer to see Numbers 11–12 not as a direct representation of conflict between holders of different social roles—prophets versus priests, whose distinctiveness is mainly a modern scholarly construct, in any case—but as a literary working out of a more complex and subtle power dynamic. At stake are the claims of a younger generation versus an older one (as already discussed) and an adaptation to new forms of and authorities for social control, specifically, a genealogically based priesthood (also already much discussed), in league with, or perhaps by now identified with, a political leadership that vests its authority in the written word. Accepting Jobling's cogent point that the text establishes Moses as the permanent channel for communicating awareness of the divine program, I shall argue further that the character 'Moses' in fact stands for this authoritative written word and, further still, that Moses' word must be appropriated as a *priestly* voice for the channel to be fully established. Numbers 11–12 articulates this process of appropriation in terms of the problem of the distribution of Mosaic authority. It does so in and through the representation of a set of kin relations.

Numbers 11–12, as a story about kinship, knowledge and the distribution of authority, actually begins in 10.29-36, where we are introduced to Hobab, 'son of Reuel, the Midianite, Moses' father-in-law'. This reminder of Moses' earlier marriage reinforces the connection of Zipporah and the Cushite wife, while at the same time signaling the motif of the brother, which, on one reading, Hobab must be to Moses' wife.[24] Hobab introduces not only the matters of brothers and (foreign) wives, but also that of the communication of divine knowledge. The name Hobab is used elsewhere for Moses' father-in-law himself. This character's appearance in Num. 10.29-36 thus foreshadows the events of ch. 11 with yet another allusion to Exodus. In Exodus 18, Moses' father-in-law (there Jethro) effectively counseled the overburdened Moses to appoint judges to help him administer the law, an event reiterated in the Numbers 11 account of the dispersion of Moses' spirit to the elders.

The Hobab pericope points to the issue of communicating divine knowledge in another way as well. In Exodus, after taking Jethro's advice about the judges, Moses 'let his father-in-law depart, and he went off to his own country' (Exod. 18.27). Numbers, however, raises a point of tension on precisely this issue. Hobab wants to go back to his own land and kin, but Moses will not let him, citing the Israelites' need for an experienced man of the wilderness to show them where to camp, and promising to extend Yhwh's blessings to him. But isn't deciding about camping location the job of the cloud of Yhwh? The latter source of knowledge is immediately asserted in 10.33-36, which displaces any

---

24. The appositives following the name Hobab create ambiguity as to his relationship with Moses. If Reuel is taken to be 'the Midianite, Moses' father-in-law' (cf. Exod. 2.18), then Hobab is Moses' brother-in-law. If all the appositives apply to Hobab, however, then Hobab is, as in Judg. 4.11, another name for Moses' father-in-law. In this case, one has to account for two different Reuels. Clearly we are dealing with conflated traditions (and we have not even mentioned Jethro). On the other hand, I find a method in the madness insofar as both figures, brother and father-in-law, are important to Num. 11–12.

response Hobab might have given Moses with information on the guidance of the cloud. We are left, then, with a question. Did Hobab agree to stay on or not? Does the cloud displace him, in other words, along with his voice and wisdom, or are we to assume the integration of divine and (foreign) human systems of guidance?

We hear no more of Hobab, but this episode serves, as it were, as a prologue to the concerns of Numbers 11–12: both to the question of knowledge and to Moses' need for human assistance. Over the course of those chapters, compensation for the failed assistance and divinely suppressed knowledge of the foreign brother/father-in-law will be offered in two ways: first, unsuccessfully, through the extension of the prophesying spirit to the 70 elders; then, with success, in Moses' union with his priestly brother.

From Strange Priest to Israelite Priest: Authorizing Leadership in Numbers 11–12

Exodus 18 and Numbers 11 represent, among other things, two efforts at organizing a leadership structure that is not dependent on Moses alone, though it claims authority from him. In Exodus 18, Jethro's focus is on helping Moses communicate and apply God's 'statutes and instructions' (Exod. 18.16, 20). The mediation of a foreign priest for Israelite law (before it's even given![25]) is surprising, but handled with military efficiency,[26] apparently creating a permanent resolution to the problem. For Yhwh in Numbers, on the other hand, it is a matter of prophecy and the spirit, a messier business even for a god. Seventy elders are placed around the tent (here assumed to be outside the camp). Yhwh places some of Moses' spirit on them and they do indeed prophesy. And then they stop. Meanwhile, back at the camp, Eldad and Medad prophesy apart from the others. Moses' response to Joshua's protest against these two is to express his wish that 'all Yhwh's people were prophets, and that Yhwh would put his spirit on them' (11.29).

---

25. The terms 'statute' (*hoq*) and 'instruction/law' (*torah*) are used several times in Exodus prior to the Sinai episode, usually to refer to specific orders given by Yhwh (12.24, 49; 15.25; 16.4, 28). In a couple of cases, however, there seems to be a proleptic reference to the body of law to be delivered to Moses (13.9; 15.26), a presupposition also embedded in Exod. 18.

26. Levine (1993: 338) comments that the new system of dividing the people into a pyramid of larger and smaller groupings resembled a military or paramilitary organization.

One might wonder how sincere this wish for an apparently useless display of divine activity is. So the elders prophesied—did this help? Did a temporary spate of babbling relieve Moses of even the smallest degree of responsibility?[27] Is this what being a prophet means? Is this the best Yhwh can do? Where, indeed, *is* Yhwh—outside the camp with 70 elders or inside, with Eldad and Medad (see above for the problem of locating the tent/tabernacle)?

Both Jethro's and Yhwh's attempts to create and authorize an extended leadership structure to assist Moses failed. But why? I shall argue that each version of the episode works through by narrative means a different aspect of the priestly problem of strangeness and holiness, with the solution finally offered in Numbers 12.

That Jethro's effort would fail is not obvious at first. It seems successful, only the repetition of the episode in Numbers indicating it was not. Why was a second effort necessary? Was the first plan's failure because of its source in a strange man, indeed, a strange priest and father to a strange wife? The narrative marks Jethro's strangeness in two ways: the obvious fact of his foreign nationality couples with a suggestion of the rhetoric of 'wrong sex' that is often entangled with that of 'wrong nationality/ethnicity'. When Moses 'sent away' his wife Zipporah with her two sons, Jethro 'took her' (Exod. 18.2). The choice of verbs in this terse sentence is striking. 'Send away' can mean 'divorce'. Relatedly, 'take' can mean 'take sexually' or 'marry'.[28] The verbs thus create the possibility of a rather intense, doubled sexual culpability on Jethro's part: he 'takes' (marries?) his (divorced?) daughter and he then returns her to her former(?) husband (18.5), a reunion forbidden by Deut. 24.1-4. The story line makes nothing directly of this sexual innuendo; it is not ready at this point to cut loose the foreign priest, for he has as yet no suitable replacement. Yet there is an intimation, a subtle casting of the aura of sexual strangeness over Jethro.

Jethro's strangeness is also conveyed, though also qualified, in the grandsons he takes along with the Strange Woman (Exod. 18.3-4). One is Gershom, a name related to *ger* ('resident alien'), once Moses' status in the land of his wife and father-in-law (Exod. 2.22). The *ger* stands on the line between the native and the true foreigner. The other son is called Eliezer, 'my god is a help'. Both the meaning of the name and its

---

27. The term for 'prophesying' (*hitnabeh*) can also mean 'raving' (Fewell and Gunn 1993: 113).

28. The usual English translation 'take *back*' misses this nuance.

similarity to Eleazar, the authorized seed of Aaron, draw this alien priest into the center. Jethro's relations—to the Strange Woman, the *ger*-child and the god-child—place him simultaneously outside, on the margin and inside. This betwixt and between status connoted by his kin relations fits well the narrative role we have already noted, that of priest of no-god, who holds open the space that Aaron will eventually occupy. Yet the strangeness Jethro represents must, in the end, be eliminated. Not only must Aaron replace Jethro as priest, moreover, but a leadership structure derived from Aaron must replace Jethro's system for teaching and applying God's statutes and instructions.

The narrative movement from the strange priest to the Israelite priest takes what may seem an odd detour in Numbers 11. One could hardly argue with Yhwh as the source of authority for creating a distribution system for divine knowledge, but what a useless mess this is. The divine spirit offers little in the form of elders who prophesy once but never again.[29] If Jethro's system for communicating knowledge of the divine is too strange in one sense—that is, too foreign—Yhwh's is too strange in another. Too close a contact with the holy is as dangerous as too much distance. We have, then, a dilemma: the foreign priest creates an orderly society based on 'statutes and instructions', while the Israelite god creates chaos with prophecy based on an unmediated bestowing of spirit. Neither can stand as such. The solution comes in Numbers 12, articulated in the intersecting binaries of kin–strange and male–female.

The otherwise anomalous inclusion of Hobab in Numbers 10 is important, for he reintroduces into Numbers's isotopies of communication and kinship the memories both of the strange priest who effectively organized the teaching of the law and of the brotherly relationship mediated through a Strange Woman. It is now time for both the relationship of brother to brother and of priest to law to be stripped of their strangeness. This purification takes place narratively by means of the

29. There is another way to look at Yhwh's apparent ineffectiveness in this context. Jobling (1978) argues that Yhwh's extension of the spirit to the elders is an intentionally partial acquiescence to Moses' complaint about the burden of leadership, his unwanted assignment as mother of Israel (11.12-13). It is an aspect of the deity's deceitful 'counter-counterprogram', which offers just enough comfort (and manifestation of power!) to quell Moses' incipient rebellion. We have already reflected on the implications of Yhwh's adoption of deceit, an element of the Strange Woman paradigm. Here, more specifically, the divine counter-counterprogram derives from the foreign father.

doubled female figuration of Miriam and the Cushite wife on whom rests the burden of All-Kinship and All-Strangeness: daughter and sister to foreign men, foreign wife and also sister to the quintessential Israelites. Through this figure of impossible identities, strangeness in all its forms is consigned to the Otherness of gender, which can then be cut off from the men who would otherwise be called kin. According to this mythic logic, Aaron first appears in identification with the strange priest, as figured through his alliance with Miriam against the exclusive authority of Moses. He emerges from the confrontation with Yhwh, however, bonded instead to the single authorized conduit of statutes and instructions from the (male) god. The proper relief of Moses has been achieved, not through secular officials as in Exodus 18, nor through un-mediated prophecy as in Numbers 11, but in the creation of the fully male, fully Israelite priest, whose seed, untainted by any Other, will now claim to be Moses' divinely authorized mouthpiece.

From the Great Communicator to the Great Communication: Priest and Canon in the Land of Canaan

Corresponding to the shifting power structures, both institutional and symbolic, of the postexilic period, Numbers 12 registers an epistemo-logical shift, not just away from prophecy received in dreams and visions (12.6), but also away from the oral transmission of revelation to its written form. While all of Numbers 11–12 is marked by an interest in communication and knowledge, 12.6-8, says Jobling, is 'the section most overtly devoted to epistemology' (1978: 45). When Yhwh speaks to Miriam and Aaron from the cloud at the entrance of the tent, he says:

> When there is a prophet among you,
> in visions (*mar'ah*) to him I make myself known,
> in dreams I speak to him.
> Not so with my servant Moses:
> in all my house he is trustworthy.
> Mouth to mouth I speak with him,
> appearance-wise (*mar'eh*),
> not in riddles,
> and the form of Yhwh he beholds (Num. 12.6b-8).

Interpreters usually focus on the phrases 'appearance-wise' and 'the form of Yhwh he beholds' as indicative of the special medium of Moses' knowledge. The first is an awkward translation for an awkward, possibly corrupt, Hebrew *umar'eh*. It is often translated as 'clearly', but this choice may gloss over the essentially *visual* (not merely conceptual) root of the word. Both these phrases, in other words, have to do with the fact that Moses *sees* the sender of the message. The interpretive problem then becomes the fact that in v. 6 Yhwh seems to denigrate visions (*mar'ah*) as a mode of revelation. Moses thus not only 'sees', he must in some sense see differently and better than anyone else: *mar'eh* rather than *mar'ah*. But what to make of this distinction?

The most telling phrase for understanding the uniqueness of Moses may be 'mouth to mouth'. On one level, this is but a variant of the phrase 'face to face' that appears in other accounts of Moses' relationship with Yhwh (Exod. 33.11; Deut. 34.10). It may, however, be a variant of crucial significance. In addition to visual and verbal apperception, 'mouth to mouth' suggests the tactile as well. This may be 'only a metaphor', but it is a powerful one. It produces, as we have already observed, at least a partial apotheosis of Moses. It also is reminiscent of Ezekiel, who also saw the form of Yhwh and had an experience of the mouth, in this case, the eating of a scroll containing the message of the deity. In both the case of Ezekiel and of Moses, the imagery lends a substance, a full physicality, to the word. The illusions of dreams, the elusions of riddles are not part of this picture. 'Mouth to mouth' suggests the impossibility that Moses could either get the message wrong or change it in transmission. His mouth has been shaped to Yhwh's. What, then, is different about the mode in which Moses receives the divine communication? Moses' reception is not merely one of seeing; rather, it is of seeing, touching, mouth-to-mouth speaking. It is, in other words, an act of recitation. It is, for all future intents and purposes, like Ezekiel's, an encounter with written text.

If this reading discloses a textual interest in its own textuality, one relevant question would be why the point is so occluded. Why not say straight out that Yhwh is now a god of a text? Why not (especially given all the other linkages with Exodus) a story about tablets of stone? Or is this episode, in fact, Numbers's version of the tablets of stone? A couple of related points might be made, in terms of both historical and literary contexts.

Historically speaking, to imagine postexilic Judah is to imagine a society in flux. It is not just a matter of who will control things, but also of how, in what institutional forms, that control will be exercised, not to mention the question of who will be included in the polity. What will be the society's defining metaphors; or, in other words, what will be the socially accepted symbols through which authority can be exercised without the need to resort to brute force? It must be granted that the answers to these questions were not entirely within Judean control: 'Persia's shadow', to use Berquist's (1995) powerful image, loomed large. Still, even if Persia were the force behind the promulgation of a holy book, one must imagine an extended and complex social-psychological process behind the ultimate acceptance of its authority. The shift in this case is a fundamental one, not just from one symbol to another, but from one epistemology to another: from knowledge communicated orally through persons to knowledge communicated in writing—in writing, and yet not, from Numbers's perspective, divorced from persons, or at least not from an institution made up of persons, to wit, a priesthood. Such a fundamental shift coupled with such contested political interests cannot be simply proclaimed to be accepted. It is the task of ideological narrative to mask social change and the will to power in a compelling tale that captures the imagination and, with it, the will to assent.

From a literary point of view, then, Numbers is a book with several interwoven agendas: ch. 12's interest in establishing the primacy of Moses and (a particular form of) his word is folded into episode after episode on discerning the priest from the *zar*; ch. 12 likewise addresses the relationship of the priest to strangeness. Yhwh, as we have seen, is not the only one Moses has been kissing. Aaron, by his own admission, has been a fool (12.11), but he has finished with the Strange Woman now. The severing takes place on more than one level: the voice of the priest is divorced from that of his most intimate of Others and married...to whom? If the text encodes at the level of gender an essential transfer of Aaron's identity from Miriam to Moses, then it encodes at the level of epistemology a shift from a god known by visions to a god known by form, by what can be seen, touched and kissed: recalling both Exodus and Ezekiel, by statutes and instructions offered to the lips in written form. The priest weds the lawgiver.

What happens if we attempt to dovetail these historical and literary observations? Let me frame the attempt, Num. 12.8 notwithstanding, as a riddle:

> Question: What do you get when you divorce a priest from a Strange
>   Woman and marry him to a lawgiver?
>
> Answer: Ezra.

Ezra, at any rate, as eponym of his edited book, the Ezra with the Aaronite genealogy and the rhetoric of Leviticus. Recalling, alongside Numbers, Ezra's similar wedding of priesthood and law, coupled with his attempted erasure of female strangeness, may explain the lingering presence in the wilderness of another figure alongside Moses, Aaron and the Strange Woman. Over and over, by a variety of names, we have evoked the Strange Priest. Why does his memory persist?[30] He opens a space, I suggested earlier, that 'Aaron' will fill. If it is finally Ezra (or his editor) who claims the name Aaron, we are led to consider whose space Ezra would fill. Is it that of a priesthood currently in power? And yet, what makes established priests strange? It is Ezra, after all, who is newly arrived from a foreign land. Do we have, then, an ideological reversal: strangeness resulting from long residence in the land, either through failure to have experienced the wilderness or through returning from it too soon? Both Jethro/Reuel/Hobab and Aaron begin, like Ezra, in the wilderness. But, narratively speaking, one fathers the line of true priests, the other is left estranged. The historical reality of the Ezraite priesthood's strange origin cannot be denied; but it can be mythically manipulated to create a *zar* from an Israelite, or vice versa.

To a biblical reader who chooses, as I have, to begin with Proverbs, there is a word in Miriam's story that stands out, that remains unaccounted for. Of Moses Yhwh says:

> Mouth to mouth I speak with him,
> by what is seen, not in riddles (Num. 12.8).

'Riddle', typically paired with 'proverb' (Ezek 17.2; Hab. 2.6; Pss. 49.5; 78.2), becomes in Proverbs wisdom's way of characterizing its own discourse.

> Let the wise also hear and gain in learning,
> and the discerning acquire skill,
> to understand a proverb and a figure,
> the words of the wise and their riddles (Prov. 2.5-6).

What, then, are riddles doing in a narrative so concerned with discourse and its transmission? Is it possible that Numbers's rejection of riddles, along with prophetic dreams and visions, is a rejection of wisdom speech (and presumably thought) and its tradents as well? With no

---

30. I owe both the pressing of this question and the formulation of an answer to David Gunn (personal communication).

more than a single word as a clue, any answer to this question will be almost entirely speculative. So I shall offer two speculations.

It is interesting, first of all, that the word 'riddles' occurs, only to be rejected, in the context of a narrative about female estrangement. If the riddle-loving narratives about Samson and Solomon can be construed in part as expressions of a wisdom-*ish* whim to play with the Strange Woman, Numbers rejects this as the dangerous game of fools. Here, all women are strange: she who begins on the inside must be pushed out, she who attempts entry from without must be killed. Wisdom's women (wise and strange) and wisdom's speech are eliminated in one narrative stroke. Or are they? I suggested earlier that the mouth-to-mouth shaping rendered by Yhwh to Moses is a shaping of female form. The tactile image of the living Moses mouth to mouth with Yhwh resists the Phallic movement toward a final, unchanging Word. In Yhwh's mouth and the brothers' rods, traces of strangeness remain even in Numbers's man-made text. A word still shaped by moving lips (not to mention the pleasure of a penis) is a word still free of the dominion of the Phallus.

My second speculation derives from a proposal I have previously made about the book of Proverbs (Camp 1985: 151-208; 1987: 102-105; and see Chapter 4 above): that in this book we are witnessing part of a self-conscious process of transformation, from the oral to the written form of a tradition. Orality hardly disappears in this predominantly non-literate culture. One might nonetheless imagine, in a context of contested authority, the *writing* of the book of Proverbs as an adaptive response to a newly dominant epistemology by a group with claims, and an ideology, of its own. What lurks between the lines in Numbers comes to full expression in Proverbs, where the female mouth is located in a female body that authorizes the written text. The strangeness that Numbers tries, unsuccessfully, to eliminate from myth, canon and corporate identity, Proverbs, in the fullness of its patriarchal wisdom, co-opts.

Chapter 7

THE (E)STRANGE(D) WOMAN IN THE LAND:
SOJOURNING WITH DINAH

The ambiguity of the narrative in Genesis 34 is legendary. Jacob's
daughter, Dinah, out visiting 'the daughters of the land', has an untoward sexual encounter with one of its sons. Shechem, however, offers
to marry her, an offer deceitfully accepted by Jacob's sons under the
condition that Shechem's men be circumcised. Dinah's brothers, with
particular focus on Simeon and Levi, then fall upon the incapacitated
men and kill them, only to be condemned by Jacob for endangering the
family. Who was in the right? What would have constituted a 'proper'
outcome?[1] Were Simeon and Levi right to avenge the honor of their sister and, presumably, their family? The ending of the story with their
rhetorical question—'Should he treat our sister like a prostitute?'—
seems to align the reader's sympathies with them. The brothers' extraordinary and self-serving violence hardly allows moral closure, however,
and Jacob is given the real last word against them in Gen. 49.5-7:

1.   Although this question plagues all interpreters of Gen. 34, it has recently
been the site of a significant methodological skirmish. Sternberg (1985, 1992) argues
strongly for the vindication of Simeon and Levi by the complex but relentless artistry
of the narrator. Fewell and Gunn (1991), on the other hand, in holding open the
possibility of an irreducibly polysemic text subject to readerly forces, maintain the
essential goodwill of Shechem and integrity of Jacob with respect to Dinah's well-
being. Noble (1996) offers a useful summary and critique of both positions, though
his own univocal thematizing of the narrative (it is 'about' crime and punishment),
based on an 'objective, reader-independent method' (1996: 203) is seriously flawed
by unsupported assumptions about ancient attitudes toward sexuality. That these
assumptions are in fact modern ones is well demonstrated by Bechtel (1994),
discussed below. Objectivity remains at large.

Simeon and Levi are brothers;[2]
weapons of violence are their swords.
In their council let me not come;
with their assembly let my honor not be united.
For in their anger they killed a man,
and at their pleasure they hamstrung an ox.
Cursed be their anger for it is strong,
and their fury, for it is fierce.
I will divide them in Jacob,
and scatter them in Israel.

The compelling arguments offered by different scholars for taking one side or the other on this question suggest that the narrative is examining issues, not requiring answers.[3] The values a reader—ancient or modern —brings to the text will determine the conclusions, if any, she or he reaches about the 'message', as will the larger literary contexts within which one chooses to read.[4] My own interest, at this point in my exploration of strangeness, concerns priestly readers and purveyors of the Dinah narrative. Thus, I shall attend particularly to traces of this voice, while, at the same time listening to it in conversation with others also audible.

The Dinah narrative reveals a complex set of antagonisms and alliances, not simply of Israelite and foreigner, but also of father and daughter, father and sons, brother and brother. As in the Miriam narratives, the issue of identity boundaries is again very much at stake, providing a warp to the weft of this tale's other major dilemma regarding the motivations for and outcome of the actions of its male characters. The problem of establishing the correct *identity* lines between Israelite and foreigner has its counterpoint, I shall argue, in the problem of

2.   Note the changes in Deut. 33. Simeon is omitted, and Levi's violence alludes to Exod. 32.25-29, the presumably justified slaughter of those who made the golden calves.

3.   This is not to say that some author did not have 'a point' to make, but only that there is no way to isolate, much less valorize, this 'intention' within the conflicted mix that now constitutes this narrative and its intertexts.

4.   The reader-response position is argued strongly by Fewell and Gunn (1991). Though Sternberg's response and Noble's article make some valid criticisms of their article, the fact that 'readers' *have* 'responded' in different (and still cogent) ways makes the basic thesis irrefutable. I owe the formulation of the insight about literary contextualization to Ramras-Rauch (1990), though I will enlarge on her single example of extending the pericope to 33.18–35.8.

drawing the correct *moral* lines within the cohort of 'Israelites'. These dynamics of morality and identity are cast in terms of sex and gender, with the Israelite sister/daughter and the strange man's penis as the foci.

In this chapter, I shall first consider the text's moral problem in terms of conflicts within and between ancient and modern ideologies, most importantly, that of honor and shame. I then turn to analyses of how the issue plays out on mythic and symbolic levels, returning to the motifs of incest and circumcision considered in the preceding chapter. Here we shall see the problem of morality intersect with that of identity, in terms that are susceptible to a priestly reading. I go on to introduce an intertextual reading of Genesis 34 with Joshua 2–7, where, again, the problem of distinguishing 'Israelites' from 'foreigners' is at issue. Finally, I consider one last canonical effort to construct a line between them in the figure of the *ger*, the resident alien, which resonates to a significant degree with that of the Levite. Here once more we shall find priestly power struggles at stake, worked out in terms of the questions of who may claim identity within The Family, and how that may be done.

Readers and their Ideologies

The difficulty in reconciling two mutually exclusive interpretations of the 'message' of the Dinah narrative results, I shall argue, from two overlapping causes. On the one hand are modern psychosocial presuppositions about the proper course of human relationships, especially male–female relationships, presuppositions that do not necessarily match those of the ancients. The contemporary ideologies of, first, love and romance and, secondly, the individual's right over her or his own body take a beating in the story of Dinah and Shechem. This makes it relatively easy for the modern reader to leap to the support of Levi and Simeon, even as we feel horror at the extremity of their response. There is, at the same time, an internal ideological contradiction embedded in this narrative that, I believe, would have produced conflicting readings among ancient interpreters as well.

Dinah's Honor: One Ideology, Two Conclusions

The competing responses by her male relatives to Dinah's sexual encounter with Shechem represent, on one level, competing cultural values. I shall suggest, however, that at least part of the conflict is internal to the larger ideology of honor and shame in which this story is grounded, a contradiction within the system that is usually suppressed by it. The eruption of ideological incoherence that comes to expression in this narrative parallels and thus mirrors contradictions in the Israelite myth of genealogically based identity, of which Genesis 34 is both part and emblem.

As Bechtel (1994) has convincingly demonstrated, many of what seem to be anomalies in the narrative only appear so to the reader informed by a modern individualistic value system. In particular, Noble's facile dismissal (1996: 189-191) of Fewell and Gunn's appeal to the cultural value of honor as a determinative of the narrative is convincingly challenged by Bechtel's excellent discussion of motivations and responses regarding sexual issues in a group-oriented society. One key issue here is the meaning of the verb *'nh* (piel), not only how it is best translated, but what it actually signifies in the ancient society. The usual understanding in this context is 'rape'. 'When Shechem, son of Hamor the Hivite, prince of the region, saw [Dinah], he took her and lay with her and raped her (*ye'anneha*)[5]' (34.2). Bechtel argues, however, that *'innah* has a range of cultural connotations that goes beyond and qualifies what the twentieth-century speaker of English means by 'rape'. The Hebrew term refers in particular to 'the "humiliation" or "shaming" of a woman through certain kinds of sexual intercourse *including rape, but not necessarily*' (Bechtel 1994: 24; my emphasis). She supports with both anthropological theory and textual detail Fewell and Gunn's point that it was not Shechem's use of force against their sister that provoked the brothers' reaction, but the imputation of dishonor that entailed.[6] A sense of honor derives from a view of the family as a closed

5.   The NRSV reduces the three verbs to two, but with the same sense: 'he seized her and lay with her by force'.

6.   To Bechtel's textual examples of *'innah* (Deut. 22.23-30; 2 Sam. 13.11-14) could be added the law on the woman taken captive in war, who cannot be sold or treated as a slave because her captor has 'shamed' her (Deut. 21.10-14) (See Bechtel 1994: 25-27). While a woman in this situation may well have experienced rape, as moderns understand it, this was hardly the basis for the law's restrictions on her master. I do not, however, agree with all the details of Bechtel's argument. I doubt, for example, that Deut. 22.28-29 does not involve rape. Where else does *tps* mean 'touch the heart', as Bechtel assumes, rather than 'seize'? While this verse is not as close a parallel to Gen. 34 as she would have it, her argument does not depend on this nuance, nor on her claim that the lack of the verb *'innah* in Deut. 22.25-27 means that there is no shame involved in the attack on the betrothed woman in the countryside. It is true that the woman in the latter case is not re-

circle, endangered by attempted incursions from without, and sees women's sexuality as the weak link in this circle.

Fewell and Gunn go farther, however, to suggest that, while the brothers' reaction is motivated by the desire to avenge the dishonor to their sister, this is, by implication, a matter of shame *to themselves*. My sister, myself: the sexual taking of a female relative is experienced as violation of the family's males, a social-psychological inference that is well-supported in the anthropological literature.[7] The reference to Shechem's 'honor' in his family (34.19) may mark inversely the lack of honor in Jacob's (cf. 49.6). Indeed, the fact that this allusion to Shechem's *kabod*—which means 'weight' as well as 'honor'—occurs almost parenthetically after the report of his undelayed submission to circumcision may constitute a bawdy taunt to the shamed brothers: even with a bit cut off, Shechem is weightier than the rest.

The complete confinement of women's sexuality inside the family circle, if only that were possible, would ease the anxiety. Indeed, the brothers' protest against their sister being 'made a harlot' reflects this wish.

> [T]hey are pointing to the fact that she has become a marginal figure by engaging in sexual activity outside her society and without the possibility of bonding... For them the relationship threatens the cohesion of the tribal structure. It is to this threat that the sons react (Bechtel 1994: 31).

The principle of family honor, defined in terms of containment of women's sexuality, thus serves an impulse toward endogamy. This impulse coalesces in the narrative, moreover, with the more explicitly political aversion to intermarriage between Israelites and non-Israelites. Violation of the family boundary through illicit sex appears as a cipher for violation of the national boundary; intermarriage is narratively classified with all other forms of illicit sex.

This double-barreled ideological salvo undermines the force of Sternberg's case for the subtle artistry involved in persuading readers to accept the brothers' violence. What kind of reader would need such per-

sponsible for her shaming—not an insignificant point—but, according to Bechtel's definition, the male perpetrator has surely violated not just the woman, but also the 'existing marital, family or community bonding and obligation' (1994: 24). This fits the definition of shame as I think she intends it.

7. A useful introduction to anthropologists' understandings of honor and shame in contemporary Mediterranean society is found in Gilmore (1987).

suasion? A modern one, to be sure, who does not share the narrative's gendered construction of shame or its identification of wrong sex with wrong nationality. Perhaps there were ancient readers as well who would have resisted such ideas, though clearly there were many who did not. To those who accepted this value system, the brothers' response may have seemed dangerous and impractical but hardly wrong, indeed, perhaps all the more admirable for its risk. As Bechtel notes, even the extent of the violence is comprehensible from the perspective of group solidarity.

> The fact that the revenge is carried out against the entire Shechemite community shows that from the sons' perspective the pollution has affected the entire Jacobite group. As a community concern, it warrants revenge on the entire Shechemite group (1994: 34).

This cultural code is reinforced by the narrative's departure from the world of 'ordinary' reality it had depicted up to that point. The ability of two men to slay all the men of an entire city becomes explicable as a mythic code for moral virtue: 'right makes might'.

As much contemporary Mediterranean anthropology shows, however, the ideology of honor and shame is not limited to the issue of male control of women's sexuality. The father Jacob also operates within this system, while manifesting a larger sense of social order that leads to a course of action different from that of his sons. Here, the important thing is that the family achieve a set of workable economic and social relationships with the outside world. Such a positive valuation of Jacob as well as Dinah can be construed when Genesis 34 is read as a continuation of Jacob's purchase of land for an altar from 'the sons of Hamor, Shechem's father' (33.19-20).[8] While the verb *yts'* ('go out') may connote the crossing of identity boundaries (Bechtel 1994: 31-32), Dinah's 'going out' to see the daughters of the land can in this larger context be understood, in alignment with her father's choice, as an appropriate act of reaching across boundaries rather than a violation of them. Jacob's purchase anticipates, moreover, the agreements negotiated later with Hamor as part of the connubial package. The latter proposes, 'You shall live with us and the land shall be open to you. Live and trade in it, and get property in it' (34.10). Jacob's initial silence, while quite different from his sons' reaction, is not so puzzling from the perspective of an

---

8.   So Ramras-Rauch (1990: 163-64); cf. Abraham's similar purchase for Sarah's tomb in Gen. 23.

honor code in a non-individualistic culture. 'He is quiescent, passive, dependent on his community and cooperative. He does not carry out independent action, but waits for mutual support' (Bechtel 1994: 35). Within this values orientation, women would be seen as natural mediators of these intergroup relationships through marriage; concomitantly, the major concern regarding women's sexuality is not its threat to male honor but the more pragmatic concern that she find her proper place as a childbearing wife in her husband's household.

I would stress that these two competing attitudes regarding women's sexuality are both very much part of the honor–shame system (cf. Sir. 42.9-10); thus the responses of Jacob and his sons represent competing priorities in establishing honor, while both assuming that honor is at stake. In each case, it is a matter of which aspect of the system one emphasizes. Jacob represents the side also expressed in the laws that require a man (whether seducer or rapist) to marry the unbetrothed woman whose virginity he has taken, while satisfying the father's economic expectation (Exod. 22.16-17; Deut. 22.28-30). Given this system, it is anachronistic to imagine that the brothers' objection to 'making their sister a harlot' is based on an objection to a marriage contract negotiated in terms of material goods and the bonding of different families (so with Bechtel 1994: 30; contra Sternberg 1985: 474). Maximizing advantage in such arrangements is the order of the day, both the prerequisite and the perquisite of honor.

In contrast to the brothers' position, the impulse on Jacob's side is exogamous. This contradiction between the desire for endogamy and need for exogamy is, then, embedded in the cultural ideology of honor and shame as well as, as we have already seen, in the Israelite myth of descent from a single family. We shall return to this point below.

Genesis 34 as a Not-So-Modern Romance

I have tried to show how the honor–shame ideology could induce both the passive response of Jacob and the bellicose response of his sons. Implicit in this discussion is the fact that, however righteous to some modern readers Simeon's and Levi's indignation may seem, the brothers' rationale of avenging offense to family honor is not our rationale of avenging offense to a woman's body. We confront another difficulty as well in understanding the ancient narrator's evaluation of these events. In part, the question hinges on the degree to which force was involved in this sexual encounter; a contemporary reader's sense of the brothers' righteousness depends on the assumption that Dinah was raped. But how, then, can one account for Shechem's tender feelings and subsequent honorable actions? A rapist falling in love with his victim departs from the modern romantic script.

A great deal hinges on the verbs used to describe Shechem's subjectivity in the encounter.

> Now Dinah, the daughter of Leah, whom she had borne to Jacob, went out to visit [lit: 'see into'] the daughters of the land. And Shechem, son of Hamor the Hivite, prince of the land, saw her and took her and lay her and humbled (*'innah*) her. And his soul cleaved to Dinah, daughter of Jacob, and he loved the young woman and he spoke to the heart of the young woman. And Shechem spoke to Hamor his father, saying, 'Get [lit: 'take'] for me this girl for a wife' (Gen. 34.1-4).

Did Shechem rape Dinah? The lack of subjectivity granted to Dinah in the encounter may suggest force to the modern reader, but perhaps less so to an ancient one, for whom male initiative in sex was the norm. We have, moreover, already observed that the 'humbling' of Dinah expresses more her male relatives' perception than her own desire or lack thereof. Finally, Shechem's 'taking' of Dinah (v. 2) anticipates both his directive to his father about his wish to marry her (v. 4), as well as the giving and 'taking' of daughters later agreed upon (v. 9). While a modern reader may well condemn a culture that describes marriage as an institution in which men unilaterally 'take' women, there is no evidence that an Israelite reader would have had such compunction. To the contrary, the anticipation of marriage adumbrated by this verb may well have cushioned the offense of the couple's premarital sex. Did, then, Shechem force Dinah to have sex with him? Perhaps so, perhaps not. Does the narrator, through the use of the verbs 'saw, took, lay, humbled', make a definitively negative judgment on Shechem *as rapist*? I do not think so.

Both Fewell and Gunn and Bechtel also stress the mitigating force of the three verbs describing Shechem's feelings and words to Dinah after the report of the sex act. What can it mean at this point in the sequence of events to say 'his soul clung to Jacob's daughter, he loved the girl, and he spoke to her heart'? There are at least two ways to think about this. One is to note the possibility that these three verbs and the four that proceed them are not to be understood as a linear temporal sequence. When Shechem 'sees, takes, lies with and humbles', only the first and maybe the second can be temporally distinguished from the others. Lying with and humbling (and maybe taking) happen coterminously. Similarly, 'cleaving, loving and speaking tenderly' do not have to be understood as happening only after the sex act; their place in the verbal sequence may be simply a bit of narrative coyness.[9] Such a reading would give weight to two other textual details. First, it sees in the initial naming of Dinah as *Leah's* daughter an allusion to Leah's status as the unloved wife, a woman who might well have wished for a man to say, 'I will give whatever you ask me; only give me the young woman to be my wife'. The opening scene offers hope that Dinah could have the happier fate of a beloved wife. Secondly, this reading finds an alignment in Dinah's and Shechem's point of view in the use of the verb 'see'. Dinah goes out to see daughters; Shechem sees a daughter. Again, coyly, the narrative does not say directly that they 'see each other', yet it suggests this mutuality (and consent?) in the common object of their seeing.

On the other hand, even if we accept the usual reading that equates the verbal sequence with a temporal sequence, and identifies the sex act as rape, I am not so sure we can make as much of that as is often done by modern readers, who find incomprehensible the change from rape (or, at best, apparently anonymous sex) to love. Our lack of comprehension is grounded in a modern, individualistic, psychological construction of love that not only provides a description of what love is and how it works, but also embeds a set of norms in this definition. We thus have a construction of 'true' love that the 'sex first, love second' sequence does not match. I do not wish to argue with this construction; I hold it as dear as most people in the modern Western world. But the few narrative constructions of 'girl–boy' encounters in the Hebrew Bible make it clear that it was not operative for them. (Note for example, the Bible's lack of what we might call a courting sequence, a quaint term, perhaps, for what is still generically required in any 'romantic' movie.) Indeed, one might with some sympathy imagine the biblical love narratives to be struggling to convey what for us is a well-parsed, though still often overwhelming, physical and emotional experience, under the dual burden of a psychological epistemology inadequate to represent an intensely personal experience and a group-oriented audience whose emotional ears are not so attuned. When, like Samson

9. Contrast 2 Sam. 13, where Amnon's emotions are explicitly depicted as involving a *change* of heart *after* engaging in a sex act that is equally explicitly resisted by Tamar.

(whose problems in love are legendary), Shechem says to his father, 'Get me this girl', perhaps he is simply doing the best he could be imagined to do.[10]

In sum, there is much to commend the construal—not in terms of modern values but in terms of understanding ancient readers—of Dinah's encounter with Shechem as appealing to emotional sympathies, rather than as appalling. This perspective on Shechem and Dinah, combined with the characterization of Jacob as 'the ideal group-oriented person' (Bechtel 1994: 35) negotiating a profitable exogamous marriage, generates an emotionally charged ideological force against the actions of Shechem and Levi equal but opposite to that which supports them.[11]

Just as modern readers have drawn different conclusions about 'who was right' by focusing on different vectors in the narrative and its intertexts, so also, I have argued, did ancient readers.[12] I shall return later in this chapter to a reading favorable, in the main, to Levi and Simeon. I do so, however, from an interest in the perspective of readers in a particular social location, namely, certain claimants to the priesthood in the postexilic period. I hope, in stressing the viability of an alternative reading, to have underlined the fact that the priests' reading, like all read-

10. Amnon's shift from love to hatred of Tamar, in a story much more explicitly of rape (2 Sam. 13), as well as Samson's awkward and sometimes unaccountable responses to women (why *does* he tell Delilah the secret of his strength?), also seem to manifest the same narratorial struggle to craft characters with emotional experiences whose terms are expressible only in rough outline (cf. Exum [1993: 61-93], who also stresses the theme of love in the Samson stories).

11. At this point I part company with Bechtel's conclusion, which has the narrative decide unisemicly in favor of Jacob.

12. To take yet another example, Freedman (1990) argues generally persuasively that Simeon's and Levi's loss of the rights of primogeniture is part of a package with Reuben's forfeiture (Gen. 35.22; 49.2-7), all of which leads to the ascendancy of the fourth son, Judah. This sequence, in turn, parallels the succession of Solomon, David's fourth son, following a succession of events that also begins with the improper sexual taking (in this case, clearly a rape) of a sister. Freedman then posits two groups of readers, one Solomonic and the other exilic, the first of whom would have cheered the demise of the older sons, the second of whom would have seen appropriately punished evil at every turn. One does not have to agree with Freedman's literary-historical assumptions (was there really a 'Super-J'?) to follow his lead in imagining varying responses to this story from ancient readers in different social locations.

ings, would have been in part the result of choices made by ideologically motivated readers.

Dinah and the Myth of Incest

Whatever else Genesis 34 is 'about', it is about drawing lines, and the problems in discerning where and how the lines should be drawn. The tension manifest here within the honor–shame system may well have generated a felt ambivalence in many ancient readers. Definitive for some, however, must have been the fact of Shechem's foreignness. A Hivite, he was one who was to be 'utterly destroyed'—and certainly not intermarried with—lest Israel turn aside to other gods (Deut. 7.1-5; 20.16-18). The conflation of illicit religion and illicit sex—both components of the idea of 'strangeness'—implicitly imposes itself on the story, as so often in biblical literature. When placed, however, in the context of cultural conversation about connubial praxis—how endogamous? how exogamous?—the opposition to marriage with foreigners, a standard feature of 'Israelite religion', discloses itself as a particular voice in particular circumstances. For the question of marriage to a foreigner is but one extreme point on a continuum of endogamy and exogamy, one (but not the only) point of contention about where one draws the line between 'us' and 'them'. Drawing the narrative to the other end of this continuum is what Kunin (1995) has called the myth of incest. It will be the purpose of this section to examine these two extremes, first in counterpoint, then as collapsing one into the other.

Endogamy or Exogamy?

In terms of the larger issue of endogamy and exogamy, let us accept, for the moment, the social-psychological truth of the idea that the 'outsider woman' (however 'outside' is defined) is a source of threat to family solidarity and group identity as perceived by the men. This granted, however, the sense of danger from the in-marrying woman has to be overcome—and, in Israel, clearly was overcome—for a society to function. Jacob represents this normative social voice expressed both in the laws on the seduction or rape of the unbetrothed young woman and also in the Holiness Code's prohibition on brother–sister sex (Lev. 18.9; 20.17). In historical terms, whatever underlying threat a woman from another family might have created, there was hardly a question during the independent political existence of Israel and Judah that marriage

would be exogamous in the sense of taking a wife from outside one's
father's house, and likely even outside the larger lineage. The latter
practice is suggested by the fact that Moses had to provide explicit
instructions that women without brothers must marry inside the lineage
in order to inherit their father's property (Num. 36). By the same token,
the opportunities for marriage to foreigners must have been few and far
between for most people. History itself provided relief from the mythological dilemma: an Israelite could marry an Israelite and still not commit incest.

One must consider, then, what the relationship is between, on the one
hand, what must have been a largely taken-for-granted practice of intra-
Israelite exogamy and, on the other, a myth so virulent against the exogamous extreme of foreign marriage and at the same time so conflicted
about incest. Whose myth is this? Does a focus on unlikely extremes
conceal a real problem in the middle? Whose identity is at stake? What
lines are really at issue? And who is the *zar*?

Decisions about endogamy and exogamy depend on prior decisions
about who is us and who is them. We have already observed, however,
the difficulty the narrative has in drawing these lines (see Chapters 5
and 6), identifying it as an expression of political tensions within postexilic Judah and, in particular, as a concern of certain groups within the
priesthood. What may have been a long-standing priestly interest in
classification becomes targeted, in this period, on the contested (and
connected) matters of establishing the identity of the 'true Israelite' (i.e.
the one with rights to the land) and the 'true priest' (i.e. the one with
control of the Jerusalem cult). Following Kunin, I have framed the narrative dynamics in mythic terms, suggesting that the problem of distinguishing 'Israelite' identity from 'foreign' when all are descended from
the same ancestor is mirrored by that of distinguishing priest from *zar*
when all are members of the same father's house.

My reading of the story of Dinah and Shechem will suggest once more
that the question of where to draw the outer periphery was as much an
intra-Israelite struggle as that of who would occupy the center. Thus,
the question of where endogamy ends and exogamy begins is a problematic one. In Kunin's analysis, the preference for endogamy in the
Israelite myth ends ultimately in a preference for incest, specifically
brother–sister incest; but it is here told in a tale apparently about exogamy. I would suggest, then, that there is a twofold mythic dynamic
involved: the binary tension between endogamy and exogamy interacts

with the infinite regression in the attempt to draw the line of in-group identity.

The Mythic Contradiction: Dinah Marries her Brothers

Kunin does not apply the full force of his insight to Genesis 34, where this inclination to sibling incest finds expression in the fact that it is Dinah's *brothers* who become outraged, while her father takes the pragmatic approach. It is to them she (mythologically) belongs as wife. Shechem and the brothers stand at opposite poles, not only in terms of national identity, but also as potential, but equally unacceptable, marriage partners for Dinah. According to the law (as opposed to the myth), either alternative, marriage to foreigners or brothers, will end in being cut off from the land or destroyed by Yhwh (Lev. 18.24-30; 20.17; Deut. 7.4). Unfortunately for Dinah, the stranger and the brother are her only alternatives. Thus, a story that appears to be about the extreme of exogamy—the sexual and potentially marital relationship between an Israelite daughter and a strange man—is (at least) equally about incest. Dinah is 'taken' (*lqh*) by Shechem in the first instance, but also in the end by Simeon and Levi who, having voided the contractual 'taking' of the Hivite daughters as wives (34.9, 16), proceed to 'take' their swords to the Hivite males.

> ...two of the sons of Jacob, Simeon and Levi, Dinah's brothers, each took his sword and came to the city unawares. They killed Hamor and Shechem with the sword and they took Dinah from Shechem's house and went out (34.25-26).

With deadly sexual innuendo, those who stand between the brothers and their sister are eliminated.[13] The three then 'go out' (*yts'*) together: in one sense, restoring the boundary line crossed by Dinah's own 'going out'; in another, perhaps, transgressing a different line.

If this mythological reading seems to stretch the bounds of the text along with the bounds of propriety, it must be noted that the marriage of Dinah and Simeon was not outside the imagination of the rabbis. Regarding Gen. 34.26, 'They took Dinah from Shechem's house and

---

13. Cf. Bechtel, who suggests that it is with the slaughter that the real rape occurs (1994: 34). One might also note the union of sex and violence adumbrated in Jacob's curse against Simeon's and Levi's 'strong' (*'az*) anger and 'fierce' (*qashatah*) fury (Gen. 49.7). The only other context in which these adjectives appear in parallel is in Song 8.6, where they describe love and passion.

went out', R. Huna glosses: 'She said, "And I, whither shall I carry my
shame" [= 2 Sam. 13.13], until Simeon took an oath that he would take
her as a wife' (*Gen. R.* 80.11). This comment surprisingly begs the
question regarding incestuous marriage. Indeed, the transfer of Tamar's
words, after her own rape by a brother, to Dinah's lips recalls the royal
daughter's apparent assumption, expressed in the same verse, that marriage to her brother could have been arranged. 'Now, therefore, I beg
you,' she says to Amnon, 'speak to the king, for he will not withhold
me from you'. Dinah is then identified in the *Rabbah* with Simeon's
unnamed 'Canaanite wife' in Gen. 46.10, an equally surprising ethnic
switch that the rabbis explain by saying, 'It is because she did what
Canaanites do', and 'She had had sexual relations with a Hivite, who
falls into the category of Canaanites'.

The rabbis make overt, I would suggest, connections and transforma-
tions implicit but readily available in the text, given the great metaphorical fluidity between the language of nationality and the language of
sexuality, and the terrible mythic contradiction of exogamy and incest.
For the impossible limitations on Dinah's marital partners are true for
her brothers as well. Whom else would they marry except sister or
Strange Woman? This problem is generally suppressed by the text as
far as the brothers are concerned (cf. Fewell 1996: 139), although it is
no accident, I would suggest, that these 12 brothers have a thirteenth
sibling. She is the means by which this suppressed contradiction is
given voice, though only by means of other contradictions. Like Miriam, this Israelite sister must be narratively estranged.

The Contradiction Resolved: Estrangement, Recuperation, Fertility
The story of Dinah has many resonances with that of Miriam, espe-
cially once the latter character is narratively and mythologically tied to
Zipporah and the Cushite woman.[14] Dinah is one of the 'sons' of Israel

---

14. Douglas also links Miriam's story to Dinah's (1993: 203-207). She argues
that Aaron's alliance with Miriam against Moses is a fifth-century representation of
Jacob's curse against Levi, Aaron's grandfather. This would have been interpreted
by fifth-century readers, according to Douglas, as a repudiation of Levi's attack on
foreigners. Although I too see Num.—and Gen. 34, for that matter—as texts dealing with postexilic (though perhaps not fifth-century) Israelite identity politics, I
find the particulars of Douglas's reading unconvincing. It depends on finding Dinah
guilty, like Miriam, of 'harlotry' and, further, fails to attend to Numbers's important
distinction between Aaron and (the) Levi(tes) (see above, Chapter 6).

but, like Miriam, she must both be distinguished from the lineage-definitive brothers and also then recuperated in order for fertility to take place.

Like Miriam, Dinah is first presented as an independent actor associated with strange women. Miriam speaks against Moses 'on account of' (*'odot*) his Cushite wife. If, as is typically understood, Miriam opposes the strange wife, the text creates the terrible paradox of the estrangement of the Israelite sister who opposes her chosen brother's marriage to a Strange Woman. Citing the rabbis, however, Eilberg-Schwartz notes that the preposition *'odot* can mean either 'because' or 'on behalf of'. The ambiguity allows for two possibilities: Miriam may either be opposed to *or aligned with* the foreign wife (Eilberg-Schwartz 1994: 150, 193).[15] There is a comparable ambiguity in Dinah's relationship with the 'daughters of the land'. The verbal phrase often translated 'to visit with' is actually *lir'ot be*, literally, 'to look into'. This relationship with the foreign women is, in other words, one that Dinah is investigating, but is not fully established. At the same time, her own activity of 'seeing' links her to Shechem, who 'sees' her in the process. Just as Miriam's coupling with the strange wife puts her outside the camp, so also Dinah must 'go out' to see about the foreign daughters, and it is this going out that eventuates in her estrangement. Whereas the sexual dimension of Miriam's estrangement is suppressed by means of other sorts of impurity language, in Dinah's case, it is overtly expressed.

Both women are, then, narratively created as strange women: Miriam through her leprosy and (paradoxically) her (possible) opposition to the Israelite man's strange wife (that is, *his* illicit sex); Dinah through her (possible) friendship with strange women and *her* illicit sex with a strange man. Both women are also recuperated into the Israelite house. The congregation waits until Miriam's time of impurity is past and she re-enters the camp.[16] The recuperation of Dinah is implied in her being taken by and going out with Simeon and Levi. In an impossible union of contradictory elements, a fully endogamous marriage has been accomplished through forbidden exogamy. Fertility results. In Gen. 35.11, God renews both the primal, priestly command and the covenant promise to Jacob: 'I am El Shaddai: be fruitful and multiply; a nation and a company of nations shall come from you and kings shall spring from

15. In the latter case, Miriam's (and Aaron's) presumed concern would be that Moses has denied sexual relations to his wife (so the rabbis) because of his competing obligation as God's wife (so Eilberg-Schwartz 1994: 150, 193).

16. Numbers 20, of course, turns the knife in Miriam once more.

you.' Similarly (though more metaphorically), the sequence of rebellions begun by Aaron and Miriam results not only in Miriam's estrangement but also, first, in the pole-borne fruit of the land and, secondly, in the enlivening of Aaron's rod: 'It put forth buds, produced blossoms and bore ripe almonds' (Num. 17.8).

The Solution Dissolved: Enter the Strange Man

Dinah's story constructs, as it were, a counterpoint to the dynamics of the Israelite myth articulated by Kunin, in which the wife must become a sister. Here, the sister is pushed outside the family identity circle to create a wife who can legitimately be married by her brothers. Read in this way, the story of Dinah deserves not the secondary place in the analysis of the myth that Kunin gives it; here, in fact, the mythic preference for endogamy comes to its fullest, and fully circular, expression. But this circularity—the story of an insider who must become an outsider in order to be accepted inside—contains a myth-exploding contradiction that is obvious when read from the other direction. For Dinah's story is also Shechem's, the story of an outsider who becomes an insider in order to be killed. Landy articulates this symbolic reversal:

> Through circumcision, the Shechemites become Israelites while remaining Canaanites. Dinah has a double allegiance—to the house that she enters and to the paternal *oikos*—and is symbolically aligned both with the land and with its future colonizers (Landy 1993: 233).

The line between foreigner and Israelite that the narrative works so hard to establish is, then, effectively demolished from two different directions: exogamy and endogamy have become moot terms.

Circumcision: Identity and Fertility

The preceding section has both used and extended Kunin's formulation of an Israelite myth that articulates the impossible—a fundamental distinction between one branch of the sons of Adam and all the rest, a uniqueness so profound that they must marry their sisters to produce offspring. I have suggested, moreover, that there is a priestly variant of this myth so wedded to the establishment of identity through male descent that, paradoxically, the sisters of priests must themselves be estranged, their outsider status revealed, as part of the process. It is no surprise, then, that the character in focus in Genesis 34 is Levi, as it was Aaron in Numbers 12. Our studies of both Numbers and Genesis 34 have shown, however, that this sort of line-drawing is an elusive and illusive business. In cutting off the female sibling from the lineage group, the group defines itself in its narrowest, most impenetrable (and most impossible) terms. The estrangement of the sister effectively excludes half the lineage, undercutting the real meaning of identity-by-descent in the same narrative that demands it. The next part of my discussion will continue to develop the notion that we are dealing here with a peculiarly priestly problem: Genesis 34 does more than ambiguate the identity status of the sister; it takes a cut at circumcision as well.

The Priestly Sister Defiled

The fact that Levi is specifically identified as a primary actor in Dinah's story is hardly irrelevant. Granted that he (and Simeon) are Dinah's full brothers, sons of Leah, so are Judah, Reuben, Issachar and Zebulun. So why these two and not the others?[17] It is precisely Levi's place as father to a priestly lineage that makes him important here. The analysis I applied to Miriam is relevant to Dinah as well. Stories of sisters seem to be a way of expressing priestly ambivalence about women. They are, to be sure, born to Israel; indeed, born to the lineage of the priests. But they cannot *be* Israel, and they can certainly not be priests. I depart here from the oversimplified view of Kunin, who equates Dinah with Israel, and sees this text as about only the issue of exogamy, and also from the more subtle and evocative reading of Alice Keefe (1993) for whom Dinah still 'is' unproblematically Israel. The narrative, I would argue, is about an Israel whose identity is fractured and displaced; thus, Dinah 'is' Israel only if Israel's aspect is that of a Cubist painting. Her identity as 'not Israel' stands in profound dialectical tension with the metaphorical 'is'. For the priests, female Otherness must be demonstrated so that none are deceived by the appearance of biological descent. Yet, of course, women are regrettably necessary for this descent to continue. Dinah must be folded into the (story) line(age).

The issue of descent, with its intimately related entailments of fertility and identity, is exemplified most dramatically by another motif in both sisters' stories—circumcision. But the sister's relationship to cir-

---

17. In this context, I address this question in terms of the priestly ideology of descent, and for this reason bracket temporarily the presence of Simeon in partnership with Levi. This omission will be rectified below with a different sort of response, in terms of tribal identity.

cumcision is a problematic one. She is of the lineage, but she is not; she certainly has no penis to circumcise. This ambiguity may be part of the reason for complications surrounding circumcision in these narratives about priests and their sisters-*cum*-wives. In the cases of both Dinah and Zipporah/Miriam, circumcision is not associated, as would be expected, with a clean separation of male Israelites from Others of both nation and gender, but rather muddied with multiply mixed sexual relations. I have dealt in the preceding chapter with circumcision in the Zipporah/Miriam material. Here we shall consider how this motif mediates the relationship between Dinah and her brothers—especially Levi—in the priestly terms of fertility and defilement.

Shechem is three times said to have 'defiled' (*tm'*) Dinah (34.5, 13, 27). Her father hears that Shechem has defiled her, but takes no action; her brothers deceive Shechem with the circumcision ruse because of her defilement; finally, the brothers plunder the city because their sister had been defiled. A term that usually means 'ritually impure', *tm'* is most often associated with priestly literature; it is not used in Genesis outside ch. 34. The unexpected priestly word is, moreover, associated with the definitive cultic act: defilement will be redressed by circumcision.[18] While the brothers up to this point seem unified, it is not surprising that the actual act of circumcision is followed immediately by an independent action by Levi (and Simeon).[19] The priestly act narratively cuts off the priestly brother from the rest.[20] It is, finally, the priestly brother who asks the chapter's seemingly decisive question:

18. The fact that circumcision is an occasion for deceit will be addressed below. For the moment, the important thing is that is was a *believable* deceit, particularly to Jacob, whose silence on learning of the 'defilement' of 'Dinah his daughter' (v. 5) seems to be given voice by his sons' plan to redress the 'defilement' (v. 13) with circumcision. The fact that the sons refer to Dinah in this context as 'our daughter' (v. 17) rather than 'our sister' further accentuates Jacob's alignment with their words.

19. In hindsight, however, one might read this distinction back into the earlier (apparent) unity. While all the sons of Jacob seem to participate in expressing the condition that, if the Hivites do not accept circumcision, 'we will take our daughter and go', it is finally Levi (and Simeon) who actualizes the ruse's reversal: after the Hivites' circumcision, they 'take' Dinah and go out anyway.

20. The last time the word 'defile' occurs, it is associated with the larger coterie of brothers, arguably *not* including Levi (and Simeon), providing the reason for their looting of the city. I offer below a possible explanation for this discrepancy.

'Should he treat our sister as a prostitute?' We have already observed the general cultural concern for shame and protection of family or tribal integrity that informs this question. To the extent that the story resonates with the myth of brother–sister marriage, however, it is the priests who stand particularly to lose; according to the law, women with sexual experience are forbidden them. As well as widows and divorcées, they may not marry 'a defiled women (*halalah*), a prostitute' (Lev. 21.14).

The subject in Levi's (Simeon's) question is, however, ambiguous: who is the 'he' that would make their sister a prostitute? Is it Shechem, the sexual aggressor, or is it Jacob, the compromising father? There is here an echo of Lev. 19.29 that may suggest the latter: 'Do not defile (*hll*, piel) your daughter by making her a prostitute, that the land not become prostituted and full of depravity.'

The rhetoric of Leviticus draws a close connection between the defilement by prostitution of Israel's daughters and the defilement of the land. This particular logic of defilement includes the priests. They may not marry a woman defiled by prostitution, and they are defiled by the prostitution of their own daughters as well. A priestly daughter who defiles herself as a prostitute must be burned to death (Lev. 21.9). Although these Leviticus texts dealing with prostituted daughters and priestly wives use the root *hll* for 'defile', Genesis 34's preferred *tm'* is used frequently elsewhere in the Holiness Code, including a dense collection of eight occurrences in Lev. 18.20-30. These verses recall the defilement of the land caused by the sexual offenses of its previous inhabitants and warn that future perpetrators will be likewise 'cut off from their people', that is, rendered infertile and without descendants.

The priestly brother's ambiguous question both articulates and challenges the identification of Shechem and Jacob. Not for Levi the defilement of a daughter *or* the defilement of the land. He, at least, will assure that Jacob/Israel neither acts like nor unites with those whom Yhwh casts out before them. From this priestly perspective, the annihilation of Shechem and his kin may have been regarded as necessary—indeed, preordained by Yhwh—to ensure the fertility of Israel. The success of Levi's intervention, involving the slaughter of those 'previous inhabitants' and the recuperation of the sister, is marked by the repetition, in the next passage, of Jacob's name change to Israel and the renewal of God's promise of fertility and land (35.9-12).

Disgrace versus Fertility

The use of the word *herpah* ('disgrace') in 34.14 is another locus for the issue of fruitfulness. Dinah's brothers say that to give their sister to one who is uncircumcised would be *herpah* to them. There are two different concerns that run together here, both centered on Shechem's penis. The first is what he has done with it: he has put it in the wrong place and thus brought disgrace on Dinah's male kin. It is a matter of honor and shame, in which the household's honor is challenged by the sexual expropriation of its woman. From this perspective, the demand for circumcision is but a ruse, though it will produce a fitting quid pro quo: the rapist will suffer a kind of rape himself.

The second concern focuses not on where Shechem's penis has been, but rather on the state it is in. Fertility is impossible with an uncircumcised penis, and the term *herpah* can connote lack of fertility. The only other usage of *herpah* in Genesis occurs in 30.23, where Rachel exclaims that the birth of her first son Joseph (which comes immediately after Dinah's birth to Leah) takes away her 'disgrace'.

Herpah also appears in Josh. 5.9, again connected with circumcision and fertility. Here, through Joshua's circumcision of an all-new generation of Israelites, Yhwh declares he has taken away 'the disgrace of Egypt'. While disgrace could be understood in a variety of ways, in this context it is closely connected to (lack of) fruitfulness. After the circumcision ritual, the Israelites eat the Passover meal for the first time and the next day manna ceased to fall (5.10-12):

> On the day after the Passover, on that very day, they ate the produce of the land, unleavened cakes and parched grain. The manna ceased on the day they ate the produce of the land, and the Israelites no longer had manna; they ate the crops of the land of Canaan that year.

Circumcision creates the conditions under which the Passover may be kept; the rite that marks Israelite identity also joins the Israelites to the fertility of the promised land.

On one reading, then, the particular form of 'disgrace' anticipated by the brothers in giving their sister to one uncircumcised is lack of fertility. Eilberg-Schwartz's (1990: 141-76) cross-cultural study of the meaning of circumcision supports this reading and, indeed, this text might echo some archaic practice of circumcision at the time of marriage or as a rite of passage to marriageable age.[21] Such a possibility, however,

---

21. The Hebrew *htn*, variously inflected as 'bridegroom', 'son-in-law' and

only creates the conditions for textual irony and brotherly deceit. For the brothers' concern is not for Shechem's fertility, but for their own: his lack of circumcision is a disgrace *to them*.[22] Shechem's sexual offense has defiled the land in a way the Israelites must not repeat, lest they be cut off. At the same time, Shechem would take away the sister necessary for their own reproduction, a means of reproduction that is also proscribed: the mythic goal of brother–sister incest is precisely one of the defiling offenses in Leviticus 18. In so many ways, it is Israelite fertility and its contradictions that are at stake. Perhaps this is why the substitutionary violence of circumcision must itself be substituted once more with real death. Israelite complicity in the sin is too strong to be atoned for by ritual violence.

Fortunately for the brothers, and especially the brother–priest, the very fact of Shechem's uncircumcision at the time he lay with Dinah is a matter of hope. Because Shechem is not circumcised, he has no possibility of fruitfulness. Dinah, that is to say, cannot be pregnant. In a sense, no 'real' sex took place, a fact that may also allow for Dinah's recuperation as sister into the family (priestly) household. We witness again the liminal status of the sister. As an unmarried woman, a priest's daughter may eat of the sacred donations to the priest. If she marries a *zar*, she may no longer eat of them unless, while still childless, she is widowed or divorced. Then, 'as in her youth, she may eat of her father's food' (Lev. 22.13). A fruitless union with the 'stranger' allows a daughter to return to her priestly 'father's' household...and become her brother's wife?

Circumcision Estranged

The sign of circumcision is in some sense a 'natural symbol' for matters of fertility and, as Eilberg-Schwartz argues, for kinship and descent as well (1990: 162-64). But the plight of Dinah and Shechem highlights the contradiction that emerges when circumcision becomes culturally connected to a myth of ethnic purity mediated through a highly lineage-conscious subgroup. Circumcision as identity marker is more ambigu-

'father-in-law', is cognate to the Arabic word that means 'circumcise' (Boling and Wright 1982: 194; cf. Chapter 6's discussion of circumcision and family relations in Exod. 4).

22. The brothers' locating the *herpah* with themselves also distinguishes its usage here from that in 2 Sam. 13.13, where Tamar asks, 'Where would I carry *my* shame (*herpah*)?'

ous than it would seem if we had only Yhwh's introduction of it in Gen.
17.9-14 as a reference. It is there prescribed as the sign of Yhwh's
covenant with the family of Abraham 'throughout your generations'.
Any male who is not so cut will be 'cut off' (17.14). This passage follows God's promise of fruitfulness and possession of Canaan (17.1-8).
Immediately afterwards, however, two complications arise. In v. 15,
God says to Abraham, 'As for Sarai your woman...' Ah, yes, as for that
woman, that one who will never be circumcised, but will always be
necessary to produce more of those who will be. Is she a part of this
covenant, too? Certainly, with her own name changed, she will be (at
least? at most?) part of the process of fertility (17.15-16). And then the
second complication. Abraham, hearing God's words, laughs and says,
'O that Ishmael may live in your sight!' Ishmael, son of the foreign
woman. Ishmael who, but a few verses later, will be inflicted with the
sign of circumcision (17.23), along with all the men of Abraham's
house, including those 'bought with money from a foreigner' (*ben-
nekar*; 17.27). Ishmael, but the first of Israel's many foreign neighbors
who, at least according to Jeremiah, also practiced circumcision: the
Egyptians, the Edomites, the Ammonites, the Moabites and others (Jer.
9.25-26; cf. Ezek. 32.21-32). Half the world will be circumcised; half
of Israel will not.

Circumcision becomes, then, the stuff of deceit. It should provide a
clear demarcation of difference, Israelite from foreigner. But it does
not. In Genesis 34, this sign of covenant is a sign of deceit with respect
to foreigners, mirroring its own aspect as deceiver among Israelites.
And who does the deceiving? From within the conventional paradigm
of covenant, with its clarity about us and them, it should be a Strange
Woman who deceives. Among the many inversions of Genesis 34,
however, we find circumcised men whose tongues are as light as, well,
as light as their cocks. Those lips need no circumcising; they indeed
speak well. Shechem, on the other hand, is the 'heaviest' (most *kabod*)
one in his father's house. And it finally takes more than circumcision to
relieve him of his physical and social weight.

Niditch has identified Genesis 34 as a trickster tale (1993a: 106-111),
manifesting that tradition's triumph of the clever (read: deceitful)
underdog. It is also more complex, however, insofar as it subverts the
easy identity claim of an underdog tale ('we' are the victorious underdogs) by refusing the obvious boundary lines: the strange man is (at least

belatedly) honorable, the Israelite woman is made strange, circumcision fails as an identity symbol.

In its figuring of circumcision, Dinah's story seems to inscribe a riddle of identity, with its heart in priestly discourse. It was the priests for whom circumcision had such important and multidimensional symbolic value: a sign of fertility, kinship, descent and maleness, it defined the turf of identity. But it must also have been priests who perceived that it was not a sufficient identity marker, for Israel or for themselves. Any man, after all, could be circumcised. Circumcision was, then, a powerful but insufficient symbol,[23] requiring reinforcement from other cultural forms.

The priestly interest in genealogy was another way of 'making the cut', reinforcing with signs on papyrus circumcision's sign on the body. Gender undermines both efforts at establishing national and priestly identity, however, even as it defines them. A patrilineally based identity system finally only reproduces the problems of circumcision: not only does it exclude all women, if traced back far enough, it includes all men. The story of Dinah and Shechem represents the first point while masking the second: the closest of women is rendered strange, while the strange man who draws near is killed. As we have already seen, moreover, patrilineal identity generates another contradiction as well, when juxtaposed with the stricture against marriage to foreigners. This contradiction is most apparent in stories of the time of origin. If they may not marry a foreigner, who else is available to the sons of Jacob other than their sister, and who else available to her? If, in a later period, the construction of ramified genealogies masks this problem, Dinah's story lays it bare.

Were the priestly reader of Genesis 34 also a wise man, perhaps he would answer its identity riddle with a proverb: 'Like the circumcision of a strange man is the sister of an Israelite.'

---

23. This is true, at least, when adult circumcision is recognized. Eilberg-Schwartz comments: 'For the priests, the salient dimension of the covenant was the fact that a male was born into it. Entrance into the covenant was not a mature, reflective decision of adult life. It is for this reason that circumcision is performed as close to birth as possible' (1990: 175). From this perspective, Shechem never had a chance. But one wonders whether the practice of infant circumcision was a reaction to precisely the problem we see in Gen. 34.

Nebalah *in Israel: Sex, Lies and (e)Strange(d) Women*

Chapter 34 is notable in the book of Genesis for breaking the pattern of typically peaceful relationships depicted there between the chosen family and outsiders. In this regard, it anticipates more directly than usual the violent conflicts of the conquest/settlement narratives, where, just as in the Dinah story, the boundary line between Israel and the Other is ruthlessly drawn, while, at the same time, both 'ethnic mixing' and internal division are represented.[24] In what follows, I shall suggest that the use of the word *nebalah* ('outrage, recklessness, folly') in Gen. 34.7, while often cited as connecting the Dinah story to other rape texts, allows a wider set of intertextual readings as well. Most important for our purposes is the series of episodes in Joshua 5–7, in which several other of our key motifs—circumcision, fertility and the Strange Woman —also appear alongside *nebalah* in the context of a bloody conquest. These intertexts highlight the connection of several entailments of the idea of strangeness: deceitful speech, illicit sex and wrong nationality are all (by now predictably) confused in the narrative in such a way as to blur, even erase, neat lines of identity or morality, even as they are being drawn. These transgressions are related, furthermore, to breakdowns in the hierarchical control of the father figure, a narrative element suggestive of intergenerational conflict in the society that produced it.

Nebalah*: Outrageous Sex and Outrageous Speech*
The violation of Dinah is described from her brothers' point of view (with narratorial agreement) with the word *nebalah*. 'When they heard of it, the men were indignant and very angry, because [Shechem] had committed *nebalah* in Israel by lying with Jacob's daughter, for such a thing ought not to be done' (Gen. 34.7). *Nebalah*, an abstract noun from the root *nbl* ('be senseless, foolish'), is sometimes translated simply as 'folly'. Its contexts suggest, however, a stronger rendering: outrage, recklessness, vileness. These contexts also typically associate *nebalah* either with illicit sex (Gen. 34.7; Deut. 22.21; Judg. 19.23, 24; 20.6, 10; 2 Sam. 13.12-13) or ungodly language (Isa. 9.16 [Eng.: 17]; 32.5-6; Job 42.8) or both (1 Sam. 25.25; Jer. 29.23). The longer phrase found in

---

24. See Fewell (1996) for further observations on the way in which the conflicts described in Judges 'rewrite Genesis'.

Gen. 34.7—'*nebalah* in Israel'—is of particular interest. This phrase or a variant of it is also found in Deut. 22.21; Josh. 7.15; Judg. 20.6, 10; 2 Sam. 13.12-13,[25] and Jer. 29.23. In every case but one, it is associated with some act of illicit sexuality, with attention drawn as much to the violation of the woman's male kin as to herself. Only Josh. 7.15, in which Achan's breaking of the ban is described as '*nebalah* in Israel', seems anomalous. As an intertextual reading of Joshua 7 with Genesis 34 will show, however, the fit here is better than it first appears.

The use of the phrase '*nebalah* in Israel' to describe a specifically sexual form of outrage links Genesis 34 with two other texts clearly dealing with rape, the story of Tamar and Amnon in 2 Samuel 13 and that of the Levite's concubine in Judges 19–20.[26] In each case, the offense against the woman's male kin is featured. The brothers of Dinah and Tamar—notably, in both cases, *not* the fathers—take action on their sisters' behalf, while the concubine's husband/master is the one who proclaims 'outrage in Israel' in Judges. Deuteronomy 22.21 deals with the case of the non-virgin bride. Violence against the woman is not the issue here, but rather the daughter's violation of her father's right of sexual control. The woman shall be stoned to death at the entrance of her father's house because '*she* committed a *nebalah* in Israel by playing the whore in her father's house'.[27] The violence against the woman's body, when it does occur, is portrayed as an appropriate response for her offense against her father's authority. Notably, however, the location of the punishment may impute failure to the father as well for not

25. The phrasing in 2 Sam. 13.12-13 is more complex: Tamar says, on being seized by Amnon, 'Do not humble me, for it is not done thus *in Israel*; do not do this *nebalah*...you will be as one of the *nebalah*-people [*hannebalim*] *in Israel*'. Repetitious in her horror, Tamar elaborates on the conventionally condensed expression '*nebalah* in Israel'.

26. This shared phrasing may say something about some commonly understood semantic force of '*nebalah* in Israel'. It may say considerably more, however, about the extent to which these three narratives were read intertextually (David Gunn, personal communication).

27. The law's attachment of guilt to the woman, along with its references to playing the harlot and the punishment at the threshold, no doubt influence the story of the Levite's concubine as well. Citation of Deut. 22.21 would have provided a clinching argument to Exum's proposal that Judg. 19's description of the woman as having 'played the whore' highlights her sexual autonomy and leads the reader to view her less sympathetically (1993: 177-80); her death on another father's threshold can be seen as to some degree fitting retribution.

guarding his daughter with proper care. Such a failure plays an important part, as we have seen, in the tensions of Genesis 34, and is at issue
in 2 Samuel and Judges as well.[28]

Jeremiah 29.23 also uses the larger phrase, '*nebalah* in Israel', in a
statement that alludes both to contexts of patriarchal sexual control and
to the typical use of *nebalah* alone in contexts referring to deceitful
speech against Yhwh (cf. Isa. 9.16; 32.5-6; Job. 42.8). Yhwh says
through Jeremiah that two prophets, Ahab and Zedekiah, will be 'roast-
ed in the fire' by Nebuchadrezzar because 'they have done *nebalah* in
Israel, and have committed adultery with their neighbors' wives, and
have spoken in my name lying words that I did not command them…'
Adultery and lying words give content to the emotive but unspecific
force of *nebalah*'s 'outrage', which, in turn, provides a portmanteau
word for speech that offends Yhwh and sex that offends male property
rights. Reading the linkage of these connotations is also encouraged in
this verse by the name Ahab, which, in turn, evokes the memory of
'Jezebel', a woman remembered, however unfairly, for her sexual mis-
behavior as well as her idolatry and lies. While accusations of sexual
misconduct, however unjustified, are often used in rhetoric against
one's enemies, Jeremiah's rhetoric goes beyond mere hyperbole. Underlying his metonymy is the metaphor he lives by: rejection of Yhwh
(here, rejection of the 'true' prophet) *is* sexual offense against the male
authority figure (Jer. 2.20-25; 3.1-3). *Nebalah* in Israel evokes, then, the
semantic field of strangeness.

Dinah and Rahab: Priests, Nebalah and the Strange Woman

Nebalah in Israel also connects two passages with extensive intertextual
resonances, Dinah's story in Genesis 34 and Achan's in Joshua 7.
Having failed to conquer Ai after the successful battle of Jericho, Joshua
and the Israelites are instructed by Yhwh to discern and expunge the
responsible sinner: 'And the one who is taken as having the devoted
things shall be burned with fire, together with all he has, for having
transgressed the covenant with Yhwh, and for having done *nebalah* in
Israel' (Josh. 7.15). Achan's *nebalah*, says Joshua, has brought 'trouble' (*'akar*) on Israel in the form of defeat by the Canaanites, and will

---

28. Genesis 34.7 is especially apposite; it reads: 'he had committed a *nebalah* in
Israel *by lying with Jacob's daughter*'. See above for the argument that whether or
not Gen. 34 depicts a rape, it is not violation of the woman, but rather dishonor to
her male kin, that is at stake.

now bring 'trouble' ('*akar*) on Achan (Josh. 7.25). 'Trouble' ('*akar*) also brews in Genesis 34, although, curiously, it is not Shechem's act of *nebalah* that brings it. Rather, according to Jacob, it is the deceit and violence of Simeon and Levi that have 'brought trouble on me by making me odious to the inhabitants of the land'; they have endangered his household, few in number, should the Canaanites and Perizzites decide to attack (Gen. 34.30).

Achan and his family must be burned (after being stoned)[29] to purge the sin from Israel and allow for a successful resumption of the conquest over the inhabitants of Canaan. God's response to Jacob's perception of danger from those Canaanites is more ambiguous, though appropriate to a story told of the pre-conquest period. God simply removes Jacob's household from danger by ordering it off to Bethel. Having removed them from danger, God promises that Jacob's family will indeed eventually inherit the land (Gen. 35.12). In this sense, Genesis 34–35 anticipates both Joshua's difficulty in overcoming the Canaanites and its resolution.

Genesis 34 stands in a clear, but tensive, relationship to Joshua 5–7. We earlier noted the similarity in the symbolism of circumcision and fertility (Josh. 5), and have now seen the connections in the language of *nebalah* and trouble, and in the threat of the Canaanites (Josh. 7). Also linking these texts is the motif of division within the house of Israel that exists alongside the effort to distinguish Israel from foreigners. In Genesis, that internal division appears primarily as contention between Jacob and his sons, but also, not inconsequentially, draws a narrative line between sons as well. Joshua, as one of only two remaining 'first generation' Israelites, also functions as a father figure who must distinguish the guilty son from the innocent, although the dynamics here play out in a somewhat different way. Are we missing a Strange Woman? Fear not: enter Rahab in Joshua 6. This is indeed a story of *nebalah* 'in Israel' after all.

One possibility opened up by this intertextual reading is further reflection on the question with which we began our consideration of Dinah's story. Who responds correctly: Jacob with his pragmatism, or the brothers with their passion? Comparison with Joshua 7, where the guilty Israelite must be singled out from his innocent brothers, encourages a

29. The doubling of the means of execution is curious. Does stoning allude to the punishment meted out to the non-virgin bride, who has also committed *nebalah* in Israel (Deut. 22.21)?

reading focusing on the sometimes subtle division between brothers made in the Genesis narrative, between references to Simeon and Levi, on the one hand, and to 'the sons of Jacob', on the other.

There is notable ambiguity in Dinah's story as to whether the two named brothers are included with the others. Up to Gen. 34.25, no brother is distinguished from the rest. All become indignant at the *nebalah* (34.7) and all speak deceitfully about circumcision because of their sense of their sister's defilement (34.13-17). As we have already observed, however, it is precisely the collocation of the latter two ideas— circumcision and defilement—that hints at priestly interests and thus foreshadows the distinctive action of Levi (if not Simeon) in killing all the city's males, including Hamor and Shechem, and taking Dinah away. Then 'the sons of Jacob' come upon the slain, plunder the city, taking booty and human prey (34.27-29). The NRSV's expansive translation ('the *other* sons of Jacob') makes the situation seem clearer than it is. Were Simeon and Levi among the plunderers? Why is it these two alone to whom Jacob addresses his anger (34.30) and they alone who take the fall in his final speech in Genesis 49?

Comparison with Joshua 7 encourages highlighting the distinction between the actions of the brothers in Genesis 34 and puts a particular evaluative spin on this doubled response. It is a matter of holy war, of *herem*.[30] Those who (appropriately) slaughter Canaanites (that is, Sime-

---

30. I use the terms 'holy war' and '*herem*' in the relatively loose sense of a war conducted for what is assumed to be a godly purpose, with the requirement that more killing be done than is necessary for practical reasons because of this 'higher' loyalty, and with possible strings attached to the spoils. This usage is looser than that in Niditch's (1993a) typology of war in the Hebrew Bible, from which I have learned much. Niditch distinguishes two types of 'banning' texts, those that represent the ban as God's portion and those that show the ban as God's justice. These she further distinguishes from what she calls the priestly ideology of war in Num. 31 and from traditional tales of victory via trickery, the latter category including Gen. 34. Though I do not dispute the distinctions Niditch makes, I wonder whether an ancient reader would have always kept them firmly in mind, especially as these stories came to be collected and read as parts of a single story. Does a traditional tale, for example, remain only a traditional tale, once placed in a larger literary context? Would a reader with priestly interests not perk up at the presence of 'Levi' dealing with the problem of 'defilement', even if the story originally had a different agenda from Num. 31? Might not the notion of an act of righteous slaughter in a trickster tale link up at some point with that of 'banning as God's justice'? I will argue, then, that the aspect of *herem* in Niditch's technical sense canonically hangs over Gen. 34, even though it may not have been composed with that in mind.

on and Levi) are to be judged differently than those who (wrongfully) take booty after the slaughter ('the sons of Jacob').[31] Although it is not impossible to see Simeon and Levi among the plunderers, the Genesis text itself provides warrant for excepting them, and reading through the lens of Joshua 7 reinforces the breakdown of Jacob's sons as a single entity. If, then, the righteous sons must be distinguished from the guilty, Jacob's wrath against Simeon and Levi is wrong-headed in more ways than one. Not only does he single them out as particularly guilty, when they were notably righteous. He also fails to respond with appropriate punishment for the sons who have ignored the difference between eradication of the enemy and enjoyment of the spoils, that is, the same greed that led Achan to break the ban. Moreover, when the 'sons' take the Hivite wives as part of the booty, this action obviates whatever rationalization may have been involved in resisting Dinah's marriage to a foreigner. It stands in contrast to the purity of Levi and Simeon, who do not participate in the taking of Shechemite wealth or women, seeming rather to understand the fundamentally endogamous meaning of their 'taking' of Dinah. On this reading, then, Jacob fails to participate actively as father to his violated daughter and to make the requisite rejection of foreign mixing; he also fails to participate correctly as father-judge to his sons.

In summary, the interreading of Genesis 34 with Joshua 7 seems to justify the slaughter of the sons of Hamor by analogy to the *herem* of the conquest, while condemning the subsequent appropriation of the Shechemites' goods and families for the same reason. Since this latter action can be ascribed to the other brothers, Simeon's and Levi's motives are kept pure.[32] Levi is both part of Israel and also separate; the

31. This reading contrasts with a typical modern readerly response that sees the slaughter as infinitely more horrific than the plundering. I do not contest this other possibility. Not only is it plausible from the point of view of modern moral sentiment, it is precisely the moral logic behind Jacob's curse of Levi and Simeon in Gen. 49; that is, it was part of ancient ethics as well—but not everybody's.

32. This reading agrees in substance with a major component of Sternberg's analysis, namely, the distinction between Simeon and Levi and the rest of the brothers. To reiterate a point made earlier, however, I do not, with Sternberg, find that the art of the narrative compels this evaluative distinction. One could argue, for example, that the story's third allusion to 'defilement' as a rationale for the looting supports a unified view of the brothers' action, or, alternatively, that Jacob's special condemnation of Simeon and Levi sets them apart only by negation. It requires, in my view, a tour de force by Sternberg to construe these possibilities as artfully con-

priests ensure the survival of all by maintaining a higher level of purity. Jacob's (= all Israel's) concern for survival is justifiable and, thus, presented sympathetically, but the priests must hold to a higher standard and it is that standard that in fact ensures communal preservation.[33]

In both Genesis 34 and Joshua 6–7, however, the tensions are complex rather than simply polar, and the heartiest condemnation does not fall where we might expect. Why is Jacob's willingness to consort with foreigners not unambiguously censured for the apostasy that it presumably is? Why instead does this potentially sharply focused conflict between 'us' and 'them' blur into a tension between brothers and between father and sons? And, similarly, why does Joshua's typically anti-foreigner ideology veer off into a scene of division within Israel? As we have seen, considering the construction of Dinah as estranged sister provides a certain kind of insight into the tensions within her story.

The Strange Woman is not absent in Joshua either. For there is the story of Rahab in Joshua 6 to consider, a narrative that shows blatant disregard, to say the least, for any form of the 'pure Israelite' stance toward foreigners and sexually strange women. As we have noted, the Achan narrative in Joshua 7 contains the one apparently anomalous usage of the phrase '*nebalah* in Israel': here it alludes neither to bad sex nor bad language, but to the breaking of the ban. Nonetheless, its proximity and its linkage by means of narrative sequence to the (however godly) deceit on the tongue of the foreign prostitute are intriguing. The phrase '*nebalah* in Israel' does not appear in the Rahab story, yet the narrative draws on precisely this set of ideas. It does so, however, only in such a way as to skew easy moral judgment. Prostitution by a father's daughter should be considered *nebalah*. Instead, Rahab saves her father and the rest of her family. The narrative highlights her kin relations four times: twice in her conversation with the Israelite spies, who agree to

ceived moral complications, while denying them the power to control the reading for real readers. What one brings to a text such as this will make a difference. A reader who comes with Josh. 7 as a real moral possibility will certainly follow Sternberg's course; however, as Niditch has shown (1993a), Josh. 7 is far from the only way real Israelites thought about war, even about holy war. Other options were real and morally valid possibilities.

33. This conclusion represents an interpretive possibility diametrically opposed to that of Bechtel, for whom Jacob's allegiance to a 'higher standard' of honor provides communal survival. Again, I do not dispute her view, but only ask what reader she envisions.

spare her 'father and mother, [her] brothers and sisters, and all that belongs to them' (2.13; cf. 2.18); again just before the destruction of Jericho, when the spies bring out Rahab from the city, 'along with her father, her mother, her brothers and all that belonged to her' (6.23); and finally in a summary statement about Joshua's sparing of 'Rahab, her father's house and all that belonged to her' (6.25).[34] The Rahab story, then, is not only about the foreign woman who saves Israel, but also about the prostitute who saves her father's house. Where the Strange Woman is involved, one must expect to have all one's expectations reversed!

The inversion of expectations surrounding the relationship between the foreign prostitute, her father and the people of Israel may be considered part of a larger set of reversals of Israelite and foreigner articulated in Hawk's comparison of the characters and fates of Rahab and Achan (1991: 79). Hawk argues that 'Rahab's story is the antithesis of Achan's'. Whereas Rahab the female foreigner hides Israelite spies on top of her house, Achan the male Israelite hides Canaanite goods under his tent. Rahab volunteers a hymn to Yhwh, but lies about what she has hidden; Achan must be enjoined to 'give glory to Yhwh', but then tells the truth about his crime. Finally, of course, the insider is taken outside to the Valley of Achor and killed, along with 'everything belonging to him', while the stranger and 'everything belonging to her' are spared, placed at first 'outside the camp', and then finally given life 'in Israel'.

The household of the Israelite man is, in effect, replaced by that of the Strange Woman, a mythological move by the narrative reflecting the extraordinary difficulty in separating Israelite identity from 'foreign'. For the myth to work, Rahab's strangeness must be displaced to Achan. I would suggest that the odd use of the phrase '*nebalah* in Israel' in Josh. 7.15 can be seen as the key to this displacement and a cipher for the whole set of inversions identified by Hawk. The phrase repeatedly invokes the improper 'taking' of a father's virgin daughter, already displaced in Joshua 2 and 6 to the figure of the foreign prostitute. But the displacement is only partial: this Strange Woman is still her father's daughter. The ground must shift again: *nebalah* in Israel becomes the taking of God's spoils. But God's spoils and foreign women are narra-

---

34. The fact that her sisters are mentioned only in the first of these four references, when Rahab herself speaks, may suggest that only one Strange Woman escaped Jericho alive. The highlighting of sisters may also signal the reader to remember sister Dinah as we ponder Rahab's story.

tive and structural analogues to each other. They are both desired, even necessary, and also forbidden. Why take the promised land if one cannot enjoy its bounty?[35] How produce, without incest, a nation, except through intercourse with foreign women (or estranged sisters)?

What is interesting in terms of our paradigm of strangeness is the accumulation of metonymic-cum-metaphoric entailments in the patri-sexual set of allusions surrounding *nebalah* in Israel. Genesis 34 makes the not unexpected liaison of strange sex with foreign people, while adding the decontextualized cultic code word, 'defile'.[36] Without leaving the first move behind (Josh. 6), Joshua 7 displaces both strange sex and strange people with an explicitly elaborated motif of ritual violation. The priests once again leave their mark on the complex ideology of foreign and female.[37]

The Father and the Strange Woman

The complex familial conflicts signaled by the phrase '*nebalah* in Israel' in Genesis 34 and Joshua 7 include, as already noted, ruptures between brothers and between father and sons. An ambiguity in the social force of the phrase highlights the latter conflict. For the violation

35. Indeed, banning texts usually permit the taking of booty (except when the ban is executed against fellow Israelites). The case of Jericho is unique in denying the Israelites all booty except that which goes into the treasury of Yhwh (Niditch 1993a: 64).

36. Bechtel also notes the intersection of the semantic fields of *nebalah* and *tm'*. 'This sexual intercourse is considered pollution because Dinah has been tainted with "outside stuff"... It is considered a "foolish thing" that is "not done" because it violates the ideals and customs of the tribal group that attempt to preserve the group boundaries' (Bechtel 1994: 32). Boundary transgression, then, is the linking concept. Bechtel does not, however, link *nebalah* to *authority* transgression, or *tm'* to priestly interests, as I attempt to do here.

37. Joshua 6–7 contains overlapping categories in terms of Niditch's typology of banning ideologies. The destruction of Jericho represents the ban as God's portion (Niditch 1993a: 41), while the annihilation of Achan's family 'moves in the direction of understanding the ban as a means of imposing justice'. The latter text, while still under the influence of the battle ideology, finds justice due precisely for the failure to give God his portion (Niditch 1993a: 63-64). Neither of these does Niditch consider 'priestly' in the sense that Num. 31 is priestly. Josh. 6 is, however, unique among her 'ban as God's portion' texts in that it designates the silver, gold, and bronze and iron vessels as sacred to Yhwh and requires their deposit in 'the treasury of Yhwh' (6.19; 'the treasury of the *house* of Yhwh' in 6.24). Achan steals, then, not just what belongs to Yhwh, but to the priests.

of the father's daughter that makes him, according to the law, a victim in need of economic compensation also makes him, according to the social code, liable to shame for failure to protect his daughter's (i.e. his family's) honor. The shame is shared by the brothers while the victim status is not, perhaps one reason why their decision to act is a simpler one than Jacob's.

Having read Genesis 34 through the lens of Joshua 7's *herem*, we can now also reverse the intertextual direction by means of this father–son dynamic. In the latter text, the role of father falls to Joshua, one of only two remaining first-generation Israelites, who addresses the beleaguered Achan with the seemingly compassionate vocative, 'my son' (7.19). If Jacob is silent regarding his shame from the *nebalah* committed against him, Joshua comes slowly to the proper understanding of the situation. First he complains to Yhwh of an *apparent* shame, the Israelites' cowardly rout by the few men of Ai (7.7-9), a complaint inversely related to Jacob's fear that his family of few numbers would be destroyed by the Canaanites. Yhwh, however, chastises Joshua with insight into the cause of the defeat (7.10-13). Yhwh, of course, as the ultimate father, cannot escape the shadow of shame himself when it comes to cultic *nebalah*. He thus guides Joshua through a ritual of judgment resulting in the proper assignment of blame, just as he saved the skin of Jacob's household by inducing 'terror' in the cities around them (Gen. 35.5). In both narratives, then, the human father fails to provide the guidance necessary to family and nation.

It is interesting to consider these negative characterizations of human fathers in relationship to the intergenerational ideology discerned by Carol Newsom (1989: 149-55) in the first nine chapters of Proverbs. Among the conflicts she finds there is the need for the older generation of fathers to establish and maintain its authority over the potentially rebellious generation of sons. The Strange Woman figures in Proverbs as one of the voices urging abandonment of filial duty, and the existence of such discourse testifies to the reality of the conflict. It is possible, and certainly tempting, to read the narrative characterizations of human fathers in Genesis and Joshua as an implicit commentary on this patriarchal ideology. The construction of Rahab on one level contests the ideology: she is the epitome of strangeness who saves and is embraced by the community, an anti-*nebalah*. For the embrace of the Strange Woman to take place, however, an Israelite man must be lost, in this sense confirming the warnings of Proverbs's sage. In the case of

Dinah, the failure of the father's authority leads to correct ritual slaughter but also to ritual violation.

In comparison with Genesis 34, the problematic is more clearly identified and more clearly resolved in Joshua 6–7. The sin of *herem* violation is foregrounded and the correct 'brother' identified as the sinner by the all-knowing father, as opposed to the muddied situation dealt with by the fallibly human Jacob. For our purposes here, it remains only to remark that the relative clarity of the Joshua narrative is achieved, at least in part, through its handling of female strangeness. Both narratives deal with the problem of Israelite identity, who is an insider and who an outsider, and both show traces of the awareness that this question has no clear answer. In Joshua 6–7, however, the myth makes use of all its resources to divide 'us' from 'them', 'them' being not only foreign but also female, sexually uncontrolled and deceitful. Only after making this careful delineation does the myth makes its equally careful—and definitively priestly—substitution of parts: one honest but ritually impure Israelite man for all of the above. Genesis 34, in contrast, begins not with the woman at the furthest distance from 'us', but the one closest. In this sense, Dinah is an emblem of the many sorts of confusion that follow in her own story, as well as of the identity confusion that proliferates in the rest of Israel's primary story.

Having considered the roles of the Levite, the Kohathite, the Strange Woman and the Estranged Woman as narrative devices that attempt to articulate an impossible line, we turn to one final liminal character: the resident alien, the *ger*.

The Ger, *the Levite and the (e)Strange(d) Woman*

I have argued that Dinah's story can be read as sharing with Miriam's a gender ideology I have characterized as priestly, evident in their working out of the contradiction of identity based on male descent through the myth of the estranged sister. In both cases, the paradox of exogamy and incest played out in the myth signals the various paradoxes of drawing boundary lines between 'us' and 'them'. In Numbers we saw the problem of the infinitely regressing line separating those in the center from those who may not approach. Miriam and the strange women of Numbers 25 step into this breach, both as the means of its suppression and its icon. In Genesis, the issue (taken at face value) is an external line, between Israelites and Others. In raising a question about the status of circumcision, however, the Dinah narrative addresses the question of what constitutes Israelite identity in terms of a priestly symbol. Again, the Israelite sister-estranged is the site on which the constitution of indeterminable boundaries, both inner and outer, comes to rest.

In spite of this congruence in gender ideology in the stories of priestly sisters, the canon reverberates with sometimes violent tensions between Aaron and the (other) descendants of Levi. These are sometimes portrayed as direct conflicts of power, as in Korah's rebellion (Num. 16) or in the Levites' slaughter of the Israelites who were worshiping the golden calf made by Aaron (Exod. 32). Other narratives, however, also focus on what must have been underlying issues at stake in postexilic priestly power struggles. Thus, as we have seen, Genesis 34 contests the meaning of circumcision, challenging an identity marker that some—and presumably some priests in particular—regarded as definitive. Related to the question of circumcision is a difference of opinion between Numbers (as well as Ezekiel and other related P material) and Genesis 34 regarding whether one not born a member of the covenant community might choose to join. The views of 'Aaron' and 'Levi' on the resident alien, the *ger*, must be considered, in relationship to the fundamental identity signifiers of circumcision, intermarriage and possession of the land. Here we shall find a remarkable structural similarity between Levites and the *gerim* as those who exist on and as the boundary line of identity. It is a similarity, however, that comes to a paradoxical narrative expression as a story of conflict between these two groups.

'Aaron' versus 'Levi'

We have already analyzed extensively the relationship of Aaronites to Levites in Numbers where, with the explosive exception of Korah's rebellion in ch. 16, the subordination of the latter to the former is portrayed as part of a divinely directed ordering process. Variations on this theme are found in notices regarding Levites in Exod. 32.25-29 and Ezek. 44.10-14.

In Exodus 32, the Israelites convince Aaron (without a great deal of difficulty!) to make for them a golden calf while Moses is on the mountain with Yhwh. When Moses returns, the 'sons of Levi' respond positively to his question, 'Who is on Yhwh's side?' and, in a scene reminiscent of Genesis 34, respond diligently to his command to slaughter the guilty. Exodus 32 thus comes out as strongly in favor of the legitimacy of Levi over Aaron as Numbers does the opposite. This text also aligns the Levites with Joshua, who had accompanied Moses up the mountain and was the first to hear the noise of the idolatrous people on their return (32.17). Just as the actions of Levi in Genesis 34 anticipate the *herem*, so do those of his 'sons' in Exodus 32. As in Joshua 7, however, here it is clearly insiders, brothers, who are subject to extermination.

If Genesis had doubts about the propriety of mass murder, Exodus has none. Exodus also ups the ante, for the victims here are identified as 'your brother, your friend, your neighbor' (v. 27; cf. v. 29's 'son' and 'brother'). Genesis had intimated, through the act of circumcision, that the slaughtered were brothers rather than outsiders; Exodus confirms this. Lasine's (1994) Girardian analysis sees an even closer kin relationship of the slayers and the slain in Exodus 32. When 'all' the Levites step to Moses' side, he argues, they in effect volunteer to serve as a sacrificial offering on behalf of the Israelites' sin: some will kill, but others, their *Levite* brothers, will be the victims. This scenario is reproduced in the deaths of Nadab and Abihu (Lev. 10) and confirmed as God's will in Numbers's various representations of the Levites as substitutes for the Israelites' firstborn and as their shield against Yhwh's wrath. Quite dramatically, in this reading, the Levites become the line between the holy and the profane by laying themselves on both sides of it at once.

The book of Ezekiel, largely if not entirely from the period of exile, provides an important perspective on the Levites that is arguably related to that in Numbers. Unlike Numbers, however, and contrary to the Torah-narrative's presupposition of the antiquity of the Aaronite lineage, Ezekiel makes no mention of Aaron or his descendants, but rather supports 'the sons of Zadok' (e.g. 44.15-31; 45.15).[38] Since Wellhausen, this passage has often been taken as evidence for a conflict between two priestly groups, an older line of Levites and the upstart Zadokites, with the Levites 'demoted' from the status of full priests to that of temple guards as the result of past idolatry. This view has

---

38. It is not necessary for my present purposes to decide whether all or parts of Ezek. 40–48 are later additions. My interest is in the postexilic situation more than in the exilic. While the 'later addition' hypothesis suits my argument perfectly, I would still assume, even if this passage is exilic, that it continued to represent the views of a later group as well.

recently been disputed by Kalinda Rose Stevenson (1996: 66-78).[39]

The text's discussion of the Levites' role is part of a larger divine pronouncement regarding who is to be admitted to and who excluded from the sanctuary (44.5). Ezekiel draws an angry line against the 'son of a foreigner' (*ben-nekar*), whom he describes as 'uncircumcised of heart and uncircumcised of flesh: his presence in the sanctuary is abomination' (vv. 6-7, 9). The 'house of Israel' (v. 6) is taken to task for admitting such persons and perhaps (the text is confused at this point) assigning them guard duty for the holy things, a task understood to be Israel's own (v. 8). According to the more typical scholarly interpretation, the Levites were regarded as particularly culpable in going astray after foreign idols, ministering to them and thereby causing Israel to stumble (vv. 10, 12). Hence their 'demotion' (vv. 11, 13). The Levites, on this reading, who slew the idol-worshipers in Exodus, here become their pimps!

In a persuasive rereading, however, Stevenson sees the force of Ezekiel's charge as directed against the house of Israel. The Levites, while involved with the people in cultic impropriety (v. 12), were not the cause of the problem and become, indeed, its solution. They 'bear the guilt' (v. 12) and the 'shame' (v. 13) of the people's abominations in a sacrificial sense, and are restored to their presumed original position as guards in the Holy Place, replacing the foreign guards, a promotion rather than a demotion.[40]

Stevenson's reading, then, brings Ezekiel 44 more in line with the Numbers perspective on the Levites' role as the divinely drawn line protecting the sanctuary and its holy personnel from foreign intrusion

---

39. See Stevenson (1996) for a brief review of the earlier consensus, with bibliography for both that and the few voices of dissent.

40. For Stevenson (1994), the Levites never held a full priestly status. As I have indicated (see Part III, Introduction n. 3), I do not find framing this question in either/or terms to be particularly helpful. The textual evidence for tensions surrounding the power and status of this group relative to other claimants for control of the cult as institution is abundant, whether or not they were ever, or ever wished to be, primary ritual actors. Note that Ezek. 44.15 refers to the sons of Zadok as 'levitical priests'. This designation may derive from the common usage in Deuteronomy that remains unaware of the political moves apparently made by 'the Levites' of a later period, or the creation of second-order clergy (cf. Blenkinsopp 1990a: 219-20). One way or the other, lineage in Levi remains definitive for the Zadokites as well as the Aaronites, at least as far as the biblical literature is concerned. In this sense, I continue to speak of the Levites as a 'priestly' group.

and protecting the rebellious people from dangerously direct contact with the holy. Like Numbers and, if Lasine is correct, Exodus 32, it establishes the Levites as the line only by first placing them, with the people, on the wrong side of it. Numbers and Ezekiel share the view that the Levites chose their sin; Exodus, on the other hand, in line with its pro-Levite politics, constructs their line-crossing as a pure sacrifice of holy brothers.

Reading Ezekiel 44 in light of the violence depicted in Numbers and Exodus has the effect of underlining the tension between the Levites and the priests permitted to approach the sacred things. This is a tension that, in my view, Stevenson's interpretation has reduced too far. For this chapter in Ezekiel slings the mud of idol-worship with the best of them, and the Levites do not emerge unsullied, even in Stevenson's more positive reading. On the other hand, assignment to temple guard duty seems an oddly mild consequence for apostasy, whether one views it as promotion or demotion. Has the rhetorical accusation of idolatry been rendered pro forma in the context of an institutional dispute wherein the antagonistic parties eventually reached a pragmatic compromise? Or has this material dealing with an early conflict between Levites and Zadokites been rewritten in terms of a later and more vicious fight between Levites and Aaronites? Answers to such particular political questions are beyond the available evidence, yet the rhetoric of priestly dispute seems consistent whichever side is producing it.

This rhetoric masks, however, more real and pressing issues in the postexilic political stakes. These lie in the identity-giving meaning of circumcision, especially as it relates to the question of intermarriage and, concomitantly, the status of the *ger*. Here too the question is one of how to deal with the line-between.

Circumcision, Intermarriage and the Ger

We have observed the insolent disregard of circumcision—what was to some a definitive mark of identity—in Genesis 34. The question of the meaning of circumcision is related there, I would suggest, to yet another problem of identity-making, namely, the status of those persons who stood on the boundary between the Israelite and the *zar/nekar*, the resident aliens, the *gerim*. The city of Shechem, which was associated with Israel from an early period, but which, according to the myth, still had at some point to be 'taken' from its 'foreign' inhabitants, provides a natural narrative locus for exploring the relationship of Israelite to *ger*. As Eilberg-Schwartz points out, the ass (*hamor*), which gives Shechem's father his name, has metaphorical associations not with persons clearly outside (*zar/nekar*), but rather with the *ger* who stands in a mediating position between Israel and the true outsider (1990: 126-28).[41] To consider the *ger*, then, is akin to our reflections in Chapter 5 on the Kohathites in Numbers 3 and the Levites in Numbers 18: it is to consider those who fill the line-between. Numbers's embrace of the *ger* requires further consideration, as does Genesis 34's rejection.

The Bible has much sympathy for the *ger* as an abstraction. Not only are *gerim* to receive the same charity as a widow or orphan, there is even provision for their functioning, ritually at least, with the same status as 'native' Israelites. If the *ger* will but circumcise himself, he may eat the Passover with Israel, and there will be but one law for the native and the *ger* (Exod. 12.48-49; cf. Exod. 12.19; Num. 9.14). Circumcision provided, moreover, not only ritual access for the *ger*, but inclusion in the fullest material and theological sense: right to inheritance of the land. Ezekiel 47.21-23 is clearly part of this momentous development:

> So you shall divide this land among you according to the tribes of Israel. You shall allot it as an inheritance for yourselves and for the *gerim* who reside among you, who have born sons among you. They shall be to you as natives among the sons of Israel. With you they shall be allotted an inheritance among the tribes of Israel. In whatever tribe the *ger* resides, there you shall give him his inheritance, says the Lord, Yhwh.

The present form of Genesis 34, on the other hand, expressly resists the integration of the *ger* into the community by means of circumcision. Genesis 34.15 adapts the wording of Exod. 12.48-49. The law says, if the *ger* wants to eat the Passover with Israel, 'all his males shall be circumcised (*himmol lo kol-zakar*); then he may draw near to celebrate it; he shall be regarded as a native of the land'. The condition for marriage laid down by Dinah's brothers is virtually identical: *lehimmol lakem kol-zakar*.[42] Genesis 34 further links the question of the inclusion of the

---

41. Shechem's people are identified as Hivites who are, to be sure, on the lists of those to be exterminated from Canaan and with whom intermarriage is forbidden. On the other hand, Gen. 33–34 is not the only context that suggests closer than expected relations between Israelites and Hivites. Josh. 9 records a ruse played out by the Hivites of Gibeon against Joshua's army that won for them a covenant of protection to live among the Israelites.

42. The connection of Passover and circumcision in Exod. 12.43-49 recalls two

circumcised *ger* to that of intermarriage. If the circumcised *ger* can draw near to eat the Passover, should he not be able to partake of the women as well? If Shechem will but circumcise himself, might he not marry Dinah, and his townsmen the other daughters of Israel? Is the *ger* one of us or one of them? The deceit surrounding circumcision in Genesis 34 would have made the answer clear, at least to readers who identified themselves with Levi.

While the text's ambivalence about marital relations with the son of Hamor may echo some earlier problem of distinguishing intra- from inter-'ethnic' relationships, its concern with connubial line-drawing carried particular force in the context of postexilic struggles to legitimize and reinforce power by controlling the definition of who was Israelite and who not. The definitional terms that finally carried the day were those constructed of sex and gender: genealogy and circumcision. As we have already seen, however, what these identity-markers actually 'say' is ambiguous and, particularly in the case of circumcision, contested. How do the genealogical lines get drawn, and by whom? What men may be circumcised; what men may marry 'our' daughters?

The *ger* stands at this contested boundary-line. The voice of Levi in Genesis 34 draws a hard line. The *ger* has land while Israel sojourns, but Israel's offer of circumcision and intermarriage to get what Shechem's got is judged by Levi as harlotry. The *ger* is here named as *zar/nekar*, not on the line but over it, a now duly (narratively) constituted 'other' that circumcision cannot homogenize with 'us'. Elsewhere the boundary-line fluctuates. Ezekiel and P take up the voice of Jacob, including what Levi would exclude. But it is important to notice that these relatively inclusive voices are hardly universalistic. If the *ger* now disappears into the inside, there is still a question of where to draw the line against the non-Israelite, the *ben-nekar* whom Ezekiel describes as 'uncircumcised of heart and uncircumcised of flesh' (44.7, 9). While Ezekiel reproduces the rhetoric of idol worship, Numbers 25, I have argued, makes a further symbolic gesture. Shifting the identity-making terms from the infinitely regressing ambiguity of the Israelite sister estranged, it offers her mirror image: the absolute Other, the Strange

other texts we have considered. The origin of Passover described just before this instruction (12.21-27) closely resembles the act of circumcision as undertaken by Zipporah in Exod. 4: sacrificial blood is wiped on a doorpost (or on a man's 'feet') to ward off an attack of the deity. Circumcision is also required before the Israelites may eat the first Passover in the land of Canaan (Josh. 5.2-12).

Woman—uncircumcised and uncircumcisable—who may be slain without guilt or residue of foreignness left on the pure of Israel.

Ger *and Levite in the Land: Sojourning with Dinah*

The structurally analogous positions of the Levites and the *gerim*, as blurring lines against inside and outside, finds a remarkable parallel in the way land distribution is described vis-à-vis these two groups. As adamantly as Genesis 34 refuses land-sharing with the circumcised foreigner, Ezekiel 47 (see quotation above) insists that the *ger* have an inheritance (the word is used three times in two verses) as a native(!) among the people of Israel, and that this inheritance be given throughout the tribes, wherever *gerim* happen to reside. And as emphatically as Ezekiel demands 'inheritance' for the *ger*, other texts deny it to the Levite (Num. 18.24; Josh. 14.3).[43] However, the Levites are finally allotted 48 cities with pastureland for their sustenance. These territories are to be yielded—like the *ger*'s—from among all the Israelite tribes (Num. 35.1-8; Josh. 21; 1 Chron. 6.54-81).

> In the plains of Moab by the Jordan at Jericho, Yhwh spoke to Moses, saying, 'Command the Israelites to give, from the inheritance that they possess, towns for the Levites to live in; you shall also give to the Levites pasture lands surrounding the towns… And as for the towns that you give from the possession of the Israelites, from the larger tribes you shall take many, and from the smaller tribes you shall take few; each in proportion to the inheritance that it obtains shall give of its towns to the Levites' (Num. 35.1-2, 8).

What might we make of this brief and subtle (too brief? too subtle?) confluence of the literary streams bearing *ger* and Levite? Dinah's story has been the source for these meanderings. Let me begin there once more, returning to a question I raised earlier regarding the distinction of Simeon and Levi from among all Dinah's brothers. I addressed this question above in terms of what I perceive as a priestly ideology of incest, an approach that accounted for Levi but not Simeon. Here I shall continue to focus on Levi as a figure read by a postexilic priestly faction, but now in the framework of traditions about tribal histories. From this vantage point, Simeon remains a shadow, although a mythically significant one. He is the product of a mythic *doubling* that clouds the bipolar structure of the myth, a structure that in this case has to do with

---

43. Cf. Num. 18.20; 26.62, where 'Aaron' is denied land.

the opposition between the landed and the landless.[44] Following this path, we shall trace a route from the territory of (the) Levi(te) to that of the *ger* and back.

Dinah is Israel's thirteenth son, if not in terms of birth order then certainly in terms of gender. Like all number 13s, she is bad luck. Once neutralized by the exposure of her strangeness, her story disappears between the lines of her brothers'. Mythically speaking, however, she does not go down without a fight. Her disappearance is registered and reproduced in Jacob's curse on Simeon and Levi in Gen. 49.5-7: 'I will divide them in Jacob, and scatter them in Israel.'

These two are a curious pair in Israel's ostensible tribal identity story. In the transition from the story of the sons of Jacob in Genesis to the tribes of the wilderness and conquest, the identities of Simeon and Levi blur in different ways. The tribe of Simeon receives land in the form of a group of towns, but these lie within the borders of the tribe of Judah.

> The inheritance of the tribe of Simeon formed part of the territory of Judah; because the portion of the tribe of Judah was too large for them, the tribe of Simeon obtained an inheritance within their inheritance (Josh. 19.9).

The towns assigned to Simeon lie on the extreme south of Judah, where more easily inhabitable land fades into the parched Negeb, the area of Israel's wilderness wandering. Simeon has territory, but no boundaries, both existing on the edge of non-identity and absorbed into the larger corporate identity. It is certainly possible, along the lines of Noth's historicizing reading of Genesis–Judges, to argue that Simeon's marginal presence, both geographically and narratively, is the result of the tribe's dispersal and relative weakness in the time of the narrator. From a more literary perspective, it seems to me also possible to find in Dinah and Simeon narrative mirrors for each other, both marginalized and absorbed, not quite forgettable but regarded as inconsequential, the brother's eponymous destiny foreshadowed by the sister's untold fate.

If Simeon in a sense reflects Dinah, Levi more directly replaces her. As we have observed, the existence of Dinah means there were actually

---

44. On this process of mythic doubling, see Kunin's analysis of the Joseph traditions, with which he includes Dinah's story (1995: 133-61, esp. 141, 161). Kunin does not, however, develop the significance of what I will suggest is a related doubling of Simeon and Levi.

thirteen 'sons of Israel'. While we might not expect a woman to 'father' a tribe in her own name, it is noteworthy that the later people of Israel were unable to divest themselves completely of the presence of a thirteenth child. Dinah apparently disposed of, her avenging brother, landless Levi, becomes, in effect, number 13 in Joshua's narrative of the tribal allotments.[45] Twelve tribes ('Joseph' now divided into 'Ephraim and Manasseh') receive inheritance in land allotments; however, '[t]o the tribe of Levi alone Moses gave no inheritance; the offerings by fire to Yhwh God of Israel are their inheritance, as he said to them' (Josh. 13.14; cf. 14.3).[46]

Both in terms of their problematized relationship to the land, as well as in their complementary mirroring/replacing of Dinah, Levi and Simeon seem a natural pairing. Yet, in another sense, their fates are quite different. Whereas Simeon fades into obscurity, Levi becomes ancestor to a lineage of crucial importance to Israelite identity. This paradox bespeaks the experientially fine line between fertility and obscurity, and perhaps also mirrors the narrative's moral tension, the undecidability of whether Dinah's brothers acted rightly or wrongly in their violence against the people of Hamor and Shechem. The connection of these two brothers may also again, in priestly fashion, manifest the arbitrary nature of God's choice of Levi for special status. As with Miriam and Aaron (and as again with Aaron's sons) both parties commit the same crime (or no crime), yet the curse against them yields different results: in the present case, landless power to the one, landed obscurity to the other.

The pairing of Simeon with Levi highlights this paradoxical relationship to the land. What may appear as a bipolar opposition—the landlessness of Levi versus the landedness of the other tribes—is, in Kunin's term, 'clouded' by the doubling. Land should be the means by which identity and power are conferred, yet 'the Levites' make a claim to be the chosen-among-God's-chosen, an honor signaled precisely in their having no land, but also narratively highlighted by offering in Simeon the possibility of the opposite, land and no honor. The clouding and mediation of the structural opposition of landedness versus landlessness

45. The list in Josh. 13–19 is similar in this respect to those in Num. 1.5-15; 2.3-31; 7.12-83; 10.14-28. Levi is one of the 12 in Gen. 29.31–30.24; 49.3-27; Deut. 27.12-13; 33.6-25 (though the last list omits Simeon); 1 Chron. 2.1-2.

46. The replacement of Levi's inheritance in land with inheritance in fire recalls the relationship of strange fire and strange women discussed in Chapter 5.

accomplished by the doubling of Dinah's avengers points, moreover, to a breakdown in practice: the Levites are not (at least in the long run) as unlanded as they are sometimes made out to be, and neither are those 'foreign' others from whom Israel has presumably taken all the land. The tribe of Levi is, in fact, given cities inside the boundaries of all the other tribes in a manner not dissimilar to the assignment of cities to Simeon within the tribe of Judah, and also not dissimilar to Ezekiel's vision of assigning land to the *gerim*. Indeed, 2 Chron. 15.9 will later allude to Simeon (along with Ephraim and Manasseh) as those who 'reside as *gerim*' among Judah and Benjamin.

The *ger*, then, joins the Levites and Kohathites, the Simeonites and the sisters: everywhere in Israel and nowhere in Israel, filling the space between, disappearing into the infinitely fine line. And land joins circumcision and genealogy as that which cannot tell us who we are.

CONCLUSION

The studies of this book have followed the textual path of the Strange Woman, attempting not only to elucidate her meanings in a variety of literary contexts, but to show that, in her, we have a powerful lens into the mythic and ideological structures of biblical thought. Strangeness necessarily depends on a notion of what is not strange, what is 'us', and thus, indeed, helps to construct that sense of identity by formulating its opposite. In the Bible, there are two different conceptual fields to which strangeness is opposed, wisdom and holiness, with different narrative effects, and yet with permeable boundaries.

Strangeness and Wisdom

I began with what I take to be the paradigm example of gendered strangeness and also, likely, its latest manifestation, the *'ishshah zarah/'ishshah nokriyyah* in Proverbs 1–9. Though this figure summons the shadows of the pre-exilic and exilic equation of adulterous sex and idolatrous worship, as well as the later preoccupation with restricting intermarriage as a way of controlling 'Jewish' identity, its major rhetorical focus is on illicit sex, with underlying concerns of maintaining patriarchal authority and temple purity. The expression of these issues in the poetic figure of the Strange Woman—at once an abstraction and embodiment of them—in tandem with the exalted female personification of Wisdom, creates in Proverbs a dualistic moral ontology that appears to be a relatively late development when compared to the monistic assumptions of most of the Bible: evil itself is, apparently for the first time, reified and personified. 'Us' is here defined not so much in terms of national identity or exclusive worship of Yhwh, but in terms of a classist, patriarchal morality. The female figuring of moral choice does more, however, than encourage adherence with offers of success and warnings of punishment; it also manages to shift the blame from Yhwh for forces that undermine the patriarchal order. The Strange Woman embodies all that is evil, shifting that burden from the shoulders of the male god to a separate, female entity, and thus offering a solution to the problem of theodicy.

The cosmic qualities assigned to both Woman Wisdom and the Strange Woman suggest, then, that more than moral pedagogy is at stake. In these two figures lies a fundamental and multidimensional expression of religious self-understanding. I have suggested that the representation of Woman Wisdom and the Strange Woman in Proverbs provides a paradigm through which other literature may be read. It is, more than likely, a late expression; that is, when we read biblical narrative through it, we perform in the first instance a reading in hindsight, yet one that lends further insight into the formulation in Proverbs as well.

Rhetorically embedded in the opposition of Woman Wisdom and the Strange Woman in Proverbs are the seeds of a dialectic: telling them apart only becomes necessary because they have been told together. I suspect that one motivation for this attempt to crystallize the wise– strange opposition as women to be grasped or avoided was a felt need to reduce to a clear binary the more overt and playful ambiguating of wisdom and strangeness—indeed, of gender and nationality/ethnicity as well—in texts like those concerning Solomon, Samson and their women. The attempt, however, was not completely successful. A reading of Proverbs through the lens of the trickster has the effect of undercutting the book's most obvious message of absolute opposition between good and evil as represented in the female figures, and highlighting their paradoxical, but experientially validated unity. This paradox also marks the Solomon and Samson narratives.

There is no biblical narrative in which the vocabulary and themes of the wisdom tradition, particularly Proverbs, are more evident than in the Solomon story (1 Kgs 1–11). The full semantic range of the concept 'wisdom' is brought to bear here, yet the narrative's evaluation of wisdom remains in doubt: it is God-given, yet it seems insufficient to prevent the wise king from succumbing to strange women. Strangeness also appears in several forms: foreign nationality and foreign gods (though the two are not always connected), illicit sexuality and (perhaps) sexuality of any sort. Wisdom and Strangeness are, in fact, perplexingly interwoven here, most notably in the characters of Bathsheba and the Queen of Sheba. The building of the temple, often regarded as Solomon's most definitive act of faithfulness, is also marked by foreign wisdom. Relatedly, the character and intentions of God, who works through female strangeness as well as other forms of (apparent) human evil, are also shadowed.

The situation is similar in the Samson story. The trickster, a narrative *mise en abyme* of language in its ambiguity and deceptiveness, here intersects both with the Strange Woman and the riddle, a figure and a language form with similar metasemiotic functions. Read through these cross-cultural and critical lenses, the dialectic of wise and strange explodes in this narrative into a full-blown deconstruction, with its necessary theological outcome, a full-blown theodicy, honoring, though only in the breach, the problems of innocent suffering and divine injustice. My reading explored the dissolution of all expected binaries and boundaries: of gender, nationality, morality. The amoral God is implicated in contradiction at every turn, generating a hero who is supposed to be a warrior, but who cannot come near a corpse on pain of pollution, and executing his plan against the foreign enemy by means of the hero's forbidden involvement with strange women, both dangerous and endangered. Solomon and Samson leave, in sum, a lot of room for tidying up to a more orderly minded sage.

Reading Text and Temple as Wise and Strange:
Proverbs Engenders a Canon

There seems to be more to the relationship of the Solomon, Samson and Proverbs texts, however, than simply satisfying a sense of order at the conceptual level. All three hint at issues, and differences of opinion, of specific importance to the development of religious identity in the postexilic period: the myth of genealogically based identity, itself closely related to the contest for leadership of the temple; the targeting of marriage to strange women in the rhetoric of exclusion, perhaps at times for pragmatic political and economic reasons but with increasingly symbolic force; and the emergence of an identity shaped by written texts.

Scholarly consensus dates the redaction of the introductory poems of the book of Proverbs (chs. 1–9), where the Strange Woman appears, to the postexilic period. Recent interpretations have drawn a connection between Proverbs's Strange Woman and the presumed attempts by Ezra and Nehemiah in the mid-to-late fifth century to eliminate marriages of Israelite men to 'foreign women'. Scholars have, however, nuanced this social analysis in an important way, observing that 'foreignness' is an epithet that was almost certainly used by some Yhwh-worshipers against others in the contest for political power and the right to define 'Israelite'

identity itself. In particular, it was used by descendants of Judahites returned from the experience of exile against those who had remained in
the land. Granting the importance of this proviso for understanding postexilic identity politics, I am still not sure that these struggles (whether
in the fifth century or later) provide the best context for understanding
the female imagery of Proverbs. Proverbs's Strange Woman is constructed most obviously in terms of sexual deviance, including not only
prostitution and adultery, but also sexual violation of the cult. This analysis provides hints bearing on the social context: the construction of a
female figure whose 'strangeness' includes violation of a series of cultic
laws found in the Torah suggests an upper-class 'sage' whose interests
include both temple purity and Torah interpretation. Illicit sexuality is
not, however, merely the topic of instruction but has become the terms
in which evil—whether failure to maintain ritual purity or failure to live
by the Torah—is understood.

Among the many upheavals provided by the tricksterish Samson to
the conventionalities of Proverbs, the evocation of a strange temple
with its pillars pushed apart, collapsing on God's randy hero, is one
capable of being read as a sort of political cartoon. Whose temple is
this, and what wisdom is to be found in Samson's separation from his
Strange Woman? Though the 'Philistine' temple is usually understood
as a transparent reference to foreign people and their gods, it could also,
it seems to me, be read as part of the intra-community conflicts of the
postexilic period. Can we envision here a postexilic reader with ties to
the school of thought that produced Proverbs, but more resistant to
nationalistic exclusivism associated at that time with the temple leadership? If so, then, like the Strange Woman who serves Yhwh's purposes
in the Samson narrative, its image of a strange temple can also be read
as ironic, the accusation of strangeness turned back on its priestly purveyors, and the threat held out of a new act of divine destruction.

The Solomon narrative also plays with the notion of a strange temple,
now explicitly Yhwh's house, and explicitly including both wisdom
and strangeness in its fabrication. Of particular interest to the question
of social location is Proverbs's shift in formulating the concept of the
'house'. The temple-house built by Solomon for Yhwh becomes a book
(Proverbs) structured as Wisdom's house, while Yhwh's promise of a
dynastic house to David issues forth from Solomon not as sons but as
wise words: Solomon's seed is wisdom itself. The process is at least

suggestive of a developing canon-consciousness, perhaps set in opposition to a temple rhetorically cast as 'foreign'.

I mentioned above that the gendered wise–strange formulation of Proverbs strikes me as an attempt to resolve the ambiguities of Solomon and Samson and, thus, as a later text. When considered from the point of view of temple politics and the emerging canon, it is possible to reach the same conclusion: over against the tensions evident in the narrative material, Proverbs seems to harmonize and consolidate, in wisdom's terms, cult and canon as the normative sources of authority and identity.[1] The gendered imagery of the narratives, now suitably tamed (or almost so!), could not have been more useful to a group whose agenda also included assertion of patriarchal control over both women and sons.

Strangeness and Holiness

Strangeness belongs not only to the tradents of wisdom, however, but also to the priests, who used it in their construction of holiness, not least the holiness of their own lineage-based identity as separate from their *zar*-brothers. When male lineage is the key to identity, however, sisters represent an unbearable contradiction; they are, by birth, of the 'right' lineage and yet, by gender, not 'us'. As the strangers-within-the-family, the sisters of priests are, in the stories of Miriam and Dinah, narratively transformed into Outsiders; they become Israelite women estranged, Miriam made unclean by leprosy and unritualized death, Dinah sexually taken by a strange man. While gender is fundamental to this construction of holiness, gender distinction is not the only issue at stake. Close attention to the concept *zar* ('strange/stranger') in priestly ideology reveals a pervasive problem of infinite regression in boundary-line drawing: the *zar* is the outsider to the chosen priestly lineage, but the line between inside and outside proves unstable, and the circle of insiders tends to shrink. The clan of Kohathites must be distinguished

---

1. Although the available evidence, such as it is, has led me to postulate a sequence of development from the narratives to Proverbs, it is certainly possible to imagine the opposite movement, that is, that the Solomon and Samson narratives are later undoings of the coherence constructed by Proverbs. My central point, in any case, does not hinge so much on the sequence as on what I perceive to be the conflictive conversation that postexilic readers could see in these texts, whether or not their authors intended it.

from the larger priestly tribe of Levites, the sub-clan of Aaronites from the Kohathites, and, finally and brutally, half of Aaron's offspring from the rest. This is the problem of the stranger-within writ large, for which the sister narratives provide both icon and displacement.

This iconic function of the relationship of the sister and priestly brother with respect to the problem of infinite regress in the marking of identity boundaries can be seen in the Miriam story (Num. 12; 20) and related texts in Exodus. The ideological problem that pervades Numbers, of dividing priest from non-priest when both are of the same lineage, plays out in the more intimate terms of acknowledging and resisting the unities of brother and sister, and brother and brother, as well as in the theo-national terms of dividing one son of Isaac from another (the conflict between Israel and Edom/Esau in Num. 20). Miriam, the Israelite sister, is a narrative transformation of Zipporah, Moses' Midianite wife, who is, in turn, identified by means of her priestly relations (her father Jethro) and function (performance of circumcision) with Aaron the would-be priest. These dangerous equations are narratized in Numbers's accounts of the Israelite sister estranged, an exorcism necessary for priestly purity to be finally established. Miriam is rendered impure first by leprosy, separating her from Aaron, then as a corpse where there is no water for purification. Yet the sister–wife is also the ideal endogamous mate, and her loss generates a new crisis: the unacceptable union of her brothers, Moses and Aaron, which is in turn veiled by the foregrounding of succeeding generations of Aaronite priests, first Eleazar, then Phineas. Phineas provides the final resolution by dispatching the 'proper' enemy, the in-marrying Strange Woman, along with his estranged brother. Thus is the line against the inner circle finally established and justified, in and through the line against the outside.

Dinah's story also hinges on the relationship between a sister and a priestly brother, in this case Levi. The ambiguity of this narrative has produced much debate regarding whether Dinah's father, Jacob, or her brothers, especially Levi and Simeon, responded properly to her sexual encounter with (rape by?) Shechem. This debate, in my view, results from a tension in the ideology of honor and shame encoded in the text. Men's desire to constrict the sexual activity of their family's women, reflecting an endogamous impulse, conflicts with the need to create, by means of the traffic in women, advantageous alliances, an exogamous impulse. This tension between endogamy and exogamy had, no doubt, practical political consequences in the struggle for identity in the post-exilic period. It also reflects, however, the contradiction involved in a story of descent from a single family, usually resolved in what Kunin calls the myth of incest: witness the wife–sister stories elsewhere in Genesis, where outsider women are narratively 'made family' before the heir to the promise can be born. For the priests, however, all women are strange; thus the wife–sister provides no satisfying resolution. The Dinah narrative represents this tension in its most extreme form, pitting premarital sex with a foreign man against the possibility of brother–sister incest, with priestly (here, Levi-tical) interests also evident in the story's concern for defilement and circumcision. As was the case with Miriam, a story of an estranged sister gives voice to the mythic contradiction.

Priestly Lines and Lineages

If the wise and strange texts of Proverbs, Samson and Solomon hint at the postexilic issues of identity, cult and canon, Numbers and Genesis provide further grist for speculating on the religious and political dynamics of this sociohistorical setting. Crucial to this consideration is the priestly rhetoric of descent and strangeness, with its emphasis on pure seed and its construction of (e)strange(d) women. Notable in our discussion has been the literary intersection of sometimes collapsing symbols of identity with allusions to what were likely real historical problems of determining membership in the community.

Dinah's story stands out in the book of Genesis, not just for its interest in the marking of boundaries and identity, but for the violence it brings to the matter. Shechem was a 'Canaanite' city with long-standing 'Israelite' connections, suggestive of the blurred boundaries found elsewhere in the form of the *ger*, the resident alien. Genesis 34 seems to argue the negative side in a debate about whether and to what degree a circumcised *ger* is part of the community of 'Israel', with access to its women and its land. The priestly law of Numbers, on the other hand, is willing to accept the *ger* as native-born (9.14; 15.14-16, 26, 29-30; 19.10; 35.15; cf. Exod. 12.19, 48-49; Lev. 19.34; 24.22; Ezek. 47.21-23). While the canon represents two sides to this debate, it also offers signs and means of resolution, beginning already in Genesis 34 and 49, where Jacob speaks with the voice of inclusion. There is, later on, considerable irony in the fact that the 'landless' Levites, who would have slaughtered the *ger* rather than gain his land by intermarriage, end up being assigned land in much the same manner as do the *gerim*, 'mixed in' among the 12 (landed) tribes of Israel. These Levites, moreover, who attempted to draw the hardest and most absolute of lines at the outside, end up, cultically speaking, on and as the line against the inside, guarding the holiness of the Aaronite priests. But here again there is a paradox, for 'Aaron' and 'Levi' are themselves sometimes in violent conflict. The priestly conflict both reproduces the struggle over where to draw the line on the *ger* and amplifies it by confusing and diffusing the force of crucial identity-giving constructs—circumcision, genealogy and land.

In Genesis 34, Levi slaughters *gerim*, making strangers of those on the line. In Exodus 32, the story of Aaron's apostasy with the golden calf, Levites slaughter their brothers, making a line where one would not expect strangers. In Numbers 16, Yhwh slaughters Korah's Levites, removing then remaking the makeshift line between brothers. These stories of Levi(tes) seem to be all pieces of the same postexilic picture of priestly conflict with respect to the specter of strangeness. It is a picture in which the insiders' struggle between priestly brothers both displaces and is displaced by the struggle at the periphery between Israel and the Other who may once have been brother. But it is the same conflict, both politically and symbolically: politically, because the two claimants to priestly centrality represent opposing views on where to draw the outer line, whether to include the *ger* or not; symbolically, because the significance of and control over the two primary priestly identity-markers, circumcision and genealogy, are at stake, as is the significance of land possession itself. The rhetoric surrounding these issues is intensified by the interwoven accusations of harlotry and idol worship. Circumcision, which may have made an effective identifying cut in exile among the uncircumcised Babylonians, draws a much blurrier line back in Judah, where it becomes a ritual invitation to (at least the landed among) those who had remained and among whom it was already likely in practice. The identity-defining capacity of genealogy is also undermined by the unmasking of its internal contradictions. In Exodus 32, the idol-making Aaron represents the 'brother' who must be slaughtered by the faithful Levites; in Numbers 16, Levi is the brother who must be slaughtered in order to be subordinated to the true priest. When the focus turns to the construction of foreigners in Genesis 34, the offer of membership through circumcision reveals genealogy as the fiction it is.

Coming at the issue from another direction, we can see how the stories of interpriestly conflict contain the seeds of their own resolution. In Exodus 32, Aaron's apostate leadership of the Israelites is redressed by the Levites' slaughter of their brothers. The narrative works on one level as a polemic against inclusivists, here styled as syncretist idolaters. On the other hand, as Lasine (1994) has pointed out, the Levites do not kill Aaron, the chief sinner, but rather their 'brothers', already making the self-sacrifice on behalf of holiness that Yhwh will institutionalize in the book of Numbers when he constitutes the Levites as the line between priests and people. Complementing this move is Numbers's otherwise paradoxical narrative depiction of the third-generation Aaronites' ultimate validation of their claim to the center over that of the Levites: the erstwhile *ger*-lovers exterminate the Strange Woman in the form of Cozbi (25.6-13) and the widows of Midian (31.1-24). If the literary tension between Levites and Aaronites expresses what was at some point in history the opposition of political parties in Judah, then one must suspect that these otherwise ironic reversals reflect some sort of compromise or, alternatively, a narrative telescoping of shifting alliances and rivalries. Using the Strange Woman as our guide, it may be possible to sort out some, though hardly all, of the circumstances whose traces remain in these biblical texts.

Ezra and the Strange Woman:
Marrying Cult and Canon

A key figure is Ezra, used often by scholars as a touchstone for historical reconstruction, yet himself something of a mystery. What was his status, his agenda, his relationship (both in terms of office and of chronology) to Nehemiah? Who were his allies and who were his enemies? In particular, how does his reported organization of the wholesale divorce of 'foreign' wives relate to the conflict situation—centered on foreigners, liminals and women—I have just described? There have been significant differences among scholars on this issue. Many have put Ezra on the side of an exclusivist priesthood, associating his (and Nehemiah's) marriage restrictions with an ultimately victorious effort to put control of land and temple in the hands of those who regarded themselves as 'pure' Jews. This consensus has, however, broken down in different and contradictory ways. Smith-Christopher still assigns Ezra to the exclusivists, but defends his radical marriage agenda as the survival mechanism of Jews who are marginal and impoverished. Douglas, attacking Ezra's exclusivism, regards him as the winner in the game of identity politics, but separates him from the losing priests who wear the white hats. Van Houten, to the contrary, finds Ezra's interests aligned with the inclusivist priests insofar as he represents a Persian government mission to unify the provinces of Samaria and Judah; she argues that the divorce action only applied to those who refused Ezra's invitation to join (his version of) the cultic community (cf. Ezra 6.21). Berquist also stresses Ezra's (and Nehemiah's) primary commitment to Persia, a commitment that enhanced the importance of the temple as an arm of state control (thereby lining priestly pockets); but (contrast van Houten) he still assumes that this agenda involved resistance to intermarriage for fear of foreign access to Yehudite land and leadership.

I confess I remain perplexed by the variety of these alternatives. Was Ezra an exclusivist or an inclusivist? Was he driven by a concern for ethnic purity or motivated mainly by his allegiance to Persian authority? As I have already suggested, I suspect, first, that there is too much we do not know to offer an airtight reconstruction and, secondly, that part of the difficulty lies in ebbs and flows of power and shifting alliances between the time of the first wave of return just after 539 BCE and the time of Nehemiah, according to the text, 90 to 100 years later. The picture is further complicated by the textual confusion about whether Ezra's mission occurred before, during or after Nehemiah's, and, most importantly, by the fact that the books of Ezra and Nehemiah were edited, if not wholly composed, at some later point—perhaps one century, perhaps two or more—after the events they purport to describe. It remains, therefore, a serious question whether we can discern anything at all about Ezra as a historical person distinct from his characterization in these books. As we have observed in the Introduction and Chapter 1, moreover, the problem with foreigners and the people of the land depicted in these books, while arguably reflective of fifth-century circumstances, was an ongoing concern, as lively in the fourth and even second centuries as it was earlier.

Let me then hold the biographical question at bay and consider three other interrelated matters of literary representation: (1) the questions raised by the depiction of Ezra's and Nehemiah's actions against foreign wives; (2) the interleafing of motifs related to gendered strangeness in the books of Numbers, Ezra and Nehemiah; and (3) the significance of Ezra's literary identification with both the priesthood (Aaron in particular) and the introduction of the Torah, itself closely related to the attack on foreign wives.

Nehemiah, Ezra and Foreign Wives

Nehemiah and Ezra are both depicted as opposing intermarriage with 'foreigners', but not in precisely the same terms. Nehemiah 13.23-31 depicts Nehemiah as cursing, beating and pulling out the hair of 'Jews who had married women of Ashdod, Ammon and Moab', then making them take an oath not to give Jewish daughters to foreign men or take their women for themselves or their sons. He also causes to flee from him the grandson of the high priest Eliashib,[2] who had married a daughter of Sanballat, the governor of Samaria, accusing 'them' (= the high priest's family only, or were there others involved as well?) of defiling 'the priesthood and the covenant of the Levites'. He then 'cleansed them of everything foreign'. Ezra (9.1–10.44) is depicted as responding to reports that 'the people of Israel, the priests and the Levites' had not 'separated themselves', but intermarried with 'the peoples of the lands' (similar phrasing is used in Neh. 9.24, 30; 10.29, 31-32). He expresses his own shame before God;[3] he utters a prayer in which he invokes words from Leviticus and Deuteronomy as accusations against the offenders; and, finally, he organizes a mass expulsion of the foreign wives of 113 men, with their children.

Doubt arises, however, as to the historicity of these accounts, both because of the uncertain relationship of Nehemiah's actions to Ezra's, and because of textual ambiguities with respect to the actual targets of their reforms. Who exactly is being accused of intermarrying, and with whom?

Nehemiah at one point maligns 'Jews' who have married women from Ashdod, Ammon and Moab (13.23). While this seems a clear reference to women of foreign nationality, the picture is elsewhere less clear. Nehemiah identifies his enemies as a Samarian (Sanballat, from Beth-Horon in what was once Ephraim), an Ammonite (Tobiah) and an

---

2.   Whether 'caused to flee from me' means that Nehemiah 'ran him out of town' or 'punched him in the nose and threw him out of the office' is impossible to decide from the text. The former would indicate a more powerful political act; the ambiguous phrasing suggests that the latter may be more accurate.

3.   Are there overtones in Ezra's 'shame' of Ezekiel's assignment of substitutionary shame to the Levites to atone for the people's failure to exclude foreigners from the temple (cf. the discussion of Ezek. 44 in Chapter 7)?

Arab (Geshem). The presence of the Samarian, who extrabiblical evidence suggests was a Yhwh-worshiper,[4] complicates any simple notion that these were 'foreigners', as does the presence of a 'Tobiah' in the list of early returnees from exile in 520 (Ezra 2.60). Notably, the three specific examples of so-called intermarriage identified by Ezra or Nehemiah involve these men or their relatives: Tobiah the Ammonite was himself the son-in-law of one leading Judean citizen and his son had married the daughter of another (Neh. 6.17-18), while one of Sanballat's daughters was wed to the high priest Eliashib's grandson (Neh. 13.28). Also striking is the use in Neh. 13.3 of the term *'ereb* to describe those from whom the people separated themselves after hearing the law. A rarely used word, it refers in Exod. 12.38 to the heterogeneous group ('mixed multitude') that joined the Israelites on their escape from Egypt. The welcome mat, once out, has apparently been rolled up, but against whom precisely? Presumably people who at some point were accepted as members of the community. The suspicion that Ezra and Nehemiah are, at least in part, drawing lines between one would-be 'Israelite' and another is reinforced by their vague use of the term 'peoples of the lands' to describe the source of forbidden brides, while vilifying them with anachronistic national labels drawn from ancient traditions of Israelite enemies (Ezra 9.1, 11; cf. Neh. 9.24, 30).

What is the connection between the peoples of the land(s) and the *gerim*, the protected resident aliens of Numbers? And how are these terms related to the powerful leaders outside Judah, some of whom were Yhwh-worshipers and some likely not? The text of Ezra–Nehemiah makes discriminating between these groups difficult. But, if they are the same, why the shift in terminology and why, especially, adopt an epithet that identifies the enemies with the land? A final complication to precise definition of those who are not to be married is the slippage in

---

4.   The Elephantine papyri supply Yahwistic names for Sanballat's two sons, Delaiah and Shelimiah (McCarter 1985). Ezra 4's account of the building of the temple also confirms in the breach the religious faithfulness of people in the north. It cites opposition to the new temple from 'adversaries of Judah and Benjamin' (4.1) who, in fact, initially ask to participate in the project. Apparently Samarians, these 'people of the land' (4.4) plead unsuccessfully that they have worshiped Yhwh 'since the days of King Esar-haddon of Assyria who brought us here' (4.2). Albertz (1994: 530) argues that the point of contention in this case was whether the community was to be defined theologically, in which case all worshipers of Yhwh, north or south, would have standing, or, as Nehemiah would have it, geographically, thus maintaining the independence of Judah.

both Ezra and Nehemiah between rejection of *all* such marriages (giving our daughters to their sons as well as taking their daughters for our sons; Ezra 9.12; Neh. 10.30; 13.25) and the rejection of foreign *wives* only (Ezra 9.2; 10.2-3, 10, 14, 17, 44; Neh. 13.23, 26-28). While it is possible that 'Israelite' men were marrying outsider women more often than vice versa, it seems just as likely that we are dealing here with the gendered rhetoric of strangeness as much as anything else.

Also curious is the difference between Ezra and Nehemiah as to who among the 'Israelites' are doing the intermarrying. In Ezra 9.1, 'the people of Israel, the priests and the Levites' are all accused of failing to separate themselves from the peoples of the lands. A few verses later, however, Ezra mourns the faithlessness of the *golah*, apparently limiting his concern to those who experienced the exile. But who constitutes this *golah*? The later one dates 'Ezra', the more diffuse a group this must be; even at the earliest (c. 458), it would have been made up mostly of second- and third-generation descendents of actual returnees. Did it also include people whose forebears had not been in exile, but had 'joined' the returnees in worshiping Yhwh (Ezra 6.21)? In contrast to Ezra, the book of Nehemiah rarely uses the term *golah*.[5] Nehemiah 10 depicts all the 'people'—along with the Levites, priests, gatekeepers, singers, temple servants, and their wives, sons, daughters, kin and nobles—making a covenant to abjure intermarriage with the peoples of the land. In ch. 13 Nehemiah refers to his troublers as 'Jews' (13.23); his focus of concern, however, is the defiling of the priesthood and the covenant of the Levites (13.29), with the grandson of the high priest the single identified marital reprobate. The Levites, far from culpable as in Ezra, seem in Nehemiah to have been disadvantaged by the priests' acceptance of outsiders: after discovering the residence of the Ammonite Tobiah in the temple, Nehemiah next finds out that 'the portions of the Levites had not been given to them', forcing them to return to their fields in order to survive instead of performing their temple duties (13.10).

At least sometimes—especially in ch. 13's identification of specific enemies and its particular concern for priestly purity and proper temple practices—the book of Nehemiah seems to represent a more historically realistic picture than does Ezra of the political situation behind these literary constructions of strangeness. To this relative realism I would

---

5. The one exception is Neh. 7.6, but this verse introduces a list of returnees substantially copied from Ezra 2.

add as well the contrast between the books in how foreign marriage was dealt with: the almost military efficiency of Ezra's divorce proceedings is rendered suspicious by Nehemiah's cursing and hair-pulling. Seen from this vantage point, Ezra's story of divorce of foreign wives does indeed appear as much of an idealization as his characterization of the peoples of the lands as Canaanites and other long-gone enemies. Was, then, the idea of compulsory divorce merely a useful political ploy, a policy designed for rhetorical appeal to the radicals but for failure in practice? Or was it even a creation of the editor of Ezra–Nehemiah, working at some later day?

Eskenazi (1988: 126) argues that concluding the redaction of Ezra–Nehemiah with the tensions and setbacks of Nehemiah 13 'protects the reader from confusing the "ideal community"…with an idyllic or idealized community'. For all its relative realism, however, political pragmatism is not the only thing at stake in this chapter. It also represents a stage in the rhetorical consolidation of 'Israelite' identity over against the outsider. Whatever the preponderance (or lack thereof) of foreign marriage taking place, and whoever these 'foreigners' may have been at one or another point in the postexilic period, Nehemiah 13 makes a crucial rhetorical move in summoning the ghosts of Balaam and, especially, Solomon to combat intermarriage of the priesthood. I shall return below to a more detailed consideration of the hermeneutics at work in this citation of authoritative texts, but the discussion up to this point has surely made the basic logic clear: right sex = right nationality = right god = true priest.

Others have argued, as we have noted, for the likelihood that the textual rhetoric against 'foreign' wives—certainly in Ezra and at least to some degree in Nehemiah—is already a step away from the literal: foreignness is as much a matter of assertion as accepted fact. But there is a rhetorical slippage in these texts that cannot be accounted for by political intention alone, a slippage between discourse on strange women and discourse on the Strange Woman. It is a slippage, then, between the politics of identity, figured in the giving and (especially) taking of daughters in marriage, and the cognitive–affective grounding of identity carried out by the religious symbol system. The latter process is figured in womanly pollution of the land, the temple and, by extension, the male body. The textual movement toward reification of the Strange Woman, along with its temporal ambiguities and its lack of coherence in describing the actions of Nehemiah and Ezra with respect to the so-called foreign women, suggest to me the work of a later literary hand. Firm conclusions about the true extent of a problem with mixed marriages in the fifth century (of whomever to whomever!) and actions (whether real or rhetorical) against them remain, in my view, outside our historical reach. Ezra, perhaps, only fakes it with the Strange Woman.

Ezra, Nehemiah and Numbers

What, then, was the relationship of this writer to the forked-tongued editor of Israel's primary story, whose narrative pastiche deconstructs circumcision and strangeness, Levite and land, sister and Strange Woman, as definitive for Israelite identity? I shall consider here the interleafing of motifs of gendered strangeness in Numbers, Ezra and Nehemiah. I suggested above that Numbers's paradoxical picture of landed Levites and priestly slaughterers of strange women represented a negotiated compromise regarding temple leadership between two priestly parties, paying at least lip service to their opposing positions on inclusion of the *ger*. A text like Numbers 25, with its vicious attack on a multivalent Strange Woman (especially the Midianite Cozbi, who threatens the tabernacle's sanctity), is easily associated with Ezra–Nehemiah's rejection of marriage to 'foreign' women who pollute land and temple. If this is also in some sense the hardline voice of 'Levi' heard in Genesis 34 and Exodus 32, however, it has taken the curious turn of speaking through the mouth (or, rather, spear) of Phineas, Aaron's grandson. It may well be that by this time the Levites were quite willing to accept a grant of land and permanent if second-class status in the temple, if their rigorous definition of Israelite identity could at least appear to have been met by the priests in charge. The Strange Woman as a literary image serves this purpose nicely: it is easier to unify contentious forces against a rhetorical construction of absolute Otherness than to negotiate that elusive line on the ground that divides us from our brothers.

One wonders, however, whether Numbers 31 might represent the other side's version of the compromise. This chapter is a quintessentially priestly depiction of the *herem*, holy war, with its concerns for ritual purification related to death and sexuality (Niditch 1993a: 78-89). Like Numbers 25, it also reflects the amalgamated terms of strangeness that mark the canon's final state: strangeness has to do with nationality, with sex and with gender. Sex takes precedence in this case over nationality as definitive of the strange: only foreign women with sexual expe-

rience were to be killed; virgins who had not known a man were reserved for Israelite use (Num. 31.17-18). Is this, then, a tacit legitimation of the leadership's 'foreign' wives (all acquired, of course, sexually
untouched)?

Numbers 31 shows other signs of Ezra and, especially, Nehemiah as
well. The characterization of Ezra's and Nehemiah's response to discovering the foreign wives of Judahite leaders is not dissimilar to that
of Moses when he finds that, along with the rest of the booty captured
from Midian, the warriors 'have allowed all the women to live'. In no
case do the offending parties seem to have any prior realization that
they had done something wrong, yet Moses gets angry, Ezra mourns
and Nehemiah curses, beats and pulls the hair from the offenders. All
three then order cleansing from the taint of foreignness (Num. 32.19-
24; Neh. 13.30; Ezra 10). Whereas Ezra's measures take the more secular legal form of ordering divorce from foreign wives, however, both
Moses' and Nehemiah's focus more on ritual purification, separating
the holy from the unclean. Nehemiah asserts that the intermarriers 'have
defiled the priesthood, the covenant of the priests and the Levites. Thus
I cleansed them from everything foreign...' (13.29-30). While Nehemiah is not explicit on exactly how this cleansing took place, Numbers
certainly is: Moses orders the foreign women with previous sexual
contact killed, then the warriors purified of contact with death.

Both Moses and Nehemiah justify their actions against foreigners
with reference to the Balaam episode, narrated in Numbers 22–24, just
before the account of Israel's 'harlotry' with the Moabite women and
Phineas's execution of Cozbi and Zimri in Numbers 25. Moses accuses
the Midianite women[6] of acting on Balaam's advice to make the Israelites 'act treacherously (*ma'al*) against Yhwh' (Num. 31.16), a feature not found in the Balaam story itself. Nehemiah 13 does not move
immediately against the women, but builds the case gradually. The
concern in Neh. 13.1-2 is to exclude Moabites and Ammonites from the
assembly of God and, paralleling Deut. 23.3-6, this exclusion is justified by reference (again, not quite as Num. 22–24 would have it) to
their hiring of Balaam to curse Israel. 'Separation' is then immediately
demanded, however, with respect to *all* non-Israelites (13.3), and the
chapter goes on to list a variety of offenses regarding foreigners. Pre-

6.   The narrative in Num. 25 and 31 shifts back and forth between 'Moabite'
women and 'Midianite'. There seems to be no clear textual distinction between
them.

dictably, the chapter concludes with an allusion to foreign women, in this case those who made Solomon sin, asking rhetorically whether its audience would 'act treacherously (*lim'ol*) against our God by marrying foreign women' (Neh. 13.26-27). While Moses in Numbers 31 collapses the Balaam story with that of the Moabite/ Midianite women who led Israel astray, Nehemiah 13 adds Solomon to the hermeneutical mix as well. It is a propitious combination: in all these contexts, what may seem the most obvious concern to resist foreign gods is complicated by metonymic and metaphoric extensions of the rhetoric of gender and sexuality. Most obvious is the equation of 'wrong religion' with 'wrong sex', and of both with 'wrong nationality/ ethnicity'. For Numbers and Nehemiah, moreover, the concern for cultic defilement is also clear, a concern perhaps adumbrated in Kings's story of the temple-builder's self-defilement.

The *herem* narrative in Numbers 31 is also notable for the role of Aaron's grandson, Phineas, who slew the intermarrying Strange Woman, the Midianite Cozbi, who was brought near the tent of meeting in ch. 25. When Moses sends the Israelites out against the Midianites, it is again Phineas who accompanies them in battle, carrying the sacred vessels (31.6). Sacred vessels are also part of Nehemiah's concern in his forays against foreigners in ch. 13. The 'vessels of Tobiah's house' must be expelled, along with their owner, from the chambers of the temple. The rooms must then be cleansed so that 'the vessels of the house of God' can be brought back in (13.8-9). It is difficult, given the concern for distinguishing virgin women from non-virgins in Numbers 31, not to read a certain sexual symbolism into all this talk of vessels. Again we see the rhetorical conflation of right sexuality and right nationality/ethnicity.[7]

Nehemiah 13 shares, then, several elements with the Phineas tradition of Numbers: reference to Balaam, loosely linked to strange women, as justification for excluding particular foreigners; concern for the sanctuary vessels; and a view of the Strange Woman as defiler of the temple. Are Phineas and Nehemiah doubles for each other? What are the implications of understanding the generation and party of 'Phineas' as the generation and party of 'Nehemiah'? If Nehemiah 'is' Phineas,

---

7. Worth noting, however, is the fact that biblical body rhetoric can use the image of 'holy (or despised) vessels' to refer to male bodies (1 Sam. 21.6 [Eng.: 5]; Jer. 22.28). I leave it to my reader to sort through the possible permutations this opens up.

where does this equation fit into the social, religious and political developments of the postexilic period, and how does it relate to the production of the corpus of the Strange Woman, of which it is also a member?

We have observed that the combination of texts involving Phineas offers something of a compromise between inclusivist and exclusivist views on 'foreigners'. Through the multivalent image of the Strange Woman in Numbers 25 and 31, the competing interests of exclusivists (presumably Levites) and more inclusive (presumably Aaronite) priests with respect to the boundaries of Israelite identity intersect and are symbolically reconciled. The Strange Woman, whose strangeness could be filled with whatever meaning her clientele might prefer—strange nationality for some, strange sexuality for others—is offered as an Other for Everyman. Both Numbers and Nehemiah also, however, show a pragmatic turn of mind, perhaps a recognition that symbolic solutions usually require a more material quid pro quo as well. Thus, Numbers offers land to the landless Levites (35.1-8) while Nehemiah protects, in addition, their right to portions of temple offerings (13.10).

This may not have been the end of priestly power struggles, however. For if Phineas, purportedly Aaron's grandson, is a guise for Nehemiah, then it is notable that Nehemiah seems never to have heard of Aaron. (Indeed, there is no clear evidence for a priestly role of Aaron before Chronicles and the priestly source of the Pentateuch.) While the text of Ezra–Nehemiah speaks regularly of *priests* and Levites, only rarely, in what seem to be later additions, does it adopt the distinction between *Aaronites* and Levites (Neh. 10.39 [Eng.: 38]; 12.47). Noteworthy is the fact that Ezra 7.5 provides Ezra with Aaronite ancestry, but this is the only time the name is mentioned in that book, and seems also to be a later addition. The animosity between Levites and Aaronites that drives Exodus 32 and Numbers 16 is of course also missing in Nehemiah (unless the failure to provide the Levites their portions is the work of hostile priests). Does the difference between Numbers and Ezra–Nehemiah on this score suggest a priestly dispute already settled or one yet to come? Or some of both? The Aaronites remain to be accounted for and, with them, Ezra.

Ezra and Aaron: Cult, Canons and the Strange Woman
Still eschewing biography, let me call attention to the text's construction of Ezra: as the bringer of the law and, not unrelatedly, as expeller of foreign wives; as the leader of the Levites in the teaching and inter-

preting of the law; and as an Aaronite priest.

Assuming that the ascription to Ezra of an Aaronite genealogy is a late addition, this means there was an earlier, Aaron-free version of Ezra–Nehemiah. This sort of editorializing must reflect a need for harmonization, even legitimation, of one party by the other. But which way does it work in this case: does Ezra legitimate the Aaronites or vice versa? The lack of textual evidence for an Aaronite priesthood before this time suggests the former, as does Numbers's tortured effort to distinguish the family of Aaron from the rest of the Levites and legitimize their hierarchical relationship.

A recent article by Blenkinsopp (1998) fills in some details. He notes certain key references to Phineas outside Numbers. In the book of Ezra, descendants of Phineas and Ithamar are said to accompany Ezra from Babylonia to Judah (Ezra 8.2), and one Eleazar, son(!) of Phineas, is apparently already a priest in Jerusalem when Ezra arrives (8.33). Blenkinsopp asserts that these names 'may provide the earliest hard evidence for the rise of the Aaronite branch of the priesthood to a position of power in the temple community in Jerusalem' (1998: 39).[8] I would make the further observation that Ezra 8–10 binds the character of Ezra together with the Phineas of Numbers, in terms similar to those that tied Phineas to Nehemiah (see above). Among the treasures brought by Ezra to Jerusalem are holy vessels for the house of Yhwh (8.27-30; cf. Num. 31.6; Neh. 13.8-9). And, having weighed out the vessels, Ezra turns to the first of his two actions of leadership in Jerusalem. In the present form of the narrative, casting out the strange women precedes even the reading of the law (Ezra 9–10; cf. Num. 25; Neh. 13.23-29). The actions of Aaron's 'grandson', then, foreshadow those of his later 'descendant'.

'Phineas, son of Eleazar, son of Aaron' is also, however, depicted as a priest at Bethel in Judg. 20.26-28, which forms part of a unit (Judg. 20–21) with clear signs of exilic and postexilic composition (Blenkinsopp 1998: 30). This characterization points to the political tensions masked by Ezra's apparently easy alignment with 'Phineas' past and present. Bethel was the southernmost cultic center of the old northern

---

8. One does not have to accept Blenkinsopp's assumption that this text reports accurately the names of leaders in 458 BCE to affirm that it provides the 'earliest' witness to the ascendancy of the Aaronites. The Ezra passage could easily be, in my view, the 'earliest' report of a later political development.

kingdom and a site of ongoing Yhwh worship in the Babylonian period, but also the location where Jeroboam I established a 'calf-worshiping' cult reminiscent of Aaron's wilderness sin. If the Aaronites had a history of cultic leadership at Bethel, and if, as Blenkinsopp persuasively argues (30-37), Bethel was the leading cultic center in the area before the rebuilding of the Jerusalem temple, this would account for the Jerusalem exclusivists' resistance to the Aaronite takeover of the Jerusalem temple and the sort of religious slander one finds in Exodus 32. This 'memory' of Aaron's apostasy with the golden calves, redressed only by the Levites' slaughter of their 'brothers', suggests that the Levites did not accept these upstarts without a fight.[9]

The Aaronites needed legitimation. Aaron as Moses' brother had a certain caché, but this had to be exploited and negative associations undermined. The text of Ezra–Nehemiah helps supply this by means of motifs that link Phineas with Ezra and Nehemiah, and also by providing Ezra with an Aaronite genealogy.[10] The particularly tightly drawn connection of Ezra and Aaron also effects a wedding of larger institutional authorities as well: Ezra the lawgiver is accorded status as an Aaronite priest.

The characterization of Ezra as lawgiver of course links him to Moses as well, and thus his text to that of Numbers, which reproduces its wedding of authorities. Numbers accomplishes this, I have argued, by a

---

9. Blenkinsopp's conclusions run in a somewhat different direction than mine. Because he assumes the basic mid-fifth-century historicity of the Ezra account, he locates the political tension between the Zadokites (presumably, following Ezekiel, the priestly caste of the exile) and the Bethel-based Aaronites. It is true that Zadok figures prominently, along with Aaron, in the priestly genealogies in Chronicles (1 Chron. 5.27-41; 6.34-38), and is also part of that provided for Ezra, likely from the same source (Blenkinsopp 1998: 38-40). This fact Blenkinsopp probably rightly takes as a sign of accommodation between the two parties. All this does not, however, account for the violent conflicts between Aaronites and *Levites* depicted in Exod. 32 and Num. 16, or the failure of Ezra–Nehemiah to offer Zadok any particular pride of place, except in the late addition of Ezra's ancestors. I return again to my sense that our present sources telescope different or multifaceted conflicts likely played out at different points in time. The tensions between Samaria and Jerusalem with respect to location of the primary temple certainly outlasted the fifth century.

10. Blenkinsopp suggests that the connecting of Phineas, associated in Ezra with the (Zadokite) Judeo-Babylonian party, to the Bethelite Aaron was itself a secondary move of harmonization. This understanding fits well with my reading of the grandfather–grandson relationship depicted in Numbers (see Chapter 6).

narrative that, after separating Aaron from the specter of female strangeness, joins him and Moses, mouth to mouth and rod to rod; thus, in terms of the structures of religious authority, joining cult—the Aaronites' particular version of cult—to law.

The character of Phineas has yet another dimension. By styling him as a 'third generation' Aaronite, Numbers puts some distance between him and his 'grandfather'. The ideological bonding of priest and lawgiver, accomplished through the narrative union of Moses and Aaron over against the Estranged Woman, comes at a high price: the suppression of one sort of strangeness allows another to surface. Moses' and Aaron's 'first-generation' leadership, understood as 'mouth to mouth' with Yhwh, remains tainted by female strangeness. Culmination of the priestly myth with Phineas seems to express the desire of a later generation to present itself as purer than the boundary-crossing, 'wilderness' generation of Moses and Aaron. The desire for separation competes, however, with the desire (and likely the need) to claim their aura of authority. Too powerful to ignore, the authority of the fathers must be both co-opted and at the same time subtly effaced in favor of the written word associated with the new generation of leaders. Thus, the 'Moses' who came down the mountain with the book of the law in Exodus comes down the mountain in Numbers with a new priest, Aaron's son. Aaron's seed is thereby identified with law. And Phineas, the seed of this seed, proves himself holy seed indeed. Surpassing even Nehemiah, he achieves, like Ezra, a conclusive victory over the Strange Woman.

I have argued that this annihilation of the Other was necessary in order to establish these priests' right to occupy the center. This was in part a mythic necessity, both arising from and suppressing the impossibility of drawing a line between the center and the rest. It was also a necessity grounded in certain historical particularities: the need to include in the polity some of the *gerim* for purposes of political support, in tension with the impulse to define a 'pure' Israel, free from 'foreign' contamination. If Blenkinsopp is correct in his reconstruction of the historical connection of the Aaronites to Bethel we can see the full force of this dilemma: 'Aaron' wishes to include the *ger* because he *is* the *ger*. At the same time, this memory of the margin must be erased or, as is so often the case, reduced to no more than a trace.

The Aaronites—perhaps in particular the generation of 'Phineas'— whatever their origins or previous stance on the politics of intermarriage, bring to this emerging ideological matrix a particular understanding of priestly purity that is well-complemented by the focus on holy writing and exclusion of the Strange Woman. The rigorous understanding of identity based on male descent means that, in effect, all women are strange. The fertility that issues from the circumcised penis is understood to issue, like holy Scripture, from God alone. Here is the enduring point to be taken from joining, in the character of Ezra, the one who brings the book and the one who expels the [Strange] Woman: holy seed and holy writ are one and the same.

The book of Proverbs—with its own, Solomonically author(iz)ed construction of holy space as holy Scripture—in one sense reflects and supports this understanding of canon and identity: the fulfillment of Yhwh's dynastic promise to David is found not in Solomon's sons but in Solomon's words. The embodied Solomon in 1 Kings had failed to distinguish the Wise Woman from the Strange, thereby endangering both seed and promise. In Proverbs, however, female Wisdom and Strangeness issue forth from Solomon's lips to build a house of words. Gender constructed is gender controlled: the flesh is made word. Or is it?

The Strange Woman is a *mise en abyme*: with her wise sister and her sometimes unholy God, she is a mirror of language itself. From her lips we hear the trickster's riddles. In her house of mirrors we see the infinite regression of boundaries written on priestly bodies, a regression built into the canonical myth of identity. In this coalescence of the wisdom and priestly traditions around the figure of the Strange Woman, we discover the presence and effect of gendered strangeness in the genesis and structure of the canon itself. Has the word become flesh once more? Perhaps not. But the taste of her honey lingers on all our tongues.

SELECT BIBLIOGRAPHY

Aichele, George, and Gary A. Phillips
    1995   'Introduction: Exegesis, Eisegesis, Intergesis', in Aichele and Phillips (eds.) 1995: 7-18.

Aichele, George, and Gary A. Phillips (eds.)
    1995   *Intertextuality and the Bible* (Semeia, 69/70; Atlanta: Scholars Press).

Albertz, Rainer
    1994   *A History of Israelite Religion in the Old Testament Period.* II. *From the Exile to the Maccabees* (OTL; trans. J. Bowden; Louisville, KY: Westminster/John Knox Press).

Aletti, Jean-Noël
    1976   'Proverbes 8, 22-31. Etudes de structure', *Bib* 57: 25-37.
    1977   'Seduction et parole en Proverbes I–IX', *VT* 27: 129-44.

Alter, Robert L.
    1981   *The Art of Biblical Narrative* (New York: Basic Books).
    1990   'Samson Without Folklore', in Niditch (ed.) 1990: 47-56.

Archer, Léonie
    1986   'The "Evil Woman" in Apocryphal and Pseudepigraphical Writings', in *Proceedings of the Ninth World Congress of Jewish Studies, August 4–12, 1985. Division A: The Period of the Bible* (Jerusalem: World Union of Jewish Studies): 239-46.

Bach, Alice
    1997   *Women, Seduction, and Betrayal in Biblical Narrative* (Cambridge: Cambridge University Press).

Bailey, Lloyd
    1979   *Biblical Perspectives on Death* (Philadelphia: Fortress Press).

Bailey, Randall C.
    1990   *David in Love and War: The Pursuit of Power in 2 Samuel 10–12* (JSOTSup, 75; Sheffield: JSOT Press).
    1991   'Beyond Identification: The Use of Africans in Old Testament Poetry and Narrative', in Cain Hope Felder (ed.) *Stony the Road We Trod* (Minneapolis: Fortress Press): 165-86.

Bal, Mieke
    1985   *Narratology: Introduction to the Theory of Narrative* (trans. C. van Boheemen; Toronto: University of Toronto Press).
    1987   *Lethal Love: Feminist Literary Readings of Biblical Love Stories* (Bloomington: Indiana University Press).
    1988a   *Death and Dissymmetry* (Chicago: University of Chicago Press).
    1988b   'Tricky Thematics', in Exum and Bos 1988: 133-56.

1993   'Metaphors He Lives By', in Camp and Fontaine 1993: 185-208.

Beal, Timothy K., and David M. Gunn (eds.)

1996   *Reading Bibles, Writing Bodies: Identity and the Book* (New York: Routledge).

Bechtel, Lyn M.

1994   'What if Dinah Is Not Raped? (Gen 34)', *JSOT* 62: 19-36.

Berquist, Jon L.

1995   *Judaism in Persia's Shadow* (Minneapolis: Fortress Press).

Bird, Phyllis

1989a   'The Harlot as Heroine: Narrative Art in Three Old Testament Texts', in Miri Amihai, George W. Coats and Anne M. Solomon (eds.) *Narrative Research on the Hebrew Bible* (Semeia, 46; Atlanta: Scholars Press): 119-40.

1989b   '"To Play the Harlot": An Inquiry into an Old Testament Metaphor', in Day 1989: 75-94.

Blenkinsopp, Joseph

1988   *Ezra–Nehemiah: A Commentary* (OTL; Philadelphia: Westminster Press).

1990a   *Ezekiel* (Louisville, KY: John Knox Press).

1990b   'The Sage, the Scribe, and Scribalism in the Chronicler's Work', in Gammie and Perdue 1990: 307-18.

1991a   'The Social Context of the "Outsider Women" in Proverbs 1–9', *Bib* 72: 457-73.

1991b   'Temple and Society in Achaemenid Judah', in Davies (ed.) 1991: 22-53.

1995   *Sage, Priest, Prophet: Intellectual and Religious Leadership in Ancient Israel* (Louisville, KY: Westminster/John Knox Press).

1998   'The Judaean Priesthood during the Neo-Babylonian and Achaemenid Periods: A Hypothetical Reconstruction', *CBQ* 60: 25-43.

Boling, Robert G.

1975   *Judges* (AB, 6A; Garden City, NY: Doubleday).

Boling, Robert G., and G. Ernest Wright

1982   *Joshua* (AB, 6; Garden City, NY: Doubleday).

Boström, Gustav

1935   *Proverbiastudien: Die Weisheit und das fremde Weib in Sprüche 1–9* (Lunds Universitets Arsskrift, 30.3; Lund: C.W.K. Gleerup).

Brenner, Athalya

1993   'Some Observations of the Figurations of Woman in Wisdom Literature', in Heather A. McKay and David J.A. Clines (eds.), *Of Prophets' Visions and the Wisdom of Sages: Essays in Honor of R. Norman Whybray on his Seventieth Birthday* (JSOTSup, 162; Sheffield: Sheffield Academic Press): 192-208 (repr. in Brenner [ed.] 1995: 50-66).

1997   *The Intercourse of Knowledge: On Gendering Desire and 'Sexuality' in the Hebrew Bible* (Biblical Interpretation, 26; Leiden: E.J. Brill).

Brenner, Athalya (ed.)

1994   *A Feminist Companion to Samuel and Kings* (Sheffield: Sheffield Academic Press).

1995   *A Feminist Companion to Wisdom Literature* (Sheffield: Sheffield Academic Press).

Brenner, Athalya, and Fokkelien van Dijk-Hemmes
    1993   *On Gendering Texts: Female and Male Voices in the Hebrew Bible* (Biblical Interpretation, 1; Leiden: E.J. Brill).

Brettler, Marc
    1991   'The Structure of 1 Kings 1–11', *JSOT* 49: 87-97.

Brueggemann, Walter
    1982   *Genesis* (Atlanta: John Knox Press).
    1990   'The Social Significance of Solomon as a Patron of Wisdom', in Gammie and Perdue 1990: 117-32.

Burns, John Barclay
    1991   'Solomon's Egyptian Horses and Exotic Wives', *Forum* 7: 29-44.

Bynum, David E.
    1990   'Samson as a Biblical φηρ ὀρεσκῷος', in Niditch (ed.) 1990: 57-74.

Camp, Claudia V.
    1985   *Wisdom and the Feminine in the Book of Proverbs* (Sheffield: Almond Press).
    1987   'Female Voice, Written Word: Women and Authority in Hebrew Scripture', in Paula M. Cooey, Sharon A. Farmer and Mary Ellen Ross (eds.), *Embodied Love: Sensuality and Relationship as Feminist Values* (San Francisco: Harper & Row): 97-114.
    1988   'Wise and Strange: An Interpretation of the Female Imagery in Proverbs in Light of Trickster Mythology', in Exum and Bos 1988: 14-36.
    1990   'The Female Sage in Ancient Israel and in the Biblical Wisdom Literature', in Gammie and Perdue 1990: 185-204.
    1991   'What's So Strange About the Strange Woman?', in Jobling, Day and Sheppard 1991: 17-32.
    1992   '1 and 2 Kings', in Carol A. Newsom and Sharon H. Ringe (eds.), *The Women's Bible Commentary* (Louisville, KY: Westminster/John Knox Press): 102-16 [repr. in expanded edition, 1998].
    1993   'Metaphor in Feminist Biblical Interpretation: Theoretical Perspectives', in Camp and Fontaine 1993: 3-32.
    1996   'Woman Wisdom and the Strange Woman: Where is Power to be Found?', in Beal and Gunn 1996: 85-115.

Camp, Claudia V., and Carole R. Fontaine
    1990   'The Words of the Wise and their Riddles', in Niditch (ed.) 1990: 127-52.

Camp, Claudia V., and Carole R. Fontaine (eds.)
    1993   *Women, War, and Metaphor: Language and Society in the Study of the Hebrew Bible* (Semeia, 61; Atlanta: Scholars Press).

Carroll, Robert P.
    1991   'Textual Strategies and Ideology in the Second Temple Period', in Davies (ed.) 1991: 108-24.
    1994   'So What Do We *Know* about the Temple? The Temple in the Prophets', in Eskenazi and Richards 1994: 34-51.

Carter, Charles E.
    1994   'The Province of Yehud in the Post-Exilic Period: Soundings in Site Distribution and Demography', in Eskenazi and Richards 1994: 106-45.

Ceresko, Anthony R.
    1990   'The Sage in the Psalms', in Gammie and Perdue 1990: 217-30.

Clines, David J.A.
1981   'Nehemiah 10 as an Example of Early Jewish Biblical Exegesis', *JSOT* 21: 110-17.
1988   'Introduction to the Biblical Story: Genesis–Esther', in J.L. Mays (ed.), *Harper's Bible Commentary* (San Francisco: Harper & Row): 74-84.
1989   'The Force of the Text: A Response to Tamara Eskenazi's "Ezra–Nehemiah: From Text to Actuality"', in Exum 1989: 199-215.
1994   'Haggai's Temple Constructed, Deconstructed, and Reconstructed', in Eskenazi and Richards 1994: 60-78.
1995   *Interested Parties: The Ideology of Writers and Readers of the Hebrew Bible* (JSOTSup, 205; GCT, 1; Sheffield: Sheffield Academic Press).

Clines, David J.A. (ed.)
1993   *The Dictionary of Classical Hebrew* (Sheffield: Sheffield Academic Press).

Coote, Robert B., and Keith W. Whitelam
1987   *The Emergence of Early Israel in Historical Perspective* (Social World of Biblical Antiquity, 5; Sheffield: Almond Press).

Crenshaw, James L.
1976   'Method in Determining Wisdom Influence', in James L. Crenshaw (ed.), *Studies in Ancient Israelite Wisdom* (New York: Ktav): 481-94.
1978   *Samson* (Atlanta: John Knox Press).

Culley, Robert C.
1984   'Stories of the Conquest: Joshua 2, 6, 7 and 8', *HAR* 8: 25-44.
1990   'Five Tales of Punishment in the Book of Numbers', in Niditch (ed.) 1990: 25-34.

Davies, Philip R.
1991   'Sociology and the Second Temple', in Davies (ed.) 1991: 11-21.
1994   'The Society of Biblical Israel', in Eskenazi and Richards 1994: 22-33.
1998   *Scribes and Schools: The Canonization of the Hebrew Scriptures* (Louisville, KY: Westminster/John Knox Press).

Davies, Philip R. (ed.)
1991   *Second Temple Studies. I. Persian Period* (JSOTSup, 117; Sheffield: JSOT Press).

Day, John, Robert P. Gordon and H.G.M. Williams (eds.)
1995   *Wisdom in Ancient Israel* (Cambridge: Cambridge University Press).

Day, Peggy L. (ed.)
1989   *Gender and Difference in Ancient Israel* (Minneapolis: Fortress Press).

Douglas, Mary
1993   *In the Wilderness: The Doctrine of Defilement in the Book of Numbers* (JSOTSup, 158; Sheffield: Sheffield Academic Press).

Eilberg-Schwartz, Howard
1990   *The Savage in Judaism: An Anthropology of Israelite Religion and Ancient Judaism* (Indianapolis: Indiana University Press).
1994   *God's Phallus and Other Problems for Men and Monotheism* (Boston: Beacon Press).

Eskenazi, Tamara C.
1988   *In an Age of Prose: A Literary Approach to Ezra–Nehemiah* (Atlanta: Scholars Press).
1989   'Ezra–Nehemiah: From Text to Actuality', in Exum 1989: 165-99.

Eskenazi, Tamara C., and Eleanore P. Judd
    1994   'Marriage to a Stranger in Ezra 9–10', in Eskenazi and Richards 1994:
            266-85.
Eskenazi, Tamara C., and Kent H. Richards (eds.)
    1994   *Second Temple Studie*s. II. *Temple and Community in the Persian Period*
            (JSOTSup, 175; Sheffield: JSOT Press).
Eslinger, Lyle
    1989   *Into the Hands of the Living God* (JSOTSup, 84; Bible & Literature, 24;
            Sheffield: Almond Press).
Exum, J. Cheryl
    1993   *Fragmented Women: Feminist (Sub)versions of Biblical Narratives* (Val-
            ley Forge, PA: Trinity Press International).
Exum, J. Cheryl (ed.)
    1989   *Signs and Wonders: Biblical Texts in Literary Focus* (SBLSS; Atlanta:
            Scholars Press).
Exum, J. Cheryl, and Johanna W.H. Bos (eds.)
    1988   *Reasoning with the Foxes: Female Wit in a World of Male Power* (Semeia,
            42; Atlanta: Scholars Press).
Fewell, Danna Nolan
    1992   'Introduction: Writing, Reading, and Relating', in Fewell (ed.) 1992: 11-20.
    1995   'Deconstructive Criticism: Achsah and the (E)razed City of Writing', in
            Gale A. Yee (ed.), *Judges and Method: New Approaches in Biblical Stud-*
            ies (Minneapolis: Fortress Press): 119-45.
    1996   'Imagination, Method and Murder: Un/Framing the Face of Post-Exilic
            Israel', in Beal and Gunn 1996: 132-52.
Fewell, Danna Nolan (ed.)
    1992   *Reading Between Texts: Intertextuality and the Hebrew Bible* (Louisville,
            KY: Westminster/John Knox Press).
Fewell, Danna Nolan, and David M. Gunn
    1991   'Tipping the Balance: Sternberg's Reader and the Rape of Dinah', *JBL*
            110: 193-211.
    1993   *Gender, Power and Promise: The Subject of the Bible's First Story*
            (Nashville: Abingdon Press).
Fontaine, Carole R.
    1982   *Traditional Sayings in the Old Testament* (Bible & Literature, 5; Shef-
            field: Almond Press).
    1986   'The Bearing of Wisdom on the Shape of 2 Samuel 11–12 and 1 Kings 3',
            JSOT 34: 61-77 (repr. in Brenner 1994: 143-60).
    1994   'A Response to "The Bearing of Wisdom"', in Brenner 1994: 161-69.
    1997   'More Queenly Proverb Performance: The Queen of Sheba in Targum
            Esther Sheni', in Michael L. Barré, SS (ed.), *Wisdom, You are my Sister:*
            Studies in Honor of Roland E. Murphy, O. Carm., on the Occasion of his
            Eightieth Birthday (CBQMS, 29; Washington, DC: Catholic Biblical
            Association of America): 216-33.
Fox, Michael V.
    1995   'The Uses of Indeterminacy', in Robinson and Culley 1995: 173-92.

Freedman, David N.
    1990   'Dinah and Shechem, Tamar and Amnon', *Austin Seminary Bulletin* 105: 51-63.

Frisch, Amos
    1991a   'Structure and Significance: The Narrative of Solomon's Reign (1 Kings 1–12.24)', *JSOT* 51: 3-14.
    1991b   'The Narrative of Solomon's Reign: A Rejoinder', *JSOT* 51: 22-24.

Frymer-Kensky, Tikva
    1989   'Law and Philosophy: The Case of Sex in the Bible', in Patrick 1989: 89-102.
    1990   'The Sage in the Pentateuch', in Gammie and Perdue 1990: 275-88.

Fuchs, Esther
    1988   '"For I Have the Way of Women": Deception, Gender, and Ideology in Biblical Narrative', in Exum and Bos 1988: 68-83.

Galambush, Julie
    1992   *Jerusalem in the Book of Ezekiel: The City as Yahweh's Wife* (SBLDS, 130; Atlanta: Scholars Press).

Galil, G.
    1985   'The Sons of Judah and the Sons of Aaron in Biblical Historiography', *VT* 35: 488-495.

Gammie, John G., and Leo G. Perdue (eds.)
    1990   *The Sage in Israel and the Ancient Near East* (Winona Lake, IN: Eisenbrauns).

Garbini, Giovanni
    1988   *History and Ideology in Ancient Israel* (trans. J. Bowden; New York: Crossroad).
    1994   'Hebrew Literature in the Persian Period', in Eskenazi and Richards 1994: 180-88.

Geertz, Clifford
    1973   *The Interpretation of Cultures* (New York: Basic Books).
    1975   'Common Sense as a Cultural System', *Antioch Review* 35: 5-26.
    1976   'Art as a Cultural System', *Modern Language Notes* 91: 1473-99.

Geller, Stephen A.
    1990   'The Sack of Shechem: The Use of Typology in Biblical Covenant Religion', *Prooftexts* 10: 1-15.

Gerbrandt, Gerald E.
    1986   *Kingship According to the Deuteronomistic History* (Atlanta: Scholars Press).

Gilbert, Maurice
    1979   'Le discours de la sagesse en Proverbes, 8', in Maurice Gilbert (ed.), *La sagesse de l'ancien testament* (BETL, 51; Leuven: Leuven University Press): 202-18.

Gilmore, David (ed.)
    1987   *Honor and Shame and the Unity of the Mediterranean* (Washington, DC: American Anthropological Association).

Glazier-McDonald, Beth
    1987   'Intermarriage, Divorce, and the *bat-el nekar*: Insights into Mal 2:10-16', *JBL* 106: 603-11.

Gordon, Robert P.
1995   'A House Divided: Wisdom in Old Testament Narrative Traditions', in
        Day, Gordon and Williams 1995: 94-105.
Grabbe, Lester L.
1991   'Reconstructing History from the Book of Ezra', in Davies (ed.) 1991:
        98-107.
1992   *Judaism From Cyrus to Hadrian* (2 vols.; Minneapolis: Fortress Press).
1994   'What was Ezra's Mission?', in Eskenazi and Richards 1994: 286-99.
1996   *An Introduction to First Century Judaism* (Edinburgh: T. & T. Clark).
1998a   *Ezra–Nehemiah* (London: Routledge).
1998b   'Introduction', in Grabbe (ed.) 1998: 11-19.
1998c   'Reflections on the Discussion', in Grabbe (ed.) 1998: 146-56.
Grabbe, Lester L. (ed.)
1998   *Leading Captivity Captive: 'The Exile' as History and Ideology* (JSOTSup,
        178; European Seminar in Historical Methodology, 2; Sheffield: Sheffield
        Academic Press).
Graetz, Naomi
1993   'Dinah the Daughter', in Athalya Brenner (ed.), *A Feminist Companion to
        Genesis* (Sheffield: Sheffield Academic Press): 306-17.
Gravatt, Sandie
1994   'That All Women May Be Warned: Reading the Sexual and Ethnic Vio-
        lence in Ezekiel 16 and 23' (dissertation, Duke University).
Gray, John
1967   *Joshua, Judges, Ruth* (NCB; London: Nelson & Sons).
Greenstein, Edward L.
1981   'The Riddle of Samson', *Prooftexts* 1: 237-60.
1989   'Deconstruction and Biblical Narrative', *Prooftexts* 9: 43-72.
Gunn, David M.
1978   *The Story of King David* (JSOTSup, 6; Sheffield: JSOT Press).
1992   'Samson of Sorrows: An Isaianic Gloss on Judges 13–16', in Fewell (ed.)
        1992: 225-56.
Gunn, David M., and Fewell, Danna Nolan
1993   *Narrative in the Hebrew Bible* (New York: Oxford University Press).
Halligan, John M.
1991   'Nehemiah 5: By Way of Response to Hoglund and Smith', in Davies
        (ed.) 1991: 146-53.
Hawk, L. Daniel
1991   *Every Promise Fulfilled: Contesting Plots in Joshua* (Lousiville, KY:
        Westminster/John Knox Press).
1992   'Strange Houseguests: Rahab, Lot, and the Dynamics of Deliverance', in
        Fewell (ed.) 1992: 98-98.
Hoglund, Kenneth
1991   'The Achaemenid Context', in Davies (ed.) 1991: 54-72.
Horsley, Richard A.
1991   'Empire, Temple and Community—But no Bourgeoisie! A Response to
        Blenkinsopp and Petersen', in Davies (ed.) 1991: 163-74.
Houten, Christiana van
1991   *The Alien in Israelite Law* (JSOTSup, 107; Sheffield: JSOT Press).

Humbert, Paul
    1937   'La femme étrangère du livre des Proverbes', *Revue des Etudes Sémitiques* 6: 40-64.
    1939   'Les adjectifs "zar" et "nokri" et la femme étrangère', in *Mélanges Syriens offerts à M. René Dussaud I* (Bibliothèque Archéologique et Historique, 30; Paris: Librairie Paul Guethner): 259-66.

Hynes, William J., and William H. Doty (eds.)
    1993   *Mythical Trickster Figures: Contours, Contexts, and Criticisms* (Tuscaloosa, AL: University of Alabama Press).

Japhet, Sara
    1991   'The Temple in the Restoration Period: Reality and Ideology', *USQR* 44: 195-251.
    1994   'Composition and Chronology in the Book of Ezra–Nehemiah', in Eskenazi and Richards 1994: 189-216.

Jenson, Philip P.
    1992   *Graded Holiness: A Key to the Priestly Conceptions of the World* (JSOTSup, 106; Sheffield: JSOT Press).

Jobling, David
    1978   *The Sense of Biblical Narrative: Three Structural Analyses in the Old Testament* (JSOTSup, 7; Sheffield: JSOT Press).
    1986   *The Sense of Biblical Narrative II* (JSOTSup, 39; Sheffield: JSOT Press).
    1991a   'Feminism and the "Mode of Production" in Ancient Israel: Search for a Method', in Jobling, Day and Sheppard 1991: 239-52.
    1991b   '"Forced Labor": Solomon's Golden Age and the Question of Literary Representation', in Jobling and Moore 1991: 57-76 (repr. as 'The Value of Solomon's Age for the Biblical Reader', in Lowell K. Handy [ed.], *The Age of Solomon* [Leiden: E.J. Brill, 1997]: 470-92).
    1991c   'Texts and the World—An Unbridgeable Gap? A Response to Carroll, Hoglund and Smith', in Davies (ed.) 1991: 175-82.

Jobling, David, and Stephen D. Moore (eds.)
    1991   *Poststructuralism as Exegesis* (Semeia, 54; Atlanta: Scholars Press).

Jobling, David, Peggy L. Day and Gerald T. Sheppard (eds.)
    1991   *The Bible and the Politics of Exegesis* (Cleveland: Pilgrim Press).

Johanson, Sheila
    1976   '"Herstory" as History: A New Field or Another Fad?', in Berenice Carroll (ed.), *Liberating Women's History* (Urbana, IL: University of Illinois Press): 400-30.

Jung, Carl G.
    1956   'On the Psychology of the Trickster Figure' (trans. R.F.C. Hull), in Radin 1956: 195-211.

Keefe, Alice A.
    1993   'Rapes of Women/Wars of Men', in Camp and Fontaine 1993: 79-98.

Kenik, Helen A.
    1983   *Design for Kingship: The Deuteronomistic Narrative Technique in 1 Kings 3:4-15* (Chico, CA: Scholars Press).

Kerenyi, Karl
    1956   'The Trickster in Relation to Greek Mythology' (trans. R.F.C. Hull), in Radin 1956: 173-91.

Kunin, Seth Daniel
    1995   *The Logic of Incest: A Structuralist Analysis of Hebrew Mythology* (JSOTSup, 185; Sheffield: Sheffield Academic Press).

Laato, Antti
    1994   'The Levitical Genealogies in 1 Chronicles 5–6 and the Formation of Levitical Ideology in Post-Exilic Judah', *JSOT* 62: 77-99.

Lakoff, George
    1987   *Women, Fire, and Dangerous Things: What Categories Reveal About the Mind* (Chicago: University of Chicago Press).

Lakoff, George, and Mark Johnson
    1980   *Metaphors We Live By* (Chicago: University of Chicago Press).

Landy, Francis
    1993   'On Metaphor, Play, and Nonsense', in Camp and Fontaine 1993: 219-37.

Lang, Bernhard
    1975   *Frau Weisheit* (Dusseldorf: Patmosverlag).
    1986   *Wisdom and the Book of Proverbs: An Israelite Goddess Redefined* (New York: Pilgrim Press).

Lasine, Stuart
    1994   'Levite Violence, Fratricide, and Sacrifice in the Bible and Later Revolutionary Rhetoric', in Mark I. Wallace and Theophus H. Smith (eds.), *Curing Violence* (Sonoma, CA: Polebridge Press): 204-29.
    1995   'The King of Desire: Indeterminacy, Audience, and the Solomon Narrative', in Robinson and Culley 1995: 85-118.

Lemaire, André
    1995   'Wisdom in Solomonic Historiography', in Day, Gordon and Williams 1995: 106-18.

Levine, Baruch A.
    1989   *Leviticus* (JPS Torah Commentary; Philadelphia: Jewish Publication Society).
    1993   *Numbers 1–20* (AB, 4; New York: Doubleday).

Lévi-Strauss, Claude
    1963   *Structural Anthropology* (trans. C. Jacobson and B.G. Schoepf; New York: Basic Books).

Linafelt, Tod
    1992   'Taking Women in Samuel: Readers/Responses/Responsibility', in Fewell (ed.) 1992: 99-114.

Linafelt, Tod and Timothy Beal
    1995   'Sifting for Cinders: Leviticus 10:1-15', in Aichele and Phillips (eds.) 1995: 19-32.

Linville, James Richard
    1998   *Israel in the Book of Kings: The Past as a Project of Social Identity* (JSOTSup, 272; Sheffield: Sheffield Academic Press).

Long, Burke O.
    1984   *1 Kings* (FOTL, 9; Grand Rapids: Eerdmans).

Maier, Christl
    1995   *Die 'fremde Frau' in Proverbien 1–9: Eine exegetische und sozialgeschichtliche Studie* (OBO, 144; Göttingen: Vandenhoeck & Ruprecht).

Margalith, Othniel
    1985   'Samson's Foxes', *VT* 35: 224-29.
    1986a   'Samson's Riddle and Samson's Magic Locks', *VT* 36: 225-34.
    1986b   'More Samson Legends', *VT* 36: 397-405.

Matthews, Victor
    1989   'Freedom and Entrapment in the Samson Narrative: A Literary Analysis', *Perpectives in Religious Studies* 16: 245-57.

McCarter, P. Kyle
    1985   'Sanballat', in P.J. Achtemeier (ed.), *Harper's Bible Dictionary* (San Francisco: Harper & Row): 904.
    1990   'The Sage in the Deuteronomistic History', in Gammie and Perdue 1990: 289-94.

McKane, William
    1970   *Proverbs: A New Approach* (OTL; Philadelphia: Westminster Press).

Mendenhall, George
    1974   'The Shady Side of Wisdom', in Howard N. Bream, Ralph D. Heim and Carey Moore (eds.), *A Light Unto My Path: Old Testament Essays in Honor of Jacob M. Myers* (Philadelphia: Temple University): 319-34.

Meyers, Carol
    1983   'Gender Roles and Genesis 3:16 Revisited', in Meyers and O'Connor 1983: 337-54.
    1988   *Discovering Eve: Ancient Israelite Women in Context* (New York: Oxford University Press).

Meyers, Carol, and M. O'Connor (eds.)
    1983   *The Word of the Lord Shall Go Forth* (Winona Lake, IN: Eisenbrauns).

Milgrom, Jacob
    1986   The Structures of Numbers: Chapters 11–12 and 13–14 and their Redaction. Preliminary Gropings', in Jacob Neusner, Baruch A. Levine and Ernest S. Frerichs (eds.), *Judaic Perspectives on Ancient Israel* (Philadelphia: Fortress Press): 49-61.
    1988   'The Rebellion of Korah, Numbers 16–18: A Study in Tradition and History', in David J. Lull (ed.), *Society of Biblical Literature: 1988 Seminar Papers* (Atlanta: Scholars Press).
    1989   'Rationale for Cultic Law: The Case of Impurity', in Patrick 1989: 103-109.
    1990   *Numbers* (JPS Torah Commentary; Philadelphia: Jewish Publication Society).
    1991   *Leviticus 1–16: A New Translation with Introduction and Commentary* (AB, 3; New York: Doubleday).

Moore, George Foot
    1901   *A Critical and Exegetical Commentary on Judges* (ICC; New York: Charles Scribner's Sons).

Myers, Jacob M.
    1965   *Ezra–Nehemiah* (AB, 14; Garden City, NY: Doubleday).

Nel, Philip
    1985   'The Riddle of Samson', *Bib* 66: 534-45.

Nelson, Richard D.
    1987   *First and Second Kings* (Louisville, KY: John Knox Press).

Neusner, Jacob
 1985 *Genesis Rabbah: The Judaic Commentary to the Book of Genesis, A New American Translation*, III (Atlanta: Scholars Press).

Newsom, Carol A.
 1989 'Women and the Discourse of Patriarchal Wisdom: A Study of Proverbs 1–9', in Day (ed.) 1989: 142-60.

Niditch, Susan
 1979 'The Wronged Woman Righted: An Analysis of Genesis 38', *HTR* 72: 143-49.
 1987 *Underdogs and Tricksters: A Prelude to Biblical Folklore* (San Francisco: Harper & Row).
 1990 'Samson as Culture Hero, Trickster, and Bandit: The Empowerment of the Weak', *CBQ* 52: 608-624.
 1993a *War in the Hebrew Bible: A Study in the Ethics of Violence* (New York: Oxford University Press).
 1993b 'War, Women, and Defilement in Numbers 31', in Camp and Fontaine 1993: 39-58.

Niditch, Susan (ed.)
 1990 *Text and Tradition: The Hebrew Bible and Folklore* (SBLSS, 20; Atlanta: Scholars Press).

Noble, Paul
 1996 'A "Balanced" Reading of the Rape of Dinah: Some Exegetical and Methodological Observations', *BibInt* 4: 173-204.

Noth, Martin
 1968 *Numbers, A Commentary* (OTL; Philadelphia: Westminster Press).

O'Brien, Julia M.
 1996 'Judah as Wife and Husband: Deconstructing Gender in Malachi', *JBL* 115: 241-250.

Oden, Robert A.
 1987 *The Bible Without Theology* (San Francisco: Harper & Row).

Ogden, Graham S.
 1988 'The Use of Figurative Language in Malachi 2:10-16', in Stine 1988: 265-73.

Olson, Dennis T.
 1996 *Numbers* (Louisville, KY: John Knox Press).

Pardes, Ilana
 1992 *Countertraditions in the Bible: A Feminist Approach* (Cambridge, MA: Harvard University Press).

Parker, Kim Ian
 1991 'The Limits to Solomon's Reign: A Response to Amos Frisch', *JSOT* 51: 15-21.
 1992 *Wisdom and Law in the Reign of Solomon* (Lewiston, NY: Edwin Mellen Press).

Patrick, Dale (ed.)
 1989 *Thinking Biblical Law* (Semeia, 45; Atlanta: Scholars Press).

Pelton, Robert D.
 1980 *The Trickster in West Africa: A Study of Mythic Irony and Sacred Delight* (Berkeley: University of California Press).

Pepicello, W.J., and Thomas A. Green
 1984   *The Language of Riddles* (Columbus: Ohio State University Press).
Perdue, Leo G.
 1977   *Wisdom and Cult* (SBLDS, 30; Missoula, MT: Scholars Press).
Petersen, David L.
 1991   'The Temple in Persian Period Prophetic Texts', in Davies (ed.) 1991: 125-45.
Pitt-Rivers, Julian
 1977   *The Fate of Shechem or the Politics of Sex* (New York: Cambridge University Press).
Polzin, Robert
 1980   *Moses and the Deuteronomist: Deuteronomy, Joshua, and Judges* (Indianapolis: Indiana University Press).
Propp, William H.
 1988   'The Rod of Aaron and the Sin of Moses', *JBL* 107: 19-26.
 1993   'That Bloody Bridegroom (Exodus 4: 24-26)', *VT* 43: 495-518.
Rad, Gerhard von
 1962   *Old Testament Theology*, I (trans. D.M.G. Stalker; New York: Harper & Row [1957]).
 1966a   *Deuteronomy: A Commentary* (trans. D. Barton; Philadelphia: Westminster Press).
 1966b   *The Problem of the Hexateuch and Other Essays* (trans. E.W.T. Dicken; Edinburgh: Oliver & Boyd [1953]).
Radin, Paul (ed.)
 1956   *The Trickster: A Study in American Indian Mythology* (New York: Philosophical Library).
Ramras-Rauch, Gila
 1990   'Fathers and Daughters: Two Biblical Narratives', in Vincent C. Tollers and John Maier (eds.), *Mappings of the Biblical Terrain: The Bible as Text* (Lewisburg, PA: Bucknell University Press): 158-69.
Rashkow, Ilona N.
 1996   'Oedipus Wrecks: Moses and God's Rod', in Beal and Gunn 1996: 72-84.
Reinhartz, Adele
 1993   'Samson's Mother: An Unnamed Protagonist', in Athalya Brenner (ed.), *A Feminist Companion to Judges* (Sheffield: Sheffield Academic Press): 157-70.
 1994   'Anonymous Women and the Collapse of the Monarchy: A Study in Narrative Technique', in Brenner 1994: 43-67.
Ricoeur, Paul
 1967   *The Symbolism of Evil* (trans. E. Buchanan; Boston: Beacon Press).
Rivkin, Ellis
 1988   'The Story of Korah's Rebellion: Key to the Formation of the Pentateuch', in David J. Lull (ed.), *Society of Biblical Literature: 1988 Seminar Papers* (Atlanta: Scholars Press): 574-81.
Robinson, Robert B.
 1995   'Introduction', in Robinson and Culley 1995: 7-16.
Robinson, Robert B., and Robert C. Culley (eds.)
 1995   *Textual Determinacy, Part II* (Semeia, 71; Atlanta: Scholars Press).

Rofé, Alexander
    1988   'The Vineyard of Naboth: The Origin and Message of the Story', *VT* 38: 89-104.

Römer, Thomas
    1994   'De l'archaïque au subversif: le cas d'Exode 4:24-26', *ETR* 69: 1-7.

Sakenfeld, Katharine D.
    1985   'Theological and Redactional Problems in Numbers 20:2-13', in James T. Butler, Edgar W. Conrad and Ben C. Ollenburger (eds.), *Understanding the Word: Essays in Honor of Bernhard W. Anderson* (JSOTSup, 37; Sheffield: JSOT Press): 133-54.

Savran, George
    1987   '1 and 2 Kings', in Robert L. Alter and Frank Kermode (eds.), *The Literary Guide to the Bible* (Cambridge: Belknap): 146-64.

Scott, R.B.Y.
    1955   'Solomon and the Beginnings of Wisdom in Israel', in M. Noth and D. Winton Thomas (eds.), *Wisdom in Israel and in the Ancient Near East* (VTSup, 3; Leiden: E.J. Brill): 262-79.
    1972   'Wise and Foolish, Righteous and Wicked', in G.W. Anderson *et al.* (eds.), *Studies in the Religion of Ancient Israel* (VTSup, 23; Leiden: E.J. Brill): 146-65.

Segovia, Fernando F.
    1995   'Cultural Studies and Contemporary Biblical Criticism: Ideological Criticism as Mode of Discourse', in Fernando F. Segovia and Mary Ann Tolbert (eds.), *Reading from This Place*, I (Minneapolis: Fortress Press): 1-34.

Sheppard, Gerald
    1980   *Wisdom as a Hermeneutical Construct* (BZAW, 151; Berlin: W. de Gruyter).

Skehan, Patrick W.
    1971   *Studies in Israelite Poetry and Wisdom* (CBQMS, 1; Worcester: Heffernan Press).

Smith, Daniel L.
    1989   *The Religion of the Landless: The Social Context of the Babylonian Exile* (Bloomington: Meyer Stone Books).
    1991   'The Politics of Ezra: Sociological Indicators of Postexilic Judaean Society', in Davies (ed.) 1991: 73-97.

Smith-Christopher, Daniel L.
    1994   'The Mixed Marriage Crisis in Ezra 9–10 and Nehemiah 13: A Study of the Sociology of Post-Exilic Judean Community', in Eskenazi and Richards 1994: 243-65.

Snijders, Lambertus A.
    1954   'The Meaning of *zar* in the Old Testament', *OTS* 10: 1-154.

Soggin, J. Alberto
    1981   *Judges: A Commentary* (OTL; trans. J. Bowden; Philadelphia: Westminster Press).
    1993   'Genesis Kapitel 34. Eros und Thanatos', in André Lemaire and Benedikt Otzen (eds.), *History and Traditions of Early Israel* (VTSup, 50; Leiden: E.J. Brill): 133-35.

Spina, Frank A.
    1983   'Israelites as *gerim*, "Sojourners," in Social and Historical Context', in Meyers and O'Connor 1983: 321-35.

Steinberg, Naomi
    1988   'Israelite Tricksters, Their Analogues and Cross-cultural Study', in Exum and Bos 1988: 1-13.

Sternberg, Meir
    1985   *The Poetics of Biblical Narrative: Ideological Literature and the Drama of Reading* (Bloomington: Indiana University Press).
    1992   'Biblical Poetics and Sexual Politics: From Reading to Counter-Reading', *JBL* 111: 463-88.

Stevenson, Kalinda Rose
    1996   *The Vision of Transformation: The Territorial Rhetoric of Ezekiel 40–48* (SBLDS, 154; Atlanta: Scholars Press).

Stine, Philip (ed.)
    1988   *Issues in Bible Translation* (UBSMS, 3; New York: United Bible Societies).

Stone, Ken
    1996   *Sex, Honor, and Power in the Deuteronomistic History* (JSOTSup, 234; Sheffield: Sheffield Academic Press).

Talmon, S.
    1963   ' "Wisdom" in the Book of Esther', *VT* 13: 419-55.

Tarlin, Jan
    1988   'The Drama of Knowledge: I Kings 3:16-28 Reexamined', *Unitarian Universalist Christian* 44: 48-56.

Thompson, Stith (ed.)
    1966   *Tales of the North American Indians* (Bloomington: Indiana University Press).

Toorn, Karel van der
    1989   'Female Prostitution in Payment of Vows in Ancient Israel', *JBL* 108: 193-205.

Toy, Crawford H.
    1899   *A Critical And Exegetical Commentary on the Book of Proverbs* (ICC; Edinburgh: T. & T. Clark).

Trible, Phyllis
    1978   *God and the Rhetoric of Sexuality* (Philadelphia: Fortress Press).
    1989   'Bringing Miriam out of the Shadows', *BR* 5: 14-25, 34.

Turner, Victor
    1969   *The Ritual Process: Structure and Anti-Structure* (Ithaca, NY: Cornell University Press).

Vickery, John
    1981   'In Strange Ways: The Story of Samson', in Burke O. Long (ed.), *Images of Man and God: Old Testament Short Stories in Literary Focus* (Bible & Literature, 1; Sheffield: Almond Press): 58-73.

Washington, Harold C.
    1994   'The Strange Woman of Proverbs 1–9 and Post-Exilic Judean Society', in Eskenazi and Richards 1994: 217-42 (repr. in Brenner 1995: 157-84).

Weinberg, Joel
    1992   *The Citizen–Temple Community* (trans. D. Smith-Christopher; JSOTSup, 151; Sheffield: JSOT Press).

Wenham, Gordon J.
    1983   'Why Does Sexual Intercourse Defile (Leviticus 15:18)?', *ZAW* 95: 432-34.

Whybray, Robert N.
    1968   *The Succession Narrative: A Study of II Samuel 9–20 and I Kings 1 and 2* (SBT, Second Series, 9; Naperville, IL: Alec R. Allenson).

Willi, Thomas
    1994   'Late Persian Judaism and its Conception of an Integral Israel According to Chronicles', in Eskenazi and Richards 1994: 146-62.

Williams, James
    1982   *Women Recounted: Narrative Thinking and the God of Israel* (Bible & Literature, 6; Sheffield: Almond Press).

Williamson, H.G.M.
    1995   'Isaiah and the Wise', in Day, Gordon and Williamson 1995: 133-41.

Wright, Christopher J.H.
    1979   'The Israelite Household and the Decalogue: The Social Background and Significance of Some Commandments', *TynBul* 30: 101-24.

Yee, Gale A.
    1989   '"I Have Perfumed my Bed With Myrrh": The Foreign Woman (*'iššâ zārâ*) in Proverbs 1–9', *JSOT* 43: 53-68 (repr. in Brenner 1995: 110-26).
    1995   'The Socio-Literary Production of the "Foreign Woman" in Proverbs', in Brenner 1995: 127-30.

Zvi, Ehud Ben
    1997   'The Urban Center of Jerusalem and the Development of the Literature of the Hebrew Bible', in Walter E. Aufrecht, Neil A. Mirau and Steven W. Gauley (eds.), *Urbanism in Antiquity: From Mesopotamia to Crete* (JSOTSup, 244; Sheffield: Sheffield Academic Press): 194-210.

INDEXES

INDEX OF REFERENCES

BIBLE